Traditional Cooking
of the
BRITISH ISLES

Traditional Cooking

of the

BRITISH ISLES

360 classic regional dishes with 1500 beautiful photographs

ENGLAND • IRELAND • SCOTLAND • WALES

Annette Yates, Christopher Trotter and Georgina Campbell

LORENZ BOOKS

This edition is published by Lorenz Books,
an imprint of Anness Publishing Ltd,
108 Great Russell Street, London WC1B 3NA;
info@anness.com

www.lorenzbooks.com; www.annesspublishing.com;
twitter: @Anness_Books

Publisher: Joanna Lorenz
Editorial Director: Helen Sudell
Executive Editor: Joanne Rippin
Additional text: Biddy White Lennon and Carol Wilson
Photographer: Craig Robertson
Food styling: Fergal Connelly and Emma MacIntosh
Props styling: Helen Trent
Designer: Nigel Partridge

A CIP catalogue record for this book is available from the British Library.

PUBLISHER'S NOTE
Although the advice and information in this book are believed to be
accurate and true at the time of going to press, neither the authors
nor the publisher can accept any legal responsibility or liability for any
errors or omissions that may have been made nor for any inaccuracies
nor for any loss, harm or injury that comes about from following
instructions or advice in this book.

The publisher would like to thank the following for the use of their
images: Alamy 48, 50t, 52t; Bridgeman Images 6, 8, 11, 14, 15, 23,
24; Corbis 12, 22, 31b, 38t; Balvenie Distillery 27b; Scottish Viewpoint
27t, 28, 29, 35; Glenfiddich 30b; VisitScotland.com 31b, 32, 33;
MacSween of Edinburgh 31t; LochFyne Fisheries 34; Failte Ireland 37;
Cephas Picture Library 38, 39; Robert Harding Picture Library 40, 43bl,
44, 45; Jamieson Irish Whiskey 43t, 46, 47t; SuperStock 41, 44tc;
National Museums and Galleries of Wales 49, 50b, 51, 53.

COOK'S NOTES
Bracketed terms are intended for American readers.

For all recipes, quantities are given in both metric and imperial
measures and, where appropriate, in standard cups and spoons.
Follow one set of measures, but not a mixture, because they
are not interchangeable.

Standard spoon and cup measures are level. 1 tsp = 5ml,
1 tbsp = 15ml, 1 cup = 250ml/8fl oz.

Australian standard tablespoons are 20ml. Australian readers
should use 3 tsp in place of 1 tbsp for measuring small quantities.

American pints are 16fl oz/2 cups. American readers should
use 20fl oz/2.5 cups in place of 1 pint when measuring liquids.

Electric oven temperatures in this book are for conventional
ovens. When using a fan oven, the temperature will probably
need to be reduced by about 10–20°C/20–40°F. Since ovens
vary, you should check with your manufacturer's instruction
book for guidance.

The nutritional analysis given for each recipe is calculated per
portion (i.e. serving or item), unless otherwise stated. If the recipe
gives a range, such as Serves 4–6, then the nutritional analysis
will be for the smaller portion size, i.e. 6 servings. Measurements
for sodium do not include salt added to taste.

Medium (US large) eggs are used unless otherwise stated.

CONTENTS

Introduction

This book is a celebration of the food and cooking of Britain. Blessed with a mild and variable climate, the country boasts a mixed landscape of fertile valleys, undulating downs and dales, rugged moors and rocky mountains. There are beautiful lakes, rushing rivers and flat, salty marshlands, as well as a long and varied coastline, much of which is dramatic and distinctive.

The British diet has been influenced not only by the landscape and the climate but also by invasion and immigration, a global empire, social development and diseases, trade and technology, politics and economics, and of course fashion.

Indigenous ingredients

The food of Britain has a history that stretches back more than six thousand years. Before that time this temperate, wooded country would have provided an abundance of small, edible mammals and fish, plus vegetation, roots, fruits

Below Roman methods of preparing food brought great changes to the way the British ate after the invasion.

Above England, Scotland, Wales and Northern Ireland share similar cuisines, but maintain strong regional variations.

and nuts that were seasonally available to early hunter-gatherers. As a group of islands, isolated off the north-west of Europe, Britain was cut off by the sea from the migration of plants and animals, and from the casual spread of new ideas and techniques as people moved about to find homes. On the other hand, for adventurous Europeans the land over the sea promised a rich

Right In medieval times the strict social feudal system meant that most communities were self-sufficient and provided all their own food.

living, with its fertile soil and mineral resources, and settlers arrived in wave after wave. Farming in Britain and Ireland began with the herding and subsistence farming techniques of one of those groups of settlers, the Celts.

The people of Britain have always taken pride in being adventurous, keen to borrow and adapt the ideas of trading partners and incomers, and this sense of adventure began to be fuelled as early as the Bronze Age, as goods were imported from mainland Europe and beyond. The British traded with many other regions, and in return for raw materials, such as tin and copper, corn and wool, they were importing wine and luxury foodstuffs from southern Europe even before the arrival of the Romans. With the Roman occupation came new varieties of plants and animals, and even more exotic ingredients such as spices from Asia.

Imports and influences

Other influences were added to the mix in later centuries: from the occupying Vikings, Saxons and Normans, and from the Arabs via trade with southern

Below Britain's ancient harbours, such as Mousehole in Cornwall, have been operating for centuries.

Above The wilder areas of Scotland still supply the locals with game, such as rabbit, venison and hare.

Europe. In the age of exploration, foods from the New World made their debut in European cuisine – foodstuffs such as beans and tomatoes, which are now regarded as staples of British cookery. Of these, the most important was the potato, which was to have such a profound influence on the history of Ireland in the 19th century. To begin with, it was more popular there than in England, as it proved a more reliable crop than oats and barley, and it was

from Ireland that the trend for planting potatoes spread to areas like Lincolnshire and Lancashire. More exotic ingredients and cooking styles arrived in Britain as its international power grew. Tropical luxuries such as spices, sugar, coffee, tea and chocolate became daily necessities, and the administrators of Britain's far-flung empire acquired a taste for the foods they had eaten in India and the Far East. Worcestershire sauce, for example, now regarded as a

Below The county of Kent in the south of England has long been known for its apple orchards.

Above A cottage kitchen in the 19th century, when a greater variety of ingredients was enjoyed than before.

typically British condiment, is a spiced fermented fish sauce, which was created in the 1830s for a family who missed the cooking of Bengal. Ironically, Worcestershire sauce made its way back to the East via European restaurants in Hong Kong and Shanghai, and is now used in Chinese cookery.

Enduring traditions

In every age, the new foodstuffs were most readily accepted, and most easily purchased, by the wealthy and fashionable, the city dwellers and the travellers. In remote rural regions, old cooking techniques and traditional ingredients persisted far longer, particularly in the highland areas of the north and west.

A primitive method of cooking meat in a pit filled with water, which was kept boiling by the addition of stones heated in a fire, seems to have been current in the Bronze Age in Ireland, Scotland, Wales and upland areas of England, but in some places the

method was still being used in the early medieval period. In the 18th and 19th centuries rural cottage dwellers continued to cook their daily soup of carrots, onions and cabbage in an iron pot over the kitchen fire, and bake their bannocks or potato cakes on a bakestone, while the wealthy and more cosmopolitan gentry were eating turtle soup, curries, ice cream and tropical

fruits. Yet it is the traditional country recipes, refined over generations, of healthy, wholesome dishes from modest ingredients, that are now a valued part of Britain's culinary heritage.

The modern age

Given the richness of Britain's food traditions and the excellence of its ingredients, it seems surprising that for much of the 20th century it had a reputation for food that was plain and boring, consisting mainly of overcooked meat and vegetables and stodgy puddings. This decline in the British approach to food probably stemmed from the 19th century, as Victorian morality inculcated a disdain for the sensory pleasure of eating, and the largely urban population lost touch with the quality of fresh produce. The emerging middle classes, locked between the wealthy and the poor, strove to keep up appearances with

Below The late Victorian kitchen in Britain still used similar cooking methods to those in medieval times.

grandiose but badly cooked meals, aided by the publications of Mrs Beeton (who, among other ill-judged recommendations, suggested boiling an egg for 20 minutes).

The lowly status of cooks, who were regarded as "below stairs" staff in the houses of the rich, the consequences of two World Wars, food shortages and rationing, periods of economic depression and the influx of processed foods all took their toll on the quality of British cooking.

Recovery from this adverse perception of its cuisine has taken a long time, but today Britain is once more able to take pride in its reputation for excellent food, and there is a welcome resurgence of interest in seasonal ingredients of high quality. The nation has the ability to embrace curry and pizza (even turning them into new national dishes) and delicacies from the Mediterranean and the Middle East, while nostalgically guarding and updating its inheritance of national and regional favourites: roast beef and Yorkshire pudding, haggis, cawl, fish

Below *Leek soup has several variations around Britain, and is probably most loved in Wales, the home of the leek.*

Above *Properly reared meat, like this joint of pork, carefully cooked and simply served with seasonal vegetables, makes the Sunday roast one of the mainstays of British cooking.*

and chips, Irish stew, bubble and squeak, and the much-loved puddings that hold memories of childhood.

The food of the British Isles

Although Britain is no longer a single political entity, its culinary heritage is very much shared between the countries of England, Ireland, Scotland

Class distinctions
The numerous French words that entered the English language following the Norman Conquest included the names of the meats that were eaten by the Norman aristocracy, such as mutton, beef, veal and pork. Meanwhile, the old Anglo-Saxon names – sheep, cow and pig – continued to be used for the live animals, as they were tended by the English peasants.

and Wales. This beautiful book illustrates the many good things that Britain has to offer. It begins with an overview of the rich food history of the the four countries, each with its own characteristics and food specialities, and describes the traditional festivals and customs of the four nations and the food associated with them. There follows a section on ingredients – vegetables, fruit, fish, meat, poultry, game and dairy produce. But the major part of this book is devoted to cooking, with a host of delicious recipes that can be traced back through the ages. Some are common to all areas of Britain, such as roast meats, crumbles, scones and cooked breakfasts to name a few, while others are unmistakeably from a particular country, such as Irish Soda Bread, Welsh Faggots, Scottish Clootie Dumpling and English Cornish Pasties.

In this fabulous collections of recipes there is something to suit every occasion. In fact, here is everything you need to know about the best of traditional British food and cooking. Enjoy it and eat well.

Below *Summer pudding was once a way of using up a glut of berries and stale bread, but is now a seasonal treat.*

Britain's food traditions

The food and eating of Britain have been shaped partly by the temperate climate and geography of the British Isles, but also by the long histories of its four nations, England, Scotland, Ireland and Wales. Local specialities and traditional recipes play a role in creating the distinctive identity of each country.

Food in England

England has a long history of invasion, settlement and immigration, and a wealth of foreign influences from continental Europe and beyond have enriched its culinary development.

Early times

Before farming began, England was mostly covered by woodland. Edible plants such as barberries, crab apples, haws, hazelnuts and sloes grew in the clearings, and the woods were home to boar, deer, and various small mammals. The rivers and seas were rich with fish and shellfish. The shift to farming from around 4000BC led to the growth of larger, settled communities. Livestock remained all-important until the Bronze Age (c2000BC), from which time the first grain crops and field systems date.

New foods from the Romans

When the Romans arrived in England in 55BC, they introduced a large range of foods and flavours, elaborately seasoned dishes and specialized cooking methods such as roasting and baking. They brought pheasants, peacocks and guinea fowl, a host of vegetables and many herbs and spices. They also introduced almonds, dates, olive oil, walnuts and wine – the customary drink of Roman soldiers – as well as orchard trees such as cherry, mulberry and plum. They established vines, using the grapes to make wine, must for cooking and vinegar for drinks, sauces and preserving.

Above *A reconstruction of a Celtic Iron Age village, when Britain was a country divided into tribes and regions.*

The Romans created hare gardens and game parks and raised cattle, pigs, sheep and goats. They also kept hens and honey bees. Oysters were highly prized. Cereals were made into porridge and gruel as well as being used in baking. Flour was mainly ground at home, though commercial bakeries existed in large towns.

Anglo-Saxons and Vikings

When the Anglo-Saxons settled in England from the 5th century, wild deer and boar were common. Domesticated pigs produced large litters that matured quickly. Sheep gave wool as well as meat, while cows produced milk, meat, hides and glue. There was fish, from both rivers and the sea.

Everyone, even children, drank weak ale, which was safer than the water. Wine imported from the continent was drunk by the wealthy. Other options were buttermilk and whey (by-products from butter and cheese-making), with mead for special occasions.

The Viking invaders of the 8th and 9th centuries ate a wide variety of fruits, nuts and grains, as well as fish

Below *The Romans brought sophisticated fishing equipment to Britain, as well as elaborate fish sauces.*

Above *Ladies of the court dressed in their finery parade a peacock re-dressed in his, for a banquet's centrepiece.*

and shellfish. Meat was available to all, not just the rich, and was preserved by salting, pickling, drying or smoking. Dairy products and eggs formed an important part of the diet. Bread – both leavened and unleavened – was made in large quantities, and the Vikings made use of wild yeasts and raising agents such as buttermilk.

Medieval extremes

What medieval people ate varied according to their social standing. Most still grew and prepared their own food, or traded it with others. Food was preserved by potting and drying, and salt was an important ingredient, kept dry in a box by the fire.

Only the rich ate white wheaten bread. The most common bread, called "maslin", was coarse and made with a mixture of wheat and rye. At the medieval table, bread was used to make trenchers – rough plates – which might be offered to the poor after the meal.

Pottage, a soupy mixture of vegetables, meat, pulses, cereals, herbs and broth, was eaten by everyone every day and was cooked in the basic utensil of the time – a three-legged iron pot that stood or hung over the fire.

Fish was very important in the diet, as it was eaten on the church's many fast days. Cattle, sheep and goats provided meat, but the mainstay of the poor was the pig. Game meats remained the privilege of the wealthy. Cooked dishes for the wealthy were flavoured with expensive imported spices such as cardamom, caraway, ginger, nutmeg and pepper, and foods were dyed with vivid colourings such as sandalwood, saffron and boiled blood.

Tudor England

The Tudor period was a time of colour and splendour. While the nobility had a reputation for overeating, even the lower classes ate well compared with most of their European counterparts.

At the table, trenchers (plates) began to be made of wood rather than bread, but bread, pottage, fish and meat still underpinned the diet. Vegetables and fruit were treated with suspicion and left for the lower classes. As a result, vitamin deficiencies were common.

Meanwhile, expeditions to the New World were bringing back new foods, such as potatoes, tomatoes and chocolate, and from southern Europe came apricots, blackcurrants, lemons, oranges, melons, pomegranates and quinces. Sugar had become more widely available and was very popular with the wealthy. A refinery was built in London and sugar was added to savoury dishes as well as being used to make preserves and sweetmeats.

Below *A wonderful picture of a kitchen in Tudor times, with its cavernous fires, and foodstuffs hung high on the walls.*

Century of upheaval

In the 17th century it became fashionable for an affluent new class – the landed gentry – to visit London, the source of both social graces and luxury foods. Standards were still set by the royal household, and French cuisine gained popularity. Fruit and vegetables were considered safe and diners began to appreciate salads, but meat formed a large part of the diet.

Baking skills improved, as local specialities were developed in the form of cakes, biscuits and buns. Puddings were tied in a cloth and cooked slowly in a pot with the meat and vegetables.

Every country house had a kitchen garden, and large estates produced a huge range of vegetables and fruit. Icehouses were built to store winter ice for cooling food and drinks in summer. Beehive ovens and stoves appeared alongside kitchen fireplaces, and ladies began to compile recipe books.

Georgian progress

In the early 1700s, the English were still growing and rearing their own food. But as landowners began to enclose their land, the poor were forced to

move to the towns, where they survived on bread, potatoes and porridge. Spirits, such as gin, were cheap, and drunkenness was rife among the poor.

Meat became more widely available as a result of new farming practices, and improved transport meant that regional foods like cheeses and fresh fish could be eaten throughout the country. Sugar was readily available, leading to the development of pickles, ketchups and bottled sauces. It was also added to drinks – wine, tea, coffee and chocolate. Coffee and tea were still

Above *The interior of an early London coffee house, c.1705, where customers were exclusively male.*

expensive treats, but tea's popularity exploded in England in the early 18th century, when people began to take afternoon tea to fill the long gap between breakfast and dinner. By the mid-18th century the dinner table

Below *From the 1600s English country houses established rooms inside that were specifically for dining.*

looked much as it does today, with plates, bowls, knives, forks, serving spoons and wine glasses.

Rebelling against fancy French sauces, the English became known for their preference for plain roast beef and their love affair with puddings – mostly loaded with butter or suet. This age of indulgence led to widespread health problems, with a high incidence of gout, diabetes, heart and liver diseases, and vitamin deficiencies.

The Victorian age

In the 19th century the growing population continued to move from the country to the city, with the poor supplying cheap factory labour. For some, life became so difficult that it prompted a humanitarian movement that offered charity in the hardest-hit areas. There were even cookery books directed at feeding the poor.

The discovery of bacteria led to advances in medicine and food preservation, and a greater awareness of food hygiene. The quality of produce in the cities improved, and international trade also took off.

With more tea and wheat in England than ever before, prices dropped. Tea became the staple drink of the poor, who drank it in copious quantities as they ate their bread or potatoes. The development of roller mills meant that white flour (and therefore white bread) was available to all. And the canning process meant that all kinds of produce – vegetables, fruit, soups, stews – could be widely transported and stored.

Victorian kitchens were large – able to hold the new cast-iron ranges, with their open fires, ovens, water tanks and hot plates. Cooks in middle-class houses could now prepare the complicated meals and delicate dishes that had been the reserve of grand kitchens. Mrs Beeton's *Book of Household Management*, published in 1861, was

popular with young, middle-class families, and was followed by many other recipe books. Kitchens were filled with new equipment and gadgets, and there was usually a walk-in pantry to keep food cool. The end of the 19th century saw the introduction of gas stoves, electric kettles and facilities for chilling and freezing meat.

The modern age

At the beginning of the 20th century the English population ate very poorly. Vitamins and their importance in a healthy diet had only recently been discovered, and the government now began to invest in dietary research.

After a period of recovery from World War I came the General Strike, during which soup kitchens were set up to feed communities, and a time of great depression and poverty followed. At the same time, the middle classes began to eat out: Indian restaurants opened in London and the first "sit-down" fish and chip cafe appeared in Guiseley, near Leeds. Milk was pasteurized and bottled, and sliced bread and instant coffee went on sale.

Above *Wealthy Victorians enjoyed imported delicacies, better cooking equipment and complex new recipes.*

In spite of shortages, World War II is now considered to have been a period of healthy eating in England. Food rationing was introduced in 1940, with the Ministry of Food advising the nation on eating healthily and allotments popping up on every corner. Children were given free milk and vitamins; calcium was added to flour, and the brown National Loaf was introduced.

The development of freezing and freeze-drying led to food scientists finding new ways to enhance and preserve foods. Ready-made meals have become popular, and shoppers are able to buy food that is convenient, but also homogenized, high in emulsified fat and high in salt.

Now there are signs of a return to more traditional ways. There is a focus on seasonal foods, local farming and environmental issues, and an interest in the past for inspiration, finding the best in the heritage of English cooking and applying it to modern methods of providing good, healthy food.

England's regions

Though it is a relatively small country, England's varied geography has led to marked regional differences, which are reflected in a host of local foodstuffs and traditional recipes.

The south-east

In spite of its dense population, centred on London, the region's mild climate and warm, rich soil makes it a prime source of fresh produce, high quality meat and fish, and dairy products. Sheep have always grazed the lowland areas, and quality lamb and mutton

Below England's temperate climate and surrounding seas make it ideal land for farming and food production.

comes from the South Downs, while pig farms abound in Hampshire. Poultry has always been important in this area, and as far back as the 1600s, the Surrey town of Dorking was said to host the greatest poultry market in England. The Aylesbury duck is the largest of the domestic ducks and has been popular for two centuries.

Historically, the south-east is better known for dairy farming than for beef. Until the mid-1800s Londoners were supplied with milk from herds that grazed on Clapham Common and Hampstead Heath. Though there is no ancient tradition of cheese-making, some fine farmhouse cheeses are now made in the area, such as Spenwood, Sussex Slipcote and Oxford Blue.

Above The southern counties of England have been famous for their fruit orchards for generations.

While the long Kent coastline has seen a huge decline in the fishing industry, fine Dover sole are still landed, with a variety of other fish. Whitstable has for centuries been known as the oyster centre of England, and still holds an annual oyster festival. Smokehouses and fish farms are dotted around the coast, and in Hampshire, the River Test yields wild trout, pike and zander.

Known as the "Garden of England", Kent grows much of the country's fruit. Spring blossoms promise apples, pears, plums and cherries, and the National Fruit Collections are based at Brogdale. There are soft fruits too, and cobnuts, a variety of hazelnut, are a local treat. Market gardens along the Sussex Weald produce fruit, vegetables and salad crops. Sussex is also known for its mushrooms. Hampshire and the Isle of Wight produce cereals, root vegetables and watercress.

Some of the oast houses in which hops for beer-making were dried still stand in the Kent countryside. The area is dotted with breweries, and Kent and

Sussex are also cider-making centres. South-facing slopes in the area are increasingly being planted with vines, following a tradition of viticulture first brought to England by the Romans.

Baked specialities range from the Bedfordshire clanger – a hefty suet pastry with a savoury filling at one end and a sweet one at the other – to puff pastry Banbury cakes from Oxfordshire and the small bread rolls known as Kentish huffkins – made with a dimple for holding jam. Sussex has its lemony Sussex pond pudding and the Isle of Wight is known for its doughnuts.

Until the early 1900s, London resounded to the cries of street traders, such as the muffin man who came bearing a tray of fresh muffins on his head. Well into the 20th century there were barrows selling shellfish, and roasted chestnuts are still sold on the winter streets. Since the 18th century, the East End of London has been home to eel and pie shops, selling stewed or jellied eels and meat pies. London is also famous for dishes such as whitebait and boiled beef and carrots. It still has pubs, chop houses and grill rooms serving specialities such as steak and kidney pudding, and game pies. Its ancient food markets include Covent Garden, Billingsgate, and Smithfield.

The south-west

This fertile region enjoys the mildest climate in England. The seas are warmed by the Gulf Stream and spring always arrives early.

Rich dairy pastures produce milk with a high butterfat content – ideal for making cream, cheese, butter and ice cream. The area is probably best known for its clotted cream, and local cream teas would not be correct without it. There are cheeses galore: Single and Double Gloucester, Stinking Bishop, with its perry-washed rind and potent smell, Dorset Blue Vinney and, in

Somerset, perhaps the most copied of English cheeses – Cheddar. Cornish Yarg, a tangy, white cheese made with cows' milk, has a distinctive rind made from nettle leaves.

Cornwall's warm climate produces the earliest fruit and vegetables, apple orchards flourish throughout the region and pear orchards feature in Devon.

The extensive coastline is dotted with bustling harbours. Huge shoals of mackerel and herring were once landed. Today's catches are small, but may include haddock, mullet, mackerel, turbot and sea bream, as well as crabs, lobsters and shellfish. Off the Cornish coast, pilchards (large sardines) were once the largest catch of the region. The River Severn is known for its salmon fishing and has been fished for elvers (baby eels) for hundreds of years.

Pig farming is the tradition of the south-west, Wiltshire in particular. Many local food specialities are based on pork and bacon, and every part of the animal is utilized, in products from fine Bradenham hams to sausages, faggots, brawn, chitterlings, trotters and black puddings (blood sausages).

Cream teas are legendary in the south-west, with scones or splits (soft

Above The wide estuary of Fowey, in Cornwall, still supports a successful sea-based community.

dough buns), strawberry jam and, of course, clotted cream. Wiltshire's lardy cake is made from white bread dough, rolled and folded with lard, sugar and dried fruit. Fairings are similar to brandy snaps but more lace-like. Apple cakes are particularly popular in Dorset and Devon, and Dorset knobs are crisp, roll-shaped biscuits.

From the Georgian city of Bath comes the Bath Oliver biscuit, the Bath bun, topped with currants and crushed lump sugar, and the Sally Lunn – a light, yeast cake, traditionally split and spread with butter or clotted cream.

Spices arrived at West Country ports from all over the world, and saffron is still a favourite baking ingredient. Last but not least is the Cornish pasty, a portable meal wrapped in thick pastry, originally designed for farmers and miners to carry to work.

With apples so abundant, cider is the traditional drink of the region, while England's oldest gin distillery in Plymouth has been supplying the Royal Navy with gin for more than 200 years.

The Midlands

This large and varied region at the heart of England is an area of rugged hills, peat bogs and moors. While it is still the home of industry, it also has rich agricultural land, orchards laden with fruit, natural spring waters and some of the best reared beef in the country.

The ginger-haired Tamworth pig is the traditional Midlands breed. Frugal cottagers used every part of their home-reared pigs, and the legacy of this practice is the wide range of pork products that remain popular, such as home-cured bacon, tripe, faggots, haslet and brawn. The most famous pork pies have been made in Melton Mowbray, Leicestershire, since the 1850s. The Hereford, one of England's oldest and best-known breeds of beef cattle, dates back to the 17th century, and the Derbyshire Dales are well known for sheep rearing.

The Nottingham Goose Fair has been held in October since the 1200s. Geese were brought to the fair to be sold before being herded to London.

A mild, wet climate produces rich pastures, making the Midlands a prolific milk-producing region. Its abundance led

Below Leicestershire's lakes and rivers are stocked with bream, carp, roach, tench and trout.

to the region's fame in cheese-making. Stilton has been popular since the 18th century and is still made with milk exclusively from Leicestershire, Nottinghamshire and Derbyshire. Cheshire cheese has been made continuously since the 12th century.

The vast orchards of the Vale of Evesham grow a large variety of apples, pears and plums, and organized Blossom Trails guide visitors along the scenic routes in spring. Numerous vegetables grow in the market gardens of Herefordshire and Worcestershire, and the local asparagus is famous.

The River Severn was once a rich source of salmon, eels and elvers and the Dee and Wye are also well-known salmon-fishing rivers, with pike and grayling running in them too.

Baked goods include brandy snaps and gingerbread, which for centuries have been sold at fairs throughout the region. Staffordshire fruitcakes are enriched with treacle (molasses) and brandy, and in Northamptonshire the making of little cheesecakes was traditional at sheep-shearing time.

Though barley and wheat are now the main crops of the region, oats were important in the 18th and 19th centuries. Still famous are Staffordshire oatcakes, which resemble pancakes. Pikelets are thick, holey pancakes, served hot and oozing with butter.

Above Oil seed rape is a modern crop that has quickly become an established part of the scenic landscape of Suffolk.

Specialities from Midland towns include crisp, lemony Shrewsbury biscuits (cookies) and Bakewell puddings, which it is claimed were invented in Bakewell in the Peak District in the 1860s. Coventry godcakes, triangular in shape to represent the Holy Trinity, were often presented by godparents to their godchildren.

While the area is important for hop growing and brewing, it is best known for its cider and perry, the latter made from the fermented juice of pears. There is also a lesser-known cider made from plums, called plum jerkum. Famous mineral waters are bottled at the springs of Ashbourne and Buxton in the Peak District and the Malvern Hills.

The eastern counties

This low-lying part of England is rich arable land. The area called the Fens spreads out from the Wash across Cambridgeshire, Lincolnshire and West Norfolk. Once a swampy wilderness, it was reclaimed with a network of

tranquil waterways. The soil is fertile and warm and tends to be dry, and all sorts of crops thrive. Lincolnshire is especially known for its peas and early crops, while East Anglia is famous for its asparagus. Numerous windmills (a few still working) are reminders of the importance of grain in this area: there are hundreds of fields growing wheat, barley and oil-seed rape. The cultivation of sugar beet is important to the local economy and yellow fields of mustard have grown here ever since Jeremiah Colman started making his condiment near Norwich in 1814. Soft fruits and orchards flourish, particularly around Wisbech in Cambridgeshire. Essex is a centre for jam-making, both cottage and commercial, and much of the produce is directed here.

Fishing has always been an important industry, with large ports including Grimsby and Lowestoft handling a range of fish – cod, haddock, plaice, skate, sprats and turbot. In Southend there is an annual festival celebrating whitebait. Great Yarmouth was once the centre for a huge herring fleet, with large smokehouses at the docks sending smoked herrings, bloaters and kippers all over the world. As with

Below Kippers are still smoked in the traditional way in East Anglia, and are enjoyed all over England for breakfast.

many coastal towns, ecological influences and over-fishing have resulted in a major industry dwindling to almost nothing.

Shellfish thrive here, especially in the relatively shallow waters of the Wash. There are small but fleshy Cromer crabs, cockles, whelks and mussels. The native oysters from the beds at Colchester (England's first recorded town) are world famous, and the fishery here dates back to the Roman occupation. In the Norfolk Broads the eel industry was once big and eels remain a local delicacy. Nowadays the waters are better known for pike and zander.

Though cattle and sheep are reared in East Anglia, pigs and poultry have always been preferred. In Essex the Dunmow Flitch trials are still held every three years, at which a flitch (side) of bacon is presented to a married couple who can prove they have not quarrelled in the previous year. Fidget (fitchet) pies with bacon, onions and apples are popular. Lincolnshire pork sausages and haslet are flavoured with sage. Stuffed chine – salt pork, slashed and filled with herbs – is a favourite. Norfolk has been famed for its turkeys since flocks of traditional Norfolk Blacks were driven on the three-month journey to London in time for the Christmas market.

The people of Cambridgeshire are said to have been the first to use a

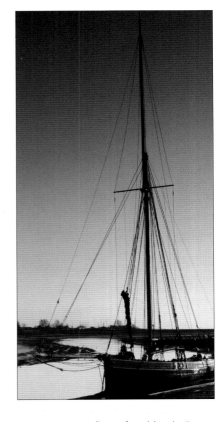

Above The seaflats of Maldon in Essex have provided superb quality salt since the 12th century.

pudding cloth for wrapping and cooking suet puddings. Lincolnshire is perhaps best known for its plum bread and Grantham has its own version of gingerbread – a crunchy, puffed-up biscuit (cookie). There are various cake recipes using saffron, which serve as a reminder that the purple saffron crocus was once grown around Saffron Walden in Essex.

The region boasts several breweries making beer by traditional methods. Norfolk cider is usually made with cooking or dessert apples rather than the cider apples used in the West Country, so is less astringent. The climate suits grape growing, and vineyards in Essex, Norfolk and Suffolk produce a range of interesting wines.

Above *The windswept and rugged landscape of the Yorkshire Dales.*

The north-east

This region is notable for its beautiful, craggy coastline, dotted with castles facing the North Sea. The Pennines lie to the west and there are dales and moors, seaside resorts and quaint fishing villages. Traditional meals tend to be simple, cheap, tasty and, in the cold climate of the North, warming.

The North Sea has been a great source of sustenance for the people of this region, providing a selection of fish and shellfish. Whitby was once a great whaling port. The Yorkshire coble, a traditional "off the beach" fishing boat designed to be launched from steep shingle, is still used to work the inshore waters. The strong fishing heritage has resulted in a love of fish and chips (French fries). This is the area to taste fish coated in a light, crisp batter, cooked in beef dripping, served with mushy peas and, of course, chips.

Northumberland has had a flourishing kipper industry based at Craster since the 19th century. Herrings are split and hung from the rafters of the smokehouses before being smoked over the fires of smouldering oak chips.

Plenty of high-quality beef is produced here – ideal for Roast Beef and Yorkshire Pudding. Yorkshire's famous batter pudding was originally cooked beneath the meat so that it caught and soaked up the juices and fat. It would often be eaten as a first course, with gravy, before the roast: an idea developed in lean days to reduce the diners' appetite for meat.

Sheep are the principal livestock of the region and the Yorkshire Moors and Yorkshire Dales are still home to some hardy breeds. Mutton was traditionally used in sausages, stews and pies, and sheep's milk is made into interesting, distinctively flavoured local cheeses. Pigs have always played an important role too. The famous York ham is traditionally eaten at Christmas. The moors are an ideal habitat for game, with fine grouse, partridge, pheasant, hare and deer to be had.

While most of the land is best suited to grazing, some is arable. Leeks grow especially well in this area and there are local competitions to discover the largest. Pulses are popular and dishes containing peas were eaten regularly during Lent when meat was forbidden. In the 1800s, pease pudding was sold as street food.

Rhubarb growing is traditional in Yorkshire, notably in the "Rhubarb Triangle" between Pontefract, Wakefield and Leeds, which supplies the country with some of the finest forced rhubarb in early spring. Bilberries (blueberries) grow wild on the moors and can be picked in late summer.

Baking is a strong northern tradition and the region's teashops serve buttered teacakes, rich fruitcakes, and Yorkshire curd tart. Bakestone, or griddle, cooking is popular here for oatcakes, drop scones, singin' hinnies and crumpets. Stottie cake, a savoury bread made with self-raising (self-rising) flour and milk, is a favourite for bacon or chip butties. Traditional sweets include Harrogate toffee and Pontefract cakes, made from liquorice, which was once grown in the area.

Below *Craster Harbour, Northumberland, is a small fishing area that is well known for its kipper and herring industry.*

The north-west

This is a region of beautiful lakes, mountains and a dramatic coastline. Between the hills and the Irish Sea lies the stunning area of the Lake District, together with manufacturing towns and plenty of farming land. Northern dishes were devised with hard-working people and big appetites in mind. Hardy sheep dot the hills and moorlands, and the choice local lamb goes into classic dishes such as Lancashire Hotpot and Shepherd's Pie. Mutton is seeing a revival and is now reared in Cumbria. Wild game, including the succulent Derwentwater duck, also thrives on the uncultivated moors and mountains.

There is plenty of pork and bacon. Cumberland hams are dry cured, salted and rubbed with brown sugar. Meaty Cumberland sausage is sold in a coil and bought by length rather than by weight. There is offal to be found that is now seldom seen in southern England: tripe and onions, brains,

Below The famous Swaledale sheep, with their distinctive black faces, roam freely over the hills of the Lake District.

chitterlings (pig's intestines), elder (pressed cow's udder), lamb's fry (testicles) and sweetbreads. Pig's trotters (feet) and cow heel are used to enrich stews and to make jellied stock for pies. The north-west is black pudding (blood sausage) country. The sausage-shaped puddings, made from pig's blood and oatmeal, vary in texture and taste according to their maker, and secret recipes abound. Faggots, potted meats, pressed tongue and brisket of beef are popular too. Hot pies, both savoury and sweet, can be bought from stalls, butchers, and fish and chip shops.

The lush pastures of this region mean there is plenty of milk to make fine cream, butter and cheese. Lancashire cheese has been made since the early 1900s and has a soft, crumbly texture and buttery flavour.

The fishing industry is centred in Fleetwood, and plaice, sole, hake and herring (often stuffed and served with mustard sauce) are particularly popular. Morecambe Bay is famous for its small brown shrimps. It was traditional to catch trout and salmon in the estuaries in wide "heave" or "haaf" nets, held by the fishermen standing in the water.

Above Gooseberries are one of the few fruits grown in the north-west.

Char, which is rare in Britain, is line-fished in the Lake District and is potted or used in pies. The Isle of Man is famed for kippers and tiny scallops.

Lancashire is one of the few areas sheltered enough to grow vegetables. Varieties are chosen to suit the harsh climate, especially potatoes, root vegetables and some salad plants. Little fruit is grown here, but damsons and gooseberries are notable exceptions.

The north-west offers a host of special cakes and pastries, such as Eccles cakes – flaky pastries stuffed full of currants – and the Cumberland rum nicky, a pie with a similar filling doused in rum. Corners are large round pies cut into serving-size quarters. Chester buns are made with yeast dough glazed with sugar and water. Gingerbread has been made in Grasmere since the mid-19th century and the gingerbread shop is still there. Dense, chewy treacle toffee is popular here, while Everton toffee is crisp and flavoured with lemon. Kendal mint cake, the strongly peppermint-flavoured glucose-based sweet (candy), is taken on walks, climbs and treks as a source of instant energy.

English feasts and festivals

Many of the annual feast days and festivals of England are linked to the Christian calendar, but their origins often stretch back to pre-Christian times, when pagan celebrations were inextricably linked with agriculture and seasonal change.

Shrove Tuesday

The last day before Lent, a period of fasting and reflection before the Christian celebration of Easter, is now often called Pancake Day. Shrove Tuesday is meant to be a day when everyone "shrives" or confesses their sins and receives absolution. It is also the last chance to feast before the period of abstinence. Pancakes are the customary treat, made with a batter containing the eggs, butter and milk that would otherwise go off during the 40 days of Lent. The traditions of tossing pancakes and pancake races are still kept up.

Good Friday

The day when Jesus Christ was crucified is a day of mourning in the Christian calendar, when churches are stripped of

Below A group of wartime evacuees celebrate Shrove Tuesday by tossing pancakes into the air.

all decoration. It is traditional to eat fish on Good Friday, and hot cross buns are eaten warm for breakfast. Though the buns predated Christianity, they were adopted as a symbol of the cross on which Christ died.

In Tudor times spiced buns could, by law, be sold only on special days. Years ago, hot cross buns were thought to have holy powers, and a bun would be hung from the ceiling to protect people in the house from harm. Bits of the stale bun would be grated off and used as a cure for illness, and if the bun went mouldy bad luck was to be had by all. There is a pub in London (The Widow's Son) where, in the early 19th century, a widow lived who was expecting her sailor son back home for Easter. On Good Friday she put a hot cross bun ready for him. Though the son never returned, his mother left the bun waiting and added a new one each year. When the house became a pub, the landlords continued the tradition.

Easter Day

Christians celebrate the resurrection of Jesus Christ on Easter Sunday, but many of the festival's symbols and traditions predate Christianity. Traditional foods include lamb (with rosemary for remembrance), simnel cake (a fruitcake layered with marzipan) and eggs (which

Above Families buy hot cross buns from a baker on a London street.

are forbidden during Lent). Customs include decorating eggs and egg hunts. In the north of England there is "egg jarping", when children tap their opponents' hard-boiled eggs with their own and the last to break is the champion, and "pace-egging", when they dress up and blacken their faces to go knocking on doors, asking in rhyme for Easter eggs. Egg rolling is still practised in England, when hard-boiled eggs are rolled down a hill. The winner might be the one that rolls the farthest or the one that survives best. Today chocolate eggs are given as gifts.

St George's Day

The patron saint of England, St George, is acknowledged on 23 April. Though there are no national celebrations people sometimes wear a red rose (the national flower), and some regions organize parades and concerts, while pubs and restaurants offer traditional English dishes.

Mothering Sunday

Also called Mother's Day, this was originally the day when people visited the "mother" church. In the 17th

century it became the occasion to acknowledge mothers. Children, mainly daughters, who had gone away to work as domestic servants were given a day off to visit their mother with flowers and simnel cake. Today it is a day when children give flowers, gifts and cards to their mothers, and the family gathers for a meal.

May Day

The first day of May is the time to celebrate spring and the coming of summer. It once marked the time when livestock was moved to the hills to graze after a winter in the lowlands. It was customary to dance around the maypole (a surviving pagan symbol of virility from the festival of Beltane) and a May queen would be crowned with hawthorn blossoms. Houses were decorated with flowers, and young girls washed their faces in morning dew for a beautiful complexion. There might be processions and Morris dancing.

Hallowe'en

The night of 31 October is All Hallows Eve, or Hallowe'en. It is traditionally a night of witches, goblins, ghouls and

ghosts, a time of mischief, magic and mystery, with customs that can be traced back to the Celts. Fires would be lit on the hillsides to ward off evil spirits, and families huddled together at home out of harm's way. These days parties are held where lanterns with menacing faces are carved from pumpkins and swedes, and games such

Below A May Day procession in a 19th century village with roots that go back to Beltane, the pagan spring festival.

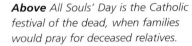

***Above** All Souls' Day is the Catholic festival of the dead, when families would pray for deceased relatives.*

as apple bobbing, when participants must remove apples from a bowl of water using only their teeth, are played.

All Souls' Day

Also with Celtic origins, All Souls' Day on 2 November was traditionally a solemn day of fasting, when Christians offered prayers for the dead. Flowers were put on graves, and candles and bonfires were lit to light the souls' way to the afterlife. It was the custom for the poor to offer prayers in return for money or food – especially fruit buns, which were called soul cakes. Spiced ale was served to the "soulers" and there were souling songs and plays.

Bonfire Night

The anniversary of the gunpowder plot on 5 November 1605 – when Guy Fawkes attempted (but failed) to blow up the Houses of Parliament in London with barrels of gunpowder – is still commemorated in England with

Above *Traditional Bonfire Night food includes baked potatoes, sausages, treacle toffee and gingerbread.*

bonfires and fireworks. It is traditional to burn an effigy, made by children from old clothes, paper and straw, to represent Guy Fawkes, and children would take their effigies onto the street asking for "a penny for the guy" with which to buy fireworks. In recent years Bonfire Night celebrations have developed into large organized events with spectacular firework displays.

Christmas

As Christians honour the birth of Jesus Christ at Christmas, families and friends come together to share customs and traditions that are centuries old. On Christmas Eve midnight mass is celebrated in churches all over the country, and children hang up stockings or pillowcases to be filled with gifts by Father Christmas (provided they have been well-behaved all year).

On Christmas Day there is much feasting and good cheer. The boar's head was the centrepiece of the medieval feast, before goose, beef, chicken, and today's turkey replaced it.

Above *Wassailers in the 16th century, carrying a bowl of spiced ale to their neighbours in seasonal greeting.*

The Yule log once burnt in every home is now represented by a cake. Plum pudding (made with prunes, eggs and meat) was the forerunner to Christmas pudding, with its rich mixture of dried fruit and spices. Similarly, mince pies were originally filled with a mixture of meat, dried fruit and spices, the meat survives in the form of suet in today's recipies. Mince pies were said to bring good luck to those who ate one on each of the twelve days of Christmas.

Wassailing was once practised all over England. "Waes hael" was an Anglo-Saxon toast meaning "Good health", and a large bowl (the wassail bowl), filled with ale, spices and honey, would be passed round. It would be taken from door to door, and gifts of Christmas fare, drink or money were offered in exchange for a goodwill toast. Greetings cards, crackers and decorated trees became fashionable in Victorian times.

Below *The flaming Christmas pudding is carried in as the finale to the traditional Christmas Day dinner.*

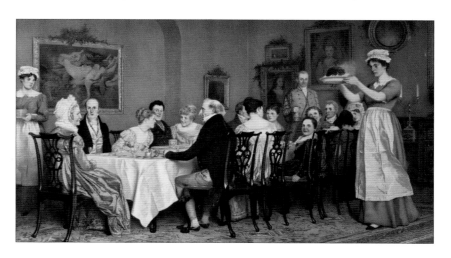

English teatime traditions

Whether teatime is a quick cup of tea and a biscuit at 4pm, a children's snack with sandwiches and cake, or a proper afternoon meal, the idea of teatime is embedded in the English psyche. Teatime might have had several changes since the 1600s, when leaf tea first arrived in England, but is still a familiar and well-loved ritual.

High tea

In the 19th century, as the working classes flocked to the cities to work in factories, the working day lengthened and the main meal of the day was served when they returned home in the evening at around 7pm. Breakfast was a modest affair, followed by a portable meal at midday. The evening meal often consisted of stews or meat puddings made with suet pastry – dishes that could be left all day to cook. Alternatively, it might be something that could be prepared quickly at the end of the working day, such as chops, kippers or perhaps cold meats, cheeses and pickles. Apple tart or milk pudding would follow and it would all be washed down with tea, which was by now England's most popular drink.

Below Afternoon tea in an Edwardian garden: a quintessentially English scene.

It came to be known as high tea because it was eaten sitting "up" at the table, unlike afternoon tea.

Afternoon tea

The English ritual of afternoon tea is said to have begun in the 1840s, when the fashionable hour for dinner, the main meal of the day, had moved to around 8pm instead of 3–4pm in the afternoon. A light meal at this time helped to ward off hunger pangs.

Left Afternoon tea in one of the many teashops in England, with elegant sandwiches, delicious cakes and tea.

When afternoon tea was introduced, it became an elegant social event with specific etiquette and smart dress, and was an ideal opportunity to show off fine china and silver. The meal was a light and leisurely affair that was conducted in the drawing room, front parlour or sitting room. China or Indian tea would be offered, together with a selection of sandwiches and cakes, the latter often made with fruit. At first gatherings were made up mainly of middle- and upper-class ladies, and provided an opportunity to gossip. In the latter half of the 19th century, when hotels installed tearooms, and teashops opened, men began to join in.

Afternoon tea at home continued as a social occasion throughout the Edwardian period. Later, teatime gave women the chance to display their baking skills, but by the latter years of the 20th century, as more and more women took jobs outside the home, the ritual more or less disappeared. However, hotels and teashops continued to serve afternoon tea, and today it is possible to enjoy it in one form or another in towns and villages anywhere in England.

Below A cup of tea and a selection of cakes will perk up an afternoon.

Food in Scotland

Scotland's magnificent culinary heritage has a long and illustrious history. The heather-clad moors and dense forests that covered much of the land ensured a plentiful supply of game; the seas, rivers and lochs teemed with fish; beef, dairy cattle and sheep thrived in pastures; wild fruits, berries and aromatic herbs were gathered from fields and hedgerows; while the cold, wet climate proved ideal for oats and barley.

Below Scotland is often carved up into three distinct areas: the rugged Highlands that dominate the northern half of the country, the bustling towns and cities of the Lowlands, and the remote, dramatic Islands that lie to the north and west.

The flavours of Scottish cuisine to this day reflect the rugged, hardy landscape. The wild mushrooms and berries complement the rich game meats, such as venison, wild boar and grouse. The smokehouses add a sumptuous taste to salmon, trout and haddock, and have resulted in local delicacies, such as Arbroath smokies and kippers.

Scottish cuisine has undergone a major progression during the past few decades, integrating new ingredients and concepts into the traditional fare. There has been an explosion of excellent restaurants offering superb dishes using local ingredients. Cottage and artisan industries have produced a wealth of speciality foods, such as jams, cheeses and breads.

A turbulent history

Scottish cuisine has been shaped not only by geography and climate but also by various social, cultural and political events. Its development was closely interwoven with the country's turbulent history – the threads producing a rich tapestry of flavours and traditions.

Over the centuries foreign invaders and settlers, particularly those from Scandinavia, had a powerful influence on Scotland's developing cuisine. The earliest impact was from the Vikings, whose lasting contribution was to teach the Scots how to make use of the rich wealth of the seas. Trade with overseas markets through Scotland's busy ports introduced new ingredients such as spices, sugar, dried fruits and wines to the Scottish kitchen. Politics too had a major role: the Auld Alliance with France, intended to curb the dynastic ambitions of English monarchs, had a great and lasting effect on the national gastronomy. All these influences brought new foods, cooking methods, ideas and skills, which over time became part of Scottish culture. Exposure to such influences occurred throughout the country's history to result in a rich and colourful cuisine based on high-quality Scottish produce.

A harsh landscape

Scotland is well known for its dramatic mountains, lochs and beautiful scenery. The geographical differences have also had a major role in shaping Scotland's cuisine and have resulted in different regional specialities according to the particular landscape and climate. The austere, rugged grandeur of the Highlands is the natural habitat of game birds, deer, rabbits and hares. The lush fertile land of the rolling countryside of the Borders and Lowlands supports beef and dairy cattle, sheep and goats while fruit and

berries thrive in the rich soils of Tayside and Fife. The islands, lochs and rivers are home to a flourishing fishing industry which exports fish and shellfish all over the world.

Traditional favourites

The Scots have always made the most of their natural resources and magnificent produce and are careful to preserve their time-honoured heritage dishes. Aberdeen Angus beef, Highland game, Tayside berries, salmon and other fish and shellfish, and of course Scotch whisky are recognized as the finest in the world.

The old traditional favourites remain popular: haggis is still widely made and is often served with "neeps and tatties" (turnips and potatoes). In addition to national foods, every region has its own unique specialities, such as Forfar

Bridies, Selkirk bannocks, Arbroath smokies, Loch Fyne kippers, Orkney, Islay and Galloway cheeses, Dundee cake, Moffat toffee, Edinburgh rock and a host of other delicious and much-loved delicacies that have been enjoyed for generations.

New speciality foods

A new generation of innovative and talented chefs has led something of a revolution in Scotland's restaurants, creating imaginative menus using Scottish produce, featuring many new and exciting signature dishes. Old favourites are given a modern twist and appear on many menus alongside traditional dishes. Restaurants in the cities of Edinburgh and Glasgow in particular blend Mediterranean with contemporary Scottish cuisine, and modern establishments serve dishes that fuse Middle Eastern and Far Eastern dishes with natural Scottish ingredients and flavours.

Food producers have also developed over the last decades, focusing on speciality quality foods, such as smoked salmon and whisky marmalades. Organic and free-range produce is increasing in popularity, with many farmers' markets springing up to promote cottage industries.

The first Scottish settlers

The early Neolithic settlers inhabited Scotland from around 4000–3000BC, coming from France and the Iberian Peninsula. They cultivated cereals and used grinding stones to make flour. They fished and hunted for food, collected shellfish from the beaches, and also kept sheep, cattle and goats.

From 2500–700BC the Beaker People from Northern and Central Europe settled, bringing bronze tools and cooking pots and thereby starting Scotland's Bronze Age, altering the cooking and eating habits of the population. Their bonding into various tribes eventually formed a group known as the Picts (painted people), named by the Romans after their body paintings.

The Celts from Ireland

The Iron-Age Celts arrived in Ireland from Scotland around 750BC. They came from today's Northern Ireland, where land shortages forced them to cross the Irish Sea to seek further pastures. The Celtic society was broken up into a caste system made up of warriors and Druids (the magicians, brehons, bards and seers), whose mystic beliefs were grounded in natural law.

Above The Neolithic settlement of Skara Brae in Orkney, where evidence of cooking and household arrangements can still be seen.

Druids performed rituals to assure the success of the hunt and the fertility of the tribe, the beasts and the land.

The Scots, as these Celts from Northern Ireland were called, brought with them the plough, horse-drawn wheeled carts and musical instruments. They lived in settlements, reared cattle and sheep, and grew crops, most commonly oats, as well as kale, cabbage and other hardy vegetables. Many used oats in soups and stews, and made oatcakes, which were originally cooked on hot stones and later on iron griddles (from the Gaelic *greadeal* meaning "hot stones").

The Celts left no written records but we know from ancient Roman and Greek writings that they ate little bread but great quantities of fish, meat and dairy produce. They farmed the land and grew oats, barley and vegetables including peas, beans and cabbage, and enjoyed wild herbs and fruits such as apples, pears, cherries and berries. They kept pigs, cattle, sheep and goats and depended on their livestock for food much more than they did their crops. Fossil records of mussel and oyster shells show that seafood was also part of their diet. The Celts roasted their food and also stewed meat and fish in pots suspended over a fire. Preservation of food was important and meat and

Left A replica Iron-Age crannog stands on Kenmore Loch. A large family or clan would have been able to live here in times of danger, surviving on stores of dried and smoked foods.

fish were salted to keep during the long winter months. Wild honey was collected and used to sweeten food and also to make mead.

The Viking raids

The 9th century was characterized by numerous Viking invasions, and Scotland became a melting pot of languages, cultures and foods. The Hebrides, Orkney and Shetland were ruled by Norway for a number of centuries, with the Hebrides passing over to the Scottish crown in 1266 and Orkney and Shetland in 1472. The Norse influence remained strong and is still in evidence today, with the traditional celebrations of Yule (Christmas) and Up-Helly-Aa.

The Vikings introduced Scandinavian methods of cooking, along with the salting, smoking and curing of fish and mutton. Many foods, following their Norse origins, are dried or salted and smoked – vivda is wind-dried mutton,

Right *The Up-Helly-Aa Viking festival at Lerwick on Shetland is a poignant link to the island's Nordic past.*

dried without salt, and is served in very thin slices, and *reested* mutton (salted and smoked) is still sold by butchers in Shetland. Cabbage appears in many dishes in the Islands, as it does in Scandinavian recipes, and is eaten with pickled pork. Herring is salted, smoked and pickled and served with onions, as it is prepared in Scandinavia.

The Scots' fondness for fish, particularly in the Northern Isles, can

partly be attributed to the Vikings, and their influence has not only survived in fish dishes but is also evident in other recipes, such as fricadellans (meatballs, from the Scandinavian 'frikadeller'). Liver muggies (fish stomachs stuffed with seasoned fish livers) are derived from the Old Norse 'magi'.

The Viking tradition of eating out of wooden bowls and plates with a sharp pointed knife was also adopted. Spoons were made from wood, horn or animal bone and were frequently carved with intricate patterns and the heads of fabulous beasts. Similarly, lavishly decorated horns were used to serve drinks and soups.

The Vikings were great drinkers, and brought with them a number of flavoursome concoctions. Whipkull, an ancient festive drink of eggs and sugar whisked over heat, is identical to the Norwegian eggedosis, the national festive dessert served with crisp biscuits. It is also similar to an Icelandic soup.

The Scottish clan system

An important influence on Scottish cuisine is the history of the clans and clan culture. The system is believed to have been founded by a group of Scots who settled on the west coast of Scotland in the 6th century. The word clan is directly drawn from the Gaelic word *clann*, meaning children. The clans were made up of both "native men" (with a direct blood relationship with their chief and with each other) and "broken men" from other clans, who sought the protection of the clan. Many clan names begin with "Mac", which means "son of".

The clan chieftain shared his home with relatives and clanspeople, who were employed by him in return for their keep. The rule of the chief over his lands was virtually autonomous, but there were frequent feuds between the clans and battles were common. Stronger, larger clans became dominant, with Clan Donald reputed to be the most powerful.

Tartan became an important symbol of clan kinship among the Highlanders, and each clan developed its own tartan

Below *Whisky was originally made by clans, and the quality and flavour was symbolic of the clan's status.*

for identification and to depict the prestige of the clan. It was worn at feasts and clan celebrations.

It was a matter of pride and honour for the clan chief to offer his very best food and drink to visitors. Reports from travellers in the 18th century praised the generous hospitality they received from the clans in the Highlands.

A breakfast of porridge (oatmeal) was typically accompanied by fresh cream, eggs, cheese, bannocks and oatcakes and was washed down with milk, buttermilk, ale or whisky. A special

Above *Highland cows were reared by the clans for beef and dairy products.*

drink for honoured guests was Auld Man's Milk – eggs, milk, honey and whisky beaten together.

Sir Walter Scott described the 14th-century funeral feast of a Highland chief in *The Fair Maid of Perth* (1828): "... Pits wrought in the hillside and lined with heated stones, served for stewing immense quantities of beef, mutton and venison; wooden spits supported sheep and goats, which were roasted entire; others were cut into joints and seethed in cauldrons made of the animals' own skins, sewed hastily together and filled with water; while huge quantities of pike, trout, salmon and char were broiled with more ceremony on glowing embers."

Clan repression

During the 18th century, the English government was determined to curtail the power of the Highland chiefs and prevent uprisings. They built roads in the previously inaccessible Highlands, and cleared much of the land (along with the Highland families) to make way for sheep farming and hunting

estates. The draconian Act of Proscription (1747) made it illegal to wear Highland dress (except in the military), and banned the use of clan names, celebrations and music.

The Highland Clearances had great repercussions for the Highlanders. Their self-sufficiency, which had relied on wild game and produce from cows, sheep, goats and hens, disappeared and they were left destitute. Many were evicted without their possessions, not even cooking utensils, as they surveyed their burning homes and lands. A few sympathetic English landlords distributed food to the stricken Highlanders, but it wasn't enough and thousands emigrated to the New World in search of a better life. The emptiness of the Highlands today is a lasting reminder of those terrible times.

The clans and other Scots attempted to bring the Stuart kings back to the throne; these episodes became known as the Jacobite Rebellions. In 1746, the "Young Pretender" or Bonnie Prince

Right Bagpipes, tartan and traditional clan celebrations can now be found throughout Scotland.

Charlie, was defeated at the Battle of Culloden. The clan lands were confiscated, and Jacobite supporters were imprisoned – including Rob Roy MacGregor. Bonnie Prince Charlie escaped and was helped to Skye by Flora Macdonald, who disguised Charlie as her maid for the crossing.

Revival of the clans

Tartan made a welcome return in 1782 when the Highland regiments, such as the Black Watch, were permitted to wear a regimental tartan. The Highlanders became keen to re-establish (or in some cases re-invent) their family tartans and celebrate their clan culture. Queen Victoria, who loved all things Scottish, encouraged the use of tartan and interest spread. Today, especially with the energy that has come from

the new Scottish Parliament, the clans are celebrated, and many traditions, foods and festivals are enjoyed throughout the country.

Below The Highland Games re-create the clan competitiveness through games such as the tug o' war.

Scottish feasts and festivals

Festivities, celebrations and parties are key to Scottish culture. There are the raucous Scottish reels accompanied by Gaelic music played on the accordion, bagpipes and fiddle. There are Highland Games, Burns Night and Hogmanay. Perhaps the best-known events in Scotland are the Edinburgh International Festival and the Edinburgh Festival Fringe, which together showcase music, theatre and dance.

Below *Fireworks light the Edinburgh streets at midnight for the Hogmanay New Year's Eve festivities.*

Hogmanay

New Year's Eve in Scotland is Hogmanay. Festivities involve street parties, fireworks and costumes, especially in Edinburgh, where the city centre is closed to normal traffic for the duration. The origins of the word Hogmanay are unknown. It may derive from the Norse *Hoggunott* or night of slaughter, when animals were killed for a midwinter feast, or from *aguillanneuf*, the old French street cry for gifts on the eve of New Year. The traditional New Year song is "Auld Lang Syne"; the version sung today was reworked and made popular by Robert Burns, the famous Scottish poet.

A great many traditions surround Hogmanay, many related to food. The "first foot" in the house after midnight must be a dark-haired man, carrying symbolic coal, black bun or shortbread. Black bun is a very rich, dark fruit cake encased in pastry, usually accompanied by a dram of whisky. Clootie dumpling (the clootie is the cloth in which the pudding is boiled) is a fruit pudding with a coin concealed inside. Traditionally, the person who got the coin was given the first newborn lambs in the spring.

In Edinburgh and other parts of Scotland the traditional Hogmanay beverage until well into the 19th century was het pint, a potent blend of hot spiced ale, eggs and whisky. A couple of hours before midnight, great gleaming copper kettles of het pint were carried through the streets. Cupbearers pressed everyone into having a "noggin".

In Kirkwall, Orkney, a New Year Ba' Game takes place in the street on 1 January. Much merriment and excitement accompanies the game where the Uppies and the Doonies fight for a cork-filled leather ball.

Burns Night

Scottish communities throughout the world commemorate the birth, on 25 January 1759, of the poet Robert Burns with the traditional Burns Supper. The intimate and magical night is heavily ritualized. Before the meal starts, Burns' "Selkirk Grace" is recited:

> *Some hae meat and canna eat*
> *And some wad eat, that want it,*
> *But we hae meat, and we can eat,*
> *Sae let the Lord be thankit.*

A piper enters, followed by the chef carrying the haggis. A waiter follows

Above A chef and piper bring in the haggis at a Burns Night supper.

behind carrying a bottle of whisky. They walk around the guests, ending at the top table, where the chairman takes the whisky and pours out two large glasses. The haggis is put on the table and the whiskies are given to the piper and to the chef. Then the haggis is "addressed" with the Burns poem "Address to a Haggis" (1786), which begins:

> *Fair fa' your honest, sonsie face,*
> *Great chieftain o' the puddin'-race!*

A dirk (dagger) is plunged into the haggis and a St Andrew's cross is cut on the top. It is served with bashed neeps and champit tatties – mashed turnips and creamed potatoes. After the meal is over there are whisky toasts to "The Immortal Memory" of Burns. The evening continues with Burns songs and ends with "Auld Lang Syne" and three cheers for absent friends.

The Edinburgh Festival

The plethora of cultural activities held over six weeks each year in the summer are collectively known as the Edinburgh International Festival. The largest arts festival in the world, the Festival has a splendid programme of events that includes art exhibitions, café concerts, talks, lectures and workshops plus live performances by internationally renowned artists. It attracts thousands of visitors from all over the world.

Food and drink are an essential part of the festival with farmers' markets offering local foods, lively food debates with top Scottish food writers and chefs, food-themed films, opportunities to sample beers from Scottish breweries, plus wine tastings from Scottish wine merchants and a chance to discover the origins of whisky with a wee dram or two on offer! There is plenty to eat and drink too as Edinburgh's finest cafés and restaurants offer a wide choice of food and drinks.

The Highland Games

Bursting with clan rivalry, the Highland Games have their roots in ancient Celtic traditions and originated with the clan meetings organized by the chiefs. The most important games are the Edinburgh Highland Games in August, and in September the Braemar Gathering and Highland Games, and the Aberdeen and Aboyne Highland Games.

Formalization and annual gatherings began around 1820 as part of the revival of tartan and Highland culture, and in 1848 the Braemar Gathering was attended by Queen Victoria. The competitions were much as they are today, with traditional stone and

Below The Edinburgh streets are crowded with performers, stalls and food fairs during the Festival.

Right The Highland Games include a traditional dance competition with brightly coloured tartans.

hammer throwing, tossing the caber, piping and dancing, along with running and jumping events.

Food and whisky are abundant, with plenty of spit roasts and local pies. Raspberries and strawberries abound, served with fresh cream and shortbreads.

Harvest celebrations

In the Celtic year, *Lammas* heralded the start of the harvest and it was an annual fair day in most parts of Scotland until the 20th century. The gathering-in of a successful *hairst* (harvest) has been celebrated since ancient times, and the climax was the harvest feast or *kirn*, also known as the *muckle supper* (big supper).

Ale-crowdie (also called meal-and-ale) always featured at the harvest feasts in Aberdeen and north-east Scotland, so much so that it gave its name to the festival. It was always made with the first of the grain, to commemorate the renewal of the food supply. The grain was put in a large bowl or small wooden tub and ale was poured over until it was of drinking consistency – if it was too thin it was an omen that next year's crops would be poor. The drink was sweetened with treacle, laced with whisky and left to stand. Charms were concealed in the bowl and everyone present took a spoonful.

In the Highlands the new grain was made into a bannock known as *moilean moire*. In Orkney a fruited bannock was given as a reward to the man who carried the last load of sheaves into the stack yard. He was then given a head start and chased by the other men and only allowed to eat it when he had out-distanced his pursuers.

Cranachan or cream crowdie (from the Gaelic *cruaidh*, meaning thick and firm), a luscious combination of toasted oatmeal, cream, honey and whisky, was also essential at harvest celebrations.

Hallowe'en

The coming of Christianity replaced the old pagan feasts with religious festivals. Samhain or Samhuinn, the most important Celtic festival marking the start of winter, became the Eve of All Hallows (the night before All Saints' Day) or Hallowe'en on 31 October. It was a mysterious time when it was

Left Traditional Scottish music is played at many celebrations, with fiddles, guitars and accordions.

Above Evening celebrations often involve a ceilidh with Scottish reels.

believed that ghosts, fairies, demons and witches wandered the earth. Bonfires were lit to ward off evil spirits, masks were worn to avoid being recognized by the spirits, and lucky charms protected against evil. Hallowe'en "guizing" and the wearing of masks and costumes is a remnant of those beliefs.

Hollowed-out turnips with a candle inside were placed on gateposts to frighten evil spirits – the origin of pumpkin lanterns today. The custom of eating special cakes probably derives from the practice of baking spiced cakes to herald the winter. Gingerbreads and biscuits were especially popular in Scotland.

Fortune-telling and magic were other traditional customs of Hallowe'en. A fortune-telling pudding (usually a large bowl of cranachan) contained small charms. Each charm had a specific meaning: a coin meant wealth, a ring foretold marriage and a thimble indicated no marriage.

Yule and Christmas festivities

Christmas festivities were banned by the Church during the Reformation. The annual holiday was abolished and church ministers checked on their parishioners to make sure no festive foods or celebrations were in evidence. Proper festivities did not resume until the mid-18th century, and still today the New Year is the more important holiday of the midwinter period in Scotland.

Whipkull or whipcol, a mixture of beaten egg yolks and sugar, was served in a special bowl to the Shetland *Udallers* (lairds) at the great Yule breakfasts. Sometimes cream was added and later still a good measure of rum or whisky. Rich, crisp shortbread is the traditional accompaniment.

Atholl brose is another popular Christmas drink enjoyed on the days running up to Christmas Day. It is made from whisky, strained honey, oatmeal and sweet cream slowly beaten together in the right order and proportion. Its creation is credited to the Duke of Atholl when, during a Highland Rebellion in 1745, he foiled his enemy by filling the well from which they drank with the heady mixture. The intoxicated men were then easily defeated and the drink became more widely known.

Up-Helly-Aa

Torches, fireworks and bonfires light the night sky in this midwinter fire festival in Lerwick on Shetland. It is rooted in an ancient Norse festival, marking the end of Yule, and the 5,000 onlookers and participants dress as Vikings.

A full-sized replica of a Norse longboat is paraded through Lerwick by the Chief Guizer, who represents Sigurd Hlodvisson – Sigurd the Stout, Earl of Orkney, who died in 1014 on the battlefield at Clontarf, Ireland. In the early evening 850 torches are lit. The guizers throw them into the ship to set it ablaze. As they do so they sing "Up-Helly-Aa". Rockets and guns are fired from ships, and the longboat burns spectacularly. Fortified with whisky, the crowds sing the anthem, "The Norseman's Home".

Below The midwinter fire festival of Up-Helly-Aa includes the burning of a Viking longboat.

Food in Ireland

Ireland is an island on the outermost edge of Europe. On the map its western coastline follows the line of Europe's continental shelf, united by the Atlantic Ocean, from Cadiz in the south of Spain to Bergen in Norway.

On this green, fertile island everything that is grown, all the animals that are reared, everything caught in the fishing grounds and all that is eaten are influenced by a temperate climate. Ireland is only rarely influenced by the cold of Northern Europe but always, especially along the western seaboard, by the warm, wet westerly winds that blow in over the warm Gulf Stream.

It is often said that Ireland does not have a climate, it has weather. For a small island the climate is extremely varied, going from sunshine to rain within minutes. Rainfall is not excessive: 1,400mm/55in in the south and west and less than 700mm/27in in the "sunny south-east". But numerous rainy days and infrequent droughts mean high humidity, which brings cloud cover and so less bright sunshine than in much of Europe.

The siren call, "Ireland the Food Island", is more than just a recent clever sales slogan. Ireland is a fast-growing food-exporting nation. Its grass-fed beef and lamb and its dairy produce are exported all over the world. Stand in any Irish fishing port and observe how foreign trawlers and fish buyers covet the fresh seafood caught in clean Atlantic waters.

All over Ireland similar crops are grown and the same foodstuffs are produced; however, the best grassland for cattle is in the counties of Kildare, Meath and the Golden Vale, and the best mountain lamb is found in the mountains of Connemara and Wicklow. Wexford and the north of County Dublin on the east coast are famous for producing high-quality soft fruits.

How Ireland's food culture developed

When trying to unravel the gradual development of Ireland's food culture, the climate, geography and history of the people merge. Plants and animals certainly existed in Ireland before the last great ice age, when ice covered most of the island and much of northern Europe. As the ice retreated, 13,000 years ago, there was a massive re-invasion of plants and animals, including the giant deer known as the great Irish elk. It is also known that over no more than a thousand years, a large number of new plants and animals appeared in Ireland, so a land bridge must have existed at a crucial time. As the ice melted, two things happened: the land started to rise and sea levels also rose.

About 7,500 years ago Ireland finally became detached from mainland Europe, limiting the varieties of flora and fauna that are indigenous – Ireland

Left There are 32 counties within Ireland and Northern Ireland. Dublin is the capital city of Ireland and other main regional towns include Cork and Galway. Belfast is the capital city of Northern Ireland.

Left *Harvesting cultivated mussels on a fish farm in the clean, clear waters of Killary Harbour, County Galway.*

has only about 70 per cent of British plants and about 65 per cent of the freshwater insects and invertebrates found in Britain.

Humans then took over, and the island's food culture was created by successive waves of settlers. The earliest were happy to find a land rich in seafood, edible nuts, fruits and plants. In their footsteps each successive group introduced new plants and animals.

Ireland's favourite food and drink

What emerges through time is that, while the Irish are always ready and willing to adopt what they like and make it their own, they rarely abandon a favourite food. Still deeply ingrained in Irish society is a love of the fish, shellfish and the wild plants and animals that first brought humans to the island: the beef and bánbhianna

Right *The warehouse of the Old Bushmills Distillery viewed over the dammed St Columb's Rill, which is the pure water source for the whiskey production at Bushmills, County Antrim, Northern Ireland.*

(white foods made from milk) and the Celts' love of feasting; the grains, fruits and vegetables of the early Christian tradition; the game birds, animals and fish brought by the Normans.

Prevented by the climate from growing vines and producing wine, the Irish became expert brewers of distinctive ciders and beers. When the secret art of distillation was brought to Ireland from the Mediterranean, the Irish discovered *uisce beatha* – whiskey – the water of life.

Even the potato, which eventually brought the misery of great famines, still has pride of place on every Irish table. Around the beginning of the 20th century, German families, who came to Ireland to escape persecution, influenced and greatly expanded the number of pork dishes, which were, for many generations, the ordinary Irish people's main fresh source of meat.

For even longer the Irish have welcomed chefs, homegrown or incomers, trained in the classic tradition. Now many talented young Irish chefs returning from "a stint abroad" are inspired to put a new spin on the traditional foods and in doing so offer essential support to a new wave of speciality food growers and producers.

The first Irish settlers

About 9,000 years ago, the first settlers in Ireland found an island full of plants and trees, growing in a climate that was a little warmer than it is today. These early settlers were hunter-fisher-gatherers and dwelt mainly on the shores of lakes, rivers or by the sea, in skin huts which they packed up and moved with them. As well as providing the raw materiais for fuel and building, the dense woods allowed them to build dugout canoes in which they could penetrate the countryside using the navigable rivers and lakes.

These early settlers knew much about edible plants. More importantly, they understood the seasonal movements of fish and animals and moved between three or four campsites in a yearly pattern governed by the migrations of fish, birds and animals, and the seasonal availability of plants, seeds,

Below An exterior view of the impressive Neolithic passage tomb at Newgrange in County Meath.

Above A curragh at sea on the Dingle peninsula, County Kerry.

nuts and berries. Early spring would find them on the coast near river estuaries where they harvested shellfish and caught fish from offshore rocks on the incoming tide. They also caught nesting seabirds (mainly auks and puffins) often taking their eggs, and fished the first-run salmon.

In summer the people followed the salmon up river to the lakes where they also harvested fruits and berries. There were large stocks of eels in the lakes too, but these were easier to catch as they began to swim downstream again in the autumn. At this time they harvested wild hazelnuts, which were an important winter food and widely available in the indigenous forests.

During the winter the people hunted and trapped game and wildfowl. Wild pig seems to have been the most important source of meat, along with hare, birds and the occasional red deer.

Mesolithic settlers

Some time after these earliest settlers, a second group arrived who had stronger, heavier tools with which they began to create small clearings in the woods. But they did not sow crops or keep domestic animals. They possessed pronged spears and possibly fish hooks. They probably preserved meat and fish,

THE FIRST IRISH SETTLERS

particularly by smoking and drying on racks. Many of the foods still most favoured in Ireland were among the very first foods eaten – wild berries, such as blackberries and rowan berries; fish, such as salmon and trout; and shellfish, such as oysters and mussels.

The first farmers

About 6,000 years ago another wave of settlers arrived: they were semi-nomadic farmers. It seems likely that they arrived in small boats made of skins stretched over wood, craft not unlike the *curraghs* which are still used today in the west of Ireland. Their arrival coincided with a change in climate and a decline in forest cover. By clearing the land for grazing and tillage they activated the growth of nettles and sorrel. They brought grains and other plants with them and animals unknown in Ireland: horses, mountain sheep, goats and small cattle.

The farming people brought pottery vessels for storage and cooking. They built wooden houses with hearths and pits for storage of their seed grain. Wild foods remained important, and the herding of animals and cereal cultivation were integrated with fishing, hunting and gathering. They ate sheep, goats and a domesticated pig, as well as wild animals such as boar, birds and occasionally even seal and bear.

An organized society develops

Over a period of more than 1,000 years, these early farmers developed a remarkable society. The most visible mark they left on the landscape is their tombs. The crowning achievement of this early society is the great series of gigantic tombs in the valley of the

Right *The valley of the River Boyne, revered in ancient Irish culture, is still valued for its fertile grazing grounds.*

River Boyne at Knowth, Dowth and Newgrange in County Meath. These are vast structures, pre-dating the Egyptian pyramids, and are unquestionably the work of an advanced organized society.

As many as 4,000 people may have been needed to provide the workers to build these great monuments, to farm the valley and provide the food to feed them. But their shallow cultivation methods quickly exhausted the soil, so they moved on, clearing more woodland. Over thousands of years successive cultures occupied the valley of the River Boyne. It remains some of the most fertile grazing land on the island. Then the climate became colder and wetter. Much of the old woodland was gradually engulfed by bogs, which crept outwards and upwards, covering many of the stone-walled field systems of the settlements.

The early Bronze Age

The next wave of settlers brought Ireland into the early Bronze Age. These Beaker People were named after the elaborate decorated pots found in their burial places, along with bronze axes and jewellery. They introduced new plants and animals into Ireland. Discovering and extracting metals meant a wider range of implements could be made, resulting in the introduction of new farming techniques.

It was these Bronze Age prospectors, roaming in search of metal-bearing rock formations, who first built *fulachta fiadh*, ancient cooking sites scattered over the countryside. A sunken trough lined with stones or wood was built near water; a fire would have been lit nearby and large stones heated in it. The hot stones were then thrown into the trough to bring the water to the boil. Large joints of meat were wrapped in straw and put into the water to cook. The stones often split when they were thrown into the water and were then thrown on to a pile on the far side of the trough.

Many of these ancient cooking-sites were discovered because of the characteristic horseshoe-shaped mounds made by the discarded stones. Sites are widespread; in County Cork alone there are over 2,500 of them. *Fulachta fiadh* remained in use into early medieval times.

Celtic cattle culture

About 2,600 years ago, during the late Bronze Age, farming activity was advanced by the development of farm implements. More domestic animals, especially cattle, were kept and wheat, barley and flax were grown.

Another group of settlers arrived in Ireland, most likely seeking copper. They slowly replaced the hunting spear with swords and shields and also brought massive cauldrons, horses, wheeled carts, saddle querns, musical instruments and the *ard* plough. This wooden plough must have seemed miraculous then, because deeper penetration of the soil meant that exhausted land could bear crops again. However, it was susceptible to damage from buried stones that would have to be removed. This labour tended to fix the early farmers to one place, quickly exhausting the newly enriched soils.

However, a rising population living on less fertile land seems to have caused unrest on Irish soil for the first time. During this period the first defensive dwelling sites appear: lake settlements (*crannogs*) and hill-forts provided protection for farmers and their domesticated animals. These hillside settlements, and the appearance of distinctive bronze artefacts, are the first signs of Celtic intruders on the island.

A farming Dark Age

It is tempting to speculate that a race of warlike Celts plundered the island bringing about the collapse of an organized society. However, there is very little real evidence of this.

Sophisticated pollen-counting techniques suggest that the Celtic period ushered in a dark age for farming, caused by soil exhaustion, which was to last for about 600 years. About 2,250 years ago, in a period known as the Pagan Iron Age, there is evidence of a gradual disappearance of agriculture: the weeds of cultivation disappear first, followed by cereals as the soils became increasingly unproductive. Tillage farming declined and semi-nomadic pastoral farming re-emerged.

The coming of the iron plough brought to Ireland by later Celts would have allowed the re-establishment of tillage in some areas, because of its ability to rip up the top layer of the acid heathlands and reveal the richer subsoils beneath. The only evidence for this is a few early ploughshares found near *crannogs*, which are thought to have been the permanent dwellings of kings or clan leaders. Generally, however, for many centuries, great

Above *The double-headed Celtic figure of Janus (meaning two-faced), near Lough Erne, Boa Island, County Fermanagh, Northern Ireland.*

herds of cattle reigned supreme. The Celts' way of life depended on cattle. Herding and protecting cattle from animal and human predators was a full-time occupation. Cattle raiding became the national pastime. A person's social standing and worth was reckoned in cattle units – a man or woman "of six heifers", or of "two milch cows", became a commonplace.

Religious festivals

The great pagan religious festivals, their myths and their rituals, mainly centred around cattle. There were four seasons in the Celtic year. The festival of *Samhain* marked the end of one year and the beginning of the next, the end of the grazing season when the herds were brought together. Grass being in short supply in the winter months, only beasts fit for breeding were spared from slaughter. Some were salted

Left *Set in superb landscape and in the middle of Doon Lough, County Donegal, are the remains of Doon Celtic fort.*

Right *The Broighter ship, found at Broighter, County Derry, represents a ship intended for high seas. It has moveable oars and a mast for a sail. Celtic merchants and traders travelled around the coasts of western Europe in boats like this. It may have been an offering, possibly to Manannan mac Lir, King of the Ocean. The Celts valued gold highly and often went in search of it.*

for winter food. The whole extended family, or *tuath*, assembled and feasted for days on end.

The festival *Imbolc* (St Brigid's Day) was associated with sheep and means "sheep's milk". *Bealtaine*, the May feast, marked the time when the herds could once again be driven out to open grazing. Two great bonfires were lit and the cattle driven between them to protect them against disease.

At *Lughnasa* sacrifices were made to the god *Lug* to ensure a good harvest of grain. These great rituals were supervised by the Druids of the tribe.

The Celtic influence

The need to keep cattle safe and productive initiated the development of Celtic farmsteads and farming practice.

As well as *crannogs* the Celts built isolated ring forts, big enough to contain a house, and a *souterrain* for underground storage and protection from raiders. A stone fort was a *cathair* or *cashel* or *dun*; those with just an earthen bank were called a *rath*.

Approximately 40,000 forts existed, and today's Irish place names reflect this, such as Cahir, Cashel, Rathkeel and Dundrum. In winter, the cattle grazed near the fort, but in the summer months the Celts drove their cattle to summer pastures and set up a *buaile* – a temporary milking shelter, anglicized as "booley".

The Celts dominated Ireland for a thousand years. When other cultures challenged their supremacy they resisted and absorbed the invaders for many hundreds of years more. Despite its semi-nomadic, pastoral nature, theirs was a developed and organized society with an enlightened, structured code of law, art and great oral traditions in literature and genealogy.

1,700 years ago Ireland emerged from the historical darkness of the Iron Age. Agricultural activity and the population increased. The Romans did not invade Ireland and as their power began to crumble in Britain, Irish tribes began to settle in Scotland, Wales, Cornwall and the Isle of Man.

For the ordinary Irish people, the cattle culture would survive the coming of Christianity, the Normans, and Cromwell and his devastations, right up to the threshold of the 18th century. Nowadays the cultural and culinary devotion to cattle is still strong and vibrant.

Left *Crannogs were used from the Bronze Age to medieval times. This replica is by the lake at Craggaunowen. They consisted of palisaded buildings on an artificial island or a platform raised on stilts over water.*

The Normans in Ireland

The English suffered more than the Irish from the Norman presence. In the Domesday Book there is no trace of the families who ruled England before 1066. In Ireland, however, leading Irish families' names were still prominent in society four hundred years later. The Normans intermarried with the Irish at the highest level, the cultures intermingled and, just as the Vikings had done before them, they became "more Irish than the Irish".

The Normans profoundly influenced agriculture and land tenure. The pre-Norman Irish farmed contentedly at subsistence levels; there was land enough for all if you counted wealth in cattle. Food was grown to feed the family and for agricultural by-products, mainly skins and hides, that were traded for more exotic items like wine, spices and olive oil. The Normans, from mainland Europe where agriculture was highly developed, counted wealth in acres of land held. They valued land for its rich soil that produced corn crops for the markets of Europe, where huge profits could be made. However, once farming depended on cash crops it was vulnerable to fluctuating demand, and Irish farming got into grave difficulties time and again.

Agricultural change

The Normans settled in the richer agricultural lands of the eastern part of the island. Within a continually shifting line they built their fortified farms and enclosed land in a manner unknown in the country. They introduced the open-field system and three-crop rotation. The feudal system of land tenure was enforced within the Norman sphere of influence. Irish kings and chieftains were displaced and their lands granted to tenants who supported the feudal lord. The day-to-day life of ordinary people changed little at first: instead of food "tributes" to their chieftain they paid food "rents" to their new master. If you were already of the old Irish "unfree class" (Irish euphemism for "slave") you became a feudal serf.

New animals

Sheep were important to the Normans for manuring arable land, and supplying wool, milk for cheese, and meat.

As well as greatly increasing the sheep flock, the Normans brought many other animals and plants to Ireland. They brought freshwater (coarse) fish to stock large ponds, rabbits to breed in great

Above *A 14th-century effigy of the Norman knight Thomas de Cantwell at Kilfane Church, County Kilkenny.*

warrens, doves to breed in dovecotes, the common hare to "course" (hunt with dogs) and the fallow deer to supplement the dwindling stocks of the native red. Peas and beans, and flax for linen were more widely grown. Markets were also established in towns.

Beyond the Normans

In the Middle Ages the climate became wetter and colder, making good wheat hard to grow. By the time of the Tudor plantations there were two distinct Irelands: the well-kept, farmed lands of The Pale and "beyond The Pale". This included large areas of undrained bog, lakes, mountains and secondary woods of "the mere Irish". It was land fit only for the old Irish way of farming called *creaghting*, where whole communities moved constantly, raiding and drifting from the land of one lord to another.

Left *Trim Castle, Leinster, is one of the sites of a Norman market.*

The big house and the cottage kitchen

The English governance of Ireland, begun by the Tudors, resulted in the emergence of two distinct food cultures. Behind demesne walls in "the big house" English landowners, well supplied with meat, game and fish, grew fruit and vegetables in walled kitchen gardens. The big house had cooking-ranges, bakehouses, storerooms and the wherewithal to store stocks of food.

In marked contrast, the vast majority of native Irish lived in small thatched cottages and cabins and, by and large, ate only the food they could grow on a tiny patch of land and cook in one pot over a turf fire set in an open hearth also used for smoking meat and fish.

Above *Muckross House in Killarney, County Kerry, was built in 1843, in English Tudor style.*

Basic cooking equipment

The three-legged iron pot was central to the food of the common people. Suspended from the "crane" (an upright pivot with an extending arm) two or three pots could be raised or lowered over the turf fire in the hearth. The bastable (an iron pot with a lid, handles and three short legs) was used for baking bread, tarts and cakes. The bread dough was set into the pot and the lid heaped with glowing turf embers giving even heat top and bottom. The *lec* (a bake stone) or a *lan* (a flat griddle with two lugs for lifting) could be set on a trivet or hung from

the crane and used to cook potato cakes, scones and griddle breads. Hard, dry oatcakes were baked on a wooden or metal stand, which was simply set in front of the fire.

Huge iron frying pans were used for pancakes and cooking rashers (strips of bacon), eggs, and fish. A "muller" was a small pot with a long handle for heating drinks, such as mulled ale, or a punch made from *poitín* or whiskey.

The poor had to be content with a small amount of pig meat, fish or seaweed, or a poached rabbit boiled with "pot-herbs". Boiled in a large pot, potatoes were drained and tipped into a skib (osier basket) to allow moisture to escape. In the "big house", silver rings, lined with a napkin, were used for the same purpose.

Given the cooking equipment and limited foods available to the poor, their ingenuity was admirable. They invented recipes that used fresh or preserved meat and seafood to add savour to one-pot stews and soups.

Left *Old cottages set in farmland at Malin Head, Innishowen, County Donegal.*

Changing cuisine

There was some crossover between the different traditions. Wealthier farmers sent their daughters into service in the big house to learn fine cooking skills and enhance their marriage prospects, since the landowners employed classically trained cooks.

Industry developed belatedly, but work became available in the cities, and country people brought their cooking traditions into urban areas. At the turn of the 20th century, before traditions might have been lost forever, pioneers like Florence Irwin travelled through Ulster learning recipes from country women. Irwin published them in her famous book *The Cookin' Woman*. Later, Theodora FitzGibbon researched in southern Ireland, delving into the handwritten receipt books of the big houses. The work of these and later pioneers awakened new interest in both the food of the ordinary people and Irish country-house cooking.

Irish feasts and festivals

The Irish have a long tradition of celebrating festivals – mainly influenced by the seasonal Celtic pagan rituals and Christian feast days. Most festivals involve food and drink of some variety and there is always singing, dancing and playing musical instruments.

Imbolc

Originally, *Imbolc,* the first day of spring, was associated with the Celtic earth goddess, Brigit, a "mother goddess". The Christian church then transformed her into St Brigid and gave her a mythical past. Like the goddess she replaced, Brigid was given the patronage of cattle, the dairy, and food.

Traditionally at *Imbolc,* presents of freshly churned butter and buttermilk were made to the poor. The festive meal was sowans (fermented oat gruel), dumplings, apple cake, cider cake, colcannon and barm brack. A *Brídeóg* (an effigy dressed in women's clothing, fashioned from a churn dash – the wooden pole with a wider head inverted through the lid of the churn) was carried from house to house by

groups of young people wearing ferocious masks. They made a collection for "the Biddy" – the anglicized name of the *Brídeóg.* Today there is no festival for *Imbolc*; it is simply the first day of spring.

Shrove Tuesday

A Christian festival, Shrove Tuesday was the day before Ash Wednesday, the start of the six-week Lenten fast, which forbade the eating of meat, milk, butter, eggs and sugar. Pancakes were cooked to use up these foods, preventing temptation during Lent. Shrove Tuesday is now commonly known as Pancake Day, when pancakes are traditionally served with butter, lemon, sugar or honey. However, chefs now produce ever more exotic fillings.

Left A postcard showing a patriotic Irishwoman on St Patrick's Day, 1916.

Right Dressed up as the patron saint of Ireland at a St Patrick's Day parade on 17 March in Dublin.

Left The Celtic earth goddess, Brigit, a "mother goddess", who was given the patronage of cattle, the dairy and food.

St Patrick's Day

Lent was set aside for St Patrick's Day, commemorating the saint who brought Christianity to Ireland. This is a day for feasting on pork and strong drink, the *pota Pádraig* (Paddy's pot), to "drown the shamrock". The shamrock, symbol of the Trinity, was placed in the last of many such pots and, after a toast, plucked from the glass and thrown over the left shoulder for luck.

Easter

On Easter Eve, to mark the end of the Lenten fast, the Whipping of the Herring was performed by butchers' boys. Herrings were whipped with sticks, then thrown in a river, and a young beribboned lamb decorated with flowers was carried in procession to the market place. Easter replaced the Celtic celebration of fertility, so decorating and eating eggs became traditional.

St Patrick's day all the Irish give
Three cheers for the banner of Erin's Isle
for her golden harp and shamrock green
And the maid that's a coming through the style.

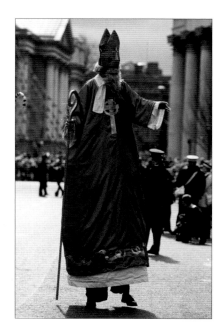

Nowadays young children are given chocolate eggs as a symbol that the fasting is over. Spring lamb is now eaten at Easter, but veal and goat kid were once equally popular. The poor received gifts of corned (salted) beef.

Echoes of fertility rituals lingered in the Cake Dance, where a cake of barm brack (decorated with birds, animals and fishes) provided by an ale-wife was set on top of a 3m/10ft high pike. Courting couples danced around it wildly until exhausted; the last couple still dancing "took the cake" and divided it up amongst them all.

Bealtaine

May Eve, or *Bealtaine*, is the start of summer when traditionally the cattle were sent to the *buaile* (booley) hill pasture. *Bealtaine* was untouched by Christianity but rich in pagan customs to guard against evil intended by the *Sióge* (malevolent fairies).

Most customs concerned cattle and their *bánbhianna*, to ensure they would survive until harvest time. Even during the 19th century, farmers drove cattle between two fires to protect them from disease. Cattle were also driven into abandoned raths and ring forts; they were bled, some of the blood was drunk, and the rest poured on the earth as a libation. Nothing was loaned or gifted on May Day lest luck "go with it". Stirabout, or hasty pudding (sweet milk thickened with flour), was prepared to show that winter supplies had held out.

Midsummer

Originally Midsummer was an ancient festival associated with the summer solstice. Small, family fires were lit to appease the fire god, and their smoke, drifting over the crops, was believed to protect the plants from blight and rust. Cattle driven though the smoke were

protected from natural ailments or magical influence. Big communal bonfires accompanied merrymaking, eating and drinking (*poitín* and beer) and food was contributed by all who could spare it.

The Twelfth of July

Of more recent origin are celebrations in Ulster commemorating King William of Orange's victory against James II at The Battle of the Boyne in 1690. At marches held by lodges of the Orange Order, spectators eat strawberries straight from the punnet. In the evening, participants have a drink or two to inspire singing and music at the great bonfires.

Lughnasa

A major Celtic festival, *Lughnasa* is now held on the first Sunday of August. Originally great assemblies and offerings were made to the god *Lugh* to thank him for the first wild fruits of the summer harvest. The pagan practice of climbing hills to gather

Above *Vendors selling yellowman and dillisk at an Auld Lammas Fair in County Antrim.*

fraughans (wild blueberries or bilberries) became a day of feasting, courting and fairs. The people feasted on meat and the first of the potato crop with summer butter, then followed this with wild *fraughans* and strawberries with cream. Unmarried girls made garlands using wheat to honour the goddess Ceres, and baked *fraughans* into cakes eaten at the bonfire dance that night.

The day is known by many names, which highlight its various aspects and traditions: Height, Garland or Fraughan Sunday and, in Northern Ireland, Lammas (an anglicization). This is the only surviving memory of an *óenach* (an ancient assembly) at which there would be a fair, chariot racing and games of strength.

An Auld Lammas Fair is held annually in Ballycastle, County Antrim during the last week of August, where the traditional treat is "yellowman", a toffee with a honeycomb texture.

Puck Fair

Held annually in August, this three-day festival takes place in Killorglin, County Kerry. On Gathering Day stalls are opened to sell food and drink, and booths are opened for trade and barter. On this first day a large billy goat is decorated with ribbons and paraded through the streets. The goat is crowned "King of the Fair" and placed on a three-storey platform in the middle of town. The second day of the fair features a livestock show. Travelling people and farmers sell and trade horses, donkeys, wagons and carts. On the evening of the third day, King Puck is led out of town by a piper to the accompaniment of traditional Irish music. This signifies the end of the fair.

Michaelmas

The goose harvest, Michaelmas, dates back to Norman times when, within the Pale, 29 September was one of two annual rent days. Geese born in spring were ready for killing and some of the flock would be paid as rent.

"Green geese", young birds under six months, were considered a delicacy because they were lean and less fatty (most geese were not killed until they had grazed on the remains of the grain harvest). Michaelmas coincided with the apple harvest, so cider was brewed for the feast. Goose, sometimes par-boiled to render the fat, was stuffed with potato, onions, celery, bacon, sage and apples and roasted in a bastable oven. In County Cavan it was covered with blue marl clay and put into the fire to bake.

Harvest Home

In grain-growing areas, a harvest supper (harvest home) was held for the farm labourers. Potato dishes such as boxty (potato cakes) were served with meat, cabbage and home-brewed beer.

Samhain (Hallowe'en)

Samhain marked the end of the Celtic year. Herds were gathered in and animals not to be kept for breeding were slaughtered. Those not eaten at

the feast were preserved by salting, or cured by smoking. A sacrifice to the gods gained good fortune for the following year and care was taken not to anger the Celtic gods; the Irish were careful to appease the *Sióge*. In mythological literature this was a time when barriers between the natural world and "the otherworld" were removed and mortals encountered fairies. Despite Christian efforts to make it a day for praying for all souls, *Samhain* remained essentially pagan.

Right up to the middle of the 20th century, the main dish was *banb samna* (the piglet of *Samhain*) and until quite recent times country people left out food for dead ancestors and to ward off fairies, especially the *púca* (Shakespeare's Puck). No wild fruits were gathered after Hallowe'en because the *púca* was believed to spit and urinate on them.

Divination customs were performed which are echoed by the charms still placed in dishes eaten at Hallowe'en: apples, roasted nuts, Hallowe'en pudding, fadge (potato apple cake), boxty pancakes, and the other two dishes that are eaten to this day – colcannon (potatoes and curly kale mashed with butter) and barm brack. In any of these traditional dishes, finding a ring meant marriage before the spring, a dried pea meant spinsterhood, a bean offered riches, a rag poverty, and a matchstick meant your husband would beat you!

Martinmas (11 November)

The Martinmas feast was supposedly established in gratitude to St Martin, who is credited with conferring the monk's habit and tonsure on his

Left Musicians playing at the Puck Fair in Killorglin, County Kerry. The fair is one of Ireland's oldest and is held on 10–12 August every year.

Above *Eating oysters and drinking a glass of Guinness at the Galway oyster festival held annually in September.*

nephew, St Patrick, Ireland's patron saint. In honour of his uncle, Patrick killed a pig for every monk and nun in Ireland. (It seems, though, that the pig was only offered to the monks in his monastery.) Martinmas was traditionally one of four days in the year when a pig was killed. This made agricultural sense, as six- to eight-month-old pigs, well-fattened by harvest gleanings, were ready for slaughter and curing by November.

Midwinter (Christmas and St Stephen's Day)

Although a Christian festival, its 12 days relate directly to pagan traditions associated with the midwinter solstice and the turn of the year. The old Celtic celebration, which celebrated the return of the dead, was replaced by a celebration of the birth of Christ.

Preparations begin in November. Rich puddings (using beef suet, mixed dried fruit, stout and/or whiskey), and whiskey-soaked fruit cakes are made and matured. Christmas dinner begins with smoked fish, followed by roasted stuffed goose (now, it is more commonly turkey) and boiled, or baked, ham. Christmas pudding with whipped cream is followed by "mince" (suet and mixed dried fruit) pies.

Spiced beef is traditionally served on St Stephen's Day, when "wren boys" in fantastical costumes play Hunt the Wren. They go round the locality singing and prancing on hobby-horses. Food is offered to the boys and money is collected to pay for a "hooley" (a party) in a local hostelry; this is still done in the south-west.

New Year (Scottish Hogmanay) has few traditions in southern Ireland but, in Dublin, church bells ring, foghorns hoot, and people "see the New Year in" at a party.

Nollaig na mBan (6 January)

Women's Christmas – *Nollaig na mBan* – is still celebrated in rural areas, especially in the south and west, with a dainty feast of scones, cream, preserves, gingerbread, iced sponge cakes and tea (rather than strong drink).

Other festivals

Two less ancient, but well established, festivals are the Wexford Strawberry Festival which is held out of doors in June when the renowned, intensely flavoured, locally grown strawberres are at their best, and the Galway Oyster Festival, held to celebrate the start of the native oyster season (they are harvested only when there is an 'r' in the name of the month). The latter takes up a whole week in September. Huge marquees are thronged with visitors from all over the world. There are oyster-eating competitions and vast quantities of raw oysters are consumed, washed down with the traditional accompaniment – a glass of Guinness stout.

Below *Traditional dishes are still popular and are often served at special occasions. From left to right: Michaelmas Goose with Apple Stuffing, Colcannon, and Spiced Beef.*

Food in Wales

The Welsh have a strong tradition of living off the land that stretches back as far as the ancient Celts. It is a tradition that was to survive well into the 20th century in parts of rural Wales. The fare was simple but wholesome and was designed to satisfy the hearty appetites of hard-working farm labourers, coal miners, quarry workers and fishermen.

Surprisingly little is documented about cooking in early Wales. Probably the best-known cookery book (and the only one in English) was *The First Principles of Good Cookery* by the Right Hon.

Below The Wye Valley and the Vale of Usk, from the northern Black Mountains to the rural valleys around Newport, are areas of outstanding natural beauty.

Lady Llanover, Lady Augusta Hall. While it made little impression at the time, it is now valued as a fascinating insight into life in a large house on the south-east border of Wales. Lady Llanover was also influential in improving Welsh culture – including sponsoring and entering competitions at the Eisteddfod, encouraging Welsh speaking, and obliging her staff, tenants and guests to wear traditional Welsh rural clothes.

Generally, however, traditional culinary skills were passed on from Welsh mothers to their daughters as they worked together in the kitchen. In fact so little had been written down that the culinary heritage of Wales was in danger of being lost completely after women began working in jobs outside the home.

That is, until Minwel Tibbott, a staff member at the Welsh Folk Museum (now the Museum of Welsh Life) began voice-recording the memories of old people all over Wales from the early 1970s to the 1990s. At this time, the people of Wales seemed unaware (and often denied the fact) that they had culinary traditions, even though they often recalled the "old foods" with enthusiasm and nostalgia. In homes and restaurants, cooks and chefs were eager to shake off the thrifty dishes made with just a few simple ingredients in favour of more elaborate dishes valued by the English. Maybe the Welsh had simply eaten them far too often in the past? Perhaps those traditional dishes, made with such limited ingredients as were available at the time, proved too uncomfortable a reminder of days when Wales experienced much poverty. Or perhaps the Welsh people simply needed to move on after the disruption of the recent world wars, a time when women discovered roles outside the home. Nevertheless, the delicious everyday dishes of Wales are a valuable part of the heritage of Wales, one that is certainly worth preserving.

Today Wales has embraced its culinary heritage and is now justifiably proud of its food culture. It enjoys world recognition for much of its produce and Welsh chefs are acknowledged to be among the best in the world.

Geography of Wales

Wales, the peninsula that projects from the western side of Britain, covers an area of about 20,000 square kilometres (7,700 square miles). At its widest point it measures 200 kilometres (124 miles) east to west and 250 kilometres (155 miles) north to south. The region is a mass of mountains deeply dissected by rivers. There are three national parks and five Areas of Outstanding Natural Beauty, which together cover a quarter of the

Then came the booming wool trade and, as in much of the rest of Britain, all efforts were switched to rearing sheep. Ever since, Wales has been known for the vast numbers of sheep to be found on its mountains and in its valleys, at home both in mountainous terrain and the damp lowland climate. Today the uplands have cattle too, often the Welsh Black, also at home in lush lowland pastures.

In common with most hilly regions in Britain, oats and barley have long been staple crops grown in the rural uplands, where the climate is cold and wet. By the end of the 19th century, oats were of considerable value to every farmer and oatmeal was one of the basic ingredients in the family's diet. The lowlands, with their fertile valleys and rivers, provide conditions more suited to growing wheat and vegetable crops. It is also where the dairy herds thrive best.

Wales has a coastline that has been a rich source of fish and other seafood, with Milford Haven formerly having one of the largest fishing fleets in Britain. The coastal marshlands are also home to a speciality of the region, saltmarsh lamb.

Below *A timeless image of a shepherd and his dogs moving a flock of sheep up to their summer pastures.*

Above *Surrounded by the sea on three sides, the peninsula of Wales is a mass of mountains divided by rivers.*

area of Wales. There are craggy peaks, peaceful valleys, picturesque lakes and reservoirs galore.

The mountains have been a rich source of minerals, yielding slate in the north, and coal and iron ore in the south, as well as lead, copper, silver and gold. The varied landscape with its strong contrasts influences the produce of the region and 80 per cent of the land is dedicated to agriculture, from livestock to crops.

The rural uplands were once dominated by goats and cattle.

Well into the 1900s the foods of Wales were mostly sourced locally from mountains, lowlands, rivers and sea. In general, the country's culinary traditions derived from those who gathered, produced and prepared the food – the labouring classes – unlike in England where trends and fashions trickled down from the upper classes. This pattern helped to preserve the traditional foods and dishes of Wales.

The Middle Ages

It was the Romans who brought herbs and vines to Wales (as well as the daffodil) but in the 10th century the Welsh *Laws of Hywel Dda* (Hywel the Good) mention the only two vegetables then cultivated in Wales – leeks and cabbages. With so few vegetables available, meat was central to the diet. When meat (usually bacon) was supplemented with some vegetables and cooked in a large pot over an open fire, it formed the basis of the traditional broth or soup called "cawl".

The 12th-century writer and cleric, Giraldus Cambrensis (Gerald the Welshman), wrote of a rural Wales with flocks, milk, cheese, butter and oats. It was on these staple foods that the

Below These huts provided some shelter for the laver gatherers at Freshwater West, Pembrokeshire, c.1930.

Above An 18th-century watermill located by the River Teifi at Cenarth, in south-west Wales.

Welsh subsisted well into the 19th century. By the 16th century, oats, rye, barley and, later, wheat were being ground in watermills. Food was cooked over open fires, directly over which cast-iron kettles, cauldrons and bakestones were placed for boiling, cooking and baking, and above which bacon was smoked and cured.

Rural life dominated in Wales, and the people, who were mostly tenant farmers, were largely self-sufficient – with the exception of sugar, salt, tea, rice and currants, which had to be bought in. Hunting was a popular sport among the upper classes. Wall ovens, either built in (stone or fire-brick) or portable (clay) ones, began to appear close to the English borders in south-east Wales in the 18th century.

The industrial revolution

During the late 17th and early 18th centuries people began to move from the rural parts of Wales to the coal-mining valleys, iron and steel works of the south, and the slate quarries of the north. Previously, even the smallest cottage would have had a small plot of land on which the cottagers could grow their own food. Now they were forced

to buy their foodstuffs. In addition, the traditional diet was influenced by those of immigrants (including English, Irish, Italians, Polish and Russians), who also flocked to the areas in search of work. Most people were poor, and the importance of meat and vegetables was reversed, with cawl now made with extra leeks, cabbage, potatoes and root vegetables and very little meat.

The increasing need to transport goods produced during the industrial revolution resulted in improved road and rail communication, at the same time bringing in a greater variety of non-native foodstuffs and refined foods – commercial flour, cheap sugar and chemical raising agents. By the mid-19th century only about one third of families in Wales were supported by agriculture, and the country became the world's second industrial nation (England was the first).

Small wall ovens became a common feature in large farmhouses, though they proved inadequate for baking bread, so home-prepared bread dough was taken to communal ovens for baking.

Above *A cattle auction at Newport cattle market with an attentive collection of local farmers.*

In 1896, the Report of the Royal Commission on Land in Wales described the conditions and circumstances under which land was held, occupied and cultivated. It mentioned home-cured meat (mainly bacon), home-grown vegetables (mostly leeks, carrots, cabbages, herbs and potatoes), dairy products (milk, butter, cheese) and cereal-based dishes.

The modern age

Cardiff became the largest exporter of coal in the world in the early 20th century. Home cooking still reigned, with home-cured meat, home-grown vegetables, dairy products, oats and barley as mainstays. Daily and weekly meals continued to follow a strict pattern – breakfast, main midday meal, tea and supper. Open chimneys with wall ovens were gradually being replaced by enclosed ranges.

After World War II the restaurant trade began to emerge but it mostly ignored the culinary heritage of Wales, instead looking to England and further afield for inspiration. The attempts were not successful and Welsh cooking acquired a poor reputation.

In homes, gas and electricity were introduced and people moved away from the monotony of cawl and stews. By the late 1900s the "old" dishes were perhaps unwelcome reminders of less affluent times though they were eaten on special occasions and promoted to tourists in particular. All the while, however, Wales continued to produce excellent quality meat, dairy foods, vegetables, fish and shellfish.

The final decades of the 20th century saw Wales at the forefront of organic farming (particularly in Ceredigion) and beginning commercial production of its own foods and drinks. The country now takes pride in supplying some of the finest produce. It enjoys international recognition for its beef and lamb, and its fresh fish and seafood, as well as its unique cheeses. Increasing numbers of skilled and innovative chefs in Wales are eager to make full use of local foods supplied by artisan food producers. There are Welsh food awards called *Taste of Wales* and many restaurants, hotels and guest houses are featured in the best-known food guides.

Cardiff is a cosmopolitan district with a range of ethnic foods available in its markets, shops and restaurants. Development is ongoing in the bay area of Cardiff, where the new National Assembly building (the *Senedd*) and the Wales Millennium Centre (the country's premier arts centre) are situated. These days, Wales is a vibrant place to live, work and eat.

Below *Late summer harvest time in the Dyfi Valley, Powys, located in the heart of rural Wales.*

Welsh food traditions

Wales has a wealth of unique traditions, many of which are related to food and hospitality. It has always had Welsh-speaking strongholds, even when the language was dwindling, and an enthusiastic revival is seeing the number of Welsh speakers rise. There is a rich folklore tradition. In addition to the set of medieval Welsh tales called *Mabinogi*, the names of Merlin and King Arthur still live on in compelling tales and place names all over Wales.

Two things intrinsic to Welsh life are music and poetry – they are found in the chapels, in competing choirs, at rugby matches and at the National Eisteddfod, one of Europe's largest and oldest cultural festivals (dating back to the 12th century). Strongly linked to the Eisteddfod is the Gorsedd of Bards, a group of poets, writers, musicians and artists who have made a distinguished contribution to Welsh language, literature, and culture.

Another important aspect of Welsh life is rugby, the nation's favourite sport since the 1800s. It started as a middle-class game but soon became very popular with the working class of the industrial south, who would turn up at matches with home-cooked pies and pasties. Today, the Welsh are as passionate as ever about rugby, and support international matches wearing leeks, daffodils and the Welsh flag.

On 1 March Wales celebrates its patron saint, *Dewi Sant*, with concerts, choir performances and other special events. Primary school children dress up in Welsh costume and it is traditional to wear a daffodil or a leek: both are considered to be national emblems, and they have Welsh names that are similar. In the past, men in Welsh armies wore leeks to distinguish them from their foes; today leeks are more likely to be seen at international rugby matches. St David's Day also sees the Welsh flag bearing the red dragon hoisted all over Wales, and mealtimes centring on traditional dishes, such as cawl and roast lamb.

Markets, drovers and country fairs

The weekly market, or mart, was important for selling livestock and food in the 18th and 19th centuries, with one in every town and several fairs during the year providing the excuse for a holiday and feasting. Drovers would walk animals (often 200 cattle or 1,000 sheep) from the local market to centres in England. With the coming of the railways, transport and ways of selling changed, and markets and fairs changed or petered out. Today, locally-produced food is sold in town markets, including Swansea, Cardiff and Carmarthen. There are also regional markets, the increasingly popular farmers' markets and annual county shows, the largest of which is the Royal Welsh Show held near Builth Wells.

Hafod and hendre

To ensure ample food for his animals throughout the year, the Welsh farmer developed the custom of dividing the year between two homes. At the end of autumn he would move his animals to the lowlands to shelter over winter and he would live in the *hendre* (or old habitation) in the valley. In spring he

Left A kettle hangs over the kitchen grate. Welsh housewives were skilled at cooking and baking on an open fire.

would move his animals to the mountains to graze while he moved to the *hafod* (his summer dwelling), leaving the valley free to grow crops during summer. This custom has long ceased, but *hafod* and *hendre* remain as farm and village names all over Wales.

Hospitality

A visitor knocking on the door of a traditional Welsh household could always be sure of a warm welcome. After being fussed over and with some bustling in the kitchen, visitors would not be allowed to leave without having a bite to eat – some quickly made pancakes or Welsh cakes to be eaten hot off the bakestone. It has always been a tradition in Wales to offer food as gifts – to celebrate weddings, childbirth and New Year's Day as well as to support friends and neighbours in times of illness or bereavement.

Baking day

It was customary, once a week, for every household to have a marathon baking day, when a huge quantity of baked goods would be prepared for the week

Below Modern bakestones are light and easy to use; they heat evenly, need little greasing and are simple to clean.

Above *Welsh black cattle in Gwynedd, Snowdonia. The beef from this breed receives international acclaim.*

ahead. Bread, bara brith, cakes and Welsh cakes were popular choices for the traditional Welsh tea (alas no longer indulged in on a regular basis) and for the packed lunches known as "boxes".

Meal times

After a traditional breakfast of bacon, eggs, laverbread and cockles (small clams), the main meal was eaten at midday. Welsh tea was the late afternoon ritual, with home-baked bread, butter, cheese and jam, and maybe bara brith or Welsh cakes. Supper, at around 8–9pm, was not considered a meal but a seasonal, light-but-savoury snack, maybe fish or wild mushrooms. Sundays and special occasions warranted roast meat and rice pudding.

Cawl

Meaning broth or soup, cawl was once eaten every day, and was an integral part of life in Wales – a broth, a stew and a soup containing all the goodness of the land in one pot. It started simply with

home-cured bacon, leeks, cabbage, potatoes and water. These basic but flavourful ingredients were left to simmer gently in an iron pot over a fire, or on a range, for hours – even days – with the fat skimmed off for frying and baking, and they turned into something that still provokes nostalgia in the older generation. It was originally served in wooden bowls and eaten with wooden spoons. So comforting was the dish that when the weather is cold, people are still heard to say "It's cawl weather".

Cooking on the open hearth

Since prehistoric times, food has been cooked in cauldrons over an open fire. In many places in Wales, this continued well into the 20th century. Such limited facilities determined what could be cooked. Stews, joints and puddings were boiled in the cooking pot, there was a spit for roasting and, for small roasts and baking bread, the iron pot would be inverted over a bakestone to form a makeshift oven, with glowing embers piled on top. A later development was the Dutch oven, a three-sided box that was hooked on to the grate with its open front facing the fire.

The bakestone

Only in Wales has such extensive use been made of the bakestone or griddle. The original bakestone was a flat stone (later it was constructed from iron or slate) that was placed over an open fire or on the hob of a range. A slender wooden spade or slice was used for turning cakes, breads, pancakes, scones, oatcakes and pastry turnovers and pies. The bakestone was used extensively until the turn of the 20th century when built-in wall ovens began to appear in farmhouses. Even then, the oven would be heated one day a week, with the bakestone used on other days.

An old, well-used bakestone is likely to need little greasing during cooking. It must be heated to an even, all-over temperature, and the heavy, traditional style needs time to achieve this, so it is put on to heat while the ingredients are prepared. The temperature needed depends on the food being cooked, and it's prudent to test it by cooking a small amount of food first.

Below *A Welsh dresser, dating from around 1880, loaded with gleaming plates and dishes.*

The British kitchen

The range of ingredients produced in Britain is varied –
from its fields, orchards and hedgerows to its hillsides
and lowland pastures; and from its rivers and lakes to
extensive coastlines. The seasonal and regional qualities
of these ingredients continue to boost Britain's growing
reputation for good food, and their diversity and
provenance encourage the cook to prepare delicious
dishes, both traditional and modern.

Vegetables

Since the Romans brought their cultivated varieties to Britain in the first century BC, vegetables have played an important role in the British diet. In a short time the Celtic diet of wild plants and roots grew to include a range of grown and harvested vegetables. Fields of beans and peas were common by the Middle Ages, and explorers returned from the New World with potatoes and other exotics.

In Scotland, medieval French monks introduced many hitherto unknown varieties of vegetables, such as spinach, French (green) beans and cauliflower. The monks of Holyrood planted orchards and laid out gardens at the base of the Castle Rock in Edinburgh, and trained laymen in horticulture. The cultivation of vegetables and fruits spread to the gardens of the nobility and other wealthy families and by the 19th century Scottish gardeners had become internationally famous. Young summer vegetables were used to make

Below The British may view vegetables as an accompaniment rather than a main dish, but they are still an important part of the weekly shop.

hairst bree, harvest broth, which is similar to Scotch broth but without the barley. The tender sweet vegetables gave the broth a special flavour. In most British kitchens vegetables were simply boiled and served plain, but when the landowners of the 17th century began to create kitchen gardens, cooking methods became more adventurous.

When transport improved, vegetables could be enjoyed outside their traditional growing areas, and by the late 20th century they were being imported from all over the world. Suddenly most vegetables were available all year round. While modern transport allows out-of-season vegetables to be imported from many parts of the world, discerning cooks still eagerly await the arrival of the new season's home-grown potatoes and vegetables such as asparagus.

Today there is revived interest in the growing and eating of local, seasonal produce, and more shops and farmers' markets are offering high-quality local produce that hasn't been transported for hundreds of miles.

Above Parsnips were once only used for animal consumption.

Organic vegetable growing is increasing, and growers, countrywide, supply local towns through wholesale markets, farmers' markets, health food shops, farm gate selling and weekly box-delivery systems. Many chefs now source organic vegetables locally.

Cooking vegetables

Although vegetables and potatoes have always been important in the traditional British diet they have most often been served as side dishes to accompany meat and fish, rather than being the central feature of a main dish. They were most often plain boiled and usually dressed with butter.

Traditional soups and stews depend upon a high vegetable and herb content, but this (and a tradition of one-pot cooking) tended to encourage the cooking of vegetables for too long, and this is a failing that many British home cooks have remedied only in the last couple of generations.

As well as accompanying main dishes, vegetables are used in soups, in first courses, as garnishes for entrées, as vegetarian dishes, and in many savoury dishes. In traditional British kitchens, carrot, onion, celery, leek, parsnip, swede (rutabaga), and herbs such as fresh parsley, thyme, garlic and bay leaf, are the mainstays of many recipes. A

Above Mashed swede (rutabaga) is used to make the traditional Scottish dish of "bashed neeps", also known as "turnip purry", which is eaten as an accompaniment to haggis.

mixture of these basic ingredients is at the heart of many stews and soups, and in Irish cooking it is often used as a "bed" that absorbs juices when roasting red meats.

Beneath the soil

Carrot Every cook's standby for a side dish to accompany meat or fish, carrots are also used to give their flavour and sweetness to soups and casseroles. In the days when sugar was still a costly imported luxury, most people relied on honey to sweeten their food, but they also used the natural sweetness of root vegetables, particularly carrots. Their inherent natural sweetness and moist texture once cooked made them a successful ingredient in many delicious cakes, puddings, pies, tarts and preserves. They store well throughout the winter.

Parsnip Now a popular vegetable, parsnip has a distinctive, sweet flavour. Steam or boil it lightly, mash it (perhaps mixed with carrots or potatoes), roast it or add it to soups and stews. It takes very well to spices, and makes a delicious curried soup.

Potato When the potato was introduced to Britain from America in

the late 16th century, it took a long time to become accepted. However, it eventually became an important crop and by the 19th century had become a staple food. In Scotland potatoes form the basis of many old dishes and in general Scots prefer floury varieties such as Maris Piper, Golden Wonder and Kerr's Pinks. Mealy tatties (boiled potatoes) were cheap and filling, and were sold from carts in Scottish cites in the 19th century. Stovies is a very old dish consisting of sliced potatoes cooked with onions. Sometimes cheese or meat was added to make the dish more substantial. In Orkney cooked potatoes and turnips or kale were mashed together to make clapshot. The curiously named rumbledethumps, from the Border region, is made with potatoes and cabbage. The name comes from "rumbled and thumped". Colcannon is a dish of boiled cabbage, carrots, turnips and potatoes mashed with butter. Today there are many varieties, and there is a potato to suit

every cooking method and every meal. In Ireland, where most of the population once depended on potatoes, they are still eaten in huge quantities, boiled or steamed "in their skins" (jackets) and dressed with butter. Potatoes are also mashed with milk (or cream) and butter, with added herbs or

Above Today's bright orange carrots have developed from an early variety that was purple in colour.

Below Home-grown potatoes played a major role in feeding the population during the two World Wars.

Above *Turnips are more popular in Scotland than in England.*

Above *When they are young the tops of beetroot can be eaten as greens.*

Above *Swede is delicious mashed with potatoes and carrots.*

other mashed vegetables. Traditional Irish dishes like boxty, colcannon, poundies, champ, stampy, potato cakes, breads and potato pastry are popular, and in some restaurants they can contain surprising additions.

Turnip The sweet, peppery flavour of the white turnip is best appreciated in spring and early summer, when it goes especially well with lamb and duck.

Below *The onion was one of the foods introduced to Britain by the Romans, and has been popular ever since.*

Turnips were introduced into Scotland in the 18th century and the Scots recognized them immediately as a tasty vegetable – unlike the English, who fed them to their cattle. Several Scottish dishes use turnips and they became the traditional accompaniment to haggis. Mashed turnips were commonly known as bashed neeps, or turnip purry (from the French purée) by the gentry. The youngest, smallest turnips have the best flavour and texture.

Swede Larger than turnip and with a leathery purple skin, swede (rutabaga) has a firm flesh and a sweet taste that is quite distinctive. It is usually eaten mashed with plenty of butter.

Onion By the Middle Ages onions, together with cabbage and beans, were one of the three main vegetables eaten by rich and poor, in all parts of the British Isles. Apart from their use in all kinds of soups and stews, they can be eaten raw in salads, fried, boiled in milk, roasted (sometimes with a cheese topping) or chargrilled. Sliced onions fried in butter until deep brown are a traditional accompaniment to steak.

Horseradish When freshly grated and mixed with cream and seasoning, this pungent root makes a sauce that is a perfect accompaniment to roast beef.

Jerusalem artichoke This knobbly root can be served roasted, boiled, or made into soup. It has an affinity with game.

Beetroot (beet) Often cooked and pickled, it can also be boiled or roasted and served hot.

Below *There are several kinds of cabbage eaten in Britain, the green variety is probably the most common.*

Above *Traditional village shows are still held in the north-east of England to find the largest leek.*

Above *For a brief few weeks in spring, England produces some of the best asparagus in the world.*

Above *Globe artichokes were once thought to be an aphrodisiac, perhaps because of the way they are eaten.*

Above the soil

Leek and spring onion (scallions) With its delicate onion flavour, the leek is good in many dishes, including soups, pies, sauces and stews. Leek is often used to flavour fish in the same way that onion is used with meat.
The market gardeners on the Lothian coast of Scotland supplied fruit and vegetables to Edinburgh and the quality of their leeks was unsurpassed. Scottish leeks are distinct from other leeks as they have almost as much green as white, so add a good colour to broths. They are essential to the famous cock-a-leekie soup, a broth made with chicken and leeks. Slice leeks down the middle and wash very well to remove any sand or grit. Chop and add to soups or stews. Spring onions are used to flavour traditional potato dishes such as champ or colcannon, and in salads.

Asparagus Once known by the name of sparrowgrass, asparagus was popular with the Romans and has been grown in English country gardens ever since the 16th century. East Anglia and the Vale of Evesham are the traditional growing areas. It has a short, six-week growing season, which makes it a

particular delicacy. It is best served steamed with melted butter or soft-boiled eggs to dip the spears into.

Cabbage One of the oldest vegetables cabbage is easy to grow. The English enjoy several varieties – green, white and red – with the wrinkly Savoy and young spring greens being particularly popular. Available all year round, cabbage can be boiled, steamed or stir-fried. It is the largest horticultural crop grown in Ireland after potatoes. The Irish prefer pointed-hearted, fresh, soft

Below *Thought to have originated in the eastern Mediterranean, cauliflower was bought to Britain by the Romans.*

green-leafed types, though stewed red cabbage is a favourite accompaniment for goose and venison. Cabbage was once a staple item of the diet in Orkney and Shetland (in common with Scandinavian countries) and was eaten both as a vegetable in its own right and as an ingredient in soups and stews. It was preserved for winter by being layered in barrels with fat, oats, salt and spices with a weight on top. It was then left to ferment, the result being very similar to sauerkraut.

Cauliflower and broccoli These popular vegetables can be cooked in similar ways. Favourite dishes are the classic cauliflower cheese and a soup incorporating cheese and cream. Cauliflower grows particularly well in the south-west of England.

Brussels sprouts These look and taste like tiny cabbages. They are served as a side vegetable (traditionally mixed with chestnuts at Christmas) or thinly sliced and served raw or stir-fried.

Globe artichoke This is an edible thistle, with layers of leaves surrounding the central heart. It was introduced to Britain from the Mediterranean, but flourishes in milder regions. It is good boiled and served

Above Spinach grows well throughout Britain. Young leaves are used in salads while more mature ones are cooked.

with lemon butter, for dipping the base of the leaves and the hearts. Inspite of the name, globe artichokes are not related to Jerusalem artichokes.

Celery An essential pot-herb, celery is eaten raw (as crudités), braised (especially the hearts), often with cheese, or as an ingredient in soup. After the Romans brought celery to England, it grew wild and tough until the 18th century, when it was cultivated and blanched to keep its stems tender. Now we enjoy both pale green summer celery and white winter celery.

Spinach When spinach first arrived in Britain from Spain, where it was introduced by the Moors, it was referred to as "the Spanish vegetable". The small young leaves add a mildly peppery taste to salads, but it is more commonly cooked as a side dish and is especially good with fish.

Chard Though similar to spinach, chard has thick stems that can be tough when older, and need to be cooked longer

than the leaves. Ruby chard has vivid red stems.

Kale or kail Dark green leafy kale is particularly popular in Scotland, and is so central to Scottish cuisine that the word kail came to mean soup and even to signify the main meal of the day. Kale grows on a long stem and has curly dark green leaves but no head. It has the advantage of flourishing in the harsher climate of northern regions and is resistant to frost – in fact the flavour improves after it has been nipped by a slight frost. Shred the leaves finely and cook for a few minutes in boiling salted water, as for cabbage. In Shetland there is a unique variety of kale that develops a head. It is believed to have ancient Scandinavian origins.

Peas and broad (fava) beans These have been grown in Britain since the Middle Ages, when they were planted in cottage gardens and dried to feed families through the winter. In summer they are deliciously sweet when small and freshly picked.

Pumpkin This squash adds colour to autumn, when they are hollowed out

Below Pumpkins are harvested in the autumn and the flesh can be roasted, baked, mashed or made into soup.

Above Unlike most vegetables, peas freeze well and are a staple vegetable standby in most English homes.

and carved into Hallowe'en lanterns, while the flesh is used for soup. There are many other varieties of squash, which can be mashed or roasted.

Wild leaves

Nettles Young nettle leaves can be cooked in the same way as spinach. Wash them well and place in a pan with just the water clinging to the leaves. Cook over a low heat for 7–10 minutes, chopping them as they cook in the pan, then add butter, salt and pepper to taste. They make a refreshing and restorative soup in early spring.

Wild rocket (arugula) This little peppery leaf grows prolifically in many areas of the country, and can be picked, washed and added to stews or made into salad.

Wild garlic leaves Also known as ramsons, these grow prolifically all round Britian for just a few weeks in the year, in spring. They add a delicate, mild garlic flavour to dishes.

Herbs

The Romans introduced most of the herbs the British use today. In the 16th century, when explorers brought home new exotic plants, the gardens of country houses filled with herbs. Some were used for culinary or medicinal purposes, or to make pomanders and scent bags. In the Victorian era, herbs remained essential to flavour food that was often stale or bad. With the 20th century came the development of artificial flavourings, and use of herbs

Above There are several kinds of mint; peppermint makes a lovely infusion.

Above Parsley is perhaps the most widely used herb, and it is particularly good with fish.

Below Combined with onion, sage makes a delicious stuffing for roast chicken or turkey.

waned until the revival of interest in seasonal and locally grown foods. Today Britain has thriving herb farms growing a huge variety of culinary plants.

Parsley The most versatile herb, parsley's leaves, stalks and roots can be used in countless ways. Its flavour goes particularly well with fish and vegetables, and it is often added to soups, sauces and stews.

Sage The strong flavour of sage goes well with cheese, potatoes and pork. It is popular as a stuffing for chicken.

Mint This summer herb is chopped and mixed with sugar and vinegar to make mint sauce for roast lamb. It is also used in salads and with new potatoes.

Tarragon French tarragon is the culinary herb. Use it with eggs and chicken, and to flavour butter, vinegar and olive oil.

Fennel/dill The aniseed flavour of dill's feathery fronds has an affinity with fish and vegetables. The seeds go well with cheese or pork.

Chives With their delicate onion flavour chives are good snipped into salads, soups, sauces and egg dishes. The flowers look good in a green salad.

Angelica The fleshy, hollow stems of angelica can be crystallized and used in cakes and desserts. Its leaves can be infused in milk or cream for desserts.

Borage The young, tender leaves can be added to salads but it is the blue,

star-shaped flowers that are so pretty for drinks or scattering over salads.

Lemon balm To add a lemony flavour to custards and ice cream, steep some lemon balm leaves in the hot milk.

Savory Often called the "bean herb". Adding a sprig or two to the cooking water of any type of bean helps to prevent flatulence.

Lavender Use the leaves and flowers to flavour sweet dishes.

Chamomile Used in lawns in the past for their apple-like scent. The leaves make a relaxing infusion.

Above Dill works very well as an accompaniment to fish.

Below The delicate blue flowers of borage can be used as a decorative ingredient in drinks and salads.

Fruits

Britain's temperate climate is ideal for growing orchard and soft fruits, and many regions still grow the same varieties that they have for centuries.

Orchard fruits

Traditional orchards have long been a distinctive feature of the landscape, but recent years have seen a severe decline in orchard-fruit crops and many old varieties have disappeared. Fortunately, traditional fruit growers are now beginning to see a turnaround, with some supermarkets responding to consumers' demand for home-grown produce, and local shops and farmers' markets helping to bring back traditional varieties.

Apples The ancestor of the modern apple is the crab apple, with its small sour fruits that make delicious jellies and other preserves. There is a huge range of traditional apple varieties, each with its own texture and unique flavour, and many are evocatively named. Dessert apples include Ashmead's Kernel, Blenheim Orange, Cox's Orange Pippin, Discovery, James Grieve, Knobby Russet, and Worcester Pearmain. Varieties that are more suitable for cooking include Bramley's Seedling, Burr Knot, Golden Hornet, Norfolk Beauty and Smart's Prince Arthur. English cider

Below The apple is Britain's oldest and most loved fruit.

Above Most medieval British pears came from stock brought from France.

apples include Bulmer's Norman, Hoary Morning and Slack-me-girdle. Apple traditions such as apple bobbing and toffee apples survive to this day.

Pears The pear's history can be traced back almost as far as the apple and for a long time it was considered the superior fruit. By the 19th century there were hundreds of varieties. Today the most popular British dessert pear is the Conference, long and thin with green skin tinged with russet, and sweet flesh. Williams pears (known as Bartlett in the USA and Australia), bred in Berkshire in the 18th century, are golden yellow or red-tinged and are ideal for cooking.

Plums Originally cultivated from hedgerow fruits – the cherry plum and the sloe (black plum) – plums vary in colour from black to pale green and yellow and can be sweet or tart. In Britain they were grown in the gardens of medieval monasteries. The Victoria plum was first cultivated in Sussex in the 1800s and, with its red and yellow skin, remains the most popular dessert plum. The greengage is a sweet amber-coloured plum that makes particularly good jam. Damsons

Above Plums are a popular filling for pies, crumbles and puddings.

are small plums with dark blue-to-purple skins and yellow flesh. They give their colour and flavour to damson gin.

Cherries These are grouped into three main types: sweet, acid and sour (known as Dukes). Sweet cherries can be firm and dry, ideal for candying into glacé cherries, or soft and juicy. Acid cherries, of which the Morello is the best known, range in colour from pale

Below Fruit pies, in particular apple, are a favourite traditional dessert.

to those with an intense crimson glow. Duke cherries are thought to be crosses between these two.

Quince The quince is an apple- or pear-shaped fruit with scented yellow flesh. Because it is very hard it needs long slow cooking. It is lovely cooked with apples or pears, when only a small amount is needed to add its flavour. Quinces make good jams and jellies that go well with pork.

Berries, currants and rhubarb

Local farmers' markets and pick-your-own farms are the best sources of traditional varieties of soft fruit. All types of berry are delicate and very perishable so keep them in the refrigerator and eat them as fresh as possible. Farm shops offer very good value, as the berries are usually freshly picked. Look for firm, plump berries, but remember that very large berries often lack flavour. To enjoy them at their best, allow them to reach room temperature before serving. Don't wash them until just before eating. Rinse strawberries very gently and hull them after washing to avoid making them soggy – the hull acts as a plug.

Below Strawberries and cream are an important part of a British summer.

Above Once only available from autumn hedgerows, blackberries are now cultivated for sale year-round.

Strawberries These luscious berries are firmly associated with the English summer. While Elsanta has become the most frequently grown variety, Cambridge Favourite, English Rose, Hapil and Royal Sovereign are becoming popular again. Strawberries are a traditional feature of the Wimbledon tennis championships.

Raspberries These are Scotland's national favourite, and Tayside is famous for its sweet fruits, which have been grown commercially since the beginning of the 20th century. New varieties such as Glen Moy and Glen Garry have recently been developed.

Blackberries Glossy, juicy blackberries are one of late summer's most delicious fruits, and the most common wild berry in Britain. Blackberries are also known as brambles and in the Scottish Highlands the bush is called *an druise beannaichte* – the blessed bramble.

Tayberries A cross between the red raspberry and a strain of blackberry, they are very juicy with a sharp taste and make particularly good jam.

Mulberries These are similar to, though larger than, blackberries. They are the fruit of large, long-lived trees of Asian origin, which have probably been grown in England since Roman times. Mulberries are very soft and easily damaged so are not widely available.

Currants Blackcurrants, with their rich, tart flavour, are the most common. Red and white currants are mixed with other summer fruits in a summer pudding.

Above Redcurrants make a jelly, often eaten with roast chicken or turkey.

Gooseberries Different varieties of these pale berries are suitable for cooking or eating raw. Gooseberries ripen when the elder tree is in flower, and elderflowers are traditionally added to impart a delicious muscatel flavour.

Rowanberries These tiny, bright orange-red berries are added to sauces and relishes for rich game meats.

Rhubarb Though botanically a vegetable, rhubarb is used like a fruit. The tender pink stems of early forced rhubarb are a spring treat, mostly grown in Yorkshire. Main crop rhubarb, with its stronger colour and more acidic flavour, is eaten in pies and crumbles.

Below Gooseberries come into season in June, a welcome early summer fruit.

Fresh fish

Britain has always enjoyed a wonderful variety of fish from its coastal waters, lakes and rivers. Recent years have seen fish stocks diminish, but an increase in fish farming has led to greater availability of certain species such as salmon and trout. Not all the fish caught in British and Irish waters are landed there; many are eagerly bought for immediate export to Europe.

Historically, fish was eaten on the Church's many "fast days" (including Friday every week) and the lengthy fasts of Lent and Advent when meat was forbidden. In Ireland this restriction affected the majority of the population until very recently, leading to an ambivalent attitude to fish, but over the past 30 years it has once again regained its place as a prized, if increasingly expensive, everyday food.

Cooking fish

Fresh fish benefits from simple methods of cooking, such as frying, grilling (broiling), steaming or baking. In restaurants fish is frequently served with classic (often French) sauces, but the vegetation from the natural habitat of the fish, and perhaps on which the fish feeds, often makes the best accompaniment, enhancing its natural flavour.

Freshwater fish from clean waters need only simple cooking and delicate herbs, perhaps with melted butter, to bring out their natural flavour. Sea fish can take more robust flavours, and oily fish such as herring and mackerel are often cooked coated in oatmeal, which absorbs their strong flavours.

Above Turbot is highly prized and can be cooked in a variety of ways.

Sea fish

Several species have been affected by overfishing and stocks are desperately low. Cod and haddock are two examples of species where reduced numbers have led to higher prices. Nevertheless, both remain popular. Haddock, while smaller than cod, has a pronounced flavour that many people consider to be finer, and in the north-east of England it is always the first choice for fish and chips. Both haddock and cod are good baked, poached, grilled or fried. Other white fish include hake, with its firm flesh, pollack, whiting and coley, all of which are excellent in pies, soups and stews.

Plaice is a popular flat fish with a good flavour and texture. Dover sole has a firm texture and a fine flavour

Above Herring is often smoked, after which it is called a kipper.

that is best appreciated when it is simply grilled (broiled) on the bone, perhaps with melted butter, chopped parsley and lemon juice. Lemon sole has softer flesh and a flavour not quite as fine as that of Dover sole, but it too is popular, being less expensive and suitable for serving with strongly flavoured sauces.

Turbot is considered by many to be the aristocrat of fish, with a sweet flavour and firm white flesh that can stand up to robust kinds of cooking. Halibut is widely available; it is best for grilling, frying or baking, but it can be poached or steamed, too.

Above Cod stocks have suffered from over-fishing in English waters.

Above *Mackerel has always been plentiful in England's coastal waters.*

Herrings, sprats, pilchards, sardines and whitebait all have a similar texture and bold flavours. Britain's thriving herring industry ensured they were always cheap and they remain good value today. The larger fish are delicious fried, grilled or baked. Tiny whitebait are deep-fried and eaten whole, and remain a popular appetizer in restaurants, particularly in London, where they were once so plentiful that they were sold from barrows in the streets. The pilchard has long been a mainstay of the Cornish fishing industry, though in greater demand abroad than at home: most of the fish has traditionally been salted and exported to France and Italy. Nowadays, with smaller catches and higher prices, the fresh fish is being more alluringly re-marketed in England under the name "Cornish sardine". Mackerel also remains inexpensive and is delicious when very fresh.

Several other species are still caught around the coast, albeit in smaller quantities, including brill, dabs, skate, sea bass, monkfish, ling, John Dory, gurnard and red mullet.

Right *Brown river trout has a lovely flavour, and is best grilled or baked.*

Freshwater fish

Britain's rivers used to team with fish, and most large country estates would have had at least one pond stocked with perch, pike and other species.

Salmon is one of today's most popular fish due to the dramatic increase in fish farming around Britain. It is perfect for cooking whole and is a favourite centrepiece for summer entertaining. Fillets and steaks are lovely pan-fried, grilled or barbecued. Wild salmon is an early summer treat worth its high price. Wild salmon, sea trout and eels are all highly prized in Ireland. When an Irishman asks an angler if he has caught "a fish" he does not mean any fish, he means a salmon.

Sea trout, otherwise known as salmon trout or sewin, has firm pink flesh and a delicate flavour, combining the best qualities of salmon and trout,

Below *Much of the salmon eaten in Britain is farmed, but wild fish is still available from good fishmongers.*

but in recent years it has become extremely scarce. It is currently even more highly prized than salmon. It can be cooked in any of the ways suitable for salmon, but is best lightly poached whole, delicately flavoured with dill.

The native brown trout, which is biologically identical to the salmon trout but not migratory, is found in lakes and streams in several regions. There is no better breakfast or supper than one or two of these freshly caught, small fish, simply dusted in seasoned flour and pan-fried whole in butter. Due to the success of fish farming, rainbow trout is now widely available and inexpensive. Both kinds of trout can be enjoyed poached, baked, fried or grilled (broiled).

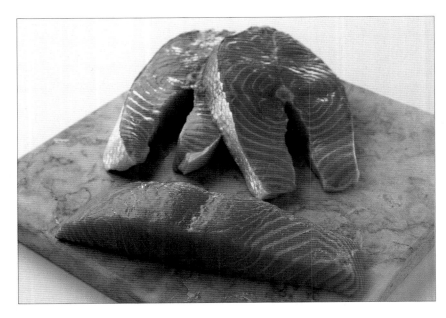

Smoked fish and shellfish

Before the days of refrigeration, freezing and easy transport, smoking over peat or wood fires was one of the chief methods of preserving fish. Smoked fish could be kept for times when fresh food was not so plentiful and for the many days when Christians were obliged to abstain from eating meat. Nowadays fish is smoked for the distinctive flavour it imparts rather than the need to preserve it. Fish that is smoked naturally is far superior to that with added dye and flavourings.

Some fish, such as salmon, trout, mackerel or herring, is hot smoked, which means it is gently cooked as it is smoked and is therefore ready for eating. Cold smoking involves smoking the fish very gently over a long period over a smouldering fire. Cold-smoked fish needs either to be cooked first, as in the case of kippers or smoked haddock, or cut into wafer-thin slices and served raw, sprinkled with lemon juice, like salmon, trout or mackerel.

Though Scotland is the main British producer of smoked fish, especially salmon, south-west England, and Cornwall in particular, is known for its smoked mackerel, kippers and bloaters. On the east coast, Great Yarmouth once bustled with fish workers and smokehouses producing bloaters and kippers. In Northumberland smoked fish

Above *Thin slices of smoked salmon are hugely popular as a starter.*

is also a speciality, especially salmon and kippers. In fact, oak-smoked kippers were first made in the fishing town of Seahouses, and kippers are still produced in traditional smokehouses there and down the coast at Craster.

Smoked herrings Bloaters are lightly smoked and dry-salted herrings that have had their heads, tails and bones removed. They are best grilled (broiled) or fried.

Buckling These are whole, hot-smoked herring that are ready to eat.

Kippers These are herrings that have been split, slightly salted and cold smoked. Kippers are poached or grilled. Red herrings are whole herrings that have been heavily smoked and salted and have a strong flavour. They are still obtainable from a few artisan smokers and can be eaten cold or lightly grilled.

Smoked haddock Traditionally served poached for breakfast or supper.

Smoked salmon is served in wafer-thin slices with lemon wedges for squeezing over, black pepper and brown bread.

Smoked trout can be bought whole or in fillets and is good as an appetizer or

made into spreads and patés. It can also be served with salad as a main course.

Smoked mackerel, with its rich flavour and smooth texture, is enjoyed in salads or made into spreads and patés.

Smoked eel is a delicacy that was formerly difficult to find, but now smokeries in East Anglia and Somerset are encouraging a revival by offering it in chunks, ready to eat.

Below *Smoked eel is a neglected delicacy that is enjoying a resurgence.*

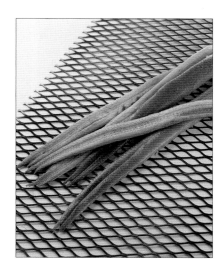

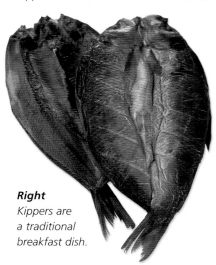

Right
Kippers are a traditional breakfast dish.

Some species of shellfish were once so plentiful that they were considered food for the poor. The coastlines of the north-east and south-west in particular have been good sources of shellfish, including lobster, crab, scallops, clams and mussels. Morecambe Bay is famous for its tiny brown shrimps, and many sandy estuaries are home to razor clams. As with other fish, shellfish stocks have been in decline in recent years, and many sheltered bays and estuaries are now home to aquaculture farms.

Oysters Once so plentiful that they were included in many dishes to eke out the ingredients, and even used as cat food, oysters are now celebrated as a delicacy. Eaten raw, they are at their best from late autumn to spring – they are traditionally eaten only "when there is an R in the month". Whitstable in Kent and Lindisfarne in Northumberland are both renowned for oysters, and they are also farmed in the unpolluted waters of Scottish sea lochs on the west coast. The Pacific oyster is often used for farming and is more elongated than the native oyster.

Below In the 17th-century, oysters were so plentiful they were fed to cats.

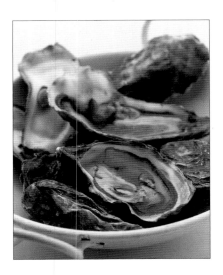

Above
Langoustines are now a speciality of many top restaurants.

Lobster Regarded as one of the tastiest shellfish, lobster has a rich, intense flavour. Originally eaten by the poor, it became a gourmet food in the 19th century. They usually boiled but can also be grilled (broiled). The dark blue-green shell becomes scarlet when cooked. Lobsters and crabs were originally fished by coaxing them from under the rocks with a stick. In the 1750s creel fishing was introduced, using special baited pots.

Langoustines These are also known as Dublin Bay prawns (jumbo shrimp), Norway lobsters or crayfish. Most fishermen regarded langoustine as a nuisance until the 1960s, when increased foreign travel began to create a demand for them. As scampi (extra large shrimp) they became a gourmet food, exported all over the world and a fixture on restaurant menus.

Crabs Known as partans in Scotland, crabs are caught around the coasts of Britain and sold live or pre-boiled. There are two main types: the common brown crab or the rarer shore variety. The flavour of the white meat is more delicate than lobster and connoisseurs regard Scottish crabs as the finest. Partan bree, a crab soup, is a famous Scottish dish.

Scallops These shellfish have a creamy white flesh with a mild flavour, enclosed in a shell that can measure up to 15cm/6in across. The orange coral is edible and has a rich flavour and smooth texture. Scallops need only a few minutes' cooking. It is important not to overcook them as the meat will become tough and rubbery, losing its sweet taste. If possible, buy them in closed shells.

Mussels make a wonderful main dish or first course. Musselburgh, near Edinburgh, was so named because of the large mussel bed at the mouth of the River Esk. Mussels must have tightly closed shells; discard any that remain open when tapped (and any that stay closed once cooked) as this indicates that they are not still alive. Steam or boil them in white wine or water, or add to fish stews.

Below Mussels are still plentiful, inexpensive and easy to prepare.

Meat

The British have always enjoyed home-reared meat of excellent quality and good flavour. For the wealthy and middle classes it was the mainstay of their diet, but the peasant class would eat it only on festivals and holidays.

Before the introduction of the modern oven, particularly in large houses, meat was cooked in huge joints, roasted on a spit in front of the kitchen fire. The less wealthy, meanwhile, would take their meat to be cooked in the baker's oven while they attended church on Sunday morning. It was customary to make the Sunday joint last for several days: it would be served hot or cold, and made into dishes such as pies, rissoles and bubble and squeak. While modern ovens are designed to cook smaller pieces of meat, the Sunday roast (especially roast beef) remains a special family and celebratory meal.

The traditional butcher, with sound knowledge and expertise, has always been the best source of meat. A good supplier will know when it is appropriate to hang meat before selling, and for how long, in order to achieve the best texture and flavour. In recent years there has been a serious decline in the number of independent butchers in Britain, but some excellent ones remain, supported by loyal customers. More and more farmers are selling direct from the farm or at farmers' markets.

Beef

Cattle are reared for both their milk and their meat. Old breeds still raised in England today include the Shorthorn (in the north) and the Red Poll (in eastern areas). The British White was always popular on the estates of large houses. Selective breeding means that there are now cattle suited to all kinds of terrain with breeds such as the Hereford, South Devon and Sussex providing meat that is marbled with fat and has an excellent flavour. Scottish beef from native breeds such as Highland cattle or Aberdeen Angus – both of which tolerate the bleak, rugged terrain and harsh weather – has achieved international renown for its superb flavour and succulent texture. Irish stock has also been bred from these Scottish cattle, and there the most prized beef breeds are Irish Hereford and Irish Angus; grass-fed Irish beef, like Irish lamb, has great flavour.

Beef needs hanging to develop the flavour and tenderize the meat. Good-quality beef is dark red with a marbling of creamy-coloured fat – bright red, wet-looking meat indicates that it has not been hung for long enough.

These days prime cuts of beef are an expensive luxury, but roast beef with all the trimmings – Yorkshire pudding, mustard and horseradish sauce – is still a favourite. The tougher cuts, which tend to be less expensive, make delicious stews (with or without dumplings), pot roasts (such as boiled beef and carrots), and traditional puddings and pies, as well as the modern burger. One of the oldest British beef dishes is Scotch collops, and the recipe appears in many old cookbooks. Originally the meat was thinly sliced, beaten with a rolling pin

Left The green, fertile grazing lands of Britain are ideal for raising cattle.

to flatten it, then seasoned with salt and pepper and fried quickly. "Scotching" meant cutting a criss-cross pattern on the meat before cooking. Potted meat and meat loaves are specialities of Scottish cuisine. The Victorians were great believers in the virtues of meat extracts, and invalids drank restorative "beef tea", made by simmering steak in water, cooling to remove all fat and residue and then reheating to serve.

Left Rib and sirloin cuts of beef.

Mutton and lamb

Lamb as we know it today was once unheard of. Sheep have always been raised more extensively than pigs or cattle and almost always grazed on grassland. Originally, sheep were kept primarily for their wool, so only older sheep were used for meat, with a strong flavour and texture that required slow cooking. Over the years, lamb has slowly replaced mutton: young, tender and sweet, it can be cooked quickly to suit modern lifestyles. Lamb joints are roasted and served with mint sauce or redcurrant jelly, while chops and steaks are grilled (broiled), fried or barbecued.

Today, there is spring lamb from mild southern regions, followed by hill lamb from northern areas and lamb (up to 18 months old) from all over the country. Hogget (one to two years

Below Herding sheep on the coastal pasture at Dunquin on the Dingle Peninsula in Kerry, Republic of Ireland.

old) and mutton (over two years) are experiencing a welcome revival. Specialist breeds are available from farmers' markets and traditional butcher shops, with interesting names such as Blackface, Blue-faced Leicester, Lincoln Longwool, Norfolk Horn, Texel and White-faced Woodland. There is the Romney from the salt marshes of Kent, and mutton from the Ryeland and Herdwick breeds.

The sheep kept by early settlers in Ireland are thought to have been dark-fleeced antecedents of the Soay breed, still found on the Hebrides. Wild goats still roam the Burren in County Clare and it is likely that goats rather than cows were the primary grazing animal of early farmers. Kid meat was traditionally used to make Irish stew, but it fell from favour many years ago.

In Ireland, native and visitor alike seek out a particular speciality: Connemara mountain lamb. In the mid-19th century black-faced lambs from the Scottish border region were introduced to Connemara, and it is probably the variety of the local wild

Below Lamb chop is one of the most popular cuts of lamb.

Above These Scottish sheep live in the spectacular Highlands on the Isle of Skye.

herbage and flora that ensures the very special flavour of this mountain lamb, which is in season in early autumn.

Mutton has been a favourite in Scotland for hundreds of years. Traditionally, every part of the animal was used – the blood was made into black pudding (blood sausage); the heart, head and trotters were used in broth. Other parts went to make haggis. Scotch pies, made with lamb, were originally sold in taverns and are now a national institution in Scotland.

There are many breeds of sheep in Scotland. Shetland sheep are a distinctive, small, hardy breed native to the Shetland Isles. Their diet of seaweed and heather, together with the sea salt carried on the strong winds to their pastures, gives them a unique, slightly gamey flavour.

Salting mutton is still done in the Hebrides, Orkney, Shetland and some northern parts of the Highlands. The meat is cured with salt, sugar and spices (in the Highlands juniper berries are used) then dried or smoked. A small piece is sufficient to flavour a pot of soup or broth.

Pork

The pig has always played a most important role in British eating, and was once known in some areas as "the gentleman who pays the rent". There was a time when at least one pig was reared in the back yard of every cottage, farm and country house in every village and town, fed on household scraps and often on the whey left over from cheese-making. The "porker" would be kept from springtime until autumn, when it was slaughtered. In small communities, pigs would be killed one or two at a

time and the meat shared out between neighbours. This practice continued until the late 19th century.

When there was plenty of meat the people ate to "lay on fat" before winter set in. The boar was saved for Christmas and went into minced meat pies, with the head being reserved for the table centrepiece. In the new year, the long sides (flitches) of bacon cured in autumn saw the family through the lean months until spring. Most parts of the pig were cured to make bacon, though the offal would be eaten immediately and some fresh pork would be cooked too. The legs were reserved for ham. Every part of the animal was eaten, including trotters (feet), stomach wall (tripe), brain, tongue, ears and tail; the blood was used for black pudding (blood sausage). Traditional breeds of pig are seeing a revival today – such as the ginger-haired Tamworth and Gloucester Old Spot, often called the orchard pig because it was fattened on windfall apples.

Left There are several regional types of sausage, including Cumberland, which is sold coiled into a circle.

Right Haggis is a famous Scottish dish, traditionally eaten at Burns Night feasts.

Above Black pudding is a much-loved breakfast food in the Midlands.

Pork is enjoyed roasted, perhaps with a stuffing of sage and onion, and served with apple sauce. It is made into sausages, pork pies, black puddings, and many other regional dishes.

Bacon and ham

As well as remaining the foundation of the traditional British breakfast, bacon is used to flavour all kinds of dishes, including soups, stews and stuffings. The hind leg from a side of pork is removed for curing separately as ham and, after brining, the rest of the side is divided into gammon (shoulder and collar joints) and back and belly bacon. Traditionally both were dry-cured; wet-curing by injecting brine into the meat was introduced in the 19th century, but dry-cured bacon and ham are now sought after by discerning consumers. Once the meat has matured over a period of weeks, some is then smoked.

Many craft pork butchers and artisan producers make speciality sausages for cooking at home. Other traditional pork products include brawn, made from various boiled and cooked cuts of pork, pigs' cheeks, tongue and feet set

Right British pig farms have very high standards of animal care and welfare.

in aspic, haslet (a cooked pork "loaf" popular in Ireland and the north of England) and the Irish street food crubeens, which is brined pigs' feet, boiled until tender, then grilled (broiled).

Haggis and black pudding

Now a great symbol of Scottish heritage, custom and tradition, the haggis is actually a type of sausage, of which only the inside is eaten. It is composed of mutton and lamb and their offal (innards), highly spiced and bound together with oatmeal, and packed into a sheep's stomach ready for lengthy boiling. Nowadays it is generally sold cooked, ready for further cooking and reheating.

Black pudding (blood sausage) is another quintessential northern food. The main ingredient is pig's blood, mixed with diced back fat, onions, herbs and spices, and oatmeal or barley, and encased in intestines, then boiled. It can be served sliced, grilled (broiled) or fried, and as an ingredient or garnish in dishes from salads to stews and casseroles, and it is sometimes served with fish or shellfish. White pudding is made with chopped offcuts of pork and bacon and offal. Though it has similar flavouring ingredients to black pudding, white pudding contains no blood.

Poultry

In rural areas the keeping of poultry was common everywhere, and was often vital to the economy of the household. Hens, ducks, geese, turkeys, sometimes guinea fowl, and less commonly pigeons were kept and bred. Their flesh provided meat for the Sunday dinner, while their eggs provided nourishing breakfasts and were an essential ingredient for cakes and tarts.

At one time poultry was reserved for Christmas and other festivities. For the rich, peacock and swan were festive fare until the 16th century, after which turkey and goose became regular features at Christmas.

Traditionally, the ducks and hens that pecked about in the yard were the province of the farmer's wife, and even in relatively grand families the mistress of the house usually took responsibility for the domestic fowl. An industrious woman could earn a good deal of "egg money" selling her produce at markets or to local stores. The profits were reserved for luxuries, such as tea (once known as "China ale"), dried fruit and spices, cloth for clothes or hair ribbons. From an early age girls were taught to care for fowl, given a few chickens to rear and allowed to spend their own egg money.

Chicken

For hundreds of years, chickens have been bred both for their meat and their eggs, and they would have been a familiar sight in farmyards, country estates and gardens all over Britain. Older hens, with their laying days behind them, used to be stewed with root vegetables or made into pies, but that was in the days when they ranged freely about the farmyard, fed on a variety of foods, grew slowly and developed a complex flavour. The methods of breeding and rearing the birds have changed drastically in the modern era, with the result that they are now plentiful and cheap. Though most chicken meat for sale is still produced by intensive methods, there is a steady increase in the demand for free-range and organic birds, which is

Above *Geese provide meat for festive roast dinners, as well as eggs for use in breakfasts and baked goods.*

being met by supermarkets as well as traditional butchers, and farmers' markets are offering birds reared by artisan producers. Smoked chicken, a fairly recent innovation, has become a tasty first course.

Goose

Roast goose is traditional fare on Michaelmas Day (29 September), sometimes called Goose Day, when eating it is said to bring good fortune to the diners. From September to Christmas, goose might also be served at wedding feasts and could be a regular Sunday roast for wealthy families. Most of the geese eaten today are raised on farms, ready for roasting and serving with sage and onion stuffing and apple or gooseberry sauce. In medieval Ireland, goose was stuffed with herbs and fruit, boiled with

Left *Free-range chickens feeding in a farmhouse yard.*

dumplings and served with apple or garlic sauce. There is no great industrial production of geese today, so the birds reared by artisan producers are a luxury food, but they are making a come-back as the bird for a special festive occasion.

Duck

There are several breeds of domesticated duck, of which the Aylesbury is one of the best. Some are more fatty than others and need longer cooking at a high temperature, so that the fat is rendered out and the skin crisps. A real farmyard duck is relatively rare now, although excellent ducks are sold by medium and small producers.

Turkey

The turkey, an American bird, was known in Britain as early as the 17th century. Only in the 20th century, however, did it become the bird of choice for the Christmas dinner, ousting the goose as the farmyard bird most likely to generate a good income. This is curious, because turkeys are difficult to rear and more prone to disease than geese. Like chicken, modern intensive production has made it plentiful, cheap and rather bland. For the true taste of turkey, look out for birds reared by specialist producers and sold at farmers' markets and traditional butchers. The Christmas turkey is served

with gravy, bread sauce, bacon rolls and small sausages, and accompanied by cranberry sauce. Guinea fowl was originally a game bird but is now farmed and usually classed as poultry.

Quail

This small bird used to be shot in the wild but grew so scarce that it eventually became a protected species. The majority of quails eaten today are farmed by artisan food producers. They also sell the tiny eggs, sometimes hard-boiled. They can be served just lightly boiled, or as a garnish, or as a party nibble dipped in celery salt. They are

Above *Free-range ducks are given access to outdoor areas during the day.*

sometimes preserved in mild, lightly spiced wine vinegar. The birds are delicious roasted, pot roasted or casseroled.

Egg production and cooking

Commercially produced hens' eggs come from a two-tiered production system: free-range (farm-fresh), which may also be organic, or battery-farmed (caged), which many customers now reject as cruel to the laying hens.

Whether simply fried, poached or scrambled with butter then served with bacon, smoked salmon, or kippers, eggs remain an essential element of the traditional British breakfast. For light meals, they can be baked, or coddled in cream, or made into an omelette.

In general cooking, eggs are used to enrich sauces, in baking, and in desserts – mousses, meringues, crème caramel and crème brûlée are very popular. Duck eggs, once reserved for men (women and children ate hens' eggs), are sought after for baking because of their stronger flavour.

Left *Over the last century, the turkey has become the most popular choice for a traditional Christmas dinner, replacing the goose.*

Game

The eating of game once helped to sustain families through the winter months when other types of fresh meat were not available. In medieval times hunting became training for war, a rite of manhood and a traditional pastime, and was then a privilege of the wealthy and the sport of kings. While aristocrats hunted prime animals and birds, such as deer, swans, peacocks and pheasant, the peasants were allowed to hunt only small creatures.

Today, thanks to organized seasonal shoots, game is widely available from game dealers throughout the country. Scotland's wild open country has long been home to a large variety of game, of unrivalled quality and flavour.

Almost all game must be hung to develop flavour and tenderize the flesh. Birds are hung by the neck, unplucked, in a cool place. Deer are gutted and skinned before hanging. The length of hanging time depends on the type of game, where it is hung and the weather: game spoils quickly when the weather is thundery, for example.

Below Red deer, Britain's largest wild animal, is a common species in Scotland.

Furred game

Venison This is the meat of the red, fallow or roe deer, which is now widely farmed, but the term once meant any furred game. In the 11th century William the Conqueror reserved the right to hunt in the royal forests, and there were severe punishments for anyone caught killing or even disturbing the animals. Venison is therefore historically a food of the wealthy and landowning classes. Scottish venison is considered to be the best in the world and is one of the glories of Scottish cuisine. In Ireland, wild deer roam Wicklow, Kerry and other highland areas. The shooting seasons depend on the species, and are different for stags and hinds. Farmed venison is less expensive than wild and the meat is more tender, with a delicate, less gamey flavour. Some deer farmers have developed a trade in venison sausages and pies. Wild venison is usually marinated in alcohol and oil to tenderize the flesh and keep it moist as it cooks. All venison is lean and low in cholesterol. The age of the animal and the hanging time greatly affect the

flavour and texture of the meat. The haunch, saddle or leg are best for roasting. Chops from the ribs can be fried or grilled (broiled). The flank is best casseroled or minced (ground). A strong-flavoured meat, venison needs to be matched with robust flavours such as spices, rowan berries, juniper berries and red wine.

Rabbit This is available all year round and is best eaten without hanging. Wild rabbit has a more pronounced flavour and a darker flesh than farmed rabbits, which are delicate in flavour and always tender. The meat tends to be dry so it should be well basted or cooked with liquid. A traditional Scottish dish, Kingdom of Fife pie, is made with rabbit and pickled pork or bacon. Rabbit is an essential ingredient in game terrines and pies.

Hare Available late summer to early spring, hare must be hung for seven to ten days before cooking. Its blood is often saved to thicken the gravy in jugged hare – a rich, dark stew.

Wild boar A few enterprising farmers are producing wild boar. Unlike pork, it is a lean, red meat with a slightly gamey flavour, which becomes more

Above Wild pheasants can be found throughout Scotland and are easy and tasty game for locals and hunters.

pronounced as the animal ages. Prized cuts are the saddle and haunches, both of which can also be smoked to produce wild boar ham.

Feathered game

Pheasant This bird is in its prime in mid-autumn and stays in season until early spring. If eaten without hanging the flavour is similar to that of chicken; after hanging, the flesh develops a mild gamey taste. The hen bird is less dry

Below Cuts of wild boar; saddle (top) with fillet (tenderloin) and chops (bottom).

than the cock and tends to have more flavour, but they are often sold as a brace – one hen and one cock bird. They can be grilled (broiled), roasted or casseroled. Roast pheasant is traditionally accompanied by bread sauce. Pheasant is a major ingredient of game pies, particularly at Christmas.

Partridge Best in mid to late autumn while young and tender, young partridge are usually roasted.

Wild duck A rare treat today, wild duck is less fatty than domesticated birds and has a more developed flavour. Mallards are the largest and most common wild ducks. Cook them in the same way as ordinary duck, but add extra oil. The smaller wild ducks, such as the teal, widgeon and pochard, are highly prized by gourmets.

Woodcock This is in season from mid-autumn to late winter. It is traditionally roasted without drawing and with its head still in place, accompanied with berries and roasted vegetables.

Pigeons For centuries, domestic pigeons were an important source of meat, housed in purpose-built cotes on farms and country

Above Wild rabbits proliferate in all parts of Scotland, providing excellent game meat.

estates. Nowadays, wild wood pigeons are shot to keep them off growing crops. The young birds, or just their breasts, can be roasted or pan-fried; older ones go into game casseroles and pies. They are available all year round.

Grouse The red grouse inhabits the Scottish moors where it feeds on heather, blueberries, grasses and herbs, which impart a unique flavour. The flavour varies according to the locality and the hanging time (usually two to seven days). They are shot from 12 August until 10 December. A native of Scotland, it is found only here and in the north of England. Grouse flesh tends to be dry, and they were originally cooked on a spit so that they basted themselves as they turned. Before roasting the bird can be stuffed with cranberries to keep it moist and complement the flavour. Wrap well in streaky (fatty) bacon or brush with butter and baste during cooking.

Dairy

The dairy has always played an important part in British country life. There was a time when even small households kept a cow in the garden to supply milk. In some areas a cow formed part of a labourer's wages, and cows were milked on the streets of London as late as the 19th century. As well as cows, there would have been ewes and goats on most mixed farms.

In some regions cattle are raised on such fertile pastures that they produce milk with an extremely high butterfat content. These areas have become justifiably renowned for their rich butter, cream and cheeses – the clotted cream of the West Country is just one example. British cookery books are full of recipes that use dairy products.

In Scotland, whey and sour milk were traditionally enjoyed as refreshing summer drinks, and buttermilk was added to mashed potatoes, porridge (oatmeal), scones and bannocks. In Shetland, whey was fermented in oak casks for several months to produce blaand, a drink that has been revived and is now produced commercially.

In the 20th century, industrialization led to a decline in the production of traditional dairy products, but the old

Below The British love cream, whether single, double, whipped or clotted.

Below The wash for Bishop Kennedy includes a generous dash of whisky, giving a lovely tasty rind.

skills are now being revived and a wealth of local products are reappearing, including milk, yogurt, cream, butter and buttermilk. In addition, there is a growing band of artisans using old-fashioned methods to make traditional cheeses with interesting characters that change along with the seasons. Locally made ice creams are becoming very popular too.

Cows' milk cheeses

Ardrahan A semi-firm Irish cheese with a washed rind and an earthy flavour, Ardrahan grows more robust and tangy as it ages.

Bishop Kennedy This is a Scottish cheese that has its origins in the medieval monasteries of France. A full-fat soft cheese, with a strong creamy taste, it is runny when ripe. The rind is washed in malt whisky to produce a distinctive orange-red crust. It has become popular for cooking.

Caboc Produced in the Scottish Highlands, Caboc is a soft-textured cream cheese shaped into logs and rolled in toasted pinhead oatmeal. The nubbly oatmeal contrasts well with the soft creamy cheese. The name is derived from kebbock, the old name for cheese.

Cairnsmore is a hard cheese from

Galloway. Aromatic and nutty, with the sweetness of caramel and burnt toffee, it ripens in seven to nine months.

Cheddar This is possibly the archetypal English hard cheese. Mature Cheddar is golden yellow with a firm, silky texture and full flavour. Some of it is matured in the caves of the Cheddar Gorge in

Below Milk is fresh and plentiful in all regions of pasture-rich Britain.

Somerset. West Country Farmhouse Cheddar has Protected Designation of Origin status, meaning that it can only be made in the four counties of Dorset, Somerset, Devon and Cornwall. A good mature piece of cheddar is ideal for the cheeseboard and to use in cooking.

Cheshire One of the oldest English cheeses, Cheshire is mentioned in the Domesday Book. It has a slightly crumbly, silky texture. Its tangy, salty flavour is due to the salt deposits found in the local pasturelands.

Coolea This is a semi-firm Irish cheese

Below Durrus (top) and Gabriel.

made only from summer milk. It is matured for between six months and two years, and becomes firm with a complex, grassy, herbal flavour that grows longer and stronger with aging.

Cooleeney A soft white mould cheese – smooth, with robust flavours of oak and mushroom and a velvety texture.

Cornish Yarg This is based on a cheese recipe from the 13th century. The cheese is pressed and brined before being wrapped in nettle leaves, which are brushed on in a prescribed pattern and attract natural moulds of white, green, grey and blue. These moulds help the cheese to ripen, and as it matures the edible nettles impart a delicate flavour.

Cotherstone From Yorkshire, this is an unpasteurized, hard cheese with a slight acidity and a fresh, citrus tang.

Crowdie This is an ancient Highland cheese made from skimmed cow's milk, similar to cottage cheese, with a sharp, acidic flavour. Uniquely Scottish, it was once used as part-payment of rent in the Highlands. After the Clearances, crowdie disappeared, but it was revived in the 1960s. It is unusual because it is half cooked. Fresh milk is left in a warm place to sour naturally, and then heated until it separates and curdles, then the curds are hung up in a large square of muslin (cheesecloth) to drain.

Curworthy A hard Devon cheese based on a 17th-century recipe and made from unpasteurized milk. It has a creamy yet open texture and a mild, buttery taste.

Derby With a smooth, mellow texture and mild, buttery flavour (similar in taste and texture to Cheddar), Derby is delicious with fruit juice.

Devon Garland An unpasteurized, semi-hard cheese made from the milk of (usually) Jersey cows. Its rind is firm and smooth with a greyish brown crust. A layer of fresh herbs is added before the cheese is matured.

Dilliskus Made with summer milk only, this is a firm Irish cheese flavoured with

Above Cornish Yarg.

dillisk or dulse (seaweed). It has a distinctive aroma with a great texture, and a sweet, tangy flavour.

Drumloch A full-fat hard pressed cheese similar to Cheddar, made from the milk of Guernsey cows in Scotland. It has a beautiful creamy texture, light golden colour and rich flavour.

Durrus A semi-soft, washed-rind cheese, moist, with a complex flavour.

Gabriel and **Desmond** Two exceptional Irish hard cheeses, made in the Swiss alpage style. Desmond has an intensely spicy, floral flavour that lingers. Gabriel is just as intense but has a sweeter, more subtle flavour.

Lancashire A creamy white cheese that can be traced back to the 13th century, with an open, crumbly texture and mild flavour. Used in sandwiches and salads, Lancashire is also one of the best melting cheeses, so is ideal for cooking.

Lavistown A semi-soft, brushed-rind Irish cheese made from skimmed milk. It has a clean buttermilk tang that is richer in flavour in winter.

Leafield A sheep's milk cheese made in Oxfordshire. Once made by the monks of Abingdon Abbey on the same site, it has been faithfully revived from its original 16th-century recipe, and is dense and chewy with a full flavour.

Lincolnshire Poacher A modern hard, unpasteurized cheese with a granite-like rind. Production began in 1992.

Above Stinking Bishop.

Milleens This is a soft, washed-rind cheese from Cork; it matures to spilling cream with a complex flavour and a herby, spicy tang.

Orkney Farmhouse Cheese Made with unpasteurized cow's milk this cheese has a wonderfully buttery, mellow flavour. Because of Orkney's isolation, traditional small-scale cheese-making on farms there has continued uninterrupted for hundreds of years.

Red Leicester A rich, russet-coloured cheese with a flaky, slightly open texture and a mellow flavour. It is good eaten with fruit or beer and can be used in cooking as it melts very well.

Single and Double Gloucester Double Gloucester is the most widely available. It was traditionally made as a large wheel with a thick rind, able to withstand the county's annual cheese-rolling races, one of which, at Cooper's Hill, is still held. Its orange colour originally came from carrot juice or saffron; today the vegetable dye annatto is used. Double Gloucester, made from whole milk, has a smooth, buttery texture with a clean, creamy, mellow flavour. It is widely available, but Single Gloucester cheese (half the size of Double) can, by law, only be made on farms in Gloucestershire with a pedigree herd of Gloucester cattle.

Right Cairnsmore (top) is aromatic and nutty, while Caboc (bottom) is creamy and rolled in toasted oatmeal.

St Andrews A creamy semi-soft cheese from Perthshire. this is one of the two Trappist-style washed-rind cheeses made in Scotland; the other is Bishop Kennedy. It has a holey texture and a sweet-sour, slightly yeasty taste.

Stinking Bishop Made in the village of Dymock in Gloucestershire, this cheese is washed with perry made with a local variety of pear called "Stinking Bishop". It has an orange rind, a meaty flavour and a pungent aroma.

Tobermory An excellent hard, full-flavoured, unpasteurized farmhouse cheese, which is matured for 18 months.

Wensleydale A moist, crumbly and flaky cheese with a flavour that is mild, slightly sweet and refreshing. Usually eaten young – one to three months old – it goes very well with apple pie. A blue variety is available.

Blue cheeses

Beenleigh Blue Made in Devon from unpasteurized sheep's milk. The rough, crusty, natural rind is slightly sticky with

Above Cashel Blue (left), a blue cheese from Tipperary, and Ardrahan (right), a vegetarian washed-rind cheese, from west Cork.

patches of blue, grey and white moulds. It is moist and crumbly, with blue-green streaks through the white interior. It is good served with a glass of mead or sweet cider.

Buxton Blue A pale orange, lightly veined cheese. Appreciate its "blue" flavour in soups, salads or on crackers. It is perfect with chilled dessert wine.

Cashel Blue Very original in flavour and texture, this is a modern blue-veined cheese from County Tipperary, sweet, tangy, rich and buttery.

Dorset Blue Vinney The name of this cheese comes from an Old English word for mould. The popularity it enjoyed in the 18th and 19th centuries declined with the introduction of factory cheese-making, and it became extinct in the 1960s, but happily is now being made again. It is a hard cheese, light in texture with a mild flavour.

Dovedale A creamy soft, mild blue cheese that is dipped in brine. It is made in Derbyshire and takes its name from a lovely valley in the Peak District.

Dunsyre Blue Renowned for its excellence, this artisan-made, blue-veined, cow's-milk cheese has a creamy yet sharp flavour. It is made solely from the milk of native Ayrshire cattle.

Lanark Blue This cheese is made from unpasteurized sheep's milk and is mottled with blue veins. Its creamy, sharp flavour is superb and it has been compared with the French Roquefort.

Oxford Blue This cheese was created less than 20 years ago as an alternative to Stilton. It is creamy with a distinct "blue" flavour and is sold wrapped in silver foil.

Shropshire Blue This cheese is not actually from Shropshire at all: having been invented in Scotland, it is now produced in Leicestershire. This distinctive orange-coloured cheese with its blue veins has a firm, creamy texture and a sharp, strong flavour. Eating Shropshire Blue with a cup of tea is said to bring out its flavour.

Stilton Historically referred to as "the king of cheeses", Stilton has narrow, blue-green veins and a wrinkled rind. Its texture is smooth and creamy and its flavour is rich and mellow with a piquant aftertaste. Never made in the village of Stilton, in Huntingdonshire, it was first sold there. The cheese

Below Stilton.

originated at Quenby near Melton Mowbray in the early 18th century. Its certification trademark and Protected Designation of Origin status allows it to be made only in the counties of Nottinghamshire, Derbyshire, and Leicestershire, to a specified recipe. At Christmas, Stilton is traditionally served with port. A white variety is available.

Strathdon Blue This cheese from the Scottish highlands has a deliciously spicy flavour and delectable creamy smooth texture dotted with knobbly blue veins, which provide a pleasing contrast. Strathdon Blue has won the Best Scottish Cheese at the British Cheese Awards twice in recent years.

Goat's milk cheeses

Blue Rathgore This is a blue cheese from Northern Ireland, moist and crumbly, with a slightly burnt taste.

Corleggy A natural rind, hard cheese, this has a fine smooth texture, with rich layers of complex flavours.

Croghan This is an unpasteurized, organic, vegetarian semi-soft cheese, made from goat's milk in the Wexford area. The

Above , Croghan (top), a vegetarian semi-soft cheese, made from goat's milk in the Wexford region, and Cooleeney (bottom), a soft white cheese from Tipperary

flavour suggests grass and hay, while the finish is aromatic without being pungent. It is made only from spring until autumn.

Inverloch This superb hard-pressed cheese, coated in red wax, is made on the Scottish Isle of Gigha, off the west coast of Kintyre.

Oisin Made with organic milk, this is Ireland's only blue goat's milk cheese.

Sheep's milk cheeses

Abbey Blue This is a flavoursome, organic, soft white-blue cheese.

Cratloe Hills Mature A hard cheese that at six months has developed a robust, fudge-caramel flavour.

Crozier Blue This cheese comes from the same maker as Cashel Blue cheese; the use of rich ewe's milk results in a distinctive cheese, smooth and buttery, with a pronounced flavour.

Tobermory Mornish This is a silky smooth, semi-soft, white, mould-ripened cheese with a wonderful creamy flavour that has hints of grass and lemon.

Alcoholic beverages

With a brewing industry dating back to the earliest times, wine imported from Europe long before the Romans came, and a long history of whisky appreciation, it is not surprising that many of Britain's favourite drinks are alcoholic. Much of their consumption traditionally happens in public houses, or "pubs". From Georgian drinking dens, to the men-only smoking clubs of the 1900s, to today's smartened up gastro-pubs, pubs have a central place in British social life.

Mead

In its simplest form, mead is a mixture of honey and water fermented with wild yeasts, and it is thought to be the oldest alcoholic drink in the world. When imports of cheap sugar reduced the importance of honey, fewer people kept bees. Mead-making declined and never really recovered, but it is still made by artisan producers.

Beer and ale

Ale is simply fermented grain, and has been drunk throughout history as a safer alternative to water, which was often contaminated. By the Middle Ages, the brewing of ale was largely the realm of women; alehouses were well established and small beer was the most common drink, even for children.

Until the 15th century ale consisted of malted barley, water and yeast. Then merchants from Flanders and Holland introduced a new hopped version, called beer. It had a bitter flavour and, unlike ale, kept well. By the 18th century all beers were hopped. Commercial brewing began in the 19th century, and various styles developed – pale beer, dark beer, porter and stout – differing according to the water supply.

Cider

Pressing and fermenting apples to make cider is an ancient art. New apple varieties reached England with the Romans and the Normans. By the middle of the 17th century, most farms had a cider orchard and an apple press and it was traditional to pay part of a farm labourer's wages in cider, with extra at haymaking time. As people moved from the farms to the towns in the 19th century, commercial cider-making developed. Although beer is more widely drunk now, cider is still very popular in England's south west.

***Above** A pint of traditionally brewed real ale, as popular as ever in Britain.*

Scotch whisky

The origins of whisky are lost in the mists of time. The word itself is derived from the Gaelic uisge beatha – the water of life. Scotland's national drink was already well established by the 15th century. Its popularity grew steadily, especially in the Lowlands where many distilleries sprang up. Highland distilleries were smaller and supplied mainly their own locality.

Malt whiskies vary in colour from palest straw to deep glowing amber and are aromatic, smooth and full of complex character. This is partly due to their long maturation in casks that have previously contained sherry, port, rum or bourbon, which augment their flavour and character as well as colour. Malt whisky is a drink of enormous variety and no two malts are the same. Single malts are the products of just one distillery and are the most highly prized. Vatted malts are a blend from several distilleries within a region. Each region produces its own character, often expressing age-old traditions.

***Left** Scotch whisky casks are specially made from woods such as oak to impart a subtle flavour to the whisky.*

Speyside is the principal whisky-producing region and makes some of the world's greatest malts, such as Macallan, Glenfiddich and Glenlivet. Speyside malt whiskies are sweet and can be highly perfumed, with scents of roses, apples and lemonade.

The central Highlands produce malt whiskies with a dry finish and a fine fragrance. Edradour is one example.

West Highland malts have a mild smokiness and a dryish finish, and include such fine whiskies as Talisker from the Isle of Skye.

East Highland malts are smooth and slightly sweet, with a hint of smokiness and a dryish finish. Royal Lochnagar, produced near Balmoral, is typical.

Lowland malts, such as Rosebank, were the first whiskies to be drunk on a large scale. They have a fruity sweetness and a dry finish.

Campbeltown malts, from Kintyre, are fully flavoured with a tang of salt.

Islay produces dry, peaty and smoky malts, such as the powerful Lavagulin.

Below Draught Guinness is a creamy stout with a refreshing, roasted flavour. Murphy's Irish Stout is light and smooth.

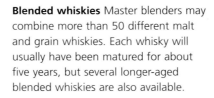

Blended whiskies Master blenders may combine more than 50 different malt and grain whiskies. Each whisky will usually have been matured for about five years, but several longer-aged blended whiskies are also available.

Irish whiskey

In the mid-16th century a tax of four pence a gallon was imposed on whiskey in Ireland, and folklore maintains the making of the illicit spirit poitín began the following day. By the 18th century 2,000 stills were in operation. Whiskey had become the spirit of the Irish nation. It is made by two methods: pot still and column still. The latter produces grain whiskey; it is more efficient but removes some of the aromatics that make pot still so flavoursome. There are three types of Irish whiskey: single malt, pure pot-stilled and a column-and-pot still blend. All are triple-distilled.

The Irish do not ice whiskey; "breaking it" with water is optional and it is often drunk neat. Some brands are soft and gentle, others "explode" in the mouth. Jameson (a blend) accounts for about 75 per cent of all Irish whiskey sold globally. Bushmills, the oldest distillery in Ireland, makes a range of single malts and blends. Premium whiskeys are matured for up to 21 years.

Recipes for whiskey liqueurs date from 1602; raisins, dates, aniseed, molasses, liquorice and herbs were used. Based on an ancient drink called heather wine, Irish Mist is made with heather honey, herbs and spices, aged whiskey and other spirits.

Invented in the 1970s, cream liqueurs such as Bailey's are made with whiskey, cream and honey. Irish coffee is a combination of whiskey, black coffee, sugar and cream.

Above Quality whisky can be enjoyed on its own or with ice.

Gin

When it was first introduced to Britain from the Netherlands, gin was drunk for medicinal purposes, but because it was very cheap it soon became a drink of the poor. By the mid-18th century London had more than 7,000 gin shops and 11 million gallons of gin were distilled there every year. Workers were given gin as part of their wages and much of it was drunk by women. The Gin Acts of 1729 and 1736 attempted to curb consumption by making the drink very expensive, but they could not be enforced; riots ensued and distilling continued. In the 1750s licensing and excise policies were introduced, and gradually the problem was resolved.

Right The famous Beefeater gin.

Breakfasts

In medieval days, most ordinary people ate bread and drank ale before a day in the fields, though the rich enjoyed meat or fish. By the late 19th century breakfast had become a very elaborate affair, with the tables of the wealthy groaning with hams, kedgeree, sausages, eggs and game. The shortages of two world wars ended such ostentation, but the British cooked breakfast is still an enjoyable tradition.

Porridge

One of Scotland's oldest foods, oatmeal porridge remains a favourite way to start the day in all parts of Britain, especially during winter. Brown sugar, golden syrup or honey are added, and for special treats in Scotland, cream and a tot of whisky.

Serves 4

1 litre/1¾ pints/4 cups water

115g/4oz/1 cup pinhead oatmeal

good pinch of salt

Variation Modern rolled oats can be used, in the proportion of 115g/4oz/ generous 1 cup to 750ml/1¼ pints/ 3 cups water, plus a sprinkling of salt. This cooks more quickly than pinhead oatmeal. Simmer, stirring to prevent sticking, for about 5 minutes. Either type of oatmeal can be left to cook overnight in the slow oven of a range.

1 Put the water, pinhead oatmeal and salt into a heavy pan and bring to the boil over a medium heat, stirring with a wooden spatula. When the porridge is smooth and beginning to thicken, reduce the heat to a simmer.

2 Cook gently for about 25 minutes, stirring occasionally, until the oatmeal is cooked and the consistency smooth. Serve hot with cold milk and extra salt, if required, topped with syrup, honey or brown sugar, and cream.

Energy 115kcal/488kJ; Protein 3.6g; Carbohydrate 20.9g, of which sugars 0g; Fat 2.5g, of which saturates 0g; Cholesterol 0mg; Calcium 16mg; Fibre 2g; Sodium 304mg

Irish brown soda breakfast scones

These unusually light scones are virtually fat-free, so they must be eaten very fresh – warm from the oven if possible, but definitely on the day of baking. Serve with generous amounts of fresh, high-quality Irish butter.

Makes about 16

225g/8oz/2 cups plain (all-purpose) flour

2.5ml/½ tsp bicarbonate of soda (baking soda)

2.5ml/½ tsp salt

225g/8oz/2 cups wheaten flour

about 350ml/12fl oz/1½ cups buttermilk or sour cream and milk mixed

topping (optional): egg wash (1 egg yolk mixed with 15ml/1 tbsp water) or a little grated cheese

1 Preheat the oven to 220°C/425°F/ Gas 7. Oil and flour a baking tray.

2 Sift the flour, bicarbonate of soda and salt in a bowl, add the wheaten flour and mix. Make a well in the centre, pour in almost all the liquid and mix, adding liquid as needed to make a soft, moist dough. Do not overmix.

3 Lightly dust a surface with flour, turn out the dough and dust with flour.

4 Press out the dough to a thickness of 4cm/1½in. Cut out 16 scones with a 5cm/2in fluted pastry (cookie) cutter. Place on the baking tray and brush the tops with egg wash, or sprinkle with a little grated cheese, if using.

5 Bake for about 12 minutes until well risen and golden brown.

Per scone Energy 117Kcal/493kJ; Protein 3.8g; Carbohydrate 20.9g, of which sugars 1.5g; Fat 2.6g, of which saturates 1.4g; Cholesterol 6mg; Calcium 49mg; Fibre 1.7g; Sodium 72mg

Scottish rowies

These are the delicious traditional breakfast rolls served in Scottish homes, originally coming from Aberdeenshire, although they are made all over the country today and are very popular in tourist areas. They are eaten like a croissant, hot from the oven with butter or fresh cream and marmalades or jams and jellies.

Makes 16

7.5ml/1½ tsp dried yeast

15ml/1 tbsp soft light brown sugar

450ml/¾ pint/scant 2 cups warm water

450g/1lb/4 cups strong white bread flour

pinch of salt

225g/8oz/1 cup butter

115g/4oz/½ cup lard or white cooking fat

1 Mix the yeast with the sugar, dissolve in a little warm water taken from the measured amount then set aside in a warm place, lightly covered to allow some air to circulate.

2 Mix the flour in a large mixing bowl with the salt. When the yeast has bubbled up pour it into the flour with the rest of the water. Mix well to form a dough and leave in a warm place, covered with a dish towel, to rise until it has doubled in size, about 2 hours.

3 Cream the butter and lard or white cooking fat together in a small bowl and then divide the mixture into three portions. The mixture should be soft enough to spread easily but not so warm that it melts. If it is melting, refrigerate for 5–10 minutes.

4 When the dough has doubled in size, knock back (punch down) until it is the original size. Roll it out on a floured surface to a rectangle about 1cm/½in thick. Spread a third of the butter mixture over two-thirds of the dough.

5 Fold the ungreased third of the dough over on to the greased middle third, then the other greased third into the middle, thus giving three layers. Roll this back to the original rectangle size. Leave to rest in a cool place for 40 minutes then repeat the procedure, including the resting period, twice more, to use up the butter mixture.

6 Cut the dough into 16 squares. Shape into rough circles by folding the edges in all the way around and place on a baking sheet. Leave to rise, covered with a clean dry dish towel, for 45 minutes. Meanwhile preheat the oven to 200°C/400°F/Gas 6.

7 When the rowies have risen, bake in the oven for 15 minutes until golden brown and flaky.

Energy 296kcal/1233kJ; Protein 3g; Carbohydrate 25.4g, of which sugars 1.5g; Fat 21g, of which saturates 11.4g; Cholesterol 41mg; Calcium 47mg; Fibre 1g; Sodium 96g.

Buttermilk pancakes

These little pancakes are a traditional Irish recipe and are made with buttermilk, which is widely available in Ireland. The pancakes are quite like the drop scones that are so familiar across the water in Scotland, with Welsh and English variations too. They are delicious served warm, with honey.

Makes about 12

225g/8oz/2 cups plain (all-purpose) flour

7.5ml/1½ tsp bicarbonate of soda (baking soda)

25–50g/1–2oz/2–4 tbsp sugar

1 egg

about 300ml/½ pint/1¼ cups buttermilk

butter and oil, mixed, or white vegetable fat (shortening), for frying

honey, to serve

1 In a food processor or a large mixing bowl, mix together the plain flour, the bicarbonate of soda and enough sugar to taste. Add the egg, mixing together, and gradually pour in just enough of the buttermilk to make a thick, smooth batter.

2 Heat a heavy pan and add the butter and oil, or white fat. Place spoonfuls of the batter on to the hot pan and cook for 2–3 minutes until bubbles rise to the surface. Flip the pancakes over and cook for a further 2–3 minutes. Remove from the pan and serve warm with honey.

Energy 1449Kcal/6098kJ; Protein 38.5g; Carbohydrate 214.2g, of which sugars 42.7g; Fat 54.9g, of which saturates 19.6g; Cholesterol 300mg; Calcium 695mg; Fibre 7g; Sodium 219mg

Irish boxty potato pancakes

Said to have originated during the Irish famine, these delicious pancakes use blended potatoes in the batter mix and can be made as thin or thick as you like. They are often served rolled around a hot savoury filling such as cooked cabbage and chopped bacon bound in a light mustard sauce, and make a lovely lunch as well as a filling breakfast.

Makes 4 pancakes

450g/1lb potatoes, peeled and chopped

50–75g/2–3oz/½–⅔ cup plain (all-purpose) flour

about 150ml/¼ pint/⅔ cup milk

salt to taste

knob (pat) of butter

1 Place the peeled and chopped potatoes in a blender or in the bowl of a food processor and process until the potato is thoroughly liquidized (blended).

2 Add the flour and enough milk to the processed potato to give a dropping consistency, and add salt to taste. The milk and flour can be adjusted, depending on how thin you like your pancake. Heat a little butter on a griddle or cast-iron frying pan.

3 Pour about a quarter of the mixture into the pan – if the consistency is right it will spread evenly over the base. Cook over a medium heat for about 5 minutes on each side, depending on the thickness of the cake. Serve rolled with the hot filling of your choice.

Per pancake Energy 163Kcal/689kJ; Protein 4.8g; Carbohydrate 30.9g, of which sugars 2.7g; Fat 3.1g, of which saturates 1.7g; Cholesterol 8mg; Calcium 69mg; Fibre 1.9g; Sodium 236mg

Scottish potato cakes

This is the traditional method of making potato cakes on a griddle or in a heavy frying pan. Commercial versions are available throughout Scotland but homemade ones are much better. Fry them with eggs for breakfast, or at teatime, buttered and sprinkled with sugar.

Makes about 12

675g/1½lb potatoes, peeled

25g/1oz/2 tbsp unsalted (sweet) butter

about 175g/6oz/1½ cups plain (all-purpose) flour

salt

1 Boil the potatoes in a large pan over a medium heat until tender, then drain thoroughly, replacing the pan with the drained poatoes over a low heat for a few minutes to allow any moisture to evaporate completely.

2 Mash the potatoes with plenty of salt, then mix in the butter and cool.

3 Turn out on to a floured work surface and knead in about one-third of its volume in flour, or as much as is needed to make a pliable dough.

4 Roll out to a thickness of about 1cm/½in and cut into triangles.

5 Heat a dry griddle or heavy frying pan over a low heat and cook the potato cakes on it for about 3 minutes on each side until browned. Serve hot.

Per batch Energy 1276kcal/5392kJ; Protein 30.4g; Carbohydrate 249.1g, of which sugars 6.7g; Fat 24.1g, of which saturates 13.4g; Cholesterol 53mg; Calcium 282mg; Fibre 14g; Sodium 203mg

Omelette Arnold Bennett

This creamy, smoked haddock soufflé omelette was created for the post-theatre suppers of the famous English novelist, who frequently stayed at the Savoy Hotel in London after World War I. It is now served all over the world as a sustaining breakfast or supper dish.

Serves 2

175g/6oz smoked haddock fillet

50g/2oz butter, diced

175ml/6fl oz/¾ cup whipping or double (heavy) cream

4 eggs, separated

40g/1½oz mature (sharp) Cheddar cheese, grated

ground black pepper

watercress, to garnish

1 Remove and discard the skin and any bones from the haddock fillet by carefully pressing down the length of each fillet with your fingertips.

2 Using two forks and following the grain of the flesh, flake the fish into large chunks.

Cook's tip It's best to buy smoked haddock that does not contain artificial colouring for this recipe. Besides being better for you, it gives the omelette an improved flavour and a lighter, more attractive colour.

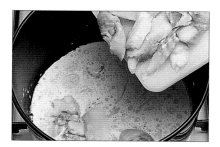

3 Melt half the butter with 60ml/4 tbsp of the cream in a small non-stick pan. When the mixture is hot but not boiling, add the fish. Stir together gently, taking care not to break up the flakes of fish. Bring slowly to the boil, stirring continuously, then cover the pan, remove from the heat and set aside to cool for at least 20 minutes.

4 Preheat the grill (broiler) to high. Mix the egg yolks with 15ml/1 tbsp of the cream. Season with ground black pepper, then stir into the fish. In a separate bowl, mix the cheese and the remaining cream. Stiffly whisk the egg whites, then fold into the fish mixture.

5 Heat the remaining butter in an omelette pan until foaming. Add the fish mixture and cook until it is browned underneath. Pour the cheese mixture evenly over the top and grill (broil) until it is bubbling. Serve immediately, garnished with watercress.

Energy 821kcal/3396kj; Protein 36.1g; Carbohydrate 2.6g, of which sugars 2.6g; Fat 74g, of which saturates 42.6g; Cholesterol 577mg; Calcium 280mg; Fibre 0g; Sodium 1123mg

Bubble and squeak

Made with leftovers from dinner the night before, the name of this dish is derived from the noises the mixture makes as it cooks. Originally, it included chopped, boiled beef. This version goes very well with bacon and eggs but can also be served with cold roast meat.

Serves 4

60ml/4 tbsp oil

1 onion, finely chopped

450g/1lb cooked, mashed potatoes

225g/8oz cooked cabbage or Brussels sprouts, chopped

salt and ground black pepper

1 Heat half the oil in a heavy, preferably non-stick frying pan. Add the onion and cook, stirring frequently, until softened but not browned.

2 Mix together the mashed potatoes and cabbage or sprouts and season to taste with salt and plenty of pepper.

Cook's tips
• Though cabbage is traditional, other cooked vegetables could be added too.
• Using bacon fat or dripping in place of oil adds extra flavour.

3 Add the vegetable mixture to the pan, stir well to incorporate the cooked onions, then flatten the mixture out over the base of the pan to form a large, even cake.

4 Cook over a medium heat for about 15 minutes, until the cake is nicely browned underneath.

5 Hold a large plate over the pan, then invert the cake onto it. Add the remaining oil to the pan and, when hot, slip the cake back into the pan, browned side uppermost.

6 Continue cooking for about 10 minutes, until the underside is golden brown. Serve hot, cut into wedges.

Energy 219kcal/908kJ; Protein 2.5g; Carbohydrate 17.2g, of which sugars 2.5g; Fat 15.9g, of which saturates 1.9g; Cholesterol 0mg; Calcium 33mg; Fibre 2.6g; Sodium 14mg

Smoked haddock with spinach and poached egg

This is a really special breakfast treat. Use young spinach leaves in season and, of course, the freshest eggs. There is something about the combination of eggs, spinach and "smoke" that really perks you up in the morning.

Serves 4

4 undyed smoked haddock fillets

milk

75ml/2½fl oz/⅓ cup double (heavy) cream

25g/1oz/2 tbsp butter

250g/9oz fresh spinach, tough stalks removed

white wine vinegar

4 eggs

salt and ground black pepper

1 Place the haddock fillets in a large frying pan and pour in just enough milk to come half way up the fish. Over a low heat, poach the fish, shaking the pan gently to keep the fillets moist, for about 5 minutes.

2 Remove the cooked fish from the pan and keep warm. Increase the heat and reduce the milk by half. Add the cream and allow to bubble. The sauce should be thickened but should pour easily. Season with salt and pepper.

3 Heat a frying pan then add the butter. Add the spinach, stirring briskly for a few minutes. Season lightly then set aside, keeping it warm.

4 To poach the eggs, bring 4cm/1½in water to a simmer and add a few drops of vinegar. Gently crack two eggs into the water and cook for 3 minutes. Remove the first egg using a slotted spoon and rest in the spoon on some kitchen paper to remove any water. Repeat with the second egg, then cook the other two in the same way.

5 Place the spinach over the fillets and a poached egg on top. Pour over the cream sauce and serve immediately.

Energy 350kcal/1455kJ; Protein 27.5g; Carbohydrate 1.5g, of which sugars 1.4g; Fat 26.3g, of which saturates 14g; Cholesterol 277mg; Calcium 170mg; Fibre 1.3g; Sodium 969mg

Creamy scrambled eggs with smoked salmon

A special treat for weekend breakfasts, scrambled eggs with smoked salmon is a popular dish in some of Britain's best guesthouses and hotels. It is a good alternative to the traditional fry-up, and is now often eaten in homes around the country.

Serves 1

3 eggs

knob (pat) of butter

15ml/1 tbsp single (light) cream or milk

1 slice of smoked salmon, chopped or whole, warmed

salt and ground black pepper

sprig of fresh parsley, to garnish

triangles of hot toast, to serve

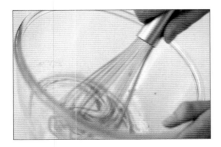

1 Whisk the eggs in a bowl together with the cream or milk, a generous grinding of black pepper and a little salt to taste if you like, remembering that the smoked salmon may be salty.

2 Melt the butter in a pan and, when it is warm, add the egg mixture and stir until nearly set.

3 Either stir in the chopped smoked salmon or serve the warmed slice alongside the egg. Serve immediately on warmed plates and garnish with the parsley and hot toast.

Below Salmon are found in the Irish Glenteenassig river, County Kerry.

Energy 447Kcal/1862kJ; Protein 37.3g; Carbohydrate 0.4g, of which sugars 0.4g; Fat 33.6g, of which saturates 13.1g; Cholesterol 734mg; Calcium 128mg; Fibre 0g; Sodium 1.37g

Smoked haddock and bacon

This is a classic combination, very much associated with Scotland. The smokiness of the fish goes well with the rich flavour of the bacon – both are complemented by the creamy sauce. Serve with warm breakfast rolls, or plenty of toast.

Serves 4

25g/1oz/2 tbsp butter

4 undyed smoked haddock fillets

8 rashers (strips) lean back bacon

120ml/4floz/½ cup double (heavy) cream

ground black pepper

chopped fresh chives, to garnish

1 Preheat the grill (broiler) to medium. Over a gentle heat, melt the butter in a frying pan.

2 Add the haddock fillets, working in two batches if necessary, and cook gently, turning once, for about 3 minutes each side. When cooked, place in a large ovenproof dish and cover. Reserve the juices from the frying pan.

3 Grill (broil) the bacon, turning once, until just cooked through but not crispy. Leave the grill on.

4 Return the frying pan to the heat and pour in the cream and any reserved juices from the haddock. Bring to the boil then simmer briefly, stirring occasionally. Season to taste with ground black pepper.

5 Meanwhile place two bacon rashers over each haddock fillet and place the dish under the grill (broiler) briefly. Then pour over the hot creamy sauce, garnish with snipped fresh chives and serve immediately.

Variation Instead of topping the smoked haddock with bacon, use wilted spinach. Thoroughly wash a good handful of spinach for each person. Then plunge it into boiling water for 3 minutes, drain well and lay across each fillet.

Energy 391kcal/1624kJ; Protein 28.8g; Carbohydrate 0.5g, of which sugars 0.5g; Fat 30.5g, of which saturates 16.5g; Cholesterol 119mg; Calcium 40mg; Fibre 0g; Sodium 1671mg

Kedgeree

Of Indian origin, kedgeree came to Britain via the British Raj. It quickly became a popular dish using smoked fish, which would be served as one of the many dishes on a wealthy family's breakfast table. It also makes a tasty supper, or a light lunch for a summer's day.

Serves 4–6

450g/1lb smoked haddock

300ml/½ pint/1¼ cups milk

175g/6oz/scant 1 cup long grain rice

pinch of grated nutmeg

pinch of cayenne pepper

1 onion, peeled and finely chopped

50g/2oz/¼ cup butter

2 hard-boiled eggs

chopped fresh parsley, to garnish

salt and ground black pepper

lemon wedges and wholemeal (whole-wheat) toast, to serve

1 Poach the haddock in the milk, made up with just enough water to cover the fish, for about 8 minutes, or until just cooked. Skin the haddock, remove all the bones and flake the flesh with a fork. Set aside.

2 Bring 600ml/1 pint/2½ cups water to the boil in a large pan. Add the rice, cover closely with a lid and cook over a low heat for about 25 minutes, or until all the water has been absorbed by the rice. Turn off the heat. Season the rice with salt and a grinding of black pepper, and the grated nutmeg and cayenne pepper.

3 Meanwhile, heat 15g/½oz/1 tbsp butter in a pan and fry the onion until soft and transparent. Set aside. Roughly chop one of the hard-boiled eggs and slice the other into neat wedges.

4 Stir the remaining butter into the rice and add the flaked haddock, onion and the chopped egg. Season to taste and heat the mixture through gently (this can be done on a serving dish in a low oven if more convenient).

5 To serve, pile up the kedgeree on a warmed dish, sprinkle generously with parsley and arrange the wedges of egg on top. Put the lemon wedges around the base and serve hot with the toast.

Variation Try leftover cooked salmon, instead of the haddock.

Energy 399Kcal/1668kJ; Protein 28.9g; Carbohydrate 38g, of which sugars 2.2g; Fat 14.6g, of which saturates 7.6g; Cholesterol 181mg; Calcium 62mg; Fibre 0.5g; Sodium 974mg

Jugged kippers

The demand in Britain for naturally smoked kippers is ever increasing. They are most popular for breakfast, served with scrambled eggs, but they're also good for an old-fashioned high tea. Jugging is the same as poaching, except that the only equipment needed is a jug and kettle. Serve with freshly made soda bread or toast and lemon.

Serves 4

4 kippers (smoked herrings), preferably naturally smoked, whole or filleted

25g/1oz/2 tbsp butter

ground black pepper

1 Select a jug (pitcher) tall enough for the kippers to be immersed when the water is added. If the heads are still on, remove them.

2 Put the fish into the jug, tails up, and then cover them with boiling water. Leave for about 5 minutes, until tender.

3 Drain well and serve on warmed plates with a knob (pat) of butter and a little black pepper on each kipper.

Energy 449Kcal/1859kJ; Protein 31.8g; Carbohydrate 0g, of which sugars 0g; Fat 35.7g, of which saturates 8.3g; Cholesterol 123mg; Calcium 96mg; Fibre 0g; Sodium 1.5g

Welsh cockle cakes

One of the simplest ways to serve Welsh cockles is to toss them in fine oatmeal and briefly fry them. Here, they are made into *teisenni cocos*, nicest when cooked in bacon fat, though you could of course simply fry them in oil or butter. They are particularly good topped with scrambled, poached or fried egg, or as part of a full breakfast.

Makes 4-8

125g/4½oz/1 cup plain (all-purpose) flour

1 egg

150ml/¼ pint/⅔ cup milk

ground black pepper

100g/3½oz shelled cooked cockles (small clams)

15–30ml/1–2 tbsp chopped fresh chives (optional)

6 bacon rashers (slices)

oil for cooking

1 Sift the flour into a bowl, make a well in the centre and break the egg into it.

2 Mix the egg into the flour, gradually stirring in the milk to make a smooth batter. Season with pepper and stir in the cockles and chives (if using).

3 Heat a little oil in a pan, add the bacon and fry quickly. Lift out and keep warm.

4 Add tablespoonfuls of batter to the hot bacon fat, leaving them space to spread. Cook until crisp and golden, turning over once. Drain and serve with the bacon.

Energy 137kcal/572kJ; Protein 7g; Carbohydrate 13.1g, of which sugars 1.2g; Fat 6.6g, of which saturates 1.7g; Cholesterol 40mg; Calcium 63mg; Fibre 0.5g; Sodium 322mg

Full British breakfast

The British cooked breakfast is a special treat, harking back to the 19th century when the buffet tables of the rich groaned with food. This is an adaptable meal, with regional variations. The basic requirements are bacon and eggs, but sausages, fried potatoes, grilled tomatoes, mushrooms, fried bread, baked beans and even black pudding can be added.

Serves 4

225–250g/8–9oz small potatoes

oil, for grilling (broiling) or frying

butter, for grilling (broiling) and frying

4 large or 8 small good-quality sausages

8 rashers (strips) of back or streaky bacon, preferably dry-cured

4 tomatoes

4 small slices of bread, crusts removed

4 eggs

1 Thinly slice the potatoes. Heat 15ml/1 tbsp oil with a knob of butter in a large, preferably non-stick frying pan, add the potatoes and cook over a medium heat for 10–15 minutes, turning them occasionally until they are crisp, golden, and cooked through.

2 Using a slotted spoon, lift the potatoes out of the pan and keep them warm on a dish in a low oven.

Cook's tip For the best flavour, fry the bread and tomatoes in the fatty juices remaining in the pan from the sausages and bacon.

3 Meanwhile, grill (broil) or fry the sausages in a little oil until golden brown all over and cooked through (test by inserting a skewer in the centre – the juices should run clear). Keep warm.

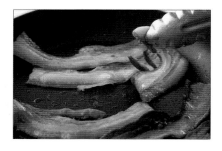

4 Grill the bacon or fry it in a little oil in the non-stick pan. Keep warm.

5 Halve the tomatoes and either top each half with a tiny piece of butter and grill until they are soft and bubbling, or fry in a little oil in the frying pan. Keep warm.

6 Fry the bread in a little oil and butter over a medium-high heat until crisp and golden brown. Keep warm.

7 Add extra oil if necessary to the hot frying pan. As soon as the oil is hot, crack the eggs into the pan, leaving space between them. Cook over a medium heat, spooning the hot fat over occasionally to set the yolks, until cooked to your liking.

8 As soon as the eggs are cooked to your liking, arrange the breakfast ingredients on warmed plates and serve immediately.

Variations
• For breakfast in a roll – warm long crusty rolls in the oven, then cut them in half vertically without slicing through the bottom crust. Fill each roll with the hot breakfast ingredients, draping the fried egg over the top. Serve with a serrated knife for cutting.
• Slices of black pudding (blood sausage) can be gently fried or grilled and served in place of the sausages.
• A few field mushrooms fried in the fat left in the pan after cooking the bacon make a delicious addition to a traditional cooked breakfast.
• Serve a spoonful of bubble and squeak in place of the fried potatoes.

Energy 731kcal/3046kJ; Protein 32.7g; Carbohydrate 35.3g, of which sugars 7.6g; Fat 52.2g, of which saturates 16.5g; Cholesterol 288mg; Calcium 185mg; Fibre 3.1g; Sodium 2049mg

Gateshead bacon floddies

This Tyneside breakfast special is traditionally cooked in bacon fat and served with eggs and sausages. A kind of potato cake, floddies are said to have originated with canal workers, who cooked them on shovels over a fire. They should be served crisp and golden brown.

Serves 4–6

250g/9oz potatoes, weighed after peeling

1 large onion

175g/6oz rindless streaky (fat) bacon, finely chopped

50g/2oz/½ cup self-raising (self-rising) flour

2 eggs

oil, for frying

salt and ground black pepper

Cook's tip Fry the floddies in oiled metal rings if you wish, for a neat circular shape.

1 Grate the potatoes onto a clean dish cloth, and then gather up the edges to make a pouch. Squeeze and twist the towel to remove the liquid.

2 Grate or finely chop the onion into a mixing bowl and add the potatoes, chopped bacon, flour and seasoning, mixing well.

3 Beat the eggs and stir into the potato mixture. Heat some oil in a large frying pan. Add generous tablespoonfuls of the potato mixture to the hot oil and flatten them to make thin cakes. Cook over a medium heat for 3–4 minutes on each side or until golden brown and cooked through. Lift out, drain on kitchen paper and serve.

Energy 214kcal/891kJ; Protein 8.8g; Carbohydrate 17.1g, of which sugars 3.5g; Fat 12.7g, of which saturates 3.4g; Cholesterol 82mg; Calcium 38mg; Fibre 1.4g; Sodium 397mg

Welsh laverbread cakes and bacon

Laverbread forms an integral part of the full Welsh breakfast – a small spoonful gives a subtle taste of the sea. Here, it is combined with oatmeal and shaped into small cakes. Grilled tomatoes and mushrooms make ideal accompaniments, as do sausages and eggs.

Serves 4

200g/7oz laverbread

70g/2½oz/½ cup fine oatmeal

10ml/2 tsp fresh lemon juice

10ml/2 tsp oil

8 bacon rashers (strips)

salt and ground black pepper

Variation Add about 100g/3½oz shelled cooked cockles (small clam) to the laverbread and oatmeal mixture in step 1. A little finely grated lemon rind is good, too.

1 Mix the laverbread, oatmeal and lemon juice, and season. Leave for 5 minutes.

2 Heat the oil in a pan, add the bacon and cook over medium-high heat until golden brown. Lift out and keep warm.

3 Drop spoonfuls of the laverbread mixture into the hot pan, flattening them gently with the back of the spoon. Cook over medium heat for a minute or two on each side until crisp and golden brown. Serve immediately with the bacon.

Energy 286kcal/1204kJ; Protein 14.1g; Carbohydrate 33.8g, of which sugars 1.4g; Fat 11.7g, of which saturates 3.1g; Cholesterol 23mg; Calcium 65mg; Fibre 3.7g; Sodium 923mg

Black pudding with potato and apple

This traditional blood sausage has come a long way from its once humble position in British cooking. Widely available, black pudding is now extremely popular. This Scottish recipe serves it with potato and apple to contrast with the rich dense flavour of the pudding.

Serves 4

4 large potatoes, peeled

45ml/3 tbsp olive oil

8 slices of Scottish black pudding (blood sausage), such as Clonakilty

115g/4oz cultivated mushrooms, such as oyster or shiitake

2 eating apples, peeled, cored and cut into wedges

25ml/1½ tbsp sherry vinegar or wine vinegar

15g/½oz/1 tbsp butter

salt and ground black pepper

1 Grate the potatoes, putting them into a bowl of water as you grate them. Drain and squeeze out any moisture.

2 Heat 30ml/2 tbsp of the olive oil in a large non-stick frying pan, add the grated potatoes and season. Press the potatoes into the pan with your hands.

3 Cook the potatoes until browned, then turn over and cook the other side. When cooked, slide on to a warmed plate.

4 Heat the remaining oil and sauté the black pudding and mushrooms together for a few minutes. Remove from the pan and keep warm.

5 Add the apple wedges to the frying pan and gently sauté to colour them golden brown. Add the sherry or wine vinegar to the apples, and boil up the juices. Add the butter, stir with a wooden spatula until it has melted and season to taste with salt and ground black pepper.

6 Cut the potato cake into portion-sized wedges and divide among four warmed plates. Arrange the slices of black pudding and cooked mushrooms on the bed of potato cake, pour over the apples and the warm juices and serve immediately.

Energy 247kcal/1034kJ; Protein 4.2g; Carbohydrate 28.8g, of which sugars 5.4g; Fat 13.6g, of which saturates 4g; Cholesterol 13mg; Calcium 16mg; Fibre 2.4g; Sodium 132mg

Laverbread and bacon omelette

Laverbread is a tasty seaweed preparation perhaps more commonly associated with the Welsh, but it has also been used in Scotland for centuries. Dried or canned versions are available and will avoid preparation time, but if you prefer, use boiled spinach instead.

Makes 1 omelette

oil, to prepare the pan

3 eggs

10ml/2 tsp butter

1 rasher (strip) lean back bacon, cooked and diced

25g/1oz prepared laverbread

salt and ground black pepper

1 Heat a little oil in an omelette pan then leave for a few minutes to help season the pan. A non-stick or small curved-sided pan may also be used.

2 Break the eggs into a bowl large enough for whisking, season then whisk until the yolk and white are well combined but not frothy.

3 Pour the oil out of the pan and reheat. Add the butter, which should begin to sizzle straight away. If it does not the pan is too cool or if it burns it is too hot. Rinse out, dry and try again.

4 Pour the whisked eggs into the pan and immediately, using the back of a fork, draw the mixture towards the middle of the pan, working from the outside and using quick circular movements going around the pan.

5 As it is beginning to cook but is not quite set, put the bacon and laverbread evenly over one half of the omelette. Cook for another 30 seconds then remove from the heat.

6 Fold one side of the mixture over the side with the bacon and laverbread, leave for a minute or two, then turn out on to a warmed plate. Serve immediately while piping hot.

Energy 355kcal/1472kJ; Protein 23.6g; Carbohydrate 0.5g, of which sugars 0.4g; Fat 29.2g, of which saturates 11.4g; Cholesterol 605mg; Calcium 131mg; Fibre 0.5g; Sodium 691mg

Lamb's kidneys with a devil sauce

This is one of those hearty dishes that the Scots are so good at, ideal served on toast as a breakfast dish, for when you are about to go out for a day's walking or stalking game in the hills and highlands. It can also be accompanied with creamy mashed potato for a delicious yet easy-to-prepare lunch or supper.

Serves 4

12 lamb's kidneys

45ml/3 tbsp vegetable oil

15ml/1 tbsp Worcestershire sauce

15ml/1 tbsp Mushroom Sauce

pinch of cayenne pepper

175g/6oz/¾ cup butter

10ml/2 tsp English (hot) mustard

10ml/2 tsp French mustard

1 Skin the kidneys and slice them in half horizontally. Push the flesh out of the way with a finger to reveal all the white gristle. Use a sharp-pointed pair of scissors or a very sharp vegetable knife to remove the central gristly core and any fat.

2 Heat the oil in a frying pan and cook the kidneys over a high heat for a few minutes on both sides, leaving them a little pink. Pour off any excess fat from the pan and set aside to allow the kidneys to cool a little.

3 Mix all the other ingredients in a bowl. Spread the mixture over the kidneys and return to the heat. Cook gently until the butter melts, then serve.

Energy 542kcal/2246kJ; Protein 26g; Carbohydrate 1.1g, of which sugars 1g; Fat 48.3g, of which saturates 25.1g; Cholesterol 566mg; Calcium 29mg; Fibre 0g; Sodium 609mg

Scottish Lorn sausage with red onion relish

The Firth of Lorn, the region from which this dish originated, cuts through Argyll between the island of Mull and the mainland on the west coast of Scotland. Prepared simply and traditionally in a loaf shape and chilled overnight, the sausage is then sliced before cooking. Accompanied by grilled tomatoes it makes a delicious breakfast.

Serves 4

900g/2lb minced (ground) beef

65g/2½oz/generous 1 cup stale white breadcrumbs

150g/5oz/scant 1 cup semolina

5ml/1 tsp salt

75ml/5 tbsp water

ground black pepper

Cranberry and Red Onion Relish, to serve

1 In a large mixing bowl, combine the beef, breadcrumbs, semolina and salt together thoroughly with a fork. Pour in the water, mix again and season to taste. Pass the beef mixture through a coarse mincer (grinder) and set aside.

2 Carefully line a 1.3kg/3lb loaf tin (pan) with clear film (plastic wrap).

3 Spoon the sausage mixture into the tin, pressing it in firmly with the back of a wooden spoon. Even out the surface and fold the clear film over the top. Chill overnight.

4 When ready to cook, preheat the grill (broiler). Turn the sausage out of the tin on to a chopping board and cut into 1cm/½in slices. Grill (broil) each slice until cooked through, turning once. Alternatively, fry until cooked through, again turning once.

Cook's tip For the best results, use standard minced (ground) beef for these sausages rather than lean minced steak, as the higher fat content is needed to bind the ingredients together and add flavour.

Energy 691kcal/2886kJ; Protein 50.1g; Carbohydrate 40.7g, of which sugars 0.4g; Fat 37.4g, of which saturates 15.6g; Cholesterol 135mg; Calcium 47mg; Fibre 1.1g; Sodium 299mg

Soups

Since the days when most cooking was done in a pot over an open fire, soups have been a staple food in Britain – from pottages and gruels made with onions, wild herbs and cereals and one-pot meals such as Welsh caul or Scotch broth, to elegant concoctions served as the first courses of elaborate dinners. Today there is a soup for every occasion, winter or summer, using rich stocks, fresh fish and seasonal vegetables.

Cream of tomato soup

When the tomato first came to Britain it was thought to be an aphrodisiac, and until the late 19th century it was viewed with great suspicion in case it caused sickness. When it was used, it was usually cooked in soups and stews, and was rarely eaten raw. This creamy soup owes its good flavour to a mix of fresh and canned tomatoes – in summer you could, of course, use all fresh, but do make sure they are really ripe and full of flavour.

Serves 4–6

25g/1oz/2 tbsp butter

1 medium onion, finely chopped

1 small carrot, finely chopped

1 celery stick, finely chopped

1 garlic clove, crushed

450g/1lb ripe tomatoes, roughly chopped

400g/14oz can chopped tomatoes

30ml/2 tbsp tomato purée (paste)

30ml/2 tbsp sugar

1 tbsp chopped fresh thyme or oregano leaves

600ml/1 pint/2½ cups chicken or vegetable stock

600ml/1 pint/2½ cups milk

salt and ground black pepper

1 Melt the butter in a large pan. Add the onion, carrot, celery and garlic. Cook over a medium heat for about 5 minutes, stirring occasionally, until soft and just beginning to brown.

2 Add the tomatoes, purée, sugar, stock and herbs, retaining some to garnish.

3 Bring to the boil, then cover and simmer gently for about 20 minutes until all the vegetables are very soft.

4 Process or blend the mixture until smooth, then press it through a sieve (strainer) to remove the skins and seeds.

5 Return the sieved soup to the cleaned pan and stir in the milk. Reheat gently.

6 Stir, without allowing it to boil. Season to taste with salt and ground black pepper. Garnish with the remaining herbs and serve.

Energy 107kcal/447kJ; Protein 2.3g; Carbohydrate 11.4g, of which sugars 10.9g; Fat 6.1g, of which saturates 3.5g; Cholesterol 13mg; Calcium 50mg; Fibre 3.9g; Sodium 71mg

Jerusalem artichoke soup

Related to the sunflower and also known as root artichoke or sunchoke, Jerusalem artichoke was introduced to Britain in the 17th century. At first it was highly prized but then became so common an ingredient that people began to lose their taste for it. The tubers can be knobbly, choose those with a fairly smooth surface for easier cleaning. Roasting the artichokes before making this soup brings out their sweet, nutty flavour.

Serves 4–6

500g/1¼lb Jerusalem artichokes

1 onion, roughly chopped

4 celery sticks, roughly chopped

2 carrots, roughly chopped

4 garlic cloves

45ml/3 tbsp olive oil

1.2 litre/2 pints/5 cups vegetable or chicken stock

60ml/4 tbsp double (heavy) cream

salt and ground black pepper

1 Preheat the oven to 200°C/400°F/Gas 6. Scrub the artichokes well and halve them lengthways.

2 Toss all the vegetables in the olive oil and spread them in a roasting pan.

3 Put the vegetables into the hot oven and roast for 30–40 minutes until they are soft and golden brown. Stir them once during cooking so that the edges brown evenly.

4 Tip the roasted vegetables into a large pan.

Cook's tip Peel the artichokes before roasting, if preferred, dropping them into water with a good squeeze of lemon to prevent them discolouring once peeled.

5 Add the stock, bring to the boil and simmer for 15 minutes. Process or blend until smooth, return to the pan, add the cream, season, and reheat gently.

Energy 310kcal/1277kJ; Protein 2.7g; Carbohydrate 4.7g, of which sugars 4.3g; Fat 31.3g, of which saturates 19.4g; Cholesterol 80mg; Calcium 116mg; Fibre 1.5g; Sodium 168mg

Watercress soup

In Roman times, eating watercress was thought to prevent baldness. Later on it became the food of the working classes and was often eaten for breakfast in a sandwich. Watercress has been cultivated in the south of England since the early 19th century. Both stalks and leaves are used in this soup for a lovely peppery flavour.

2 Melt the butter in a large pan and add the onion. Cook over a medium heat for about 5 minutes, stirring occasionally, until the onion is soft and just beginning to brown.

3 Stir in the potato and the chopped watercress, then add the stock. Bring to the boil, cover the pan and simmer gently for 15–20 minutes until the potato is very soft.

4 Remove from the heat, leave to cool slightly and then stir in the milk.

5 Process or blend the mixture until the soup is completely smooth. Return the soup to the pan and adjust the seasoning to taste.

6 Reheat gently and top each serving with a spoonful of cream and a few watercress leaves.

Serves 6

2 bunches of watercress, about 175g/6oz in total

25g/1oz/2 tbsp butter

1 medium onion, finely chopped

1 medium potato

900ml/1½ pints/3¾ cups chicken or vegetable stock

300ml/½ pint/1¼ cups milk

salt and ground black pepper

single (light) cream, to serve

1 Roughly chop the watercress, reserving a few small sprigs to garnish.

Cook's tip Try adding a little finely grated orange rind and the juice of an orange in step 5.

Energy 68kcal/280kJ; Protein 1.5g; Carbohydrate 1.4g, of which sugars 1g; Fat 6.3g, of which saturates 2.4g; Cholesterol 8mg; Calcium 79mg; Fibre 0.9g; Sodium 45mg

Country vegetable soup

Vegetable soups have always been particularly popular in the north of England. In the reign of Victoria, during extreme food shortages, vegetable soup kitchens were opened in Manchester. Soup-making is a good way to make the most of seasonal vegetables. Serve this one as an appetizer or with crusty bread and perhaps a wedge of cheese as a light meal.

Serves 6

15ml/1 tbsp oil

25g/1oz/2 tbsp butter

2 medium onions, finely chopped

4 medium carrots, sliced

2 celery sticks, sliced

2 leeks, sliced

1 potato, cut into small cubes

1 small parsnip, cut into small cubes

1 garlic clove, crushed

900ml/1½ pints/3¾ cups vegetable stock

300ml/½ pint/1¼ cups milk

25g/1oz/4 tbsp cornflour (cornstarch)

handful of frozen peas

30ml/2 tbsp chopped fresh parsley

salt and ground black pepper

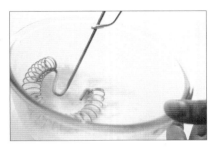

2 Add the stock to the pan and stir into the vegetables. Bring the mixture slowly to the boil, cover and simmer gently for 20–30 minutes until all the vegetables are soft.

3 Whisk the milk into the cornflour, making a paste. Stir into the vegetables. Add the frozen peas. Bring to the boil and simmer for 5 minutes Adjust the seasoning, stir in the parsley and serve.

1 Heat the oil and butter in a large pan and add the onions, carrots and celery. Cook over a medium heat for 5–10 minutes, stirring occasionally, until soft and just beginning to turn golden brown. Stir in the leeks, potato, parsnip and garlic.

Energy 160kcal/665kJ; Protein 3.6g; Carbohydrate 11.5g, of which sugars 10g; Fat 11.4g, of which saturates 6.8g; Cholesterol 27mg; Calcium 72mg; Fibre 5.4g; Sodium 106mg

Celery soup with Stilton

Stilton – known as the "king of English cheeses" – and celery are traditional partners, whether on the cheeseboard or in this warming winter soup. The two flavours complement each other beautifully, with the fresh, clean taste of the celery setting off the rich, creamy texture and tang of the famous blue-veined cheese.

3 Add the stock, bring to the boil, then cover the pan and simmer gently for about 30 minutes, until all the vegetables are very soft.

4 Process or blend about three-quarters of the mixture until smooth, then return it to the pan with the rest of the soup.

5 Bring the soup just to the boil and season to taste with salt and ground black pepper.

Serves 6

40g/1½oz/3 tbsp butter

1 large onion, finely chopped

1 medium potato, cut into small cubes

1 whole head of celery, thinly sliced

900ml/1½ pints/3¾ cups vegetable or chicken stock

100g/3¾oz Stilton cheese, crumbled

150ml/¼ pint/⅔ cup single (light) cream

salt and ground black pepper

1 Melt the butter in a large pan and add the onion. Cook over a medium heat for 5 minutes, stirring occasionally, until soft but not browned.

2 Stir in the potato and celery and cook for a further 5 minutes until the vegetables soften and begin to brown.

6 Remove the pan from the heat and stir in the cheese, reserving a little for the garnish. Stir in the cream and reheat the soup gently without boiling.

7 Serve topped with the reserved crumbled cheese.

Cook's tip In the place of Stilton try using another cheese, either a blue-veined variety or a strong Cheddar.

Energy 199kcal/826kJ; Protein 5.9g; Carbohydrate 7.5g, of which sugars 2.4g; Fat 16.2g, of which saturates 10.4g; Cholesterol 44mg; Calcium 117mg; Fibre 1.4g; Sodium 233mg

Parsnip and apple soup

The Romans introduced apple orchards to England. Since then the country has been proud of its wonderful range of apples, and many fine apple juices are now available, often made from single varieties. For this soup, choose a fairly sharp-tasting juice – it will complement the sweetness of the parsnips and the warmth of the spices.

Serves 4–6

25g/1oz/2 tbsp butter

1 medium onion, finely chopped

1 garlic clove, finely chopped

500g/1¼lb parsnips, peeled and thinly sliced

5ml/1 tsp curry paste or powder

300ml/½ pint/1¼ cups apple juice

600ml/1 pint/2½ cups vegetable stock

300ml/½ pint/1¼ cups milk

salt and ground black pepper

thick natural yogurt, to serve

chopped fresh herbs such as mint or parsley, to serve

1 Melt the butter in a large pan and add the onion, garlic and parsnips. Cook gently, without browning, for about 10 minutes, stirring often.

2 Add the curry paste or powder and cook, stirring, for 1 minute.

Variation This recipe is also delicious when the parsnips are replaced with butternut squash or an equal mixture of the two.

3 Add the juice and stock, bring to the boil, cover and simmer gently for about 20 minutes until the parsnips are soft.

4 Process or blend the mixture until smooth and return it to the pan.

5 Add the milk and season to taste with salt and pepper.

6 Reheat the soup gently and serve topped with a spoonful of yogurt and a sprinkling of herbs.

Energy 130kcal/548kJ; Protein 3.4g; Carbohydrate 18.5g, of which sugars 12.6g; Fat 5.3g, of which saturates 2.9g; Cholesterol 12mg; Calcium 101mg; Fibre 4g; Sodium 56mg

Shropshire pea and mint soup

Peas have been grown in England since the Middle Ages, while mint was made popular by the Romans. Peas and mint picked fresh from the garden are still true seasonal treats and make a velvety, fresh-tasting soup. When fresh peas are out of season, use frozen peas.

Serves 6

25g/1oz/2 tbsp butter

1 medium onion, finely chopped

675g/1½lb shelled fresh peas

1.5ml/¼ tsp sugar

1.2 litres/2 pints/5 cups chicken or vegetable stock

handful of fresh mint leaves

150ml/¼ pint/⅔ cup double (heavy) cream

salt and ground black pepper

snipped fresh chives, to serve

1 Melt the butter in a large pan and add the onion. Cook over a low heat for about 10 minutes, stirring occasionally, until soft and just brown.

2 Add the peas, sugar, stock and half the mint. Cover and simmer gently for 10–15 minutes until the peas are tender.

3 Leave to cool slightly. Add the remaining mint and process or blend until smooth. Return the soup to the pan and season to taste.

4 Stir in the cream and reheat gently without boiling. Serve garnished with snipped chives.

Energy 121kcal/506kJ; Protein 6.1g; Carbohydrate 9.2g, of which sugars 5.2g; Fat 7g, of which saturates 4.2g; Cholesterol 18mg; Calcium 113mg; Fibre 3g; Sodium 123mg

London particular

Victorian London was regularly covered with a thick winter fog, known as a "pea-souper", or "London particular", because it had the colour and consistency of yellow pea soup. The original version would probably have included pig's trotters and a marrow bone.

Serves 4–6

350g/12oz/1½ cups dried split yellow or green peas

25g/1oz/2 tbsp butter

6 rashers (strips) rindless lean streaky (fatty) bacon, finely chopped

1 medium onion, finely chopped

1 medium carrot, thinly sliced

1 celery stick, thinly sliced

1.75 litres/3 pints/7½ cups ham or chicken stock

60ml/4 tbsp double (heavy) cream

salt and ground black pepper

croûtons and fried bacon, to serve

1 Put the split peas into a large bowl, cover well with boiling water (from the kettle) and leave to stand.

2 Meanwhile, melt the butter in a large pan. Add the bacon, onion, carrot and celery and cook over a medium heat for 10–15 minutes, stirring occasionally until the vegetables are soft and beginning to turn golden brown.

3 Drain the peas and add them to the pan. Stir in the stock. Bring to the boil, cover and simmer gently for about 1 hour or until the peas are very soft.

4 Process or blend until smooth and return the soup to the pan. Season to taste and stir in the cream. Heat until just bubbling and serve with croûtons and pieces of crisp bacon on top.

Energy 378kcal/1584kJ; Protein 20.2g; Carbohydrate 34.9g, of which sugars 3.1g; Fat 18.5g, of which saturates 8.7g; Cholesterol 47mg; Calcium 45mg; Fibre 3.4g; Sodium 527mg

Welsh leek soup

This is an adaptation of the traditional Welsh method, where a piece of bacon flavours the *cawl cennin*. Two generations ago, bacon, vegetables and water were put into the pot early in the morning and left to simmer over the fire all day. It often made two courses or even two meals – the bacon and vegetables for one and the cawl or broth for the other.

Serves 4–6

1 unsmoked bacon joint, such as corner or collar, weighing about 1kg/2¼lb

500g/1lb 2oz/4½ cups leeks, thoroughly washed

1 large carrot, peeled and finely chopped

1 large main-crop potato, peeled and sliced

15ml/1 tbsp fine or medium oatmeal

handful of fresh parsley

salt and ground black pepper

1 Trim the bacon of any excess fat, put into a large pan and pour over enough cold water to cover it. Bring to the boil, then discard the water. Add 1.5 litres/ 2¾ pints fresh cold water, bring to the boil again, then cover and simmer gently for 30 minutes.

2 Meanwhile, thickly slice the white and pale green parts of the leeks, reserving the dark green leaves.

Cook's tip For a quicker version fry 4 finely chopped bacon rashers in butter before adding the vegetables in step 3, and use chicken or vegetable stock in place of water.

3 Add the sliced leek to the pan together with the carrot, potato and oatmeal. Then bring the mixture back to the boil, and cover and simmer gently for a further 30–40 minutes until the vegetables and bacon are tender.

4 Slice the reserved dark green leeks very thinly and finely chop the parsley.

5 Lift the bacon out of the pan and either slice it and serve separately or cut it into bitesize chunks and return it to the pan.

6 Adjust the seasoning to taste, adding pepper, but please note it may not be necessary to add salt. Then bring the soup just to the boil once more. Finally, add the sliced dark green leeks along with the parsley and simmer very gently for about 5 minutes before serving the leek soup.

Energy 273kcal/1135kJ; Protein 18.8g; Carbohydrate 10.9g, of which sugars 3.5g; Fat 17.3g, of which saturates 6.3g; Cholesterol 53mg; Calcium 33mg; Fibre 2.7g; Sodium 1550mg

Avocado, spinach and sorrel soup

Sorrel, with its sharp lemony flavour, grows wild throughout the UK, Europe, North America and Asia. In some parts of Scotland it is known as "sourocks", a reference to its sharp or sour flavour. It is delicious in salads and soups.

Serves 4

30ml/2 tbsp olive oil

2 onions, chopped

1kg/2¼lb spinach

900ml/1½ pints/3¾ cups light chicken stock

4 garlic cloves, crushed with salt

1 bunch sorrel leaves

2 avocados, peeled and stoned (pitted)

1 Pour the olive oil into a large heavy pan and sweat the onions over a gentle heat until soft but not coloured. Meanwhile, wash the spinach thoroughly and remove the stalks.

2 Add the spinach to the onions and cook for about 2 minutes, stirring, to wilt the leaves. Cover and increase the heat slightly then cook for a further 3 minutes. Add the stock, cover again and simmer for about 10 minutes.

3 Add the garlic, sorrel and avocados to the soup and once heated through remove from the heat.

4 Allow the soup to cool then purée in a blender. Reheat the soup before serving with warmed crusty bread.

Cook's tips
• Crushing garlic in salt helps to bring out the oils of the garlic and also stops any being wasted in a garlic press. Use a coarse salt and try to keep a chopping board or at least a corner of one for this sole purpose, as it is hard to get rid of the scent of garlic and it can taint other foods.
• When using avocados in soup do not let them boil as this makes them taste bitter. They are best added at the end and just heated through.
• This soup freezes for up to a month. Freeze it the day you make it.

Energy 282kcal/1161kJ; Protein 9.3g; Carbohydrate 11.4g, of which sugars 8.3g; Fat 22.1g, of which saturates 4.1g; Cholesterol 0mg; Calcium 452mg; Fibre 8.9g; Sodium 357mg

Irish leek and oatmeal soup

This traditional leek and oatmeal soup is known as *brotchán foltchep* or *brotchán roy* and combines leeks, oatmeal and milk – three ingredients that have been staple foods in Ireland for centuries. Serve with freshly baked bread and Irish butter.

Serves 4–6

about 1.2 litres/2 pints/5 cups chicken stock and milk, mixed

30ml/2 tbsp medium pinhead oatmeal

25g/1oz/2 tbsp butter

6 large leeks, sliced into 2cm/¾in pieces

sea salt and ground black pepper

pinch of ground mace

30ml/2 tbsp chopped fresh parsley

1 Bring the stock and milk mixture to the boil over medium heat and sprinkle in the oatmeal. Stir well to prevent lumps forming, and then simmer gently.

2 Wash the leeks in a bowl. Melt the butter in a separate pan and cook the leeks over a gentle heat until softened slightly, then add them to the stock mixture. Simmer for a further 15–20 minutes, or until the oatmeal is cooked. Extra stock or milk can be added if the soup is too thick.

3 Season with salt, pepper and mace, stir in the chopped parsley and serve in warmed bowls. Decorate with a swirl of cream if you like.

Energy 199Kcal/834kJ; Protein 10g; Carbohydrate 19.5g, of which sugars 12.4g; Fat 9.6g, of which saturates 5.1g; Cholesterol 22mg; Calcium 243mg; Fibre 5.8g; Sodium 219mg

Leek and cheese soup

The cheese is an integral part of this substantial soup, which makes full use of ingredients that have always been important in Irish cooking. It can be a good way to use up cheeses left over from the cheeseboard. Serve with freshly baked brown bread.

Serves 6

3 large leeks

50g/2oz/¼ cup butter

30ml/2 tbsp oil

115g/4oz blue farmhouse cheese, such as Cashel Blue or Stilton

15g/½oz/2 tbsp plain (all-purpose) flour

15ml/1 tbsp wholegrain Irish mustard, or to taste

1.5 litres/2½ pints/6¼ cups chicken stock

ground black pepper

50g/2oz/½ cup grated cheese and chopped chives or spring onion (scallion) greens, to garnish

1 Slice the leeks thinly. Heat the butter and oil together in a large heavy pan and gently cook the leeks in it, covered, for 10–15 minutes, or until just softened but not brown.

2 Grate the cheese coarsely and add it to the pan, stirring over a low heat, until it is melted.

3 Add the flour and cook for 2 minutes, stirring constantly with a wooden spoon, then add ground black pepper and wholegrain mustard to taste.

4 Gradually add the stock, stirring constantly and blending it in well; bring the soup to the boil.

5 Reduce the heat, cover and simmer very gently for about 15 minutes. Check the seasoning.

6 Serve the soup garnished with the extra grated cheese and the chopped chives or spring onion greens, and hand fresh bread around separately.

Energy 187Kcal/773kJ; Protein 5.6g; Carbohydrate 4.3g, of which sugars 1.9g; Fat 16.6g, of which saturates 8.6g; Cholesterol 32mg; Calcium 118mg; Fibre 1.8g; Sodium 407mg

Scottish cabbage and potato soup with caraway

Earthy floury potatoes are essential to the success of this soup, so choose your variety carefully. Caraway seeds are aromatic and nutty, with a delicate anise flavour, and are a favourite in Scotland. They impart a subtle accent to this satisfying dish.

Serves 4

30ml/2 tbsp olive oil

2 small onions, sliced

6 garlic cloves, halved

350g/12oz/3 cups shredded green cabbage

4 potatoes, unpeeled

5ml/1 tsp caraway seeds

5ml/1 tsp sea salt

1.2 litres/2 pints/5 cups water

1 Pour the olive oil into a large pan and soften the onion. Add the garlic and the cabbage and cook over a low heat for 10 minutes, stirring occasionally to prevent the cabbage from sticking.

2 Add the potatoes, caraway seeds, sea salt and water. Bring to the boil then simmer until all the vegetables are cooked through, about 20–30 minutes.

3 Remove from the heat and allow to cool slightly before mashing into a purée or passing through a seive.

Cook's tip Use a floury variety of potatoe to achieve the correct texture for this soup. King Edward or Maris Piper (US russet or Idaho) are excellent choices.

Energy 144Kcal/601kJ; Protein 3.1g; Carbohydrate 20.4g, of which sugars 8.1g; Fat 6g, of which saturates 0.9g; Cholesterol 0mg; Calcium 60mg; Fibre 3.3g; Sodium 507mg

Scottish rocket soup with kiln-smoked salmon

Kiln-smoked salmon, also referred to as "hot" smoked salmon, has actually been "cooked" during the smoking process, producing a delicious flaky texture. This is in contrast to traditional cold-smoked salmon, which is not actually cooked but does not spoil because it has been preserved first in brine. This is a beautifully rich and attractive soup.

Serves 4

15ml/1 tbsp olive oil

1 small onion, sliced

1 garlic clove, crushed

150ml/¼ pint/⅔ cup double (heavy) cream

350ml/12fl oz/1½ cups vegetable stock

350g/12oz rocket (arugula)

4 fresh basil leaves

salt and ground black pepper

flaked salmon, to garnish

1 Put the olive oil in a high-sided pan over a medium heat and allow to heat up. Add the sliced onion and sweat for a few minutes, stirring continuously. Add the garlic and continue to sweat gently until soft and transparent, although you should not allow the onion to colour.

Variation
• Cold-smoked salmon is also very good with this soup, and can be used if you can't find the kiln-smoked variety. Simply cut a few slices into medium to thick strips and add to the hot soup.
• Warming the smoked salmon for a few minutes increases the flavour.

2 Add the cream and stock, stir in gently and bring slowly to the boil. Allow to simmer gently for about 5 minutes. Add the rocket, reserving a few leaves to garnish, and the basil. Return briefly to the boil and turn off the heat. Add a little cold water and allow to cool for a few minutes.

3 Purée in a blender until smooth, adding a little salt and pepper to taste. When ready to serve, reheat gently but do not allow to boil. Serve in warmed bowls with a few flakes of salmon, a leaf or two of rocket and a drizzle of virgin olive oil over the top.

Energy 258kcal/1063kJ; Protein 6.8g; Carbohydrate 3.2g, of which sugars 2.8g; Fat 24.3g, of which saturates 13.1g; Cholesterol 56mg; Calcium 174mg; Fibre 2.1g; Sodium 395mg

Fish soup

With some fresh crusty home-made brown bread or garlic bread, this quick-and-easy soup can be served like a stew and will make a delicious first course or supper.

Serves 6

25g/1oz/2 tbsp butter

1 onion, finely chopped

1 garlic clove, crushed or finely chopped

1 small red (bell) pepper, seeded and chopped

salt and ground black pepper

2.5ml/½ tsp sugar

a dash of Tabasco sauce

25g/1oz/¼ cup plain (all-purpose) flour

about 600ml/1 pint/2½ cups fish stock

450g/1lb ripe tomatoes, skinned and chopped, or 400g/14oz can chopped tomatoes

115g/4oz/1½ cups mushrooms, chopped

about 300ml/½ pint/1¼ cups milk

225g/8oz white fish, such as haddock or whiting, filleted and skinned, and cut into bitesize cubes

115g/4oz smoked haddock or cod, skinned, and cut into bitesize cubes

12–18 mussels, cleaned (optional)

chopped fresh parsley or chives, to garnish

1 Melt the butter in a large heavy pan and cook the chopped onion and crushed garlic gently in it until softened but not browned. Add the chopped red pepper. Season with salt and pepper, the sugar and Tabasco sauce.

2 Sprinkle the flour over and cook gently for 2 minutes, stirring. Gradually stir in the stock and add the tomatoes, with their juices, and the mushrooms.

3 Bring to the boil, stir well and then reduce the heat and simmer gently until the vegetables are soft. Add the milk and bring back to the boil.

4 Add the fish to the pan and simmer for 3 minutes, then add the mussels, if using, and cook for another 3–4 minutes, or until the fish is just tender but not breaking up. Discard any mussels that remain closed. Adjust the consistency with a little extra fish stock or milk, if necessary. Check the seasoning and serve immediately, garnished with parsley or chives.

Energy 142Kcal/597kJ; Protein 13.9g; Carbohydrate 10.7g, of which sugars 7.1g; Fat 5.2g, of which saturates 2.9g; Cholesterol 36mg; Calcium 84mg; Fibre 1.7g; Sodium 91mg

Seafood chowder

This filling fish soup is infinitely adaptable according to the availability of fresh fish and shellfish. Hand around freshly made brown bread separately.

Serves 4–6

50g/2oz/¼ cup butter

1 large onion, chopped

115g/4oz bacon, rind removed, diced

4 celery sticks, diced

2 large potatoes, diced

450g/1lb ripe, juicy tomatoes, chopped or 400g/14oz can chopped tomatoes

about 450ml/¾ pint/2 cups fish stock

450g/1lb white fish fillets, such as cod, plaice, flounder or haddock, skinned and cut into small chunks

225g/8oz shellfish, such as prawns (shrimp), scallops or mussels

about 300ml/½ pint/1¼ cups milk

25g/1oz/¼ cup cornflour (cornstarch)

sea salt and ground black pepper

lightly whipped cream and chopped parsley, to garnish

1 Melt the butter in a large pan, add the onion, bacon, celery and potatoes and coat with the butter. Cover and leave to sweat over very gentle heat for 5–10 minutes, without colouring.

2 Meanwhile purée the tomatoes in a blender, and sieve them to remove the skin and pips. Add the tomato purée and fish stock to the pan.

3 Bring to the boil, cover and leave to simmer gently until the potatoes are tender, skimming the top occasionally as required.

4 Prepare fresh prawns by plunging briefly in a pan of boiling water. Remove from the pan as the water boils. Cool and peel.

5 If using mussels, scrub the shells and discard any that do not open when tapped. Put the mussels into a shallow, heavy pan, without adding any liquid. Cover tightly and cook over a high heat for a few minutes, shaking occasionally, until all the mussels have opened. Discard any that fail to open. Remove the cooked mussels from their shells. Raw shelled scallops can be left whole.

6 Add the shellfish to the soup. Blend the milk and cornflour together in a small jug (pitcher), stir into the soup and bring to the boil again. Reduce the heat, and cover and simmer for a few minutes until the fish is just tender. Adjust the texture with milk or stock if necessary and season to taste with sea salt, if required, and freshly ground black pepper. Serve in warm soup bowls, garnished with a swirl of cream and some parsley.

Variation To make cockle and mussel chowder, replace the mixed fish and shellfish with 175g/6oz shelled cooked mussels and 115g/4oz shelled cooked cockles (small clams); include any liquor left from cooking the mussels and cockles. Reserve a few in their shells for garnish, if you like.

Energy 488Kcal/2050kJ; Protein 46g; Carbohydrate 36.2g, of which sugars 11.3g; Fat 18.7g, of which saturates 9.6g; Cholesterol 127mg; Calcium 163mg; Fibre 3.5g; Sodium 771mg

Devon crab soup

Locals will tell you that crab caught around the Devon coastline is especially sweet. Although crab is available all the year round, it is at its best and is least expensive during the summer months – the perfect time to make this lovely creamy soup.

Serves 4–6

25g/1oz/2 tbsp butter

1 medium onion, finely chopped

1 celery stick, finely chopped

1 garlic clove, crushed

25ml/1½ tbsp flour

225g/8oz cooked crab meat, half dark and half white

1.2 litres/2 pints/5 cups fish stock

150ml/¼ pint/⅔ cup double (heavy) cream

30ml/2 tbsp dry sherry

salt and ground black pepper

1 Melt the butter in a pan and add the onion, celery and garlic. Cook over a medium heat for about 5 minutes, stirring frequently, until the vegetables are soft but not browned.

2 Remove from the heat and quickly stir in the flour, then the brown crab meat. Gradually stir in the stock.

3 Bring the mixture just to the boil, then reduce the heat and simmer for about 30 minutes. Process or blend the soup and return it to the cleaned pan. Season to taste with salt and pepper.

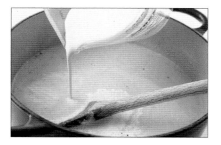

4 Chop the white crab meat and stir it into the pan with the cream and sherry. Reheat the soup and serve immediately.

Energy 209kcal/867kJ; Protein 7.8g; Carbohydrate 4.6g, of which sugars 1.2g; Fat 17.3g, of which saturates 10.6g; Cholesterol 70mg; Calcium 69mg; Fibre 0.3g; Sodium 241mg

Scottish Cullen skink

The famous Cullen skink comes from the small fishing port of Cullen on the east coast of Scotland, the word "skink" meaning an essence or soup. The fishermen smoked their smaller fish and these, with locally grown potatoes, formed their staple diet.

Serves 6

1 Finnan haddock, about 350g/12oz

1 onion, chopped

bouquet garni

900ml/1½ pints/3¾ cups water

500g/1¼lb potatoes, quartered

600ml/1 pint/2½ cups milk

40g/1½oz/3 tbsp butter

salt and pepper

chopped chives, to garnish

1 Put the haddock, onion, bouquet garni and water into a large pan and bring to the boil. Skim the surface with a slotted spoon, discarding any fish skin, then cover the pan. Reduce the heat and gently poach for 10–15 minutes, until the fish flakes easily.

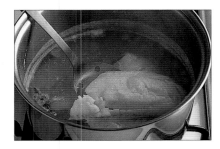

2 Lift the fish from the pan, using a fish slice, and remove the skin and any bones. Return the skin and bones to the pan and simmer, uncovered, for a further 30 minutes. Flake the cooked fish flesh and leave to cool.

Cook's tip If you can't find Finnan haddock, substitute it with a good quality smoked haddock.

3 Strain the fish stock and return to the pan, then add the potatoes and simmer for about 25 minutes, or until tender.

4 Carefully remove the poatoes from the pan using a slotted spoon. Add the milk to the pan and bring to the boil.

5 In a separate pan, mash the potatoes with the butter. A little at a time, whisk this thoroughly into the pan until the soup is thick and creamy.

6 Add the flaked fish to the pan and adjust the seasoning. Sprinkle with chives and serve immediately with fresh crusty bread.

Energy 205kcal/864kJ; Protein 16.1g; Carbohydrate 19g, of which sugars 6.4g; Fat 7.8g, of which saturates 4.7g; Cholesterol 41mg; Calcium 137mg; Fibre 1g; Sodium 132mg

Shore crab soup

These little crabs have a velvet feel to their shell. They are mostly caught off the west coast of Scotland, although they can be quite difficult to find in fishmongers. If you have trouble finding them, you can also use common or brown crabs for this recipe.

Serves 4

1kg/2¼lbs shore or velvet crabs

50g/2oz/¼ cup butter

50g/2oz leek, washed and chopped

50g/2oz carrot, chopped

30ml/2 tbsp brandy

225g/8oz ripe tomatoes, chopped

15ml/1 tbsp tomato purée (paste)

120ml/4fl oz/½ cup dry white wine

1.5 litres/2½ pints/6¼ cups fish stock

sprig of fresh tarragon

60ml/4 tbsp double (heavy) cream

lemon juice

1 Bring a large pan of water to a rolling boil and plunge the live crabs into it. They will be killed very quickly, and the bigger the pan and the more water there is, the better. Once the crabs are dead – a couple of minutes at most – take them out of the water, place in a large bowl and smash them up. This can be done with either a wooden mallet or the end of a rolling pin.

2 Melt the butter in a heavy pan, add the leek and carrot and cook gently until soft but not coloured.

3 Add the crabs and when very hot pour in the brandy, stirring to allow the flavour to pervade the whole pan. Add the tomatoes, tomato purée, wine, stock and tarragon. Bring to the boil and simmer gently for 30 minutes.

4 Strain the soup through a metal sieve, forcing as much of the tomato mixture through as possible. (If you like, you could remove the big claws and purée the remains in a blender.)

5 Return to the heat, simmer for a few minutes then season to taste. Add the cream and lemon juice, and serve.

Cook's tip If you don't have fish stock then water will do, or you could use some of the water used to boil the crabs initially.

Energy 419kcal/1741kJ; Protein 35.1g; Carbohydrate 3.8g, of which sugars 3.6g; Fat 25.7g, of which saturates 15.1g; Cholesterol 196mg; Calcium 252mg; Fibre 1.1g; Sodium 1122mg

Scotch broth

Sustaining and warming, Scotch broth is custom-made for the chilly Scottish weather, and makes a delicious winter soup anywhere. Traditionally, a large pot of it is made and this is dipped into throughout the next few days, the flavour improving all the time.

Serves 6–8

1kg/2¼lb lean neck (US shoulder or breast) of lamb, cut into large, even-sized chunks

1.75 litres/3 pints/7½ cups cold water

1 large onion, chopped

50g/2oz/¼ cup pearl barley

1 bouquet garni

1 large carrot, chopped

1 turnip, chopped

3 leeks, chopped

1 small white cabbage, finely shredded

salt and ground black pepper

chopped fresh parsley, to garnish

1 Put the lamb and water in a large pan over a medium heat and gently bring to the boil. Skim off the scum with a spoon. Add the onion, pearl barley and bouquet garni, and stir in thoroughly.

2 Bring the soup back to the boil, then reduce the heat, partly cover the pan and simmer gently for a further 1 hour. Make sure that it does not boil too furiously or go dry.

3 Add the remaining vegetables to the pan and season with salt and ground black pepper. Bring to the boil, partly cover again and simmer for about 35 minutes, until the vegetables are tender.

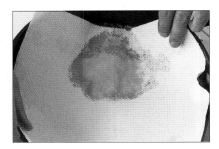

4 Remove the surplus fat from the top of the soup with a sheet of kitchen paper. Serve the soup hot, garnished with chopped parsley, with chunks of fresh bread.

Energy 387kcal/1619kJ; Protein 36.2g; Carbohydrate 17.7g, of which sugars 9.1g; Fat 19.5g, of which saturates 8.8g; Cholesterol 127mg; Calcium 86mg; Fibre 4.3g; Sodium 157mg

Lamb and vegetable broth

This is a good modern adaptation of the traditional recipe for Irish mutton broth, *brachán caoireola*, and is delicious served with wholemeal bread.

Serves 6

675g/1½lb neck of lamb on the bone, trimmed of excess fat

1 large onion

2 bay leaves

3 carrots, chopped

½ white turnip, diced

½ small white cabbage, cored and shredded

2 large leeks, thinly sliced

15ml/1 tbsp tomato purée (paste)

30ml/2 tbsp chopped fresh parsley

salt and ground black pepper

1 Place the lamb in a large pan. Chop the onion, add to the pan with the bayleaf and 1.5 litres/2½ pints/6¼ cups water. Bring to the boil. Skim the surface and simmer for about 1½–2 hours. Remove the lamb on to a board and leave to cool until ready to handle.

2 Remove the meat from the bones and cut into small pieces. Discard the bones and return the meat to the broth. Add the vegetables, tomato purée and parsley, and season. Simmer for another 30 minutes, until the vegetables are tender. Ladle into soup bowls and serve.

Energy 162Kcal/675kJ; Protein 13.1g; Carbohydrate 8.5g, of which sugars 7g; Fat 8.6g, of which saturates 3.8g; Cholesterol 44mg; Calcium 42mg; Fibre 3g; Sodium 55mg

Irish beef and barley soup

This traditional farmhouse soup makes a wonderfully restorative dish on a cold day.
The flavours develop particularly well if it is made in advance and reheated to serve.

Serves 6–8

450–675g/1–1½lb rib steak, or other stewing beef on the bone

2 large onions

50g/2oz/¼ cup pearl barley

50g/2oz/¼ cup green split peas

3 large carrots, chopped

2 white turnips, chopped

3 celery stalks, chopped

1 large or 2 medium leeks, thinly sliced

sea salt and ground black pepper

chopped fresh parsley, to serve

1 Bone the meat, put the bones and half an onion, roughly sliced, into a large pan. Cover with cold water, season and bring to the boil. Skim if necessary, then leave to simmer until required.

2 Meanwhile, trim any fat or gristle from the meat and cut into small pieces. Chop the remaining onions finely. Drain the stock from the bones, make it up with water to 2 litres/3½ pints/9 cups, and return to the rinsed pan with the meat, onions, barley and split peas.

3 Season, bring to the boil, and skim if necessary. Reduce the heat, cover and simmer for about 30 minutes.

4 Add the rest of the vegetables to the pan and allow to simmer for 1 hour, or until the meat is tender. Add salt and pepper to taste. Ladle the hearty soup into large warmed bowls and serve, generously sprinkled with the fresh parsley.

Energy 194Kcal/816kJ; Protein 20.3g; Carbohydrate 21.6g, of which sugars 12g; Fat 3.5g, of which saturates 1.2g; Cholesterol 50mg; Calcium 84mg; Fibre 5g; Sodium 88mg

Oxtail soup

This hearty soup is an English classic, stemming from the days when it was natural to make use of every part of an animal. Oxtail may start off tough and full of bone, but long slow cooking produces a flavour that is rich and delicious, and meat that is beautifully tender.

Serves 4–6

1 oxtail, cut into joints, total weight about 1.3kg/3lb

25g/1oz/2 tbsp butter

2 medium onions, chopped

2 medium carrots, chopped

2 celery sticks, sliced

1 bacon rasher (strip), chopped

2 litres/3½ pints/8 cups beef stock

1 bouquet garni

2 bay leaves

30ml/2 tbsp flour

squeeze of fresh lemon juice

60ml/4 tbsp port, sherry or Madeira

salt and ground black pepper

1 Wash and dry the pieces of oxtail, trimming off any excess fat. Melt the butter in a large pan, and when foaming, add the oxtail a few pieces at a time and brown them quickly on all sides. Lift the meat out onto a plate.

2 To the same pan, add the onions, carrots, celery and bacon. Cook over a medium heat for 5–10 minutes, stirring occasionally, until the vegetables are softened and golden brown.

3 Return the oxtail to the pan and add the stock, bouquet garni, bay leaves and seasoning. Bring just to the boil and skim off any foam. Cover and simmer gently for about 3 hours or until the meat is so tender that it is falling away from the bones.

4 Strain the mixture, discarding the vegetables, bouquet garni and bay leaves, and leave to stand.

5 When the oxtail has cooled sufficiently to handle, pick all the meat off the bones and cut it into small pieces.

6 Skim off any fat that has risen to the surface of the stock, then tip the stock into a large pan. Add the pieces of meat and reheat.

7 With a whisk, blend the flour with a little cold water to make a smooth paste. Stir in a little of the hot stock then stir the mixture into the pan. Bring to the boil, stirring, until the soup thickens slightly. Reduce the heat and simmer gently for about 5 minutes.

8 Season with salt, pepper and lemon juice to taste. Just before serving, stir in the port, sherry or Madeira.

Energy 459kcal/1914kJ; Protein 45.4g; Carbohydrate 6.5g, of which sugars 2.6g; Fat 26.8g, of which saturates 11.8g; Cholesterol 176mg; Calcium 36mg; Fibre 0.7g; Sodium 403mg

Brown Windsor soup

Another classic hearty soup, this was particularly popular during the reign of Queen Victoria, when it is said to have featured regularly on state banquet menus at Windsor Castle in Berkshire. It is smooth, meaty, full of flavour and pleasantly substantial.

Serves 4

225g/8oz lean stewing steak

30ml/2 tbsp flour

25g/1oz/2 tbsp butter

1 medium onion, finely chopped

1 medium carrot, finely chopped

1 small parsnip, finely chopped

1 litre/1¾ pints/4 cups beef stock

1 bouquet garni

salt, black pepper and chilli powder

cooked rice, to garnish

3 Add the vegetables to the hot pan and cook over a medium heat for about 5 minutes, stirring occasionally until softened and golden brown.

4 Return the steak to the pan and add the stock, bouquet garni and seasoning.

5 Bring just to the boil, cover and simmer very gently for about 2 hours until the steak is very tender.

6 Process or blend the soup until smooth, adding a little extra hot stock or water to thin it if necessary. Return it to the pan, adjust the seasoning to taste and reheat. When the soup is in the serving bowls, add a spoonful of cooked rice to each one.

1 Cut the stewing steak into 2.5cm/1in cubes and coat with the flour.

2 Melt the butter in a large saucepan. Add the steak a few pieces at a time and brown them on all sides. Lift the meat out and set aside.

Energy 182kcal/757kJ; Protein 13.8g; Carbohydrate 8g, of which sugars 3.4g; Fat 10.7g, of which saturates 5.5g; Cholesterol 46mg; Calcium 25mg; Fibre 1.7g; Sodium 81mg

Appetizers

Delicious starters whet the appetite with savoury
flavours and an exciting combination of ingredients.
The fine fish and meat and cheese of the British Isles,
and traditional methods of smoking and curing, have
engendered a wealth of recipes, from elegant
seafood salads, pâtés and terrines to spicy devilled
dishes and new guises for traditional foods such as
black pudding and oysters.

Irish goat's cheese salad with hazelnut dressing

The milder-flavoured goat's cheeses are popular in Ireland. Corleggy Quivvy (small chunks preserved in oil) and Boilié (little balls of cheese) are examples of excellent handmade soft cheeses, both from County Cavan. Serve the salad with crusty bread or Melba toast.

Serves 4

175g/6oz mixed salad leaves, such as lamb's lettuce, rocket (arugula), radicchio, frisée or cress

a few fresh large-leafed herbs, such as chervil and flat leaf parsley

15ml/1 tbsp toasted hazelnuts, roughly chopped

15–20 goat's cheese balls or cubes

For the dressing

30ml/2 tbsp hazelnut oil, olive oil or sunflower oil

5–10ml/1–2 tsp sherry vinegar or good wine vinegar, to taste

salt and ground black pepper

1 Tear up any large salad leaves. Put all the leaves into a large salad bowl with the fresh herbs and most of the toasted, chopped nuts (reserve a few for the garnish).

2 To make the dressing, whisk the hazelnut, olive or sunflower oil and vinegar together, and then season to taste with salt and pepper.

3 Just before serving, toss the salad in the dressing and divide it among four serving plates. Arrange the drained goat's cheese balls or cubes over the leaves, sprinkle over the remaining chopped nuts and serve.

Cook's tip A grilled (broiled) slice from a goat's cheese log can replace the cheese balls or cubes if you prefer.

Energy 225Kcal/931kJ; Protein 11g; Carbohydrate 1.4g, of which sugars 1.3g; Fat 19.5g, of which saturates 8.7g; Cholesterol 41mg; Calcium 138mg; Fibre 1.2g; Sodium 325mg

Pears with Irish Cashel Blue cream and walnuts

The success of this dish depends on the quality of the pears, which must be very succulent, and, of course, the cheese. Cashel Blue, made from cow's milk in County Tipperary, is one of Ireland's great artisan food success stories and is widely available.

Serves 6

115g/4oz fresh cream cheese

75g/3oz Cashel Blue cheese

30–45ml/2–3 tbsp single (light) cream

115g/4oz/1 cup roughly chopped walnuts

6 ripe pears

15ml/1 tbsp lemon juice

mixed salad leaves, such as frisée, oakleaf lettuce and radicchio

6 cherry tomatoes

sea salt and ground black pepper

walnut halves and sprigs of fresh flat leaf parsley, to garnish

For the dressing

juice of 1 lemon

a little finely grated lemon rind

pinch of caster (superfine) sugar

60ml/4 tbsp olive oil

1 Mash the cream cheese and Cashel Blue cheese together in a mixing bowl with a good grinding of black pepper, then blend in the cream to make a smooth mixture. Add 25g/1oz/¼ cup chopped walnuts and mix to distribute evenly. Cover and chill until required.

2 Peel and halve the pears and scoop out the core. Put them into a bowl of water with the 15ml/1 tbsp lemon juice to prevent them from browning. To make the dressing: whisk the lemon juice, lemon rind, caster sugar and olive oil together and season to taste.

3 Arrange a bed of salad leaves on six plates – shallow soup plates are ideal – add a tomato to each and sprinkle over the remaining chopped walnuts.

4 Drain the pears well and pat dry with kitchen paper, then turn them in the prepared dressing and arrange, hollow side up, on the salad leaves. Divide the Cashel Blue mixture between the six halved pears, and spoon the dressing over the top. Garnish each pear with a walnut half and a sprig of flat leaf parsley before serving.

Variation Crozier Blue or other mature blue cheese can be used instead.

Energy 331Kcal/1373kJ; Protein 6.7g; Carbohydrate 16.3g, of which sugars 16.1g; Fat 27g, of which saturates 9.8g; Cholesterol 30mg; Calcium 120mg; Fibre 4.1g; Sodium 219mg

Asparagus with lime butter dip

British asparagus has the shortest of seasons – just a few weeks – but it is worth the wait, and while it is at its freshest you should find as many ways as possible to enjoy it. This recipe is based on the traditional butter sauce but it has lime added to lift the flavour.

Serves 4

40 medium asparagus spears

1 litre/1¾ pints/4 cups water

15g/½oz coarse salt

For the lime butter dip

90ml/6 tbsp dry white wine

90ml/6 tbsp white wine vinegar

3 shallots or 1 onion, finely chopped

225g/8oz/1 cup very cold unsalted (sweet) butter, cut into chunks

juice of 1 lime

salt and ground black pepper

lime wedges, to serve

1 Wash the asparagus spears and trim the bases off evenly to give about 10cm/4in lengths. Bring a pan of water to the boil, add the salt then plunge in the asparagus. Cook for about 7 minutes or until you can just spear a stem with a knife and the blade slips out easily. Drain immediately, cover and set aside, keeping the asparagus warm while you make the sauce.

2 A stainless steel pan with a handle is essential for the lime butter dip. If you are using a gas ring make sure the flame does not come round the side of the pan, as the sauce can burn easily.

3 Combine the wine and vinegar in the pan with the shallots or onion, and simmer until the liquid has reduced to about 15ml/1 tbsp.

4 Off the heat, vigorously whisk in the butter until the sauce thickens. Whisk in the lime juice until thoroughly combined. Taste the sauce and adjust the seasoning if necessary.

5 Arrange ten asparagus spears per serving on warmed individual plates. Coarsely grind some black pepper over the top. Serve the warm lime butter dip in a bowl for handing round or in four small bowls.

Cook's tips
• There are two important points to remember when you add the butter to the sauce. Firstly, don't allow the sauce to boil. If the butter is taking a long time to melt, put the pan back over a very gentle heat to speed it up. Secondly, you must not stop whisking for a moment until the butter is completely incorporated.
• You can use the asparagus trimmings to make soup or a lovely rich stock for stews or casseroles.

Variations Use cider instead of vinegar, and orange or lemon juice instead of lime juice.

Energy 527kcal/2166kJ; Protein 7.8g; Carbohydrate 6.7g, of which sugars 6.1g; Fat 50.9g, of which saturates 31.5g; Cholesterol 128mg; Calcium 84mg; Fibre 4.5g; Sodium 1841mg

Potted cheese

The potting of cheese became popular in England in the 18th century, and it is still a great way to use up odd pieces left on the cheeseboard. Blend them with your chosen seasonings, adjusting the flavour before adding the alcohol. Serve with oatcakes or toast.

Serves 4–6

250g/9oz hard cheese, such as mature Cheddar

75g/3oz/6 tbsp soft unsalted butter, plus extra for melting

1.5ml/¼ tsp ready-made English (hot) mustard

1.5ml/¼ tsp ground mace

30ml/2 tbsp sherry

ground black pepper

fresh parsley, to garnish

1 Cut the cheese into rough pieces and put them into the bowl of a food processor. Use the pulse button to chop the cheese into small crumbs.

2 Add the butter, mustard, mace and a little black pepper and blend again until smooth. Taste and adjust the seasoning. Finally, blend in the sherry.

3 Spoon the mixture into a dish just large enough to leave about 1cm/½in to spare on top. Level the surface.

Variations
• Use Stilton in place of the Cheddar and port in place of sherry.
• Some finely chopped chives could be added instead of mustard.

4 Melt some butter in a small pan, skimming off any foam that rises to the surface. Leaving the sediment in the pan, pour a layer of melted butter on top of the cheese mixture to cover the surface. Refrigerate until required.

5 Garnish with parsley and serve spread on thin slices of toast or crispbread.

Energy 262kcal/1082kJ; Protein 10.7g; Carbohydrate 0.2g, of which sugars 0.2g; Fat 23.6g, of which saturates 15.2g; Cholesterol 70mg; Calcium 290mg; Fibre 0g; Sodium 363mg

Anglesey eggs

This delicious Welsh dish of potatoes, leeks, eggs and cheese sauce, *wyau Ynys Môn*, is traditional to Anglesey. A nice variation is to add a little freshly grated nutmeg to the cheese sauce. Instead of browning the dish in the oven, you may prefer to finish it by putting it under a medium-hot grill.

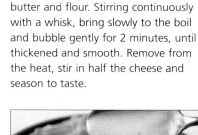

4 Pour the milk into a pan and add the butter and flour. Stirring continuously with a whisk, bring slowly to the boil and bubble gently for 2 minutes, until thickened and smooth. Remove from the heat, stir in half the cheese and season to taste.

Serves 4

500g/1lb 2oz potatoes, peeled

3 leeks, sliced

6 eggs

600ml/1 pint/2½ cups milk

50g/2oz/3 tbsp butter, cut into small pieces

50g/2oz/½ cup plain (all-purpose) flour

100g/3½oz/1 cup Caerphilly cheese, grated

salt and ground black pepper

1 Cook the potatoes in boiling, lightly salted water for about 15 minutes or until soft. Meanwhile, cook the leeks in a little water for about 10 minutes until soft. Hard-boil the eggs, drain and put under cold running water to cool them.

2 Preheat the oven to 200°C/400°F/ Gas 6. Drain and mash the potatoes.

3 Drain the leeks and stir into the potatoes with a little black pepper to taste. Remove the shells from the eggs and cut in half or into quarters lengthways.

5 Arrange the eggs in four shallow ovenproof dishes (or use one large one). Spoon the potato and leek mixture around the edge of the dishes. Pour the cheese sauce over and top with the remaining cheese.

6 Put into the hot oven and cook for about 15–20 minutes, until bubbling and golden brown.

Cook's tip The leeks could just as easily be cooked in the microwave in a covered dish: there is no need to add any water. Stir the leeks once or twice during cooking.

Energy 540kcal/2259kJ; Protein 26.6g; Carbohydrate 41.3g, of which sugars 12.3g; Fat 30.6g, of which saturates 16.2g; Cholesterol 345mg; Calcium 471mg; Fibre 5g; Sodium 443mg

Salad of Carmarthen ham with smoked salmon

This famous dry-cured Carmarthen ham is Wales' answer to Italian prosciutto or parma ham. Carmarthen ham's flavour is rich and deep and a little can go a long way. In this salad the ham is paired with hot-smoked salmon, and served in a warm dressing of olive oil, lemon juice and spring onion.

Serves 4

90ml/6 tbsp olive oil

100g/3½oz Carmarthen ham slices, cut into wide strips

4 spring onions (scallions), thinly sliced

300g/10½oz hot-smoked salmon, skin removed and roughly flaked

30ml/2 tbsp lemon juice

mixed salad leaves, such as spinach, watercress, frisée, little gem and lollo rosso

1 Heat the oil in a pan. Toss in the ham and cook quickly until crisp and tinged with golden brown. Lift the ham out on to a plate.

2 Add the spring onions and salmon to the hot pan and sprinkle in the lemon juice. Once warm, return the ham to the pan. Arrange the salad leaves on plates and spoon the ham and salmon over.

Energy 288kcal/1196kJ; Protein 24.1g; Carbohydrate 1g, of which sugars 1g; Fat 20.9g, of which saturates 3.3g; Cholesterol 41mg; Calcium 27mg; Fibre 0.4g; Sodium 1712mg

Salmon mousse

This type of light and delicate mousse often features at the wedding feasts of English brides. It is ideal for a summer lunch or buffet, garnished with thinly sliced cucumber, cherry tomatoes and lemon wedges. Serve it with crisp crackers or Melba toast.

Serves 6–8

300ml/½ pint/1¼ cups milk

1 small onion, thinly sliced

1 small carrot, thinly slIced

2 bay leaves

2 sprigs of parsley or dill

4 whole peppercorns

15ml/1 tbsp powdered gelatine

350g/12oz salmon fillet

75ml/5 tbsp dry white vermouth

25g/1oz/2 tbsp butter

25g/1oz/4 tbsp flour

75ml/5 tbsp mayonnaise

150ml/¼ pint/⅔ cup whipping cream

salt and ground black pepper

1 Put the milk in a pan with half the onion, carrot, herbs and peppercorns. Bring to the boil, remove from the heat, cover and leave to stand. Sprinkle the gelatine over 45ml/3 tbsp cold water.

2 Put the salmon in a pan with the remaining onion, carrot, herbs and peppercorns, the vermouth and 60ml/ 4 tbsp water. Simmer, covered, for 10 minutes. Flake the fish, discarding the skin and bones. Boil the juices in the pan to reduce by half, strain and reserve.

3 Strain the infused milk into a clean pan and add the butter and flour. Whisking continuously, cook until the sauce thickens, then simmer for 1 minute. Pour into a food processor, add the soaked gelatine and blend. Add the salmon and reserved juices and blend.

4 Tip into a bowl. Season, and stir in the mayonnaise. Whip the cream and fold in gently. Transfer to an oiled mould, cover and refrigerate for about 2 hours. Turn out onto a plate to serve.

Energy 285kcal/1183kJ; Protein 12.6g; Carbohydrate 5.8g, of which sugars 3.2g; Fat 22.7g, of which saturates 8.7g; Cholesterol 57mg; Calcium 73mg; Fibre 0.2g; Sodium 103mg

Potted shrimps

Tiny brown shrimps found in the seas around England (most famously those from Morecambe Bay) have been potted in spiced butter since about 1800. If your fishmonger doesn't have them you can use small cooked prawns instead.

Serves 4

225g/8oz cooked, shelled shrimps

225g/8oz/1 cup butter

pinch of ground mace

salt

cayenne pepper

dill sprigs, to garnish

lemon wedges and thin slices of brown bread and butter, to serve

1 Chop a quarter of the shrimps. Melt 115g/4oz/½ cup of the butter slowly.

2 Skim off any foam that rises to the surface of the butter. Stir in all the shrimps, the mace, salt and cayenne and heat gently without boiling. Pour the mixture into four individual dishes and leave to cool.

3 Melt the remaining butter in a small pan, then spoon the clear butter over the shrimps, leaving the sediment behind. When the butter is almost set, place a dill sprig in the centre of each dish. Cover and chill.

4 Remove from the refrigerator 30 minutes before serving with lemon wedges and brown bread and butter.

Prawn cocktail

This 1960s dinner-party appetizer is a delight, so long as it includes really crisp lettuce and is assembled at the last minute. The traditional accompaniment is brown bread and butter.

Serves 6

60ml/4 tbsp double (heavy) cream, lightly whipped

60ml/4 tbsp mayonnaise

60ml/4 tbsp tomato ketchup

5–10ml/1–2 tsp Worcestershire sauce

juice of 1 lemon

450g/1lb cooked peeled prawns (shrimp)

½ crisp lettuce, finely shredded

salt, ground black pepper and paprika

thinly sliced brown bread, butter and lemon wedges, to serve

1 Mix the cream, mayonnaise, ketchup, Worcestershire sauce and lemon juice in a bowl. Stir in the prawns and season.

2 Part-fill six glasses with lettuce. Spoon the prawns over and sprinkle with paprika. Serve immediately.

Energy 460kcal/1895kJ; Protein 9.6g; Carbohydrate 0.4g, of which sugars 0.4g; Fat 46.7g, of which saturates 29.4g; Cholesterol 193mg; Calcium 83mg; Fibre 0g; Sodium 555mg

Energy 193kcal/802kJ; Protein 13.9g; Carbohydrate 4g, of which sugars 3.9g; Fat 13.6g, of which saturates 4.6g; Cholesterol 167mg; Calcium 79mg; Fibre 0.4g; Sodium 374mg

Smoked Wicklow trout with cucumber

Rainbow trout is farmed in Ireland's Wicklow Hills and the smoked trout fillets are widely available in vacuum packs. They need no further cooking or preparation except for any accompanying salad or sauce, making them an excellent fresh convenience food and a deservedly popular cold first course or light meal. Allow one or two fillets per person.

Serves 4

1 small cucumber

4–8 smoked trout fillets

sprigs of dill, to garnish

brown bread and butter, to serve

For the dressing

90ml/6 tbsp extra virgin olive oil

30ml/2 tbsp white wine vinegar

15ml/1 tbsp chopped fresh dill

sea salt and ground black pepper

1 To make the dressing, whisk the oil and vinegar together vigorously, or shake in a screw-top jar, then blend in the dill and seasoning to taste.

2 Peel the cucumber, if you prefer, and slice it thinly. Arrange with the trout fillets on four serving plates.

3 Sprinkle the fish with the dressing, and garnish with sprigs of dill. Serve with brown bread and butter.

Above *The clear waters of the Glendasin river flowing through Glendalough, County Wicklow.*

Energy 467Kcal/1943kJ; Protein 55g; Carbohydrate 0.7g, of which sugars 0.6g; Fat 27g, of which saturates 4.7g; Cholesterol 226mg; Calcium 92mg; Fibre 0.3g; Sodium 206mg

Smoked salmon with Irish potato cakes

Although the ingredients are timeless, this combination makes an excellent modern dish, which is deservedly popular as a first course or as a substantial canapé to serve with drinks. It also makes a perfect brunch dish, served with lightly scrambled eggs and freshly squeezed orange juice. Choose wild fish if possible.

Serves 6

450g/1lb potatoes, cooked and mashed

75g/3oz/⅔ cup plain (all-purpose) flour

2 eggs, beaten

2 spring onions (scallions), chopped

a little freshly grated nutmeg

50g/2oz/¼ cup butter, melted

150ml/¼ pint/⅔ cup sour cream

12 slices of smoked salmon

salt and ground black pepper

chopped fresh chives, to garnish

1 Put the potatoes, flour, eggs and spring onions into a large bowl. Season with salt, pepper and a little nutmeg, and add half the butter. Mix thoroughly and shape into 12 small potato cakes.

Cook's tip If it is more convenient, you can fry the potato cakes in advance and keep them overnight in the refrigerator. When required, warm them through in a hot oven 15 minutes before serving and assembling.

2 Heat the remaining butter in a non-stick pan and cook the potato cakes in batches until browned on both sides.

3 Removed the cakes from the pan, and keep them warm until all the batches are cooked.

4 To serve, mix the sour cream with some salt and pepper. Fold a piece of smoked salmon and place on top of each potato cake. Top with the cream and chives and serve immediately.

Variation Top the potato cakes with smoked mackerel and a squeeze of lemon juice, if you like.

Energy 326Kcal/1365kJ; Protein 21.9g; Carbohydrate 22.9g, of which sugars 2.3g; Fat 17g, of which saturates 8.6g; Cholesterol 119mg; Calcium 70mg; Fibre 1.2g; Sodium 1315mg

Devilled whitebait

Whitebait are the tiny, silver fry (young) of sprats or herring and the English enjoy them crisply fried and eaten whole. They used to be caught in large numbers every summer in the Thames estuary, and, for most of the 19th century, an annual whitebait dinner was held at Greenwich to mark the end of each parliamentary session.

Serves 4

oil, for deep-frying

150ml/¼ pint/⅔ cup milk

115g/4oz/1 cup flour

450g/1lb whitebait

salt and ground black pepper

cayenne pepper

1 Heat the oil in a large pan or deep-fryer. Put the milk in a shallow bowl. Spoon the flour into a paper bag or freezer bag and season the flour with salt, pepper and a little cayenne.

2 Dip a handful of the whitebait into the milk, drain them well, then put them in the bag. Shake gently to coat in the flour. Repeat until all the fish have been coated. Don't add too many of the fish at once or they will stick together.

3 Heat the oil to 190°C/375°F or until a cube of stale bread browns in 20 seconds. Add a small batch of whitebait and fry for 2–3 minutes, until crisp and golden brown. Lift out, drain and keep hot while you fry the rest. Sprinkle with more cayenne and serve very hot.

Energy 696kcal/2881kJ; Protein 25.8g; Carbohydrate 7g, of which sugars 0.1g; Fat 63g, of which saturates 5.8g; Cholesterol 0mg; Calcium 1140mg; Fibre 0.3g; Sodium 305mg

Sussex smokies

England's smokehouses produce some fine products. The flavour and colour of this Sussex dish is best when made with pale, undyed smoked haddock rather than the bright yellow artificially dyed variety. Follow this filling appetizer with a light main course or serve it with crusty bread as a light meal or snack.

Serves 4

350g/12oz smoked haddock

450ml/¾ pint/scant 2 cups milk

25g/1oz/2 tbsp butter

25g/1oz/4 tbsp flour

115g/4oz mature Cheddar cheese, grated

60ml/4 tbsp fresh breadcrumbs

salt and ground black pepper

crusty bread, to serve

1 Remove and discard all skin and bones from the haddock and cut the fish into strips.

2 Put the milk, butter, flour and seasoning into a pan. Over a medium heat and whisking constantly, bring to the boil and bubble gently for 2–3 minutes until thick and smooth.

3 Add the haddock and half the cheese to the hot sauce and bring it just back to the boil to melt the cheese.

4 Divide the mixture between individual flameproof dishes or ramekins. Toss together the remaining cheese and the breadcrumbs and sprinkle the mixture over the top of each filled dish.

5 Put the dishes under a hot grill (broiler) until bubbling and golden. Serve immediately with crusty bread.

Energy 363kcal/1525kJ; Protein 30.1g; Carbohydrate 21.8g, of which sugars 5.8g; Fat 17.4g, of which saturates 10.8g; Cholesterol 79mg; Calcium 396mg; Fibre 0.5g; Sodium 1073mg

Langoustines with saffron and tomato

The best Scottish langoustines come from the west coast, where everything from a tiny shrimp to just smaller than a lobster is called a prawn. Langoustines, also known as Dublin Bay prawns or Norway lobsters, look like miniature lobsters, although they taste more like jumbo prawns or shrimp, and these can be substituted if you prefer.

Serves 4

5ml/1 tsp sea salt

20 live langoustines or Dublin Bay prawns (jumbo shrimp)

1 onion

15ml/1 tbsp olive oil

pinch of saffron threads

120ml/4fl oz/½ cup dry white wine

450g/1lb ripe fresh or canned tomatoes, roughly chopped

chopped fresh flat leaf parsley, to garnish

salt and ground black pepper

1 Bring a large pan of water to the boil, add the salt and plunge the shellfish into the pan. Let the water return to the boil then transfer the shellfish to a colander to cool.

Variation You can also use other kinds of shellfish for this dish, if available, such as mussels or clams. You will need to adjust the cooking times. Lobster also goes well in this recipe if you are serving a large number of people for a special occasion.

2 When cooled, shell the langoustines or prawns and reserve four heads with two claws each. Keep the rest of the shells, heads and claws to make a flavourful stock for the sauce.

3 Chop the onions. Heat a large heavy pan and add 15ml/1 tbsp olive oil. Gently fry the chopped onion to soften.

4 Stir in the saffron threads. Then add the shellfish debris, including the heads and the pincers. Stir to mix thoroughly then reduce the heat.

5 Add the wine and then the tomatoes. Simmer to soften the tomatoes – this will take about 5 minutes. Do not allow the mixture to become too dry; add water if necessary.

6 Strain through a sieve, pressing the debris to get as much moisture out as possible. The resulting sauce should be light in texture; if it's too thick add some water. Check the seasoning.

7 Add the langoustines or prawns and warm over a gentle heat for a few minutes. Serve in warmed soup plates garnished with the reserved langoustine or prawn heads and scattered with chopped fresh flat leaf parsley.

Cook's tip Crushing the langoustine or prawn shell debris with a rolling pin before adding it to the pan helps to extract more flavour into the juices.

Energy 107kcal/449kJ; Protein 9.8g; Carbohydrate 4.9g, of which sugars 4.5g; Fat 3.4g, of which saturates 0.6g; Cholesterol 98mg; Calcium 54mg; Fibre 1.3g; Sodium 598mg

Langoustines with garlic butter

There is nothing quite like the smell of garlic butter melting over shellfish. Freshly caught langoustines or jumbo shrimp are ideal for this simple yet extremely tasty first-course dish. Serve with plenty of fresh crusty white bread to soak up the delicious garlicky juices.

Serves 4

2 garlic cloves

5ml/1 tsp coarse salt

10ml/2 tsp chopped fresh flat leaf parsley, plus extra to garnish (optional)

250g/9oz/generous 1 cup butter, softened

juice of 2 lemons

pinch of cayenne pepper

20 freshly caught langoustines or Dublin Bay prawns (jumbo shrimp), cooked and peeled

ground black pepper

1 Preheat the grill (broiler) to medium. Using a blender or food processor, blend the garlic cloves, salt and chopped parsley until quite well mixed. Then add the butter, lemon juice and cayenne pepper and blend again until all the ingredients are thoroughly combined.

2 Scrape the butter mixture out of the food processor and into a bowl.

3 Place the langoustines or prawns on a metal baking tray and put a blob of garlic butter on each one. Place under the preheated grill for about 5 minutes, or until the shellfish are cooked and the butter is bubbling.

4 Lift five shellfish on to each plate and spoon over the collected pan juices. Serve immediately with a grind or two of black pepper and garnished with chopped fresh flat leaf parsley if you like. Accompany with fresh bread for mopping up the juices.

Cook's tip To cook the langoustines or prawns, plunge them into boiling water until the water returns to the boil and then drain and cool. Shell them by pulling off the head, legs and outer shell. Reserve a few heads to garnish, if you like.

Energy 616kcal/2552kJ; Protein 29.7g; Carbohydrate 4.9g, of which sugars 0.6g; Fat 53.3g, of which saturates 33.1g; Cholesterol 192mg; Calcium 68mg; Fibre 0.5g; Sodium 1098mg

Scottish oysters with Highland heather honey

Highland honey is very fragrant, the pollen gathered by bees late in the season when the heather on the moors is in full flower. Beekeepers in Scotland will take their hives up to the hills once the spring and early summer blossoms are over, so the flavour is more intense.

Serves 4

1 bunch spring onions (scallions), washed

20ml/4 tsp heather honey

10ml/2 tsp soy sauce

16 fresh oysters

1 Preheat the grill (broiler) to medium. Chop the spring onions finely, removing any coarser outer leaves.

2 Place the heather honey and soy sauce in a bowl and mix. Then add the finely chopped spring onions and mix them in thoroughly.

3 Open the oysters with an oyster knife or a small, sharp knife, taking care to catch the liquid in a small bowl. Leave the oysters attached to one side of the shell. Strain the liquid to remove any pieces of broken shell, and set aside.

4 Place a large teaspoon of the honey and spring onion mixture on top of each oyster.

5 Place under the preheated grill until the mixture bubbles, which will take about 5 minutes. Take care when removing the oysters from the grill as the shells retain the heat. Make sure that you don't lose any of the sauce from inside the oyster shells.

6 Allow the oysters to cool slightly before serving with slices of bread to soak up the juices. Either tip them straight into your mouth or lift them out with a spoon or fork.

Energy 81kcal/343kJ; Protein 9.2g; Carbohydrate 9.1g, of which sugars 6.9g; Fat 1.2g, of which saturates 0.2g; Cholesterol 46mg; Calcium 121mg; Fibre 0.3g; Sodium 588mg

Dressed crab with asparagus

Crab is the juiciest and most flavoursome seafood, possibly better even than lobster and considerably cheaper. This dish is a combination of two paragons: crab as the king of seafood and asparagus as a prince among vegetables.

Serves 4

24 asparagus spears

4 dressed crabs

30ml/2 tbsp mayonnaise

15ml/1 tbsp chopped fresh parsley

1 Cook the asparagus (as for Asparagus with Lime Butter Dip), but when cooked plunge the stems into iced water to stop them from cooking further. Drain them when cold and pat dry with kitchen paper.

2 Scoop out the white crab meat from the shells and claws and place it in a bowl. If you can't find fresh crabs, you can use the same amount of canned or frozen white crab meat.

3 Add the mayonnaise and chopped fresh parsley and combine with a fork. Place the mixture into the crab shells and add six asparagus spears per serving. Serve with crusty bread.

Energy 207kcal/859kJ; Protein 19.5g; Carbohydrate 3g, of which sugars 2.8g; Fat 13g, of which saturates 1.9g; Cholesterol 72mg; Calcium 157mg; Fibre 2.6g; Sodium 540mg

Hot crab soufflés

These delicious little soufflés must be served as soon as they are ready, so seat your guests at the table before taking the soufflés out of the oven. Use local freshly caught crabs if possible, although canned or frozen will do if necessary.

Serves 6

50g/2oz/¼ cup butter

45ml/3 tbsp fine wholemeal (whole-wheat) breadcrumbs

4 spring onions (scallions), finely chopped

15ml/1 tbsp Malaysian or mild Madras curry powder

25g/1oz/¼ cup plain (all-purpose) flour

105ml/7 tbsp coconut milk or milk

150ml/¼ pint/⅔ cup whipping cream

4 eggs, separated, plus 2 extra egg whites

225g/8oz white crab meat

mild green Tabasco sauce, to taste

salt and ground black pepper

1 Use a little of the butter to grease six ramekins or a 1.75 litre/3 pint/7½ cup soufflé dish. Sprinkle in the fine wholemeal breadcrumbs, roll the dish(es) around to coat the base and sides completely, then tip out the excess breadcrumbs. Preheat the oven to 200°C/400°F/Gas 6.

2 Melt the remaining butter in a pan, add the spring onions and Malaysian or mild Madras curry powder and cook over a low heat for about 1 minute, until softened. Stir in the flour and cook for 1 minute more.

3 Gradually add the coconut milk or milk and cream, stirring continuously until each batch is thoroughly absorbed. Cook over a low heat until the mixture is smooth and thick.

4 Off the heat, stir in the egg yolks, then the crab meat. Season with salt, black pepper and Tabasco sauce.

5 In a grease-free bowl, beat the egg whites stiffly with a pinch of salt. Using a metal spoon, stir one-third into the crab mixture to lighten it; fold in the rest. Spoon into the dish(es).

6 Bake in the preheated oven until well risen and golden brown, and firm to the touch. Individual soufflés will be ready in 8 minutes; a large soufflé will take 15–20 minutes. Serve immediately.

Variation Lobster or salmon can be used instead of crab in these soufflés. You will need to cook the fish before adding it to the mixture.

Energy 234kcal/972kJ; Protein 11.8g; Carbohydrate 8.7g, of which sugars 1.8g; Fat 17.1g, of which saturates 9.3g; Cholesterol 97mg; Calcium 37mg; Fibre 0.3g; Sodium 322mg

Irish garlic-stuffed mussels

Mussels are plentiful on the West coast of Ireland, and safe to gather from the rocks in areas where the water is clean. Wild garlic has been used in Ireland for hundreds of years, so this way of cooking mussels is more traditional than it might sound.

Serves 4–6

2kg/4½lb fresh mussels, washed and well scrubbed

175g/6oz/¾ cup butter

4–6 garlic cloves

50g/2oz/1 cup fresh white breadcrumbs

15ml/1 tbsp chopped fresh parsley

juice of 1 lemon

brown bread, to serve

1 Remove the beards from the washed mussels. Discard any with broken shells, or that don't close when tapped.

2 Put the mussels into a shallow, heavy pan, without adding any liquid. Cover tightly and cook over a high heat for a few minutes, until all the mussels have opened. Discard any that fail to open.

3 Remove the top shell from each mussel and arrange the bottom shells with the mussels in a shallow flameproof dish.

4 Melt the butter in a small pan, add the crushed garlic, breadcrumbs, parsley and lemon juice. Mix well and sprinkle this mixture over the mussels.

5 Cook under a hot grill (broiler) until golden brown. Serve very hot, with freshly baked brown bread.

Above *Cockles, mussels and clams are a popular catch all over Ireland.*

Energy 500Kcal/2082kJ; Protein 27.7g; Carbohydrate 10g, of which sugars 0.6g; Fat 39.2g, of which saturates 23.3g; Cholesterol 153mg; Calcium 319mg; Fibre 0.3g; Sodium 675mg

Scottish smoked haddock pâté

Arbroath smokies come from the Scottish city of that name. They are small haddock, gutted, with their heads removed, but they are not split before being salted and hot-smoked. You can also use kippers or any other kind of smoked fish for this recipe.

Serves 6

3 large Arbroath smokies, approximately 225g/8oz each

275g/10oz/1¼ cups soft cheese

3 eggs, beaten

30–45ml/2–3 tbsp lemon juice

ground black pepper

sprigs of chervil, to garnish

lettuce and lemon wedges, to serve

1 Preheat the oven to 160°C/325°F/ Gas 3. Butter six ramekin dishes. Lay the smokies in a baking dish and heat through in the oven for 10 minutes.

2 Remove the fish from the oven, carefully remove the skin and bones then flake the flesh into a bowl.

3 Mash the fish with a fork then work in the cheese, then the eggs. Add lemon juice and pepper to taste.

4 Divide the fish mixture among the ramekin dishes and place them in a large roasting pan. Pour hot water into the roasting pan to come halfway up the dishes. Bake in the oven for 30 minutes, until just set.

5 Leave to cool for 2–3 minutes, then run a sharp knife around the edge of each dish and carefully invert the pâté on to warmed plates. Garnish with chervil sprigs and serve with the lettuce leaves and lemon wedges.

Energy 206kcal/859kJ; Protein 25.3g; Carbohydrate 1.7g, of which sugars 0.1g; Fat 11g, of which saturates 5.8g; Cholesterol 153mg; Calcium 82mg; Fibre 0g; Sodium 940mg

Irish three-fish terrine

This attractive striped terrine uses haddock, salmon and turbot – all native fish to Irish seas and rivers. Serve with a small salad, freshly made brown bread or Melba toast and butter.

Serves 8–10

450g/1lb spinach

350–450g/12oz–1lb haddock, cod or other white fish, skinned and chopped

3 eggs

115g/4oz/2 cups fresh breadcrumbs

300ml/½ pint/1¼ cups fromage blanc

a little freshly grated nutmeg

350–450g/12oz–1lb fresh salmon fillet

350–450g/12oz–1lb fresh turbot fillet, or other flat fish

oil, for greasing

salt and ground black pepper

lemon wedges and sprigs of fresh dill or fennel, to garnish

1 Preheat the oven to 160°C/325°F/ Gas 3. Remove the stalks from the spinach and cook the leaves briskly in a pan without any added water, shaking the pan occasionally, until the spinach is just tender. Drain and squeeze out the excess water.

2 Put the spinach into a food processor or blender with the haddock or other white fish, eggs, breadcrumbs, fromage blanc, salt, pepper and nutmeg to taste. Process until smooth.

3 Skin and bone the salmon fillet and cut it into long thin strips. Repeat with the turbot.

4 Oil a 900g/2lb loaf tin (pan) or terrine and line the base with a piece of oiled baking parchment or foil, cut to fit. Make layers from the spinach mixture and the strips of salmon and turbot, starting and finishing with the spinach.

5 Press down carefully and cover with lightly oiled baking parchment. Prick a few holes in it, then put the terrine into a roasting pan and pour enough boiling water around it to come two-thirds of the way up the sides.

6 Bake in the preheated oven for 1–1½ hours, or until risen, firm and set. Leave to cool, then chill well before serving.

7 To serve, ease a sharp knife down the sides to loosen the terrine and turn the terrine on to a flat serving dish. Using a sharp knife, cut the terrine into slices and serve garnished with lemon wedges and fresh dill or fennel.

Cook's tip If you cannot find fromage blanc, substitute it with low-fat soft cream cheese.

Below *Boats moored on the tranquil waters of the Kenmare River, Ring of Kerry, County Kerry.*

Energy 290Kcal/1216kJ; Protein 32.5g; Carbohydrate 13.7g, of which sugars 2.8g; Fat 12.1g, of which saturates 3.9g; Cholesterol 112mg; Calcium 203mg; Fibre 1.5g; Sodium 306mg

Haddock and smoked salmon terrine

This substantial terrine makes a superb dish for a summer buffet, or an impressive starter, accompanied by dill mayonnaise or a fresh cucumber salad.

Serves 10–12 as a first course, 6–8 as a main course

15ml/1 tbsp sunflower oil, for greasing

350g/12oz oak-smoked salmon

900g/2lb haddock fillets, skinned

2 eggs, lightly beaten

105ml/7 tbsp crème fraîche

30ml/2 tbsp drained capers

30ml/2 tbsp drained soft green or pink peppercorns

salt and ground white pepper

crème fraîche, peppercorns, fresh dill and rocket (arugula), to garnish

1 Preheat the oven to 200°C/400°F/ Gas 6. Grease a 1 litre/1¾ pint/4 cup loaf tin (pan) or terrine with the oil. Use half of the salmon to line the tin or terrine, letting some of the ends overhang the mould. Reserve the remaining smoked salmon.

Variations
• Use any thick white fish fillets for this terrine – try halibut or Arctic bass.
• Cod is also good, although it is better to use a firm, chunky piece that will not crumble easily after being cooked.
• You could also use fresh salmon for a truly salmony flavour.

2 Cut two long slices of haddock the length of the tin or terrine and set aside. Cut the rest of the haddock into small pieces. Season all the haddock.

3 Combine the eggs, crème fraîche, capers and peppercorns in a bowl. Season, then stir in the small pieces of haddock. Spoon the mixture into the tin or terrine until one-third full. Smooth the surface with a spatula.

4 Wrap the reserved long haddock fillets in the reserved smoked salmon. Lay them on top of the fish mixture in the tin or terrine.

5 Fill the tin or terrine with the rest of the fish mixture, smooth the surface and fold the overhanging pieces of smoked salmon over the top. Cover tightly with a double thickness of foil. Tap the terrine to settle the contents.

6 Stand the terrine in a roasting pan and pour in boiling water to come halfway up the sides. Place in the preheated oven and cook for 45–60 minutes.

7 Take the terrine out of the roasting pan, but do not remove the foil cover. Place two or three large heavy tins on the foil to weight it and leave until cold. Chill in the refrigerator for 24 hours.

8 About 1 hour before serving, lift off the weights and remove the foil. Carefully invert the terrine on to a serving plate and lift off the terrine. Serve the terrine in thick slices with crème fraîche, peppercorns, fronds of dill and rocket leaves.

Energy 187kcal/785kJ; Protein 27.5g; Carbohydrate 0.3g, of which sugars 0.2g; Fat 8.5g, of which saturates 3.7g; Cholesterol 95mg; Calcium 31mg; Fibre 0g; Sodium 735mg

Duck liver pâté with redcurrant sauce

For this classic recipe, duck or chicken livers are interchangeable, depending on availability. Redcurrant sauces are much favoured by British chefs, who appreciate the colour, lightness of texture and piquancy of the pretty little berries. This recipe is easy to prepare and keeps for about a week in the refrigerator if the butter seal is not broken.

Serves 4–6

1 onion, finely chopped

1 large garlic clove, crushed

115g/4oz/½ cup butter

225g/8oz duck livers

10–15ml/2–3 tsp chopped fresh mixed herbs, such as parsley, thyme or rosemary

15–30ml/1–2 tbsp brandy

bay leaf (optional)

50–115g/2–4oz/¼ –½ cup clarified butter (see Cook's tip for method), or melted unsalted (sweet) butter

salt and ground black pepper

a sprig of flat leaf parsley, to garnish

For the redcurrant sauce

30ml/2 tbsp good quality redcurrant jelly

15–30ml/1–2 tbsp port

30ml/2 tbsp redcurrants

For the Melba toast

8 thin slices white bread, crusts removed

Cook's tips

• To make clarified butter, melt ordinary butter and pour off the clear liquid on top – this is the clarified butter. Discard any sediment left behind.
• Cumberland sauce can be used as an alternative to the redcurrant sauce.
• If game livers are not available then use chicken livers, trimming off any fat or connective tissue before cooking. This makes it easier to pass them through the sieve (strainer) later.

1 Cook the onion and garlic in 25g/1oz/ 2 tbsp of the butter in a pan over gentle heat, until just turning colour.

2 Trim the duck livers. Add to the pan with the herbs and cook together for about 3 minutes, or until the livers have browned on the outside but are still pink in the centre. Allow to cool.

3 Dice the remaining butter, then process the liver mixture in a food processor, gradually working in the cubes of butter by dropping them down the chute on to the moving blades, to make a smooth purée.

4 Add the brandy, then check the seasoning and transfer to a 450–600ml/ ½–1 pint/scant 2 cups dish. Lay a bay leaf on top if you wish, then seal the pâté with clarified or unsalted butter. Cool, and then chill in the refrigerator until required.

5 To make the redcurrant sauce, put the redcurrant jelly, port and redcurrants into a small pan and bring gently to boiling point. Simmer to make a rich consistency. Leave to cool.

6 To make the Melba toast, toast the bread on both sides, then slice through the middle of each slice to make 16 very thin slices.

7 Place the untoasted side up on a grill (broiler) rack and grill until golden brown, making sure it doesn't catch and burn. (The toast can be stored in an airtight container for a few days, then warmed through to crisp up again just before serving.)

8 Serve the chilled pâté garnished with parsley and accompanied by Melba toast and the redcurrant sauce.

Energy 794Kcal/3312kJ; Protein 101.3g; Carbohydrate 11.3g, of which sugars 9.9g; Fat 36.8g, of which saturates 19g; Cholesterol 2213mg; Calcium 73mg; Fibre 1.3g; Sodium 608mg

Scottish mallard pâté

Mallard ducks are shot during the game season, which in Scotland is during the winter months. This recipe needs two days to prepare, as the birds need to be briefly cooked and allowed to rest overnight before making the rest of the pâté.

Serves 4

2 young mallards

a little groundnut (peanut) oil

185g/6½oz streaky (fatty) bacon

300g/11oz wild duck livers

10ml/2 tsp salt

ground black pepper

pinch each of grated nutmeg, ground ginger and ground cloves

275ml/9fl oz/generous 1 cup double (heavy) cream

4 egg yolks

37.5ml/2½ tbsp brandy

50g/2oz/scant ⅓ cup sultanas (golden raisins)

1 Preheat the oven to 240°C/475°F/Gas 9. Remove the legs from the ducks. Season the birds and sprinkle with oil. Roast in the preheated oven for 15 minutes then remove from the oven and leave to rest, overnight if possible.

2 The next day, preheat the oven to 190°C/375°F/Gas 5. Put the bacon, livers, salt, pepper and spices into a blender and purée to a smooth cream.

3 Add the cream, egg yolks and brandy, and purée for a further 30 seconds. Push the mixture through a sieve into a mixing bowl and add the sultanas.

4 Remove the breasts from the ducks and skin them. Dice the meat finely then mix into the liver mixture.

5 Put the mixture in a terrine, cover with foil and cook in the oven in a roasting pan of hot water for 40–50 minutes. The centre should be slightly wobbly. Cool then chill for at least 4 hours. Serve with toast.

Energy 771kcal/3203kJ; Protein 48.5g; Carbohydrate 9.8g, of which sugars 9.8g; Fat 59.3g, of which saturates 28.4g; Cholesterol 636mg; Calcium 81mg; Fibre 0.3g; Sodium 1782mg

Strawberry and smoked Scottish venison salad

The combination of strawberries, balsamic vinegar and smoked venison creates a perfect trio of flavours. The tang of the vinegar sets off the sweetness of the strawberries, which must be ripe, and adds a fruity contrast to the rich, dry, smoky venison.

Serves 4

12 ripe Scottish strawberries

2.5ml/½ tsp caster (superfine) sugar

5ml/1 tsp balsamic vinegar

8 thin slices of smoked venison

mixed salad leaves

For the dressing

10ml/2 tsp olive oil

5ml/1 tsp balsamic vinegar

splash of strawberry wine (optional)

salt and ground black pepper

1 Slice the strawberries vertically into three or four pieces then place in a bowl with the sugar and balsamic vinegar. Leave for 30 minutes.

Cook's tips
• Suitable salad leaves include lollo rosso for colour, rocket (arugula) and lamb's lettuce (corn salad) for a peppery flavour and colour, and Little Gem (Bibb) for crunch.
• The sugar brings out the moisture in the strawberries, which combines with the balsamic vinegar to create a lovely shiny coat. Do not leave them to stand for too long as they can become tired looking, 30 minutes is about right.

2 Meanwhile, make the dressing by placing the olive oil and balsamic vinegar in a small bowl and whisking them together with the wine, if you are using it. Add salt and ground black pepper to taste.

3 Cut the smoked venison into little strips. Mix the salad leaves together then toss with the dressing. Distribute the salad leaves among four plates, sprinkle with the strawberries and venison and serve immediately.

Energy 116kcal/486kJ; Protein 11.6g; Carbohydrate 3.1g, of which sugars 3.1g; Fat 6.8g, of which saturates 1.2g; Cholesterol 25mg; Calcium 16mg; Fibre 0.6g; Sodium 31mg

Leek and bacon tart

This versatile tart soon becomes a favourite. While it makes a deliciously savoury appetizer, it is equally suitable served in more generous proportions with a mixed leaf salad as a light main course for lunch or supper.

2 Preheat the oven to 200°C/400°F/ Gas 6. Roll out the pastry thinly and use to line 6–8 tartlet cases or a 28cm/11in tart dish. Remove any air pockets and prick the base with a fork. Line the pastry loosely with baking parchment, weigh down with baking beans and bake the pastry shell blind for 15–20 minutes, or until golden.

3 To make the filling, cook the bacon in a hot pan until crisp. Add the leeks and continue to cook for 3–4 minutes until just softening. Remove from the heat. In a bowl, beat the eggs, cream cheese, mustard, cayenne pepper and seasoning together, then add the leeks and bacon.

Makes 6–8 individual tartlets

275g/10oz/2½ cups plain
(all–purpose) flour

pinch of salt

175g/6oz/¾ cup butter

2 egg yolks

about 45ml/3 tbsp very cold water

lettuce leaves and tomato,
to garnish

For the filling

225g/8oz streaky (fatty) bacon, diced

4 leeks, sliced

6 eggs

115g/4oz/½ cup cream cheese

15ml/1 tbsp mild mustard

pinch of cayenne pepper

salt and ground black pepper

1 Sieve the flour and salt into a bowl, and rub in the butter until it resembles fine breadcrumbs. Add the egg yolks and just enough water to combine the dough. Alternatively, you can use a food processor. Wrap the dough in clear film (plastic wrap) and place in the refrigerator for 30 minutes.

4 Remove the paper and baking beans from the tartlet or tart case, pour in the filling and bake for 35–40 minutes.

5 To serve, plate the tartlets on to individual serving plates or cut the tart into narrow wedges and serve warm.

Energy 487Kcal/2026kJ; Protein 15.4g; Carbohydrate 28.2g, of which sugars 1.6g; Fat 35.7g, of which saturates 19.1g; Cholesterol 265mg; Calcium 107mg; Fibre 2.1g; Sodium 681mg

Bacon salad with Irish cheese dressing

This recipe combines complementary products: really good quality dry-cured bacon together with one of Ireland's finest farmhouse cheeses, Cooleeney Camembert, from County Tipperary – an area also known for its apple production.

Serves 4

30ml/2 tbsp olive oil

50g/2oz diced streaky (fatty) bacon rashers (strips), preferably dry-cured, diced

1 eating apple, cored and chopped

2 small heads of cos or romaine lettuce

squeeze of lemon juice

salt and ground black pepper

warm soda bread, to serve

For the dressing

150ml/¼ pint/⅔ cup sour cream

15ml/1 tbsp cider

50g/2oz Cooleeney, or other Camembert-style cheese, chopped

a dash of cider vinegar

◄ 3 To make the dressing, heat the sour cream, cider, cheese and vinegar together in a small pan over a low heat until smooth and creamy. Dress the lettuce with some of the remaining oil and the lemon juice and season to taste, then divide among four plates. Place the warm apple and bacon on top, then drizzle over the dressing.

1 Heat 15ml/1 tbsp of the olive oil in a large frying pan and add the diced streaky bacon. Cook over a medium heat until crisp and golden. Add the chopped apple and cook gently for 1–2 minutes until golden brown and softened.

2 Tear the cos or romaine lettuce carefully into bitesize pieces.

Energy 219Kcal/905kJ; Protein 6.7g; Carbohydrate 4g, of which sugars 4g; Fat 19.3g, of which saturates 9g; Cholesterol 41mg; Calcium 138mg; Fibre 0.6g; Sodium 300mg

Angels on horseback

This recipe dates back to the 19th century, when oysters were plentiful and cheap. It became fashionable in England to serve a small, strongly flavoured dish at the end of a meal, mainly to revive the palates of the gentlemen after dessert and before the arrival of the port. Nowadays, this little dish makes a delicious appetizer.

Serves 4

16 oysters, removed from their shells

fresh lemon juice

8 rindless rashers (strips) of streaky (fatty) bacon

8 small slices of bread

butter, for spreading

paprika (optional)

1 Preheat the oven to 200°C/400°F/ Gas 6. Sprinkle the oysters with a little lemon juice.

2 Lay the bacon rashers on a board, slide the back of a knife along each one to stretch it and then cut it in half crosswise. Wrap a piece of bacon around each oyster and secure with a wooden cocktail stick (toothpick). Arrange them on a baking sheet.

3 Put the oysters and bacon into the hot oven for 8–10 minutes until the bacon is just cooked through.

4 Meanwhile, toast the bread. When the bacon is cooked, butter the hot toast and serve the bacon-wrapped oysters on top. Sprinkle with a little paprika, if using.

Devils on horseback

This is another popular English savoury, designed to be served at the end of a lavish dinner, that makes a good appetizer. The prunes are sometimes filled with paté, olives, almonds or nuggets of cured meat. They may be served on crisp, fried bread instead of buttered toast.

Serves 4

16 stoned prunes

fruit chutney, such as mango

8 rindless rashers (strips) of lean streaky bacon

8 small slices of bread

butter for spreading

1 Preheat the oven to 200°C/400°F/ Gas 6. Ease open the prunes and spoon a small amount of fruit chutney into each cavity.

2 Lay the bacon rashers on a board, slide the back of a knife along each one to stretch it and then cut in half crosswise. Wrap a piece of bacon around each prune and lay them close together (if they touch each other, they are less likely to unroll during cooking) on a baking sheet.

3 Put into the hot oven for 8–10 minutes until the bacon is cooked through.

4 Meanwhile, toast the bread. Butter the hot toast and serve the bacon-wrapped prunes on top.

Energy 326kcal/1365kJ; Protein 20.3g; Carbohydrate 26.4g, of which sugars 1.4g; Fat 16.2g, of which saturates 6.9g; Cholesterol 79mg; Calcium 147mg; Fibre 0.8g; Sodium 1483mg

Energy 309kcal/1303kJ; Protein 14.7g; Carbohydrate 41.7g, of which sugars 18.3g; Fat 10.4g, of which saturates 3.5g; Cholesterol 30mg; Calcium 75mg; Fibre 3.6g; Sodium 1132mg

Glamorgan sausages

When is a sausage not a sausage? When it is a Glamorgan sausage! These meat-free concoctions were made at least as far back as the 1850s. George Borrow recorded his appreciation of them during his travels in Wales, when *selsig morgannwg* were served for breakfast. They are delicious served with a crisp salad and a fruit-based sauce or chutney.

Makes 8

150g/5½oz/3 cups fresh breadcrumbs, plus extra for coating

100g/3½oz/1 cup mature (sharp) Caerphilly cheese, grated

1 small leek, washed and thinly sliced

15–30ml/1–2 tbsp chopped fresh herbs, such as parsley, thyme and a little sage

5ml/1 tsp mustard powder

2 eggs

milk to mix, if necessary

plain (all-purpose) flour, for coating

oil, for deep-frying

salt and ground black pepper

1 In a large mixing bowl, stir together the breadcrumbs, cheese, leek, herbs, mustard and seasoning. Separate 1 egg and lightly beat the yolk with the whole egg (reserving the white). Stir the beaten eggs into the breadcrumb mixture. You need to add sufficient milk to make a mixture that can then be gathered together into a sticky (although not wet) ball.

2 Using your hands, divide the mixture into eight and shape into sausages of equal size. Cover and refrigerate for about 1 hour, or until needed.

Cook's tip They won't be quite as crispy, but you can fry the sausages in shallow oil in a frying pan, turning them occasionally, until they are golden brown on all sides.

3 Lightly whisk the reserved egg white. Coat each sausage in flour, egg white and then in fresh breadcrumbs.

4 Heat some oil in a deep fat fryer or large pan to 180°C/350°F. Lower the sausages into the oil and cook for 5 minutes until crisp and golden brown. Lift out, drain on kitchen paper and serve immediately.

Energy 202kcal/844kJ; Protein 7.6g; Carbohydrate 17.6g, of which sugars 1g; Fat 11.5g, of which saturates 3.8g; Cholesterol 60mg; Calcium 134mg; Fibre 1g; Sodium 251mg

Salad with warm black pudding

A traditional sausage containing pig's blood flavoured with spices, black pudding is considered a Lancashire or Midland speciality in England, but similar sausages are made all over Britain. Fried rapidly so that the outside is crisp, and the inside still moist, slices of black pudding are delicious in salads.

Serves 4

250g/9oz black pudding (blood sausage)

45ml/3 tbsp olive oil

1 small crusty loaf, plain or flavoured with herbs, cut into small chunks

1 romaine lettuce, torn into bite size pieces

250g/9oz cherry tomatoes, halved

For the dressing

juice of 1 lemon

90ml/6 tbsp olive oil

5ml/1 tsp English (hot) mustard

15ml/1 tbsp clear honey

30ml/2 tbsp chopped fresh herbs, such as chives and parsley

salt and ground black pepper

1 Slice the black pudding with a sharp knife, then dry-fry the slices on both sides over a high heat in a non-stick frying pan for 5–10 minutes, until crisp.

2 Remove the black pudding from the pan using a slotted spoon and drain the slices on kitchen paper. Keep warm.

3 Mix together the ingredients for the salad dressing and season to taste with salt and pepper.

4 Add the olive oil to the juices in the frying pan and cook the bread cubes in two batches, turning often, until golden on all sides. Drain the croûtons on kitchen paper.

5 Mix together the croûtons, black pudding, lettuce and cherry tomatoes in a large bowl. Pour the dressing over the salad, mix well and serve at once.

Variation Try this salad with pieces of bacon, fried until crispy, or chunks of grilled, herby sausages in place of the black pudding.

Energy 683kcal/2858kJ; Protein 16.4g; Carbohydrate 66.5g, of which sugars 9.5g; Fat 41g, of which saturates 9g; Cholesterol 43mg; Calcium 234mg; Fibre 3.5g; Sodium 1156mg

Lamb's kidneys with mustard sauce

This piquant recipe is simple and flexible, so the exact amounts of any one ingredient are unimportant. It makes a tasty first course, served with crusty bread or thin toast, but would be equally suitable as a supper dish for two, in which case plain rice makes a good accompaniment, followed by a dressed green salad.

Serves 4

4–6 lamb's kidneys

butter, for frying

Dijon mustard or other mild mustard, to taste

250ml/8fl oz/1 cup white wine

5ml/1 tsp chopped fresh mixed herbs, such as rosemary, thyme, parsley and chives

1 small garlic clove, crushed

about 30ml/2 tbsp single (light) cream

salt and ground black pepper

fresh parsley, to garnish

1 Skin the kidneys and slice them horizontally. Remove the cores with scissors, and then wash them thoroughly in plenty of cold water. Drain and dry off with kitchen paper.

2 Heat a little butter in a heavy frying pan and gently cook the kidneys in it until cooked as you like them, but be careful not to overcook. Remove the kidneys from the pan and keep warm. Add a spoonful of mustard to the pan with the wine, herbs and garlic. Simmer gently to reduce the sauce by about half.

3 Add enough cream to the pan to make a smooth sauce.

4 Return the kidneys to their sauce and reheat gently, without cooking any further, or the kidneys will be tough. Serve garnished with parsley, and with rice or a green salad.

Cook's tip Look for kidneys that are firm, with a rich, even colour. Avoid those with dry spots or a dull surface.

Energy 138Kcal/578kJ; Protein 15.6g; Carbohydrate 0.6g, of which sugars 0.6g; Fat 3.8g, of which saturates 1.7g; Cholesterol 288mg; Calcium 20mg; Fibre 0g; Sodium 140mg

Fish and shellfish

Britain has always enjoyed wonderful fish and shellfish from its extensive coastline, lakes and rivers. Before the days of refrigeration and fast transportation, most fresh fish was eaten locally, leading to a large number of regional specialities and distinctive recipes. Cooking methods range from simple pan-frying, steaming and baking to hearty casseroles, pies and fishcakes.

Poached salmon with hollandaise sauce

Though it was once plentiful, wild salmon is now a rare and expensive treat. These days farmed salmon is readily available and is an economical choice. A whole poached fish makes an elegant party dish, and served cold it is perfect for a summer buffet.

Serves 8–10

300ml/½ pint/1¼ cups dry (hard) cider or white wine

1 large carrot, roughly chopped

2 medium onions, roughly chopped

2 celery sticks, roughly chopped

2 bay leaves

a few black peppercorns

sprig of parsley

sprig of thyme

2–2.5kg/4½–5½lb whole salmon, gutted, washed and dried

For the hollandaise sauce

175g/6oz/¾ cup unsalted butter

5ml/1 tsp sugar

3 egg yolks

10ml/2 tsp cider vinegar or white wine vinegar

10ml/2 tsp lemon juice

salt and ground white pepper

1 Put all the ingredients except the salmon into a large pan and add 1 litre/1¾ pints/4 cups water. Bring to the boil and simmer gently for 30–40 minutes. Strain and leave to cool.

2 About 30 minutes before serving, pour the cooled stock into a fish kettle. Lay the salmon on the rack and lower it into the liquid.

3 Slowly heat the kettle until the stock almost comes to the boil (with small bubbles forming and rising to the surface), cover and simmer very gently for 20–25 minutes until the fish is just cooked through – test the thickest part with a knife near the backbone.

4 Meanwhile, to make the hollandaise sauce, heat the butter with the sugar (on the stove or in the microwave) until the butter has melted and the mixture is hot but not sizzling – do not allow it to brown.

5 Put the egg yolks, vinegar, lemon juice and seasonings into a processor or blender and blend on high speed for about 15 seconds, or until the mixture is creamy.

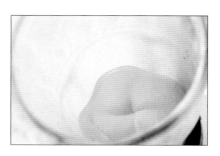

6 Keep the processor or blender on high speed and add the hot butter mixture in a slow stream until the sauce is thick, smooth and creamy.

7 Lift the salmon out of its cooking liquid. Remove the skin carefully, so the flesh remains intact, and lift the salmon on to a warmed serving plate. Garnish with watercress and serve with the warm hollandaise.

Variation To cook salmon that is to be served cold, in step 3 slowly heat until the stock just comes to the boil, let it bubble two or three times then cover, remove from the heat and leave to cool completely (this will take up to 12 hours). When cold, lift out the fish and slide it on to a serving plate. Strip off the fins and peel away the skin, then garnish with wafer-thin cucumber slices arranged like scales, salad leaves, baby tomatoes or black olives. Serve the salmon with mayonnaise.

Energy 450kcal/1868kJ; Protein 34.6g; Carbohydrate 0.5g, of which sugars 0.5g; Fat 34.4g, of which saturates 12.8g; Cholesterol 182mg; Calcium 44mg; Fibre 0g; Sodium 183mg

Salmon with herb butter

A delicious fish with a delicate flavour, salmon needs to be served simply. Here, fresh dill and lemon are combined to make a slightly piquant butter.

2 Spoon the butter on to a piece of baking parchment and roll up, smoothing with your hands into a sausage shape. Twist the ends tightly, wrap in clear film (plastic wrap) and put in the freezer for 20 minutes, until firm.

3 Meanwhile, preheat the oven to 190°C/375°F/Gas 5. Cut out four squares of foil to encase the salmon steaks and grease with butter. Place a salmon steak into the centre of each.

4 Remove the herb butter from the freezer and slice into eight rounds. Place two rounds on top of each salmon steak with a halved lemon slice in the centre and a sprig of dill on top. Lift up the edges of the foil and crinkle them together until well sealed. Place on a baking tray.

5 Bake for 20 minutes. Place the unopened parcels on warmed plates. Open the parcels and slide the contents on to the plates with the juices.

Serves 4

50g/2oz/¼ cup butter, softened, plus extra for greasing

finely grated rind of 1 lemon

15ml/1 tbsp lemon juice

15ml/1 tbsp chopped fresh dill

4 salmon steaks

2 lemon slices, halved

4 sprigs of fresh dill

salt and ground black pepper

1 Place the butter, lemon rind, lemon juice and chopped fresh dill in a small bowl and mix together with a fork until blended. Season to taste with salt and ground black pepper.

Energy 409kcal/1700kJ; Protein 35.6g; Carbohydrate 0.2g, of which sugars 0.2g; Fat 29.6g, of which saturates 9.8g; Cholesterol 114mg; Calcium 47mg; Fibre 0.2g; Sodium 156mg

Salmon fishcakes

The secret of a good fishcake is to make it with freshly prepared fish and potatoes, homemade breadcrumbs and plenty of interesting seasoning.

Serves 4

450g/1lb cooked salmon fillet

450g/1lb freshly cooked potatoes, mashed

25g/1oz/2 tbsp butter, melted

10ml/2 tsp wholegrain mustard

15ml/1 tbsp each chopped fresh dill and chopped fresh flat leaf parsley

grated rind and juice of ½ lemon

15g/½oz/1 tbsp plain (all-purpose) flour

1 egg, lightly beaten

150g/5oz/generous 1 cup dried breadcrumbs

60ml/4 tbsp sunflower oil

salt and ground white pepper

rocket (arugula) leaves and fresh chives, to garnish

lemon wedges, to serve

1 Flake the cooked salmon, watching carefully for and discarding any skin and bones. Place the flaked salmon in a bowl with the mashed potato, melted butter and wholegrain mustard. Mix well then stir in the chopped fresh dill and parsley, lemon rind and juice. Season to taste.

2 Divide the mixture into eight portions and shape each into a ball, then flatten into a thick disc. Dip the fish cakes first in flour, then in egg and finally in breadcrumbs, making sure they are evenly coated.

3 Heat the oil in a frying pan until very hot. Fry the fishcakes in batches until golden brown and crisp all over. As each batch is ready, drain on kitchen paper and keep hot.

4 Warm some plates and then place two fishcakes on to each warmed plate, one slightly on top of the other. Garnish with rocket leaves and chives, and serve with lemon wedges.

Cook's tip
• Almost any fresh white or hot-smoked fish is suitable; smoked cod and haddock are particularly good.
• A mixture of smoked and unsmoked fish also works well.

Energy 586kcal/2453kJ; Protein 29.8g; Carbohydrate 49.9g, of which sugars 3.2g; Fat 31g, of which saturates 7.2g; Cholesterol 117mg; Calcium 79mg; Fibre 1.3g; Sodium 266mg

Pan-cooked salmon with Welsh sorrel sauce

Sorrel leaves add a lovely lemony flavour to the sauce of this salmon dish. In its absence (sorrel is at its best in spring and early summer) try using tender young spinach leaves or, better still, a tablespoon or two of laverbread with a squeeze of lemon juice added.

2 Turn the fish over and continue cooking the second side for about 3 minutes until it is almost cooked through. Lift out and keep warm (the salmon will finish cooking while you make the sauce).

3 Add the sorrel to the hot pan and cook, stirring, until wilted and soft. If the sorrel gives off lots of liquid, bubble it gently until reduced to a tablespoonful or two.

4 Stir in the double cream, bring just to the boil and bubble gently for no more than 1 minute. Add seasoning to taste and serve with the salmon.

Serves 4

15g/½oz/1 tbsp butter

10ml/2 tsp olive oil

4 pieces salmon fillet, each weighing about 175g/6oz

large handful of fresh sorrel leaves (about 100g/3½oz), chopped

150ml/¼ pint/⅔ cup double (heavy) cream

salt and ground black pepper

1 Heat the butter and oil in a pan, add the salmon and cook over medium heat for 3–5 minutes until golden brown.

Variation This recipe also works well with other fish, such as sewin (sea trout), trout and sea bass.

Energy 549kcal/2274kJ; Protein 36.7g; Carbohydrate 1.1g, of which sugars 1g; Fat 44.2g, of which saturates 18.1g; Cholesterol 147mg; Calcium 98mg; Fibre 0.5g; Sodium 145mg

Trout with almonds

The shallow streams and rivers of southern England and many other regions of Britain once supplied an abundance of wild trout, now the freshwater trout available will most likely be farmed. Their earthy flavour goes particularly well with buttery juices and toasted almonds.

Serves 4

4 whole trout, cleaned

45–60ml/3–4 tbsp seasoned flour,

75g/3oz/6 tbsp butter

15ml/1 tbsp olive oil

50g/2oz/½ cup flaked (sliced) almonds

juice of ½ lemon

lemon wedges, to serve

1 Wash the fish, dry with kitchen paper and coat them with seasoned flour, shaking off any excess.

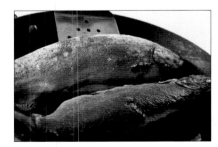

2 Heat half the butter with the oil in a large frying pan. When the mixture begins to foam, add one or two fish.

3 Cook over medium heat for 3–5 minutes on each side or until golden brown and cooked through. Lift out, drain on kitchen paper and keep warm.

4 Cook the remaining fish, then wipe the pan out with kitchen paper. Add the remaining butter and when foaming add the almonds. Cook gently, stirring frequently, until the almonds are golden brown. Remove from the heat and add the lemon juice.

5 Sprinkle the almonds and pan juices over the trout and serve immediately with lemon wedges for squeezing over.

Cook's tip When buying the trout, choose a size that will fit inside your frying pan.

Variation The trout can be grilled (broiled) if preferred. Omit the flour coating. Melt half the butter and brush over both sides of the fish. Put the fish under a medium-hot grill (broiler) and cook for 5–7 minutes on each side until golden brown and cooked all the way through. Cook the almonds in butter as in step 4.

Energy 475kcal/1978kJ; Protein 39.2g; Carbohydrate 7.6g, of which sugars 0.8g; Fat 32.2g, of which saturates 12.4g; Cholesterol 187mg; Calcium 101mg; Fibre 1.2g; Sodium 249mg

Mackerel with onions

Perhaps more than most fish, mackerel is best cooked within hours of being caught. When buying, look for really fresh fish with bright eyes and bluish-green tinges on the skin. In this recipe the sweetness of the onions and the sharpness of the apple and vinegar complement the rich, oily flesh of the mackerel.

Serves 2

2 mackerel, cleaned

15ml/1 tbsp oil

1 large onion, very thinly sliced

1 garlic clove, finely chopped or crushed

1 bay leaf

150ml/¼ pint/⅔ cup medium apple juice or cider

30ml/2 tbsp wine vinegar

15ml/1 tbsp finely chopped fresh parsley or coriander (cilantro)

salt and ground black pepper

1 Make two or three shallow slashes down each side of each mackerel.

2 Heat the oil in a frying pan, add the mackerel and cook over medium heat for about 5–8 minutes on each side or until just cooked through. Lift out and keep warm.

3 Add the onion, garlic and bay leaf to the pan, cover and cook gently for 10–15 minutes, stirring occasionally, until soft and beginning to brown. Remove the lid, increase the heat and continue cooking until the onions are golden brown.

4 Add the apple juice and vinegar. Boil until the mixture is well reduced, thick and syrupy. Remove from the heat, stir in the parsley and seasoning to taste. Remove the bay leaf. Serve the onions with the mackerel.

Cook's tip To serve this dish cold, flake the cooked fish, discarding skin and bones, cover with the onion mixture and leave to cool.

Energy 451kcal/1876kJ; Protein 30.5g; Carbohydrate 15.9g, of which sugars 13.5g; Fat 29.9g, of which saturates 5.6g; Cholesterol 80mg; Calcium 87mg; Fibre 2.4g; Sodium 98mg

Welsh herrings with mustard

The west coast of Wales was famous for its herring catches, when the fish was sold door-to-door and the remainder salted and cured. Whole fish would be fried or grilled for serving with jacket potatoes, while fillets were spread with mustard, rolled and cooked with potato, onion and apple. The latter was the inspiration for this dish.

Serves 2

4–6 herrings, filleted

20–30ml/4–6 tsp wholegrain mustard

4–6 small young sage leaves

1 eating apple

wholemeal (whole wheat) bread, to serve

1 Preheat the oven to 180°C/350°F/ Gas 4. Rinse the herrings and dry inside and out with kitchen paper.

2 Open the fish and lay them, skin side down, on a board or the surface. Spread with 5ml/1 tsp mustard and tear 1 sage leaf over each one.

3 Quarter and core the apple and cut into thin wedges. Lay the wedges lengthways along one side of each fish, overlapping them as you go. Fold the other half of the fish over the apple.

4 Oil a baking tray (or line it with baking parchment) and carefully lift the filled herrings on to it.

5 Cook the herrings in the hot oven for about 20 minutes, until they are cooked through and just beginning to brown on the edges. Serve, freshly cooked, with wholemeal bread.

Energy 209kcal/870kJ; Protein 18.5g; Carbohydrate 3.5g, of which sugars 3.5g; Fat 13.5g, of which saturates 3.3g; Cholesterol 50mg; Calcium 102mg; Fibre 1.6g; Sodium 128mg

Herrings in oatmeal

Herrings are very popular in Scotland, and with their wonderfully strong flavour they are ideal for simple recipes. Traditional to the Northern Isles and the east coast, these herrings coated in oats make for hearty meals, and are also easy to prepare and cook.

Serves 4

175ml/6fl oz/¾ cup thick mayonnaise

15ml/1 tbsp Dijon mustard

7.5ml/1½ tsp tarragon vinegar

4 herrings, approximately 225g/8oz each

juice of 1 lemon

115g/4oz/generous 1 cup medium rolled oats

salt and ground black pepper

1 Place the mayonnaise in a small mixing bowl and add the mustard and vinegar. Mix thoroughly and then chill for a few minutes.

2 Place one fish at a time on a chopping board, cut side down, and open out. Press gently along the backbone with your thumbs. Turn the fish over and carefully lift away the backbone.

3 Squeeze lemon juice over both sides of the fish, then season with salt and ground black pepper. Fold the fish in half, skin side outwards.

4 Preheat the grill (broiler) to medium hot. Place the rolled oats on a plate then coat each herring evenly in the oats, pressing it in gently.

5 Place the herrings on a grill rack and grill (broil) the fish for 3–4 minutes on each side, until the skin is golden brown and crisp and the flesh flakes easily when the fish is cut into. Serve immediately on warmed plates with the mustard sauce handed round in a separate dish or bowl.

Energy 755kcal/3143kJ; Protein 36.7g; Carbohydrate 32.6g, of which sugars 0.6g; Fat 54g, of which saturates 9.3g; Cholesterol 98mg; Calcium 149mg; Fibre 3g; Sodium 459mg

Mackerel with Scottish gooseberry relish

Off Scotland's west coast it is still possible to fish for mackerel yourself, quite often at the weekends part-time fishermen can be found selling their catch at the harbours. The cool Northern climate suits gooseberries well, and they give a wonderful tartness to this dish.

Serves 4

4 whole mackerel

60ml/4 tbsp olive oil

For the sauce

250g/9oz gooseberries

25g/1oz/2 tbsp soft light brown sugar

5ml/1 tsp wholegrain mustard

salt and ground black pepper

1 For the sauce, wash and trim the gooseberries and then roughly chop them, so there are some pieces larger than others.

2 Cook the gooseberries in a little water with the sugar in a small pan. A thick and chunky purée will form. Add the mustard and season to taste with salt and ground black pepper.

Cook's tips
• Turn the grill (broiler) on well in advance as the fish need a fierce heat to cook quickly. If you like the fish but hate the smell, use a barbecue.
• The foil lining in the grill pan is to catch the smelly drips. Simply roll it up and throw it away afterwards, leaving a nice clean grill (broiling) pan.

3 Preheat the grill (broiler) to high and line the grill pan with foil. Using a sharp knife, slash the fish two or three times down each side then season and brush with the olive oil.

4 Place the fish in the grill pan and grill (broil) for about 4 minutes on each side until cooked. You may need to cook them for a few minutes longer if they are particularly large. The slashes will open up to speed cooking and the skin should be lightly browned. To check that they are cooked properly, use a small sharp knife to pierce the skin and check for uncooked flesh.

5 Place the mackerel on warmed plates and spread generous dollops of the gooseberry relish over them. Pass the remaining sauce around at the table.

Energy 576kcal/2390kJ; Protein 38.1g; Carbohydrate 8.4g, of which sugars 8.4g; Fat 43.5g, of which saturates 8.2g; Cholesterol 108mg; Calcium 43mg; Fibre 1.5g; Sodium 128mg

Pan-fried Dover sole

For many, Dover sole is one of the finest of the flat fish, often called "the Englishman's fish of choice" because in the days when transport was slow its flavour actually improved during the journey from the Kent coast. Use herbs such as dill, parsley or tarragon.

2 Add one or two fish to the pan and cook over a medium heat for 3–5 minutes on each side until golden brown and cooked through. Lift them out and keep them warm while you cook the remaining fish.

3 Add the remaining oil and the butter to the hot pan and heat until the butter has melted. Stir in the lemon juice and chopped herbs. Drizzle the pan juices over the fish and serve immediately, garnished with watercress sprigs.

Cook's tips
• Leaving the white skin on the fish helps to keep its shape during cooking; it is also full of flavour and good to eat, particularly the crisp edges.
• To grill (broil) the fish, omit the flour coating and brush both sides with melted butter. Put the sole under a medium-hot grill (broiler) and cook for 5–7 minutes on each side until golden brown and cooked through.

Serves 4

4 small Dover sole, dark skin and fins removed

30–45ml/2–3 tbsp flour seasoned with salt and pepper

45ml/3 tbsp olive oil

25g/1oz/2 tbsp butter

juice of 1 lemon

15ml/1 tbsp chopped fresh herbs

watercress sprigs, to garnish

1 Spread the seasoned flour on a plate, and coat each fish, shaking off any excess. Heat a large non-stick frying pan and add the oil.

Energy 177kcal/739kJ; Protein 18.6g; Carbohydrate 3g, of which sugars 0.2g; Fat 10.2g, of which saturates 1.2g; Cholesterol 50mg; Calcium 42mg; Fibre 0.3g; Sodium 101mg

Skate with black butter

Skate wings were especially popular in the early 20th century and in southern England were often sold in fish and chip shops. Black butter, a traditional sauce, is in fact a deep nutty brown colour. Serve this classic dish simply with boiled, small new potatoes.

Serves 4

4 pieces of skate wing, total weight about 1kg/2¼lb

1 small onion

1 bay leaf

50g/2oz/4 tbsp butter

30ml/2 tbsp cider vinegar or white wine vinegar

10–15ml/2–3 tsp capers, rinsed and drained

15ml/1 tbsp chopped fresh parsley

salt

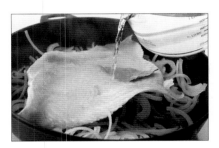

1 Wash and dry the skate wings and put them into a shallow pan large enough to accommodate the fish in a single layer. Thinly slice the onion and add to the pan with the bay leaf. Season with a little salt and pour over boiling water (from the kettle) to cover.

2 Heat until bubbles rise to the surface then lower the heat and simmer gently for 10–15 minutes until the flesh parts easily from the bones.

3 Using a slotted fish slice, lift the skate wings out of the pan on to a warmed serving plate. Carefully peel off and discard any skin. Cover the fish and keep it warm while you cook the sauce.

4 Melt the butter in a small pan and cook gently until it turns golden brown. Drizzle it over the cooked fish.

5 Add the vinegar to the hot pan and allow it to bubble gently until slightly reduced. Drizzle this over the fish.

6 Scatter the capers and parsley over the top and serve immediately.

Cook's tip If the skate is not already skinned by your fishmonger, you will find it much easier to remove the skin after cooking.

Energy 246kcal/1029kJ; Protein 35.5g; Carbohydrate 0.5g, of which sugars 0.4g; Fat 11.2g, of which saturates 6.5g; Cholesterol 27mg; Calcium 125mg; Fibre 0.8g; Sodium 356mg

Fish and chips

Here is one of Britain's national dishes. Use white fish of your choice – cod, haddock, hake, huss, plaice, skate or whiting – and cook in batches so that each piece of fish and all the chips are perfectly crisp. Salt and vinegar are the traditional accompaniments.

Serves 4

115g/4oz/1 cup self-raising (self-rising) flour

150ml/¼ pint/⅔ cup water

675g/1½lb potatoes

oil, for deep frying

675g/1½lb skinned cod fillet, cut into four pieces

salt and pepper

lemon wedges, to serve

1 Stir the flour and salt together in a bowl, then make a well in the centre. Gradually whisk in the water to make a smooth batter. Leave for 30 minutes.

2 Using a sharp knife, cut the potatoes into strips about 1cm/½in wide and 5cm/2in long. Put the potatoes in a colander and rinse them with cold water, then drain and dry well.

3 Heat the oil in a deep-fat fryer or large heavy pan to 150°C/300°F. Using a wire basket, lower the potatoes in batches into the hot oil and cook for 5–6 minutes, shaking the basket occasionally until the chips are soft but not browned. Remove the chips from the oil and drain them thoroughly on kitchen paper.

4 Increase the heat of the oil in the fryer to 190°C/375°F. Season the pieces of fish with salt and pepper. Stir the batter, then dip the fish into it, one piece at a time, allowing the excess to drain off.

5 Working in two batches if necessary, lower the fish into the hot oil and fry for 6–8 minutes, until crisp and brown. Drain the fish on kitchen paper and keep warm.

6 Make sure the oil is hot again then add a batch of chips, cooking for 2–3 minutes, until brown and crisp. Keep hot while cooking the other batches. Sprinkle with salt and serve with the fish, accompanied by lemon wedges.

Energy 521kcal/2188kJ; Protein 36.3g; Carbohydrate 48.9g, of which sugars 2.6g; Fat 21.3g, of which saturates 2.7g; Cholesterol 78mg; Calcium 126mg; Fibre 2.6g; Sodium 223mg

Haddock in cheese sauce

A relative of cod, haddock is one of the nation's preferred white fish, though unfortunately North Sea supplies have declined considerably in recent years. Other white fish can be used in place of haddock in this flavourful dish – try hake, coley or whiting.

Serves 4

1kg/2¼lb haddock fillets

300ml/½ pint/1¼ cups milk

1 small onion, thinly sliced

2 bay leaves

a few black peppercorns

25g/1oz/2 tbsp butter

25g/1oz/2 tbsp flour

5ml/1 tsp English (hot) mustard

115g/4oz mature hard cheese such as Cheddar, grated

salt and ground black pepper

1 Put the fish in a pan large enough to hold it in a single layer. Add the milk, onion, bay leaves and peppercorns and heat slowly until small bubbles are rising to the surface.

2 Cover and simmer very gently for 5–8 minutes, until the fish is just cooked. Lift out with a slotted spoon, straining and reserving the cooking liquid. Flake the fish, removing any bones.

Variation This dish can be made with smoked haddock; use fillets that have been mildly smoked. You can also use half smoked and half unsmoked.

3 To make the sauce, melt the butter in a saucepan, stir in the flour and cook gently, stirring all the time, for about 1 minute (do not allow it to brown). Remove from the heat and gradually stir in the strained milk. Return the pan to the heat and cook, stirring, until the mixture thickens and comes to the boil. Stir in the mustard and three-quarters of the cheese and season to taste.

4 Gently stir the fish into the sauce and spoon the mixture into individual flameproof dishes. Sprinkle the remaining cheese over the top. Put under a hot grill (broiler) until bubbling and golden. Serve with crusty bread.

Cook's tip The fish can be left whole, simply spoon the sauce over them before grilling (broiling).

Energy 430kcal/1809kJ; Protein 58.2g; Carbohydrate 9.6g, of which sugars 4.5g; Fat 17.4g, of which saturates 10.6g; Cholesterol 136mg; Calcium 351mg; Fibre 0.4g; Sodium 446mg

Plaice fillets with sorrel and lemon butter

Sorrel is a wild herb that is now grown commercially. It is very good in salads and, roughly chopped, partners this slightly sweet-fleshed fish very well. Plaice – such a pretty fish with its orange spots and fern-like frills – is a delicate fish that works well with this sauce. Cook it simply like this to get the full natural flavours of the ingredients.

Serves 4

200g/7oz/scant 1 cup butter

500g/1¼lb plaice fillets, skinned and patted dry

30ml/2 tbsp chopped fresh sorrel

90ml/6 tbsp dry white wine

a little lemon juice

1 Heat half the butter in a large frying pan and, just as it is melted, place the fillets skin side down. Cook briefly, just to firm up, reduce the heat and turn the fish over. The fish will be cooked in less than 5 minutes. Try not to let the butter brown or allow the fish to colour.

2 Remove the fish fillets from the pan and keep warm between two plates. Cut the remaining butter into chunks. Add the chopped sorrel to the pan and stir. Add the wine then, as it bubbles, add the butter, swirling it in piece by piece and not allowing the sauce to boil. Stir in a little lemon juice.

3 Serve the fish with the sorrel and lemon butter spooned over, with some crunchy green beans and perhaps some new potatoes, if you like.

Variation Instead of using sorrel, you could try this recipe with fresh tarragon or thyme.

Energy 494kcal/2047kJ; Protein 25.7g; Carbohydrate 0.5g, of which sugars 0.5g; Fat 43.3g, of which saturates 26.4g; Cholesterol 170mg; Calcium 98mg; Fibre 0.3g; Sodium 501mg

Scottish quenelles of sole

Traditionally, these light fish "dumplings" were made with pike, but they are even better made with sole or other white fish. If you are feeling extravagant, serve them with a creamy shellfish sauce studded with crayfish tails or prawns. They make a great lunchtime meal or late-night supper, with bread and a crisp salad.

Serves 6

450g/1lb sole fillets, skinned and cut into large pieces

4 egg whites

600ml/1 pint/2½ cups double (heavy) cream

freshly grated nutmeg

salt and ground black pepper

chopped fresh parsley, to garnish

For the sauce

1 small shallot, finely chopped

60ml/4 tbsp dry vermouth

120ml/4fl oz/½ cup fish stock

150ml/¼ pint/⅔ cup double (heavy) cream

50g/2oz/¼ cup butter, diced

1 Check the sole for stray bones, then put the pieces in a food processor. Season. Switch the machine on and, with the motor running, add the egg whites one at a time through the feeder tube to make a smooth purée. Press the purée through a metal sieve placed over a bowl. Stand the bowl of purée in a larger bowl and surround it with plenty of crushed ice or ice cubes.

2 Whip the cream until very thick, but not stiff. Gradually fold it into the fish mixture. Season, then stir in nutmeg to taste. Cover the bowl and refrigerate for several hours.

3 To make the sauce, combine the shallot, vermouth and fish stock in a small pan. Bring to the boil and cook until reduced by half. Add the cream and boil until it has a thick consistency.

4 Strain and return to the pan. Whisk in the butter, one piece at a time, until the sauce is creamy. Season and keep hot, but do not allow to boil.

5 Bring a wide shallow pan of lightly salted water to the boil, then reduce the heat so that the water surface barely trembles. Using two tablespoons dipped in hot water, shape the fish mousse into ovals. As each quenelle is shaped, slip it into the simmering water.

6 Poach the quenelles in batches for 8–10 minutes, until just firm to the touch but still slightly creamy inside. Lift out using a slotted spoon, drain on kitchen paper and keep hot. When all the quenelles are cooked, arrange them on warmed plates. Pour the sauce around, garnish with parsley and serve.

Energy 771kcal/3180kJ; Protein 17.7g; Carbohydrate 3.3g, of which sugars 3g; Fat 75.4g, of which saturates 46.1g; Cholesterol 227mg; Calcium 89mg; Fibre 0.1g; Sodium 195mg

Stuffed white fish wrapped in bacon

Caught mainly off the east coast of Ireland, and available all year round, plentiful but rather bland fish such as whiting and lemon sole, plaice and flounder, are good for this recipe. Serve with boiled new potatoes and a green vegetable.

Serves 4

4 good-size or 8 small fish fillets, such as whiting, trimmed

4 streaky (fatty) bacon rashers (strips)

For the stuffing

50g/2oz/¼ cup butter

1 onion, finely chopped

50g/2oz/1 cup fine fresh brown breadcrumbs

5ml/1 tsp finely chopped fresh parsley

a good pinch of mixed dried herbs

sea salt and ground black pepper

1 Preheat the oven to 190°C/375°F/ Gas 5. Trim the fish fillets. If they are big, cut them in half lengthways. Remove the rind and any gristle from the streaky bacon rashers.

2 For the stuffing, melt the butter in a pan, add the onion and cook until soft but not brown. Add the breadcrumbs, parsley, herbs, salt and pepper.

3 Divide the stuffing between the fillets, roll them up and wrap a bacon rasher around each one. Secure with wooden cocktail sticks (toothpicks) and lay in a single layer in a buttered baking dish.

4 Cover with foil and bake in the oven for 15 minutes, removing the cover for the last 5 minutes. Serve with potatoes and green beans.

Energy 344Kcal/1436kJ; Protein 38.1g; Carbohydrate 12.5g, of which sugars 2.4g; Fat 15.9g, of which saturates 8.2g; Cholesterol 120mg; Calcium 44mg; Fibre 0.8g; Sodium 662mg

Poached turbot with saffron sauce

The saffron sauce complements the firm white flesh of the turbot well. Turbot is a treat by any standards and this is a rich elegant dish, most suitable for entertaining. Offer rice, or new boiled potatoes, and mangetouts or peas with the turbot.

Serves 4

pinch of saffron threads

50ml/2fl oz/¼ cup single (light) cream

1 shallot, finely chopped

175g/6oz/¾ cup cold unsalted (sweet) butter, cut into small cubes

175ml/6fl oz/¾ cup dry sherry

475ml/16fl oz/2 cups fish stock

4 medium turbot fillets, about 150–175g/5–6oz each, skinned

flat leaf parsley leaves, to garnish

1 Put the saffron threads into the single cream and allow them to infuse (steep) for 10 minutes. Cook the chopped shallot very gently in a large heavy-based frying pan with 15g/½oz/1 tbsp of the butter until it is soft.

2 Put the cooked shallot, with the dry sherry and fish stock, into a fish kettle or other large pan. Lay the turbot fillets in the pan, without overlapping them, and bring gently to the boil. Reduce the heat immediately and simmer gently for about 5 minutes, depending on the thickness of the fillets.

Cook's tip White fish such as plaice fillets can also be used in this recipe.

3 When cooked, remove the fillets from the poaching liquid with a slotted fish slice or metal spatula and lay them on a heated dish. Cover and keep warm.

4 To make the sauce: bring the poaching liquor to the boil and boil fast to reduce it to 60ml/4 tbsp.

5 Add the cream and saffron and bring back to the boil. Remove from the heat, add the butter, whisking constantly until a smooth sauce has formed.

6 Pour the sauce on to warmed serving plates, lay the turbot on top and sprinkle with parsley leaves to serve.

Energy 544Kcal/2256kJ; Protein 27.4g; Carbohydrate 1.4g, of which sugars 1.4g; Fat 42.4g, of which saturates 25.4g; Cholesterol 100mg; Calcium 97mg; Fibre 0.1g; Sodium 376mg

Monkfish kebabs

Although it was until recently seen as little more than a cheap alternative to using Dublin Bay prawns to make scampi, monkfish is now almost equally prized. This firm-fleshed fish is ideal for the barbecue, as it won't fall apart when cooked.

Serves 4

900g/2lb fresh monkfish tail, skinned

3 (bell) peppers, preferably red, green and yellow

juice of 1 lemon

60ml/4 tbsp olive oil

bay leaves, halved (optional)

salt and ground black pepper

rolls or pitta bread and lemon juice (optional), to serve

For the spicy barbecue sauce

15ml/1 tbsp olive oil

1 onion, finely chopped

1 garlic clove, finely chopped

300ml/½ pint/1¼ cups water

30ml/2 tbsp wine vinegar

30ml/2 tbsp soft brown sugar

10ml/2 tsp mild mustard

grated rind and juice of ½ lemon

pinch of dried thyme

30ml/2 tbsp Worcestershire sauce

60–75ml/4–5 tbsp tomato ketchup

30ml/2 tbsp tomato purée (paste) (optional)

1 Trim the skinned monkfish and cut it into bitesize cubes. Cut each pepper into quarters, and then seed and halve each quarter.

2 Combine the lemon juice and oil in a bowl and add seasoning. Turn the fish and pepper pieces in the mixture and leave to marinate for 20 minutes (this will add flavour and offset the natural dryness of the fish). Soak four wooden skewers in cold water for 30 minutes. This prevents them from burning during cooking.

3 To make the sauce, heat the oil in a pan and fry the onion and garlic until soft but not browned. Add all the remaining ingredients, bring to the boil and simmer for 15 minutes.

4 Preheat a very hot grill (broiler) or barbecue, and oil the grill rack. Thread pieces of fish and pepper alternately, with the occasional half bay leaf, if you like. Cook for about 10 minutes, turning and basting frequently.

5 Remove the fish and vegetables from the kebabs and serve in rolls or pitta bread, with the sauce, or simply with a squeeze of fresh lemon juice.

Energy 377Kcal/1586kJ; Protein 37.4g; Carbohydrate 24.1g, of which sugars 23.1g; Fat 15.3g, of which saturates 2.4g; Cholesterol 32mg; Calcium 54mg; Fibre 2.8g; Sodium 382mg

Crusted garlic and wild thyme monkfish

Monkfish is a lovely juicy fish; it is hard to believe that until recently it was thrown back into the sea because its firm texture was not fashionable. Now it is considered a prime fish that needs simple cooking, and can carry strong flavours such as garlic and thyme.

Serves 4

4 monkfish tails (see Cook's tips)

garlic and herb butter
(see Langoustines with Garlic Butter, but use wild thyme in place of parsley)

115g/4oz/generous 1 cup dried breadcrumbs (see Cook's tips)

salt and ground black pepper

1 Preheat the oven to 220°C/425°F/ Gas 7. Make two or three diagonal slashes down each side of the fish, working from the bone to the edge.

Cook's tips
• Buy monkfish tails weighing about 250g/9oz each. Ask your fishmonger to trim off all the skin and purple membrane surrounding the fillets but to leave the fish on the bone.
• The best breadcrumbs are made with day-old bread. Break the bread up with your fingers and then chop roughly in a food processor to make coarse breadcrumbs. Leave to dry out further overnight. The next day process the dried bread again to obtain fine dry crumbs. If you are really fussy you can then pass them through a coarse sieve to produce a very fine crumb.

2 Season the fish with salt and freshly ground black pepper. Using your fingertips, rub the garlic butter liberally all over, ensuring that you have pushed a good quantity into each of the diagonal slashes.

3 Sprinkle on the breadcrumbs, place on a baking tray and bake for 10–15 minutes. The cooked tails should be golden brown, with white slashes where the cuts have opened up to reveal the succulent flesh inside.

Energy 272kcal/1130kJ; Protein 11.4g; Carbohydrate 9.9g, of which sugars 0.5g; Fat 21.1g, of which saturates 13.1g; Cholesterol 62mg; Calcium 26mg; Fibre 0.3g; Sodium 258mg

Gratin of cod with wholegrain mustard

While the cod crisis continues in European waters, those in north-west Europe are advised not to buy Atlantic cod. However, you can now buy good-quality farmed cod, and elsewhere in the world cod or its local equivalents are still available. If you need an alternative then a thick, flaky-textured, moist white-fleshed fish is what is required.

Serves 4

4 cod steaks, approximately 175g/6oz each

200g/7oz/1¾ cups grated Cheddar cheese, such as Isle of Mull

15ml/1 tbsp wholegrain mustard

75ml/5 tbsp double (heavy) cream

salt and ground black pepper

1 Preheat the oven to 200°C/400°F/Gas 6. Check the fish for bones. Butter the base and sides of an ovenproof dish then place the fish fillets skin side down in the dish and season.

2 In a small bowl, mix the grated cheese and mustard together with enough cream to form a spreadable but thick paste. Make sure that the cheese and mustard are thoroughly blended to ensure an even taste. Season lightly with salt and ground black pepper.

3 Spread the cheese mixture thickly and evenly over each fish fillet, using it all up. Bake in the preheated oven for 20 minutes. The top will be browned and bubbling and the fish underneath flaky and tender. Serve immediately on warmed plates.

Energy 445kcal/1852kJ; Protein 46g; Carbohydrate 0.4g, of which sugars 0.4g; Fat 27.7g, of which saturates 17.3g; Cholesterol 157mg; Calcium 395mg; Fibre 0g; Sodium 474mg

Fish pie

A well-made fish pie is absolutely delicious, and is particularly good made with a mixture of fresh and smoked fish – ideal in the winter when the fishing fleets are hampered by gales and fresh fish is in short supply. Cooked shellfish, such as mussels, can be included too.

Serves 4–5

450g/1lb haddock or cod fillet

225g/8oz smoked haddock or cod

150ml/¼ pint/⅔ cup milk

150ml/¼ pint/⅔ cup water

1 slice of lemon

1 small bay leaf

a few fresh parsley stalks

450g/1lb potatoes, boiled and mashed

25g/1oz/2 tbsp butter

For the sauce

25g/1oz/2 tbsp butter

25g/1oz/¼ cup plain (all-purpose) flour

5ml/1 tsp lemon juice, or to taste

45ml/3 tbsp chopped fresh parsley

ground black pepper

1 Preheat the oven to 190°C/375°F/Gas 5. Put the fish into a pan with the milk, water, lemon, bay leaf and parsley stalks. Heat slowly until bubbles are rising to the surface, then cover and simmer gently for about 10 minutes until the fish is cooked.

2 Lift out the fish and strain and reserve 300ml/½ pint/1¼ cups of the cooking liquor. Leave the fish until cool enough to handle, then flake the flesh and discard the skin and bones. Set aside.

3 To make the sauce, melt the butter in a pan, add the flour and cook for 1–2 minutes over low heat, stirring constantly. Gradually add the reserved cooking liquor, stirring well until smooth. Simmer gently for 1–2 minutes, then remove from the heat and stir in the fish, parsley and lemon juice. Season to taste with black pepper.

4 Turn into a buttered 1.75 litre/3 pint/7½ cup ovenproof dish, top with the potato and dot with butter. Cook for about 20 minutes, until heated through and golden brown on top.

Energy 458kcal/1921kJ; Protein 29.4g; Carbohydrate 32.8g, of which sugars 5.8g; Fat 25g, of which saturates 3.7g; Cholesterol 74mg; Calcium 216mg; Fibre 1g; Sodium 867mg

Welsh cockle pie

This Pembrokeshire dish is sprinkled with grated cheese and browned under the grill, though it could equally well be topped with shortcrust or puff pastry and cooked in a hot oven. Serve the former with crusty bread and the latter with a crisp salad.

Serves 2

425ml/¾ pint/scant 2 cups milk

25g/1oz/2 tbsp butter, cut into small pieces

25g/1oz/¼ cup plain (all-purpose) flour

150–200g/5½–7oz shelled cooked cockles (small clams)

100g/3½oz/1 cup mature cheese, such as Llanboidy or Llangloffan, grated

about 60ml/4 tbsp fresh breadcrumbs

salt and ground black pepper

1 To make the sauce, put the milk, butter, flour and seasoning into a pan. Over medium heat and stirring constantly with a whisk, bring to the boil and bubble gently for 2–3 minutes until thick, smooth and glossy.

2 Stir in two-thirds of the cheese. Add the cockles and bring just to the boil.

3 Spoon the mixture into one large dish or four individual flameproof dishes. Then toss together the remaining cheese and the breadcrumbs.

4 Sprinkle the cheese and breadcrumb mixture over the cockle sauce. Put under a hot grill (broiler) until bubbling and golden. Serve immediately.

Cook's tips
• Add some chopped fresh herbs (chives or parsley are good), laverbread, softened sliced leeks or some crisp-fried bacon pieces to the white sauce.
• This dish is equally delicious made with mixed seafood, such as mussels, clams, squid and cockles.

Energy 294kcal/1231kJ; Protein 16.8g; Carbohydrate 21.6g, of which sugars 5.6g; Fat 15.7g, of which saturates 9.9g; Cholesterol 64mg; Calcium 376mg; Fibre 0.5g; Sodium 562mg

Dublin Bay prawns in garlic butter

Dublic bay prawns aren't actually a prawn at all, but a small lobster, also known as langoustine. This all-time favourite is equally popular as a first or main course. Serve them with lemon wedges, rice and a side salad.

Serves 4

32–36 large live Dublin Bay prawns (jumbo shrimp)

225g/8oz/1 cup butter

15ml/1 tbsp olive oil

4 or 5 garlic cloves, crushed

15ml/1 tbsp lemon juice

sea salt and ground black pepper

1 Drop the live Dublin Bay prawns into a large pan of briskly boiling salted water. Bring rapidly back to the boil, cover with a lid and simmer for a few minutes; the time required depends on their size and will be very short for small ones – do not overcook. They are ready when the underside of the shell has lost its translucency and becomes an opaque whitish colour.

2 Drain, refresh under cold water, and leave in a colander until cool. Twist off the heads and the long claws, then peel the shell off the tails and remove the meat. If the claws are big it is worthwhile extracting any meat you can from them with a lobster pick.

3 Make a shallow cut along the back of each prawn. Remove the trail (the dark vein) that runs along the back.

4 Heat a large heavy pan over medium heat, add the butter and oil and the garlic. When the butter is foaming, sprinkle the prawns with a little salt and a good grinding of pepper, and add them to the pan. Cook for about 2 minutes until the garlic is cooked and the prawns thoroughly heated through.

5 Add lemon juice to taste, and adjust the seasoning, and then turn the prawns and their buttery juices on to warmed plates and serve immediately.

Cook's tips
• Dublin Bay prawns can weigh up to 225g/8oz each, although the average weight is 45g/1³/₄oz. You'll need 8–9 per person for a main course.
• These crustaceans are also known as Norway lobsters.

Variation This recipe works very well with scallops (puréed Jerusalem artichokes are a good accompaniment), small queen scallops, or with a firm-fleshed fish such as monkfish.

Energy 498Kcal/2054kJ; Protein 13g; Carbohydrate 0.4g, of which sugars 0.4g; Fat 49.4g, of which saturates 29.8g; Cholesterol 260mg; Calcium 67mg; Fibre 0g; Sodium 478mg

Fisherman's casserole

For many years the favourite fish of the English has probably been cod or herring, but this fish pie can include whichever firm-fleshed fish is available, and is made even more versatile by the addition of shellfish, adding texture and flavour.

Serves 4

500g/1¼lb mixed fish fillets, such as haddock, bass, red mullet, salmon

500g/1¼lb mixed shellfish, such as squid strips, mussels, cockles (small clams) and prawns (shrimp)

15ml/1 tbsp oil

25g/1oz/2 tbsp butter

1 medium onion, finely chopped

1 carrot, finely chopped

3 celery sticks, finely chopped

30ml/2 tbsp plain (all-purpose) flour

600ml/1 pint/2½ cups fish stock

300ml/½pt/1¼ cups dry (hard) cider

350g/12oz small new potatoes, halved

150m/¼ pint/⅔ cup double (heavy) cream

small handful of chopped mixed herbs such as parsley, chives and dill

salt and ground black pepper

1 Wash the fish fillets and dry on kitchen paper. With a sharp knife, remove the skin, feel carefully for any bones and extract them. Cut the fish into large, even chunks.

2 Prepare the shellfish, shelling the prawns if necessary. Scrub the mussels and cockles, discarding any with broken shells or that do not close when given a sharp tap. Pull off the black tufts (beards) attached to the mussels.

3 Heat the oil and butter in a large saucepan, add the onion, carrot and celery and cook over a medium heat, stirring occasionally, until beginning to soften and turn golden brown. Add the flour, and cook for 1 minute.

4 Remove the pan from the heat and gradually stir in the fish stock and cider. Return the pan to the heat and cook, stirring continuously, until the mixture comes to the boil and thickens.

Cook's tip This simple recipe can be adapted according to the varieties of fish and shellfish that are obtainable on the day – it is delicious whatever mixture you choose.

5 Add the potatoes. Bring the sauce back to the boil, then cover and simmer gently for 10–15 minutes until the potatoes are nearly tender.

6 Add all the fish and shellfish and stir in gently.

7 Stir in the cream. Bring back to a gentle simmer, then cover the pan and cook gently for 5–10 minutes or until the pieces of fish are cooked through and all the shells have opened. Adjust the seasoning to taste and gently stir in the herbs. Serve immediately.

Energy 583kcal/2439kJ; Protein 49.3g; Carbohydrate 25.3g, of which sugars 6.1g; Fat 30.2g, of which saturates 16.5g; Cholesterol 354mg; Calcium 199mg; Fibre 2.5g; Sodium 404mg

Welsh mussels in cider

Mussel harvesting is concentrated around north Wales, and Conwy in particular, where there is also a mussel museum. They are delicious when steamed and lifted out of their shells, and quickly fried with bacon. Here they are cooked with a broth of cider, garlic and cream.

2 Melt the butter in a very large pan and add the leek and garlic. Cook over medium heat for about 5 minutes, stirring frequently, until very soft but not browned. Season with pepper.

3 Add the cider and immediately pour in the mussels. Cover with a lid and cook quickly, shaking the pan once or twice, until the mussels have just opened (take care not to overcook and toughen them).

4 Remove the lid, add the cream and parsley and bubble gently for a minute or two. Serve immediately in shallow bowls.

Serves 4 as a starter, 2 as a main course

1.8kg/4lb mussels in their shells

40g/1½oz/3 tbsp butter

1 leek, washed and finely chopped

1 garlic clove, finely chopped

150ml/¼ pint/⅔ cup dry (hard) cider

30–45ml/2–3 tbsp double (heavy) cream

a handful of fresh parsley, chopped

ground black pepper

1 Scrub the mussels and scrape off any barnacles. Discard those with broken shells or that refuse to close when given a sharp tap with a knife. Pull off the hairy beards with a sharp tug.

Cook's tip Eat mussels the fun way! Use an empty shell as pincers to pick out the mussels from the other shells. Don't try to eat any whose shells have not opened during cooking.

Energy 261kcal/1092kJ; Protein 21.1g; Carbohydrate 6.5g, of which sugars 2.1g; Fat 15.6g, of which saturates 8.2g; Cholesterol 104mg; Calcium 82mg; Fibre 1g; Sodium 498mg

Mussels in tomato broth

Once considered fit only to feed the poor because they were so abundant, mussels remain reasonably plentiful and inexpensive, and are farmed in several places around the British Isles. These days they appear in a myriad of dishes, from simple to sophisticated.

Serves 4

1.8kg/4lb mussels in their shells

1 medium onion

1 garlic clove

30ml/2 tbsp oil

5ml/1 tsp sugar

pinch of cayenne or chilli powder

150ml/¼ pint/⅔ cup dry (hard) cider

400g/14oz can chopped tomatoes

small handful of chopped fresh parsley

salt and ground black pepper

crusty bread, to serve

4 Add the cider, tomatoes and a little seasoning. Bring to the boil.

Cook's tip Do not be tempted to prise open and eat any mussels that have not opened up during cooking, they are unsafe and should be discarded.

5 Add the mussels, all at once. Cover tightly with a lid and cook quickly for about 5 minutes, until the shells have opened, shaking the pan occasionally.

6 Serve in warmed shallow dishes with parsley scattered over and crusty bread.

1 Scrub the mussels in cold water, discarding any that have broken shells and any with open shells that do not close when given a sharp tap. Pull off the black tufts (beards) attached to the shells.

2 Finely chop the onion and garlic.

3 Heat the oil in a very large pan and add the onion, garlic and sugar. Cook, stirring occasionally, over medium heat for about 5 minutes, or until the onion is soft and just beginning to brown. Stir in the cayenne or chilli.

Energy 211kcal/891kJ; Protein 21.1g; Carbohydrate 9.3g, of which sugars 4.9g; Fat 9g, of which saturates 1.2g; Cholesterol 72mg; Calcium 77mg; Fibre 1.2g; Sodium 444mg

Scottish clam stovies

Clams are now harvested in some Scottish lochs, especially in Loch Fyne where some of the best Scottish clams are grown on ropes. Limpets or cockles can also be used if you can buy them fresh or collect them yourself along the seashore.

Serves 4

2.5 litres/4 pints/10 cups clams

potatoes (see step 3 for quantity)

oil, for greasing

chopped fresh flat leaf parsley, to garnish

50g/2oz/¼ cup butter

salt and ground black pepper

1 Wash the clams and soak them overnight in fresh cold water. This will clean them out and get rid of any sand and other detritus.

2 Preheat the oven to 190°C/375°F/ Gas 5. Put the clams into a large pan, cover with water and bring to the boil. Add a little salt then simmer until the shells open. Reserve the cooking liquor. Shell the clams, reserving a few whole.

3 Weigh the shelled clams. You will need three times their weight in unpeeled potatoes.

4 Peel and slice the potatoes thinly. Lightly oil the base and sides of a flameproof, ovenproof dish. Arrange a layer of potatoes in the base of the dish, add a layer of the clams and season with a little salt and ground black pepper. Repeat until the ingredients are all used, finishing with a layer of potatoes on top. Finally, season lightly.

5 Pour in some of the reserved cooking liquor to come about halfway up the dish. Dot the top with the butter then cover with foil. Bring to the boil on the stove over a medium-high heat, then bake in the preheated oven for 2 hours until the top is golden brown.

6 Serve hot, garnished with chopped fresh flat leaf parsley.

Energy 320kcal/1348kJ; Protein 17.3g; Carbohydrate 36.7g, of which sugars 3.3g; Fat 12.6g, of which saturates 7g; Cholesterol 57mg; Calcium 188mg; Fibre 2.9g; Sodium 262mg

Queenies with smoked Ayrshire bacon

This recipe uses the classic combination of scallops with bacon, but this time using queen scallops, known in Scotland as "Queenies", which are cooked with a flavoursome cured bacon known as smoked Ayrshire bacon.

Serves 4

6 rashers (strips) smoked Ayrshire bacon, cut into thin strips

5ml/1 tsp ground turmeric

28 queen scallops

1 sprig each of parsley and thyme

1 bay leaf

6 black peppercorns

150ml/¼ pint/⅔ cup dry white wine

75ml/2½ fl oz/⅓ cup double (heavy) cream

30ml/2 tbsp chopped fresh chives, to garnish

1 Using a pan with a close-fitting lid, fry the bacon in its own fat until well cooked and crisp. Remove the bacon.

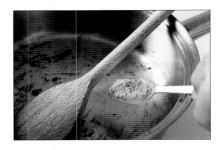

2 Reduce the heat, stir the turmeric into the juices and cook for 1–2 minutes.

3 Add the scallops to the pan with the herbs and peppercorns. Carefully pour in the wine (it will steam) and then cover with the lid. The scallops will only take a few minutes to cook. Test them by removing a thick one and piercing with a sharp knife to see if they are soft. Once they are cooked, remove from the pan and keep warm.

4 Stir in the cream and increase the heat to allow the sauce to simmer. This should be a light sauce; if it becomes too thick then add a little water.

5 Serve the scallops in warmed bowls or on plates with the sauce ladled over. Sprinkle with the crisp bacon and garnish with chopped fresh chives.

Energy 353kcal/1476kJ; Protein 36.5g; Carbohydrate 4.8g, of which sugars 0.5g; Fat 18.4g, of which saturates 9.1g; Cholesterol 106mg; Calcium 51mg; Fibre 0g; Sodium 904mg

East Neuk lobster with mustard and cream

The East Neuk of Fife is the "corner" of Fife on the east coast of Scotland, an area bounded by the sea almost all around. From Elie to St Andrews, there is a proliferation of fishing villages, which in their time provided the vast majority of jobs in the area. Today, Pittenweem is the only real fishing port with its own fish and shellfish market.

Serves 2

1 lobster, approximately 500g/1¼lb

10ml/2 tsp butter

splash of whisky (grain not malt)

1 shallot or ½ onion, finely chopped

50g/2oz button (white) mushrooms

splash of white wine

175ml/6fl oz/¾ cup double (heavy) cream

5ml/1 tsp wholegrain mustard

10ml/2 tsp chopped fresh chervil and a little tarragon

60ml/4 tbsp breadcrumbs

50g/2oz/¼ cup butter, melted

salt and ground black pepper

1 Bring a large pan of salted water to the boil. Make sure it is boiling hard, as this will kill the lobster immediately. Cook the lobster in the boiling water for about 7 minutes then remove from the pan and set aside to cool.

Cook's tip You can use a precooked lobster or prepared lobster meat for this recipe if you prefer.

2 Once cool, cut the lobster down the middle, top to bottom, and remove the intestinal tract down the back.

3 Remove the meat from the tail, taking care not to let it break into pieces.

4 Cut the tail meat into slanted slices. Remove the meat from the claws, keeping it as whole as possible. Wash the two half-shells out and set aside.

5 Heat a frying pan over a low heat, add the butter and wait for it to bubble. Gently add the lobster meat and colour lightly (don't overcook or it will dry out). Pour in the whisky. If you have a gas hob, allow the flames to get inside the pan to briefly flame the pieces and burn off the alcohol; if the hob is electric, don't worry as it isn't vital. Remove the lobster meat.

6 Add the chopped shallot or onion and the mushrooms to the pan, and cook gently over a medium-low heat for a few minutes until the mushrooms are soft and the onion or shallot is transparent. Add a little white wine, then the cream, and allow to simmer to reduce to a light coating texture.

7 Add the mustard to the pan with the chopped herbs and mix well. Season to taste with a little salt and freshly ground black pepper. Meanwhile preheat the grill (broiler) to high.

8 Place the two lobster half-shells on the grill pan. Distribute the lobster meat evenly throughout the two half-shells and spoon the sauce over. Sprinkle with breadcrumbs, drizzle with melted butter and brown under the preheated grill. Serve immediately.

Energy 812kcal/3357kJ; Protein 23.6g; Carbohydrate 12g, of which sugars 3.7g; Fat 74.9g, of which saturates 46g; Cholesterol 287mg; Calcium 127mg; Fibre 0.9g; Sodium 580mg

Seafood pancakes

English pancakes can be traced back as far as the 15th century, when the batter would have been made with eggs, flour and water. Three hundred years later, the water was replaced with beer or ale and later still with milk.

Serves 4

For the pancakes

115g/4oz/1 cup plain (all-purpose) flour

pinch of salt

1 egg

300ml/½ pint/1¼ cups milk

15ml/1 tbsp melted butter

oil or melted butter, for cooking

For the filling

300ml/½ pint/1¼ cups milk

150ml/¼ pint/⅔ cup fish stock

25g/1oz/2 tbsp flour

25g/1oz/2 tbsp butter

350g/12oz skinless fish fillets, such as haddock and salmon, cut into bite size pieces

115g/4oz peeled prawns (shrimp)

large handful of baby spinach leaves

50g/2oz cheese, such as Cheddar or Lancashire, grated

1 To make the pancakes, sift the flour and salt into a bowl and break the egg into it. Gradually beat in the milk to make a smooth batter and then stir in 15ml/1 tbsp melted butter.

2 Put a 20cm/8in non-stick frying pan over a medium heat and brush with oil or butter. When hot, add 45ml/3 tbsp batter, tilting to cover the surface. Cook until the underside is golden brown then flip over and briefly cook the other side. Repeat with the remaining batter to make eight pancakes. Keep warm.

3 To make the filling, put the milk, stock, flour and butter into a pan. Bring to the boil, whisking continuously, until the sauce thickens. Add the fish pieces and simmer gently for 3–4 minutes or until the fish is just cooked. Stir in the prawns and spinach.

4 Cook until the prawns are heated through and the spinach is wilted. Stir in the cheese. Remove from the heat.

5 Spoon the fish mixture into the centre of the pancakes and roll up or fold into triangles. Serve immediately.

Energy 393kcal/1647kJ; Protein 26.7g; Carbohydrate 25.4g, of which sugars 5.7g; Fat 21.2g, of which saturates 11.9g; Cholesterol 203mg; Calcium 273mg; Fibre 0.8g; Sodium 513mg

Welsh scallops with bacon and sage

Scallops are fished off the west coast and, in particular, off Anglesey. Their sweetness is complemented by the addition of bacon. This dish is delicious served with marsh samphire, found on the marshy coastlines of Wales when it is in season – from June to September.

Serves 4 as a starter, 2 as a main course

15ml/1 tbsp olive oil

4 streaky (fatty) bacon rashers (strips), cut into 2.5cm/1in strips

2–3 fresh sage leaves, chopped

small piece of butter

8 large or 16 small scallops

15ml/1 tbsp fresh lemon juice

100ml/3½fl oz dry cider or white wine

1 Heat a frying pan and add the oil, bacon and sage. Cook over medium heat, stirring occasionally, until the bacon is golden brown. Lift out and keep warm.

2 Add the butter to the pan and when hot add the scallops. Cook for about 1 minute on each side until browned. Lift out and keep warm with the bacon.

3 Add the lemon juice and cider to the pan and, scraping up any sediment, bring just to the boil. Continue bubbling gently until the mixture has reduced to a few tablespoons of syrupy sauce.

4 Serve the scallops and bacon with the sauce drizzled over.

Cook's tips
• Scallops that are particularly large can be sliced in half so that they form two discs before cooking (cut off the corals and cook these separately in the pan).
• To prepare samphire, wash it thoroughly and pick off the soft fleshy branches, discarding the thicker woody stalks. Drop it into boiling water for just 1 minute before draining and serving.

Energy 179kcal/745kJ; Protein 15.6g; Carbohydrate 1.9g, of which sugars 0.2g; Fat 10.4g, of which saturates 3.3g; Cholesterol 42mg; Calcium 19mg; Fibre 0g; Sodium 414mg

Meat and venison

The traditional Sunday roast is still a meal the British
greatly enjoy and take pride in: a succulent joint of
beef, lamb or pork served with all the trimmings
is often the focus of a weekend family gathering.
Then there are savoury pot roasts, stews and braises,
and comforting puddings and pies, not to mention
chops, steaks and a wonderful variety
of sausages.

Rib of beef with Yorkshire puddings

Mention English food and most people think of this quintessential dish, which is traditionally served for Sunday lunch and on special occasions. In Victorian days in the north-east of England, roast beef would have been traditional fare on Christmas day. The accompanying batter pudding was not served alongside it until well into the 18th century and in Yorkshire it is still sometimes eaten with gravy before the meat course.

Serves 6–8

rib of beef joint, weighing about 3kg/6½lb

oil, for brushing

salt and ground black pepper

For the Yorkshire puddings

115g/4oz/1 cup plain (all-purpose) flour

1.5ml/¼ tsp salt

1 egg

200ml/7fl oz/scant 1 cup milk

oil or beef dripping, for greasing

For the horseradish cream

60–75ml/4–5 tbsp finely grated fresh horseradish

300ml/½ pint/1¼ cups soured cream

30ml/2 tbsp cider vinegar or white wine vinegar

10ml/2 tsp caster (superfine) sugar

For the gravy

600ml/1 pint/2½ cups good beef stock

1 Preheat the oven to 220°C/425°F/ Gas 7. Weigh the joint and calculate the cooking time required as follows: 10–15 minutes per 500g/1¼lb for rare beef, 15–20 minutes for medium and 20–25 minutes for well done.

Cook's tip To avoid the pungent smell (and tears) produced by grating horseradish, use a jar of preserved grated horseradish.

2 Put the joint into a large roasting pan. Brush it all over with oil and season with salt and pepper. Put into the hot oven and cook for 30 minutes, until the beef is browned. Lower the oven temperature to 160°C/325°F/Gas 3 and cook for the calculated time, spooning the juices over the meat occasionally during cooking.

3 For the Yorkshire pudding, sift the flour and salt into a bowl and break the egg into it. Make the milk up to 300ml/½ pint/1¼ cups with water and gradually whisk into the flour to make a smooth batter. Leave to stand while the beef cooks. Generously grease eight Yorkshire pudding tins (muffin pans) measuring about 10cm/4in.

4 For the horseradish cream, put all the ingredients into a bowl and mix well. Cover and chill until required.

5 At the end of its cooking time, remove the beef from the oven, cover with foil and leave to stand for 30–40 minutes while you cook the Yorkshire puddings and make the gravy.

6 Increase the oven temperature to 220°C/425°F/Gas 7 and put the prepared tins on the top shelf for 5 minutes until very hot. Pour in the batter and cook for about 15 minutes until well risen, crisp and golden brown.

7 To make the gravy, transfer the beef to a warmed serving plate. Pour off the fat from the roasting pan, leaving the meat juices. Add the stock to the pan, bring to the boil and bubble until reduced by about half. Season to taste.

8 Carve the beef and serve with the gravy, Yorkshire puddings, roast potatoes and horseradish cream.

Energy 1037kcal/4338kJ; Protein 129g; Carbohydrate 15.1g, of which sugars 4.1g; Fat 51.5g, of which saturates 24.3g; Cholesterol 352mg; Calcium 123mg; Fibre 0.5g; Sodium 249mg

Pot-roasted beef with English stout

Stout is a dark ale developed in Britian and Ireland, a direct descendant of porter, it is generally darker and stronger in flavour than other real English ales.

Serves 6

30ml/2 tbsp vegetable oil

900g/2lb rolled brisket of beef

2 medium onions, roughly chopped

2 celery sticks, thickly sliced

450g/1lb carrots, cut into
large chunks

675g/1½lb potatoes, peeled and cut
into large chunks

30ml/2 tbsp plain (all-purpose) flour

450ml/¾ pint/ 2 cups beef stock

300ml/½ pint/1¼ cups stout

1 bay leaf

45ml/3 tbsp chopped fresh thyme

5ml/1 tsp soft light brown sugar

30ml/2 tbsp wholegrain mustard

15ml/1 tbsp tomato purée (paste)

salt and ground black pepper

1 Preheat the oven to 180°C/350°F/ Gas 4. Heat the oil in a large flameproof casserole and brown the beef until golden brown all over.

2 Lift the beef from the pan and drain on kitchen paper. Add the onions to the pan and cook for about 4 minutes, until just beginning to soften and brown.

3 Add the celery, carrots and potatoes to the casserole and cook over a medium heat for 2–3 minutes, or until they are just beginning to colour.

4 Add the flour and cook for a further 1 minute, stirring continuously. Gradually pour in the beef stock and the stout. Heat until the mixture comes to the boil, stirring frequently.

5 Stir in the bay leaf, thyme, sugar, mustard, tomato purée and seasoning. Place the meat on top, cover tightly and transfer the casserole to the hot oven.

6 Cook for about 2½ hours, or until the tender. Add salt and pepper, to taste. To serve, carve the beef into thick slices and serve with the vegetables and plenty of gravy.

Energy 415kcal/1743kJ; Protein 36g; Carbohydrate 35.6g, of which sugars 13.1g; Fat 14g, of which saturates 4.4g; Cholesterol 81mg; Calcium 66mg; Fibre 4.2g; Sodium 284mg

East Anglian braised beef with herb dumplings

Dumplings, probably originally made from bread dough, have been added to English stews for centuries to satisfy hearty appetites, and are particularly associated with Norfolk.

Serves 4

25g/1oz/2 tbsp butter

30ml/2 tbsp oil

115g/4oz/⅔ cup streaky (fatty) bacon, chopped

900g/2lb lean braising steak, cut into chunks

45ml/3 tbsp plain (all-purpose) flour

450ml/¾ pint/scant 2 cups beer

450ml/¾ pint/scant 2 cups beef stock

1 bouquet garni

8 shallots

175g/6oz/2 cups small mushrooms

salt and ground black pepper

For the herb dumplings

115g/4oz/1 cup self-raising (self-rising) flour

50g/2oz/scant ½ cup shredded suet

2.5ml/½ tsp salt

2.5ml/½ tsp mustard powder

15ml/1 tbsp chopped fresh parsley

15ml/1 tbsp fresh thyme leaves

1 In a large frying pan, melt half the butter with half the oil, add the bacon and brown. Transfer to a casserole.

2 Brown the beef quickly in the frying pan in batches, then transfer it to the casserole using a slotted spoon.

3 Stir the flour into the fat in the pan. Add the beer, stock and seasoning and bring to the boil, stirring constantly. Pour over the meat, add the bouquet garni, cover and place in a cold oven set to 200°C/400°F/Gas 6. Cook for 30 minutes then reduce the temperature to 160°C/325°F/Gas 3 and cook for 1 hour.

4 Heat the remaining butter and oil in a frying pan and cook the shallots until golden. Lift out and set aside. Add the mushrooms and cook quickly for 2–3 minutes. Stir the vegetables into the stew, cover and cook for 30 minutes.

5 In a bowl, mix together the dumpling ingredients. Add cold water to make a soft, sticky dough. Roll into 12 balls and place on top of the stew. Cover, cook for a further 25 minutes, and serve.

Energy 754kcal/3148kJ; Protein 60.8g; Carbohydrate 36.6g, of which sugars 3.8g; Fat 41.4g, of which saturates 14.9g; Cholesterol 163mg; Calcium 147mg; Fibre 2.1g; Sodium 700mg

Steak and kidney pudding

This classic dish is in fact a 19th-century invention that has, in a relatively short time, become one of England's most famous dishes. In Victorian days it would also have included oysters, then incredibly cheap, and some versions also contain mushrooms.

Serves 6

500g/1¼lb lean stewing steak, cut into cubes

225g/8oz beef kidney or lamb's kidneys, skin and core removed and cut into small cubes

1 medium onion, finely chopped

30ml/2 tbsp finely chopped fresh herbs, such as parsley and thyme

30ml/2 tbsp plain (all-purpose) flour

275g/10oz/2½ cups self-raising (self-rising) flour

150g/5oz/1 cup shredded suet

finely grated rind of 1 small lemon

about 120ml/4fl oz/½ cup beef stock or water

salt and ground black pepper

1 Put the stewing steak into a large mixing bowl and add the kidneys, onion and chopped herbs. Sprinkle the plain flour and seasoning over the top and mix well.

2 To make the pastry, sift the self-raising flour into another large bowl. Stir in the suet and lemon rind. Add sufficient cold water to bind the ingredients and gather into a soft dough.

3 On a lightly floured surface knead the dough gently, and then roll out to make a circle measuring about 35cm/14in across. Cut out one-quarter of the circle, roll up and put aside.

4 Lightly butter a 1.75 litre/3 pint heatproof bowl. Line the bowl with the rolled out dough, pressing the cut edges together and allowing the pastry to overlap the top of the bowl slightly.

5 Spoon the steak mixture into the lined bowl, packing it in carefully, so as not to split the pastry.

6 Pour in sufficient stock to reach no more than three-quarters of the way up the filling. (Any stock remaining can be heated and poured into the cooked pudding to thin the gravy if desired.)

7 Roll out the reserved pastry into a circle to form a lid and lay it over the filling, pinching the edges together to seal them well.

8 Cover with greaseproof paper or baking parchment, pleated in the centre to allow the pudding to rise, and then with a large sheet of foil (again pleated at the centre). Tuck the edges under and press them tightly to the sides of the basin until securely sealed (alternatively, tie with string). Steam for about 5 hours.

9 Carefully remove the foil and paper, slide a knife around the sides of the pudding and turn out on to a warmed serving plate.

Energy 436kcal/1835kJ; Protein 31.1g; Carbohydrate 49.5g, of which sugars 4.8g; Fat 13.9g, of which saturates 3.6g; Cholesterol 166mg; Calcium 201mg; Fibre 1.9g; Sodium 380mg

Braised oxtail

While oxtail requires long, slow cooking to tenderize the meat, the resulting flavour is rich and well worth the effort. Braised oxtail is traditionally served with plain boiled potatoes to soak up the rich gravy, though mashed potatoes would be good too.

Serves 6

1.5kg/3lb 6oz oxtails, cut into pieces

30ml/2 tbsp flour

45ml/3 tbsp oil

2 large onions, sliced

2 celery sticks, sliced

4 medium carrots, sliced

1 litre/1¾ pints/4 cups beef stock

15ml/1 tbsp tomato purée (paste)

finely grated rind of 1 small orange

2 bay leaves and sprigs of thyme

salt and ground black pepper

chopped fresh parsley, to garnish

1 Preheat the oven to 150°C/300°F/ Gas 2. Coat the pieces of oxtail in the seasoned flour, shaking off and reserving any excess.

2 Heat 30ml/2 tbsp oil in a large flameproof casserole and add the oxtail in batches, cooking quickly until browned all over.

3 Lift the oxtail out of the pan and set aside. Add the remaining oil to the pan, and stir in the sliced onions, then the celery and carrots.

4 Cook the vegetables quickly, stirring occasionally, until beginning to brown. Tip in any reserved flour then add the stock, tomato purée and orange rind.

5 Heat until bubbles begin to rise to the surface, then add the herbs, cover and put into the hot oven. Cook for 3½–4 hours until the oxtail is very tender.

6 Remove from the oven and leave to stand, covered, for 10 minutes before skimming off the surface fat. Adjust the seasoning and garnish with parsley.

Cook's tip This dish benefits from being made in advance. When cooled completely, any fat can be removed before reheating.

Energy 341kcal/1426kJ; Protein 30.9g; Carbohydrate 13.6g, of which sugars 7.7g; Fat 18.6g, of which saturates 0.7g; Cholesterol 0mg; Calcium 54mg; Fibre 2.3g; Sodium 203mg

Irish smoked beef with potato pancakes

In the west of Ireland, turf (peat) is an integral part of the way of life and was once used to to smoke meat. Chargrilled beef fillet is a delicious alternative to the turf-smoked original, and this recipe was devised for an Irish cookery competition by a chef from the region.

Serves 4

500g/1¼lb trimmed beef fillet

salt and ground black pepper

oil, for chargrilling

herb sprigs, to garnish

broccoli florets, white turnip and courgettes (zucchini), to serve

For the potato pancakes

250g/9oz potatoes, cooked

50g/2oz/½ cup plain (all-purpose) flour

1 egg

freshly grated nutmeg

oil, for frying

For the sauce

4 shallots, finely diced

200ml/7fl oz/scant 1 cup chicken stock

120ml/4fl oz/½ cup white wine

200ml/7fl oz/scant 1 cup double (heavy) cream

15ml/1 tbsp chopped fresh herbs, such as flat leaf parsley, tarragon, chervil and basil

lemon juice, to taste

1 To make the potato pancakes, blend the potatoes with the flour and egg to make a thick purée. Add nutmeg and seasoning to taste.

2 Heat and lightly oil a heavy pan, then use the potato purée to make eight small pancakes, cooking on both sides until golden brown. Keep warm.

3 To make the sauce, put the shallots, stock, wine and half the cream into a pan and cook over a medium heat until reduced by two-thirds. Purée the mixture and strain it, then mix in enough herbs to turn the sauce green.

4 Season the beef with salt and freshly ground black pepper. In a heavy, pan, seal the meat on all sides over a high heat. Place the meat in a smoker for about 10 minutes until medium-rare.

5 Alternatively, if you don't have a smoker, continue cooking in the pan for another 3–5 minutes, covered, turning once. Keep warm.

6 When ready to serve, whip the remaining cream and fold it into the sauce, adjusting the flavour with salt, black pepper and a little lemon juice.

7 Divide the sauce between four warm plates. Cut the beef fillet into eight slices and place two slices on top of the sauce on each plate.

8 Arrange potato pancakes around the meat. Garnish with sprigs of herbs and serve with the broccoli florets, white turnip and courgettes.

Energy 683Kcal/2834kJ; Protein 32.9g; Carbohydrate 23g, of which sugars 3g; Fat 49.5g, of which saturates 27.5g; Cholesterol 219mg; Calcium 82mg; Fibre 1.9g; Sodium 166mg

Irish spiced beef

This is quite a traditional Irish dish, although it is a modern version of the old recipe, as it omits the initial pickling stage, does not include the preservative saltpetre, and takes only three or four days to cure rather than. Serve on thinly sliced brown bread, with chutney.

Serves 8

1.8kg/4lb corned beef, silverside or tail end

300ml/½ pint/1¼ cups Guinness

15ml/1 tbsp coarsely ground black pepper

10ml/2 tsp ground ginger

15ml/1 tbsp juniper berries, crushed

15ml/1 tbsp coriander seeds, crushed

5ml/1 tsp ground cloves

15ml/1 tbsp ground allspice

45ml/3 tbsp soft dark brown sugar

2 bay leaves, crushed

1 small onion, finely chopped

fruit chutney and bread, to serve

1 First, spice the beef: blend the pepper, spices and sugar thoroughly, then mix in the bay leaves and onion. Rub the mixture into the meat, then put it into a suitable lidded container and refrigerate for 3–4 days, turning and rubbing with the mixture daily.

2 Put the meat into a pan and barely cover with cold water. Place a tight lid on the pan and bring to the boil. Reduce the heat and cook very gently for about 3½ hours. For the last hour add the Guinness to the cooking liquid.

3 When the joint is cooked, leave it to cool in the liquid. Wrap in foil and keep in the refrigerator until required, then slice to serve. It will keep for about 1 week.

Variation Spiced beef is excellent as finger food for parties, sliced thinly and served with sour cream lightly flavoured with horseradish and black pepper.

Energy 309Kcal/1301kJ; Protein 53.6g; Carbohydrate 2g, of which sugars 2g; Fat 9.7g, of which saturates 3.6g; Cholesterol 137mg; Calcium 15mg; Fibre 0g; Sodium 140mg

Irish beef and Guinness casserole

Stouts, such as Guinness, and beef make natural partners and occur frequently in Irish cooking. This richly flavoured version of a popular dish is suitable for any occasion, including informal entertaining. Serve with creamy well-buttered mashed potatoes.

Serves 4

30ml/2 tbsp olive oil

900g/2lb stewing beef (such as rib steak or shoulder), cut into thin slices

1 onion, chopped

2 leeks, sliced

2 carrots, sliced

2 celery sticks, sliced

2 garlic cloves, finely chopped

300ml/½ pint/1¼ cups well-reduced beef stock

150ml/¼ pint/⅔ cup Guinness

50g/2oz/¼ cup butter

75g/3oz streaky (fatty) bacon, trimmed and diced

115g/4oz wild or cultivated mushrooms, quartered or sliced

50g/2oz shallots or small onions, left whole

25g/1oz/¼ cup plain (all-purpose) flour

salt and ground black pepper

1 Heat the oil in a pan and brown the meat. Transfer to a casserole.

2 Sauté the vegetables for 5 minutes in the pan. Add the vegetables to the meat, and add the garlic.

3 Add the stock and the Guinness. Season. Cover the casserole and bring to the boil, then reduce the heat and simmer for about 1½ hours.

4 Remove the meat from the casserole and strain the cooking liquid and reserve. Discard the vegetables.

5 Clean the casserole and sauté the bacon, mushrooms and shallots in the butter for 5–10 minutes. When the shallots are tender, sprinkle in the flour and stir in, then slowly blend in the reserved cooking liquid. Return the meat to the casserole, and reheat. Serve with mashed potatoes.

Energy 670Kcal/2786kJ; Protein 57.5g; Carbohydrate 14g, of which sugars 7.3g; Fat 42g, of which saturates 17.5g; Cholesterol 169mg; Calcium 71mg; Fibre 3.7g; Sodium 478mg

Scottish beef with chanterelle mushrooms

The trick here is to use really good beef with no fat and to rapidly fry the dried pieces quickly so the outside is well-browned and the inside very rare. Chanterelle mushrooms are the most delicious wild mushrooms, yellowy orange and resembling small umbrellas. They are often found wild in pine woods in Scotland, Northern Europe and North America.

Serves 4

115g/4oz chanterelle mushrooms

2 rump (round) steaks, 175g/6oz each, cut into strips

45ml/3 tbsp olive oil

1 garlic clove, crushed

1 shallot, finely chopped

60ml/4 tbsp dry white wine

60ml/4 tbsp double (heavy) cream

25g/1oz/2 tbsp butter

salt and ground black pepper

chopped fresh parsley, to garnish

Cook's tips
• Mushrooms should ideally never be washed in water as they will absorb too much moisture.
• When browning meat in a hot pan don't put too much in at once as this lowers the temperature too quickly and the meat will poach instead of fry. Put in a few pieces at first, then wait 10–15 seconds before adding more.

1 Clean the mushrooms. If you have collected them from the wild cut off the ends where they have come from the ground and, using kitchen paper, wipe off any leaf matter or moss that may be adhering to them. Cut the mushrooms in half through the stalk and cap.

2 Dry the beef thoroughly on kitchen paper. Heat a large frying pan over a high heat then add 30ml/2 tbsp olive oil. Working in batches (*see* Cook's tips) put the meat in the pan and quickly brown on all sides.

3 Remove the meat, which should still be very rare, from the pan, set aside and keep warm. Add the remaining olive oil to the pan and reduce the heat. Stir in the garlic and shallots and cook, stirring, for about 1 minute. Then increase the heat and add the mushrooms. Season and cook until the mushrooms just start to soften. Add the wine, bring to the boil and add the cream. As the liquid thickens, return the beef to the pan and heat through.

4 Remove the pan from the heat and swirl in the butter without mixing fully. Serve on warmed plates, garnished with chopped fresh parsley.

Energy 415kcal/1725kJ; Protein 29.9g; Carbohydrate 0.7g, of which sugars 0.6g; Fat 31g, of which saturates 14.2g; Cholesterol 122mg; Calcium 21mg; Fibre 0.4g; Sodium 124mg

Welsh braised beef with vegetables

Stews such as this were the mainstay of the Welsh kitchen, when everything was left to cook gently all day in one large pot on the range or (in earlier times) at the edge of the fire. Gentle simmering in a modern oven produces an equally delicious dish. "Trollies", a form of dumpling made with oatmeal and currants, often replaced potatoes.

Serves 4–6

1kg/2¼lb lean stewing steak, cut into 5cm/2in cubes

45ml/3 tbsp plain (all-purpose) flour,

45ml/3 tbsp oil

1 large onion, thinly sliced

1 large carrot, thickly sliced

2 celery sticks, finely chopped

300ml/½ pint/¼ cup beef stock

30ml/2 tbsp tomato purée (paste)

5ml/1 tsp dried mixed herbs

15ml/1 tbsp dark muscovado (molasses) sugar

225g/8oz baby potatoes, halved

2 leeks, thinly sliced

salt and ground black pepper

1 Preheat the oven to 150°C/300°F/ Gas 2. Season the flour and use to coat the beef cubes.

2 Heat the oil in a large, flameproof casserole. Add a small batch of meat, cook quickly until browned on all sides and, with a slotted spoon, lift out. Repeat with the remaining beef.

Variation Replace the potatoes with dumplings. Sift 175g/6oz/1½ cups self-raising (self-rising) flour and stir in 75g/3oz/½ cup shredded suet, 30ml/2 tbsp chopped parsley and season. Stir in water to make a soft dough and divide the mixture into 12 balls. In step 6, stir in the leeks and put the dumplings on top. Cover and cook for 15–20 minutes more.

3 Add the onion, carrot and celery to the casserole. Cook over medium heat for about 10 minutes, stirring frequently, until they begin to soften and brown slightly on the edges.

4 Return the meat to the casserole and add the stock, tomato purée, herbs and sugar, at the same time scraping up any sediment that has stuck to the casserole. Heat until the liquid nearly comes to the boil.

5 Cover with a tight fitting lid and put into the hot oven. Cook for 2–2½ hours, or until the beef is tender.

6 Gently stir in the potatoes and leeks, cover and continue cooking for a further 30 minutes or until the potatoes are soft.

Energy 450kcal/1880kJ; Protein 41.3g; Carbohydrate 23.6g, of which sugars 10.3g; Fat 21.7g, of which saturates 7.3g; Cholesterol 97mg; Calcium 63mg; Fibre 3.5g; Sodium 137mg

Beef with oysters and Scottish Belhaven beer

Oysters have been collected from the waters south of Edinburgh since Roman times. They were very cheap and readily available in the 18th and 19th centuries, with "oyster lassies" wandering through the streets of Edinburgh selling them, calling their familiar cry, "Wha'll o' caller ou?" – "Who will have fresh oysters?"

Serves 4

1kg/2¼lb rump (round) steak

6 thin rashers (strips) streaky (fatty) bacon

12 oysters

50g/2oz/½ cup plain (all-purpose) flour

generous pinch of cayenne pepper

butter or olive oil, for greasing

3 shallots, finely chopped

300ml/½ pint/1¼ cups Belhaven Best beer

salt and ground black pepper

1 Preheat the oven to 180°C/350°F/ Gas 4. You need thin strips of beef for this recipe, so place the steaks one at a time between sheets of clear film (plastic wrap) and beat it with a rolling pin until it is flattened and thin. Slice the meat into 24 thin strips, wide enough to roll around an oyster.

2 Stretch the bacon rashers lengthways by placing them on a chopping board and, holding one end down with your thumb, pulling them out using the thick side of a sharp knife. Cut each rasher into four pieces.

3 Remove the oysters from their shells, retaining the liquid from inside their shells in a separate container. Set aside.

4 Cut each oyster in half lengthways and roll each piece in a strip of bacon, ensuring that the bacon goes around at least once and preferably covers the oyster at each end. Then roll in a strip of beef so no oyster is visible.

5 Season the flour with the cayenne pepper and salt and black pepper, then roll the meat in it.

6 Lightly grease a large flameproof casserole with butter or olive oil. Sprinkle the shallots evenly over the base. Place the floured meat rolls on top, evenly spaced.

7 Slowly pour over the beer, bring to the boil then cover and cook in the oven for 1½–2 hours.

8 The flour from around the meat will have thickened the stew sauce and produced a lovely rich gravy. Serve with creamy mashed potatoes and fresh steamed vegetables.

Cook's tip To open the oysters use an oyster knife, grasping the oyster in your other hand with a dish towel. If you don't have an oyster knife, use a small knife or a pen knife, although you should be careful of cutting yourself as the blade can easily slip.

Variations
• Belhaven Best, beautifully honey coloured, is a Scottish draught (draft) ale. You could substitute your favourite ale or even Guinness if you prefer.
• If you want to create the dish without beer, use a good beef stock. Half a glass of red wine would also make a good addition if you are using stock.

Energy 528kcal/2208kJ; Protein 61.4g; Carbohydrate 12.7g, of which sugars 2.5g; Fat 24.4g, of which saturates 10.1g; Cholesterol 182mg; Calcium 52mg; Fibre 0.6g; Sodium 634mg

Fillet steak with pickled walnut sauce

This is a traditional Scottish way of cooking beef, which makes it go a little further with the use of the onions. Filet mignons are the small pieces from the end of the fillet, known as "collops" in Scotland. If you prefer, you can use Mushroom Sauce instead of pickled walnuts.

Serves 4

15ml/1 tbsp vegetable oil

75g/3oz/6 tbsp butter

8 slices of beef fillet (filet mignon)

4 onions, sliced

15ml/1 tbsp pickled walnut juice

salt and ground black pepper

pickled walnut slices to garnish

1 Heat the oil and half the butter in a frying pan and cook the steaks until almost done. Keep them warm.

2 Once you have taken your steaks out of the pan, melt the remaining butter then add the sliced onions. Increase the heat and stir to brown and soften the onions, scraping the base of the pan.

3 Add the pickled walnut juice and cook for a few minutes. Season to taste with salt and pepper. Serve the steams on warmed plates, with the onions and juices spooned over, and garnished with slices of pickled walnut.

Energy 490kcal/2036kJ; Protein 43.4g; Carbohydrate 6.1g, of which sugars 4.3g; Fat 32.6g, of which saturates 17g; Cholesterol 167mg; Calcium 31mg; Fibre 1.1g; Sodium 219mg

Scottish collops of beef with shallots

Once again, the beef is paired with the sweetness of onions – a combination you will find time and again in traditional Scottish cooking. In this dish shallots are being used, left whole to impart a wonderful texture and flavour to the meal.

Serves 4

4 fillet steaks (beef tenderloin)

15ml/1 tbsp olive oil

50g/2oz/¼ cup butter

20 shallots, peeled

5ml/1 tsp caster (superfine) sugar

150ml/¼ pint/⅔ cup beef stock

salt and ground black pepper

1 Take the steaks out of the refrigerator well before you need them and dry with kitchen paper. Heat the oil and butter in a large frying pan then cook the steaks as you like them.

2 Once cooked remove the steaks from the pan and keep warm. Put the shallots in the pan and brown lightly in the meat juices. Add the sugar and then the stock. Reduce the heat to low and allow the liquid to evaporate, shaking the pan from time to time to stop the shallots sticking.

3 The shallots will end up slightly soft, browned and caramelized with a shiny glaze. Season to taste with salt and ground black pepper.

4 Serve the steaks on warmed plates and spoon over the caramelized shallots and juices from the pan.

Energy 424kcal/1767kJ; Protein 43.2g; Carbohydrate 6.1g, of which sugars 4.6g; Fat 25.4g, of which saturates 12.5g; Cholesterol 149mg; Calcium 27mg; Fibre 0.9g; Sodium 166mg

Irish corned beef with dumplings and cabbage

Once the traditional favourite for Easter, corned beef now tends to be associated with
St Patrick's Day. If lightly cured, the meat may need to be soaked before cooking, but check
with the butcher when buying; if in doubt, soak in cold water overnight.

Serves 6

1.3kg/3lb corned silverside or brisket

1 onion

4 cloves

2 bay leaves

8–10 whole black peppercorns

1 small cabbage

For the dumplings

1 small onion, finely chopped

small bunch of parsley, chopped

115g/4oz/1 cup self-raising
(self-rising) flour

50g/2oz shredded beef suet (chilled,
grated shortening) or similar

salt and ground black pepper

1 Soak the meat in cold water, if
necessary, for several hours or overnight.
When ready to cook, drain the meat
and put it into a large heavy pan or
flameproof casserole. Cover with fresh
cold water.

2 Stick the cloves into the onion and
add it to the pan with the bay leaves
and peppercorns. Bring slowly to the
boil, cover and simmer for 2 hours,
or until the meat is tender.

3 Meanwhile, make the dumplings:
mix the onion and parsley with the
flour, suet and seasoning, and then
add just enough water to make a soft,
but not too sticky, dough. Dust your
hands with a little flour and shape the
dough into 12 small dumplings.

4 When the meat is cooked, remove
it from the pan and keep warm. Bring
the cooking liquid to a brisk boil, put
in the dumplings and bring back to
the boil. Cover tightly and cook the
dumplings briskly for 15 minutes.

5 Meanwhile, slice the cabbage leaves
finely and cook lightly in a little of the
beef stock (keep the remaining stock
for making soup). Serve the beef sliced
with the dumplings and shredded
cabbage. Boiled potatoes and parsley
sauce are traditional accompaniments.

Energy 451Kcal/1895kJ; Protein 54.6g; Carbohydrate 21g, of which sugars 4.5g; Fat 17.4g, of which saturates 7.7g; Cholesterol 139mg; Calcium 86mg; Fibre 2.4g; Sodium 142mg

Shepherd's pie

This dish developed during Victorian days as a thrifty way of using up leftovers. By the 1930s it had become part of a regular weekly pattern of eating, made with leftover meat from the Sunday roast and served to the family on Monday or Tuesday.

Serves 4

1kg/2¼lb potatoes, peeled

60ml/4 tbsp milk

about 25g/1oz/2 tbsp butter

15ml/1 tbsp oil

1 large onion, finely chopped

1 medium carrot, finely chopped

450g/1lb cold cooked lamb, minced (ground)

150ml/¼ pint/⅔ cup lamb or beef stock

30ml/2 tbsp finely chopped fresh parsley

salt and ground black pepper

1 Preheat the oven to 190°C/375°F/Gas 5. Boil the potatoes in salted water for about 20 minutes or until soft. Drain, and mash with the milk, adding butter and seasoning to taste.

Variations Add extra ingredients to the meat base, such as a clove or two of chopped garlic, a few mushrooms, a spoonful of tomato purée (paste) or ketchup, or a splash of Worcestershire sauce. You could also mix the potatoes with parsnip or swede (rutabaga), and add a dollop of wholegrain mustard.

2 Heat the oil in a frying pan and add the onion and carrot. Cook over medium heat for 5–10 minutes, stirring occasionally, until soft. Stir in the minced meat, stock and parsley.

3 Spread the meat mixture in an ovenproof dish and spoon the mashed potato evenly over the top. Cook in the hot oven for about 30 minutes until the potatoes are crisped and browned.

Energy 487kcal/2045kJ; Protein 29.4g; Carbohydrate 50.1g, of which sugars 15.2g; Fat 20.2g, of which saturates 8.4g; Cholesterol 69mg; Calcium 54mg; Fibre 5.3g; Sodium 379mg

Lancashire hotpot

This famous hotpot was traditionally cooked in a farmhouse or communal bread oven, in time for supper at the end of the day. The ingredients would have been layered straight into the pot, but here the meat is first browned to add colour and extra flavour to the dish.

Serves 4

15–30ml/1–2 tbsp oil

8–12 lean best end of neck (cross rib) lamb chops

about 175g/6oz lamb's kidneys, skin and core removed and cut into pieces

2 medium onions, thinly sliced

few sprigs of fresh thyme or rosemary

900g/2lb potatoes, thinly sliced

600ml/1 pint/2½ cups lamb or vegetable stock

25g/1oz/2 tbsp butter, in small pieces

salt and ground black pepper

1 Preheat the oven to 180°C/350°F/ Gas 4. Heat the oil in a large frying pan and brown the lamb chops quickly on all sides. Remove the meat from the pan and set aside.

Variation Add sliced carrots or mushrooms to the layers. Replace 150ml/¼ pint/⅔ cup of the stock with dry (hard) cider or wine.

2 Add the kidney to the hot pan and brown lightly over a high heat. Lift out.

3 In a casserole, layer the chops and kidneys with the onions, herbs and potatoes, seasoning each layer.

4 Finish off with a layer of potatoes. Pour over the stock, sprinkle with herbs and dot the top with butter. Cover, put into the oven and cook for 2 hours. Remove the lid, increase the oven temperature to 220°C/425°F/Gas 7 and cook, uncovered, for a further 30 minutes until the potatoes are crisp.

Energy 810kcal/3400kJ; Protein 76.7g; Carbohydrate 43.7g, of which sugars 9.3g; Fat 37.8g, of which saturates 13.2g; Cholesterol 363mg; Calcium 140mg; Fibre 6.2g; Sodium 285mg

Roast shoulder of lamb with mint sauce

Lamb is one of the three meats (with beef and pork) that is traditionally roasted and served for a British Sunday lunch. It is particularly popular at Easter. Mint sauce, with its sweet-sour combination, has accompanied roast lamb since at least the 17th century.

Serves 6–8

boned shoulder of lamb, weighing 1.5–2kg/3¼–4½lb

30ml/2 tbsp fresh thyme leaves

30ml/2 tbsp clear honey

150ml/¼ pint/⅔ cup dry (hard) cider or white wine

30–45ml/2–3 tbsp double (heavy) cream (optional)

salt and ground black pepper

For the mint sauce

large handful of fresh mint leaves

15ml/1 tbsp caster (superfine) sugar

45–60ml/3–4 tbsp cider vinegar or wine vinegar

1 Preheat the oven to 220°C/425°F/ Gas 7. To make the mint sauce, finely chop the mint leaves with the sugar (the sugar draws the juices from the mint) and put the mixture into a bowl.

2 Add 30ml/2 tbsp boiling water (from the kettle) to the mint and sugar, and stir well until the sugar has dissolved. Add the vinegar to taste and leave the sauce to stand for at least 1 hour for the flavours to blend.

3 Open out the lamb with skin side down. Season with salt and pepper, sprinkle with the thyme leaves and drizzle the honey over the top. Roll up and tie securely with string in several places. Place the meat in a roasting pan and put into the hot oven. Cook for 30 minutes until browned all over.

4 Pour the cider and 150ml/¼ pint/ ⅔ cup water into the tin. Lower the oven to 160°C/325°F/Gas 3 and cook for about 45 minutes for medium (pink) or about 1 hour for well done meat.

5 Remove the lamb from the oven, cover loosely with a sheet of foil and leave to stand for 20–30 minutes.

6 Lift the lamb on to a warmed serving plate. Skim any excess fat from the surface of the pan juices before reheating and seasoning to taste. Stir in the cream, if using, bring to the boil and remove from the heat. Carve the lamb and serve it with the pan juices spooned over and the mint sauce.

Energy 351kcal/1468kJ; Protein 36.9g; Carbohydrate 2.5g, of which sugars 2.5g; Fat 21g, of which saturates 9.8g; Cholesterol 143mg; Calcium 23mg; Fibre 0g; Sodium 202mg

Welsh cawl

Traditionally, *cawl mamgu*, "granny's broth", would have been made with bony pieces of lamb and beef, usually from the neck or shin – full of flavour and cheap. A large pot of cawl fed a family for several days, with ingredients added each time it was reheated.

Serves 4

30ml/2 tbsp olive oil

2 onions, roughly chopped

2 celery sticks, thickly sliced

2 carrots, thickly sliced

2 parsnips, roughly chopped

1 small swede (rutabaga), roughly chopped

800g/1¾lb lamb, such as boned shoulder, trimmed and cut into bitesize pieces

lamb or vegetable stock

30ml/2 tbsp chopped fresh thyme leaves or 10ml/2 tsp dried thyme

3 potatoes

2 leeks, trimmed

handful of chopped fresh parsley

salt and ground black pepper

1 Heat a large pan, add half the oil and stir in the onions, celery, carrots, parsnips and swede. Cook all the vegetables quickly, stirring occasionally until golden brown and then lift them out.

2 Add the remaining oil to the pan, quickly brown the lamb in batches and then lift it out.

3 Return the browned lamb and vegetables to the pan and pour over enough stock to cover the ingredients. Add the thyme and a little seasoning.

4 Bring to the boil and skim off any surface scum. Cover and cook gently, so that the liquid barely bubbles, for about 1½ hours, until the lamb is tender.

5 Peel and cut the potatoes into cubes and add to the pan. Cover and cook gently for 15–20 minutes until just soft.

6 Thinly slice the white part of the leeks and add to the pan, adjust the seasoning to taste and cook for 5 minutes.

7 Before serving, thinly slice the green parts of the leeks and add to the broth with the parsley. Cook for a few minutes until the leeks soften and serve.

Energy 594kcal/2488kJ; Protein 45.2g; Carbohydrate 39.4g, of which sugars 17.9g; Fat 29.6g, of which saturates 11.5g; Cholesterol 152mg; Calcium 151mg; Fibre 8.5g; Sodium 224mg

Welsh saltmarsh lamb with laverbread sauce

Laverbread goes particularly well with saltmarsh lamb. It makes a delicious sauce with milk that has been infused with vegetables and spices. This is particularly good served with mixed root vegetables such as carrots, parsnips and swede.

Serves 6

100g/3½oz fresh breadcrumbs

50g/2oz/½ cup fine oatmeal

1 small onion, finely chopped

5ml/1 tsp fresh rosemary leaves

grated rind of ½ orange

boned loin of saltmarsh lamb, weighing about 1kg/2¼lb

425ml/¾ pint/scant 2 cups milk

1 small onion, roughly chopped

1 small carrot, roughly chopped

1 small celery stick, roughly chopped

a few black peppercorns

a few allspice berries (optional)

1 bay leaf

30ml/2 tbsp plain (all-purpose) flour

30ml/2 tbsp laverbread

salt and ground black pepper

1 Preheat the oven to 200°C/400°F/Gas 7. Mix the breadcrumbs, oatmeal, onion, rosemary, orange rind and seasoning.

2 Open up the lamb and place on a board, skin side down. Place the stuffing down the centre in a thick sausage shape.

3 Roll the lamb back into shape to enclose the stuffing. Tie securely with string in several places along the roll. Place in a roasting tin (pan).

4 Put into the hot oven and cook for 15 minutes, then reduce the temperature to 160°C/325°F/Gas 3 and cook for a further 30–40 minutes or until the lamb is cooked to your liking.

5 Meanwhile, put the milk in a pan with the onion, carrot, celery, peppercorns, allspice (if using) and bay leaf. Heat slowly and, as soon as the milk boils, remove from the heat and leave to stand for the flavours to infuse for at least 15 minutes.

6 When the lamb is cooked, lift it out and leave in a warm place to rest for 15 minutes.

7 Pour any excess fat from the tin, leaving 15–30ml/1–2 tbsp. Strain the milk into the tin and, with a whisk, stir in the flour. Cook over medium heat, stirring with the whisk, until the sauce thickens and comes to the boil. Stir in the laverbread and bubble gently for a minute or two.

8 Adjust the seasoning, and add any juices that may have seeped from the lamb. Serve the lamb with the sauce.

Energy 406kcal/1704kJ; Protein 36.4g; Carbohydrate 21.6g, of which sugars 2.9g; Fat 20g, of which saturates 8.8g; Cholesterol 127mg; Calcium 77mg; Fibre 2.1g; Sodium 256mg

Lamb with honey, rosemary and cider

Welsh mountain lamb with honey and rosemary are traditional partners. Here they are teamed with dry cider and cooked until the lamb is meltingly soft and the sweet juices are caramelized and golden. There are several cider producers operating in Wales today, concentrated mainly in the south-east of the country. Every year the Welsh Cider Festival is held in the City Hall, Cardiff. Serve with roast potatoes and leafy greens.

Serves 4–6

1.5kg/3lb 6oz shoulder of lamb

2 garlic cloves, halved

fresh rosemary sprigs

75ml/5 tbsp clear honey

300ml/½ pint/1¼ cups dry (hard) cider, plus extra if necessary

lemon juice (optional)

salt and ground black pepper

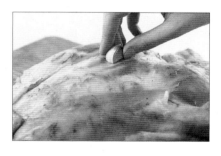

1 Preheat the oven to 220°C/425°F/Gas 7. Rub the lamb with the cut garlic. Put the meat and the garlic in a deep roasting tin (pan). Season with salt and pepper.

2 Make small slashes in the meat with a knife and push in a few small sprigs of rosemary.

3 Stir the honey into the cider until it has fully dissolved and then pour it over the lamb.

4 Put the roasting tin into the hot oven and cook the lamb for 20–30 minutes until it has browned and the juices have reduced, begun to caramelize and turn golden brown. Keep checking to make sure the liquid does not dry up and brown too much.

5 Stir 300ml/½ pint water into the pan juices and spoon them over the lamb. Cover with a large tent of foil, scrunching the edges around the rim of the tin to seal them.

6 Put the roasting tin back into the oven, reduce the temperature to 180°C/350°F/Gas 4 and cook for about another hour.

7 Remove the foil and spoon the juices over the lamb again. Turn the oven temperature back up to 220°C/425°F/Gas 7 and continue cooking, uncovered, for a further 10–15 minutes, until the outside of the lamb is crisp and brown.

8 Lift the lamb on to a serving plate and leave in a warm place to rest for 15 minutes before carving.

9 While the lamb is resting, spoon any excess fat off the top of the juices in the tin. Then taste the juices and adjust the seasoning, if necessary, adding lemon juice to taste. Put the roasting tin on the hob and bring just to the boil.

10 Serve the carved lamb and vegetables with the meat juices.

Cook's tip Though it looks attractive when the rosemary stands proud of the lamb, it is likely to burn. So make sure the slashes are deep and that you push the rosemary sprigs into the lamb.

Variation Apple juice, light vegetable stock or water could be used in place of cider.

Energy 524kcal/2180kJ; Protein 35.3g; Carbohydrate 10.9g, of which sugars 10.9g; Fat 36.5g, of which saturates 17g; Cholesterol 153mg; Calcium 17mg; Fibre 0g; Sodium 130mg

Barnsley chops with mustard sauce

Named after the Yorkshire town of Barnsley, this double-sized lamb chop is cut from the saddle – the two loins with the backbone intact between them. It is served here with mustard sauce, also a Yorkshire favourite with lamb.

Serves 4

15ml/1 tbsp tender rosemary leaves

60ml/4 tbsp olive oil

4 Barnsley chops or 8 lamb loin chops

100ml/3½fl oz/scant ½ cup lamb or beef stock

30ml/2 tbsp wholegrain mustard

5ml/1 tsp Worcestershire sauce

salt and ground black pepper

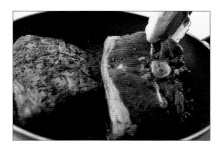

1 Chop the rosemary and mix with the oil. Rub the mixture over the chops and leave to stand, covered, for 30 minutes.

2 Heat a large frying pan. Season the chops with salt and pepper.and fry over a medium heat for 5–8 minutes on each side until cooked.

3 Lift the chops out of the pan, and keep warm. Pour the stock into the hot pan, scraping up any sediment.

4 Add the mustard to the stock. Heat until the mixture comes to the boil and leave to bubble gently until reduced by about one third. Stir in the Worcestershire sauce and adjust the seasoning. Serve the chops with the mustard sauce spooned over.

Energy 582kcal/2401kJ; Protein 18.8g; Carbohydrate 0.9g, of which sugars 0.8g; Fat 55.9g, of which saturates 23.6g; Cholesterol 96mg; Calcium 17mg; Fibre 0g; Sodium 313mg

Scottish mutton hotpot

Another traditional cottage favourite, this mutton hotpot would have been a Sunday treat in the remote highlands of Scotland. Mutton is hard to come by today but it really is worth looking out for. Try your local farmers' market or ask your butcher if he could get it for you. It often has a superior flavour to lamb, although it does require longer, slower cooking.

Serves 6

6 mutton chops

6 lamb's kidneys

1 large onion, sliced

450g/1lb potatoes, sliced

600ml/1 pint/2½ cups dark stock

salt and ground black pepper

1 Preheat the oven to 180°C/350°F/ Gas 4. Trim the mutton chops, leaving a little fat but no bone. Slice the kidneys in two horizontally and remove the fat and core with sharp scissors.

2 Place three of the chops in a deep casserole and season well with salt and ground black pepper.

3 Add a layer of half the kidneys, then half the onion and finally half the potatoes. Season lightly.

4 Repeat the process, seasoning as you go and making sure that you finish with an even layer of potatoes.

5 Heat the stock and pour it into the casserole, just about covering everything but leaving the potatoes just showing at the top. Cover and cook in the preheated oven for 2 hours, removing the lid for the last 30 minutes to allow the potatoes to brown.

Variation If you prefer, you can use lamb chops instead. Use 2 chops per person and reduce the cooking time by 30 minutes as lamb does not need 2 hours.

Energy 626kcal/2629kJ; Protein 76.9g; Carbohydrate 23.1g, of which sugars 5g; Fat 25.8g, of which saturates 11.6g; Cholesterol 374mg; Calcium 76mg; Fibre 2g; Sodium 269mg

Welsh minted lamb with leeks and honey

Mint, together with thyme and savory, have always been significant culinary herbs in Wales, and mint's particular affinity with lamb is indisputable. For this dish the lamb is marinated in a mixture of oil, lemon juice and mint before it is pan-fried.

2 Heat a frying pan and add the remaining oil and the lamb. Cook over medium heat for 6–8 minutes each side or until browned and cooked to your liking. Lift out and keep warm.

3 Drain off any excess fat from the pan, leaving about 15ml/1 tbsp. Add the leeks and garlic, and scrape up any sediment from the base of the pan. Cover and cook over medium heat for about 5 minutes, stirring occasionally, until the leeks are soft.

Serves 2

30ml/2 tbsp olive oil

15ml/1 tbsp fresh lemon juice

30ml/2 tbsp finely chopped fresh mint leaves

4 lamb chops or steaks

250g/9oz/2 cups leeks, thinly sliced

1 garlic clove, finely chopped or crushed

45ml/3 tbsp double (heavy) cream

10ml/2 tsp clear honey

salt and ground black pepper

1 In a shallow, non-metal container, mix 15ml/1 tbsp of the oil with the lemon juice, a little seasoning and 15ml/1 tbsp of the mint. Add the lamb and turn until well coated with the mint mixture. If time allows, cover and leave to stand for 30 minutes (or longer in the refrigerator), turning the lamb over occasionally.

4 Stir in the remaining mint, cream and honey and heat gently until bubbling. Adjust the seasoning if necessary. Serve the leeks in sauce with the lamb.

Variation This recipe also works well with rosemary instead of mint. Strip the tender young leaves from a small sprig and chop them finely.

Energy 521kcal/2166kJ; Protein 31.8g; Carbohydrate 7.9g, of which sugars 7g; Fat 40.5g, of which saturates 17g; Cholesterol 145mg; Calcium 54mg; Fibre 2.8g; Sodium 137mg

Irish stew

Ireland's national dish was traditionally made with mature mutton, but lamb is now usual.
There are long-standing arguments about the correct ingredients for an authentic Irish stew
This is a modern variation using lamb chops.

Serves 4

1.3kg/3lb best end of neck
of mutton or lamb chops

900g/2lb potatoes

small bunch each of parsley
and thyme, chopped

450g/1lb onions, sliced

salt and ground black pepper

1 Trim all the fat, bone and gristle from
the meat, and cut it into fairly large
pieces. See Variations if using chops.
Slice one-third of the potatoes and cut
the rest into large chunks.

2 Arrange the potatoes in a casserole,
and then add a sprinkling of herbs,
then half the meat and finally half the
onion, seasoning each layer. Repeat
the layers, finishing with the potatoes.

3 Pour over 450ml/¾ pint/scant 2 cups
water, and cover tightly; add a sheet of
foil before putting on the lid if it is not
a very close-fitting one.

4 Simmer the stew very gently for
about 2 hours, or cook in the oven at
120°C/250°F/Gas ½, if you prefer. Shake
the casserole from time to time to
prevent sticking.

5 Check the liquid level occasionally
during the cooking time and add extra
water if necessary; there should be
enough cooking liquor to have made a
gravy, thickened by the sliced potatoes.

6 Serve hot on warmed serving plates.
This stew tastes even better heated up
the next day.

Variations

• Trimmed lamb or mutton chops can
be arranged around the edge of the
pan, with the sliced onions and
chopped potatoes, herbs and
seasonings in the middle. Add the
water and cook as above.

• Hogget – lamb over a year old – is
available in the spring and early summer.

Energy 869Kcal/3627kJ; Protein 69.1g; Carbohydrate 47.6g, of which sugars 7.7g; Fat 45.9g, of which saturates 20.8g; Cholesterol 244mg; Calcium 53mg; Fibre 4.5g; Sodium 218mg

Rack of lamb with herb crust

This dish is very popular in Irish restaurants and for special occasions at home. Serve with creamy potato gratin, baby carrots and a green vegetable such as mangetouts or green beans. Offer some traditional mint jelly as an accompaniment.

Serves 6–8

2 racks of lamb (fair end), chined and trimmed by the butcher

salt, ground black pepper and a pinch of cayenne pepper

For the herb crust

115g/4oz/½ cup butter

10ml/2 tsp mustard powder

175g/6oz/3 cups fresh breadcrumbs

2 garlic cloves, finely chopped

30ml/2 tbsp chopped fresh parsley

5ml/1 tsp very finely chopped fresh rosemary

mint jelly, to serve

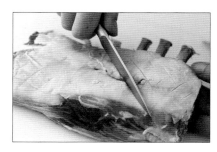

1 Preheat the oven to 200°C/400°F/ Gas 6. Remove any fat from the top of the bones and scrape clean, then wrap in foil to prevent burning. Remove almost all the fat from the lamb and score the thin layer remaining to make a lattice pattern; this will help to hold the herb crust in place later.

2 Season the lamb with salt, pepper and cayenne pepper, and cook the racks in the preheated oven for 20 minutes. Remove from the oven and allow to cool to room temperature.

3 Next make the herb crust: when the lamb is cold, blend 75g/3oz/6 tbsp of the butter with the mustard to make a smooth paste, and spread it over the fatty sides of the lamb.

4 Mix the breadcrumbs, garlic, parsley and rosemary together in a bowl. Melt the remaining butter, add it to the bowl and combine well. Divide the herb mixture between the two racks, laying it on top of the butter paste and pressing it well on to the lamb. Set aside and keep at room temperature until ready to finish cooking.

5 When ready to cook the meat, preheat the oven to 200°C/400°F/ Gas 6, and roast for a final 20 minutes. To serve, remove the foil from the bones; finish them with paper cutlet frills, if you wish. Carve into cutlets, allowing 2 or 3 per person, and replace any of the crust that falls off.

Cook's tip This modern dish is convenient for entertaining as it is made in two stages, allowing the main preparation to be done ahead.

Energy 455Kcal/1899kJ; Protein 26.4g; Carbohydrate 22.7g, of which sugars 0.9g; Fat 29.4g, of which saturates 16.1g; Cholesterol 130mg; Calcium 51mg; Fibre 0.7g; Sodium 438mg

Irish lamb and carrot casserole with barley

Barley and carrots make natural partners for lamb and mutton. In this convenient casserole the barley ekes out the meat and adds to the flavour and texture as well as thickening the sauce. The dish is comfort food at its best. Serve with a green vegetable, such as cabbage.

Serves 6

675g/1½lb stewing lamb

15ml/1 tbsp oil

2 onions, sliced

675g/1½lb carrots, thickly sliced

4–6 celery sticks, sliced

45ml/3 tbsp pearl barley, rinsed

stock or water

salt and ground black pepper

chopped fresh parsley, to garnish

1 Trim the lamb and cut it into bitesize pieces. Heat the oil in a flameproof casserole and brown the lamb.

2 Add the vegetables to the casserole and fry them briefly with the meat. Add the barley and enough stock or water to cover, and season to taste.

3 Cover the casserole and simmer gently or cook in a slow oven, 150°C/300°F/Gas 2 for 1–1½ hours until the meat is tender. Add extra stock or water during cooking if necessary. Serve garnished with the chopped fresh parsley.

***Right** A flock of sheep grazing in summertime, Owenmore Valley, Dingle, County Kerry.*

Energy 304Kcal/1263kJ; Protein 23.2g; Carbohydrate 13g, of which sugars 11.3g; Fat 18g, of which saturates 7.5g; Cholesterol 84mg; Calcium 53mg; Fibre 3.6g; Sodium 110mg

Roast pork with crackling and apple sauce

A roast joint makes a traditional centrepiece for Sunday lunch with family or friends. Since Roman times it has been customary to offset the richness of the pork with sharp fruit flavours. Serve this fruit-stuffed loin of pork with freshly cooked seasonal vegetables.

Serves 6

15ml/1 tbsp light olive oil

2 leeks, chopped

150g/5oz/⅔ cup ready-to-eat dried apricots, chopped

150g/5oz/1 cup dried dates, stoned (pitted) and chopped

75g/3oz/1½ cups fresh white breadcrumbs

2 eggs, beaten

15ml/1 tbsp fresh thyme leaves

1.5kg/3¼lb boned loin of pork

salt and ground black pepper

For the apple sauce

450g/1lb cooking apples

30ml/2 tbsp cider or water

25g/1oz/2 tbsp butter

about 25g/1oz/2 tbsp caster (superfine) sugar

1 Preheat the oven to 220°C/425°F/ Gas 7. To make the stuffing, heat the oil in a large pan and cook the leeks until softened. Remove from the heat and stir in the apricots, dates, breadcrumbs, eggs and thyme and season with salt and pepper.

2 Lay the pork skin side up, and use a very sharp knife to score the rind into diamonds. (You may find it easier to do this with a clean craft knife or scalpel.)

3 Turn the joint over and cut vertically down the centre of the meat to within 1cm/½in of the rind and fat, then cut horizontally from the middle outwards towards each side to open out the joint for stuffing.

4 Spoon half the stuffing into the cut surfaces, then fold the meat over. Tie the joint back into its original shape, then place in a roasting pan and rub the skin liberally with salt.

5 Put the joint into the hot oven and cook for 40 minutes. Reduce the temperature to 190°C/375°F/Gas 5 and cook for a further 1½ hours, or until the meat is cooked through – the juices should run clear when the meat is pierced with a sharp knife.

6 Meanwhile, shape the remaining stuffing into walnut-sized balls. Arrange on a tray, cover with clear film (plastic wrap) and chill until 30 minutes before the pork is cooked. Then add the balls to the roasting pan and baste them with the cooking juices from the meat.

7 To make the apple sauce, peel, core and chop the apples, then place in a small pan with the cider or water and cook, stirring occasionally, for 5–10 minutes, or until very soft. Beat well or blend in a blender or food processor until smooth. Beat in the butter and sugar to taste. Reheat the apple sauce just before serving, if necessary.

8 When the meat is cooked, cover it closely with foil and leave to stand in a warm place for 10 minutes to rest before carving. Carve the pork into thick slices and serve with pieces of the crackling, the stuffing balls and the apple sauce.

Energy 582kcal/2452kJ; Protein 59.9g; Carbohydrate 48.3g, of which sugars 38.6g; Fat 17.9g, of which saturates 6.5g; Cholesterol 230mg; Calcium 91mg; Fibre 5.2g; Sodium 327mg

Irish stuffed pork steak

Pork steak is the Irish name for the cut known as pork fillet, tenderloin or boneless fillet.
It is lean, tender but expensive, so it is usually served stuffed to make the meat go further.
The stuffing also help to keep the meat moist.

2 Put the breadcrumbs, herbs, onion, butter, egg, orange rind and salt and pepper in a bowl. Mix together with a fork, including as much of the orange juice as is required to bind the stuffing. Set aside any leftover juice.

3 To cook the pork steaks individually, divide the stuffing mixture in half and lay it down the centre of each steak; fold the flaps up towards the middle and secure with cotton string or skewers to make a roll. Alternatively, turn all the stuffing on to one of the steaks, spread evenly, and then cover with the second steak. Secure with string or skewers.

4 Rub the pork steaks with a little softened butter. Season with salt and pepper and put into a shallow dish or roasting pan with 300ml/½ pint/ 1¼ cups water to prevent the meat drying out during cooking.

Serves 6

2 evenly sized pork steaks, about 400g/14oz each

115g/4oz/2 cups fresh white breadcrumbs

small bunch of parsley and thyme, leaves chopped

1 onion, chopped

25g/1oz/2 tbsp butter, melted

1 egg, lightly beaten

finely grated rind and juice of 1 small orange

softened butter, for the steaks

15ml/1 tbsp plain (all-purpose) flour (optional)

salt and ground black pepper

1 Preheat the oven to 180°C/350°F/Gas 4. Slit the pork steaks along the length with a sharp knife; do not cut right through. Hold out each of the flaps this has created and slit them lengthways in the same way, without cutting right through. Flatten out gently.

Cook's tip Be careful to use cotton string to secure the stuffing, as synthetic twine will melt in the oven.

5 Cover with a lid or foil and cook in the preheated oven for 1 hour, turning and basting after 30 minutes cooking.

6 When the meat is cooked, remove from the tin and make a gravy by thickening the meat juices with a little flour in the roasting pan. Add the reserved orange juice to the gravy, heat through and serve with the steaks.

Energy 279Kcal/1173kJ; Protein 32g; Carbohydrate 16.1g, of which sugars 1.4g; Fat 10.1g, of which saturates 4.3g; Cholesterol 125mg; Calcium 44mg; Fibre 0.6g; Sodium 276mg

Somerset pork casserole

Right up until the 20th century, many country folk kept and reared a pig, and not one bit of it was wasted. Apple is its perfect partner in this modern West Country dish. The extensive orchards of Somerset supply apples from which both juices and cider are made.

Serves 4

500g/1¼lb lean belly pork, weighed after removing rind and bones

15ml/1 tbsp oil

1 medium onion, chopped

2 celery sticks, sliced

600ml/1 pint/2½ cups chicken stock

300ml/½ pint/1¼ cups medium-dry apple juice

15ml/1 tbsp clear honey

pinch of ground cloves

15ml/1 tbsp fresh thyme leaves

4 fresh sage leaves, finely chopped

2 medium carrots, sliced

2 leeks, sliced

2 x 400g/14oz can haricot beans, drained

salt and ground black pepper

chopped parsley, to garnish

1 Cut the pork into 2.5cm/1in cubes. Heat the oil in a large heavy pan.

2 Add the cubed pork to the pan and cook over a medium-high heat, turning each piece so they are golden brown all over.

3 Add the onion and celery and cook for about 5 minutes.

4 Add the stock, apple juice, honey, cloves, thyme and sage. Bring to the boil, cover and simmer for 1 hour, stirring occasionally. Stir in the carrots and leeks.

5 Stir in the beans and add a little seasoning. Bring just to the boil and simmer gently for a further 20–30 minutes, or until the pork is very tender.

6 Adjust the seasoning to taste and sprinkle some chopped parsley over the casserole before serving.

Energy 619kcal/2594kJ; Protein 39g; Carbohydrate 52g, of which sugars 22.8g; Fat 29.7g, of which saturates 9.8g; Cholesterol 89mg; Calcium 189mg; Fibre 15g; Sodium 891mg

Roast belly of pork with root vegetables

Nothing quite compares with the rich flavour of belly of pork, particularly when it is topped with a crisp layer of crackling. The secret with this Welsh recipe is to make sure the vegetables do not dry out during roasting. Let them, and the pan juices, reach a deep golden brown before topping up with additional water.

2 Cut the vegetables into small cubes and stir them with the oil in a roasting tin (pan), tossing until evenly coated. Place the pork on top of the vegetables, skin side uppermost. Pour in 300ml/½ pint/1¼ cups water.

3 Put the roasting tin into the oven and cook for 30 minutes, by which time the liquid will have almost evaporated to leave a crust in the bottom of the tin.

4 Add 600ml/1 pint/2½ cups cold water to the tin. Reduce the oven temperature to 180°C/350°F/Gas 4, and cook for 1½ hours, or until the pork is tender and the juices run clear when the centre of the meat is pierced with a skewer. Add a little extra water if necessary.

Serves 4–6

1.5kg/3lb 6oz belly of pork, well scored

1 small swede (rutabaga)

1 onion

1 parsnip

2 carrots

15ml/1 tbsp olive oil

15ml/1 tbsp fresh thyme leaves or 5ml/1 tsp dried thyme

sea salt and ground black pepper

1 Preheat the oven to 220°C/425°F/ Gas 7. Sprinkle the pork rind with thyme, salt and pepper, rubbing them well into the slashes in the pork belly.

5 If the crackling is not yet crisp enough, increase the oven temperature to 220°C/425°F/Gas7 and continue cooking for another 10–20 minutes, adding extra water if necessary.

6 With a sharp knife, slice off the crackling. Serve it with thick slices of the pork, some vegetables and the golden juices spooned over.

Energy 1014kcal/4194kJ; Protein 39.5g; Carbohydrate 9.4g, of which sugars 7.3g; Fat 91.2g, of which saturates 33.1g; Cholesterol 180mg; Calcium 81mg; Fibre 3.3g; Sodium 202mg

Ham with mustard sauce and crispy cabbage

This is an updated version of the traditional Irish dish of boiled bacon and cabbage, in which the meat – either gammon or any cut of boiling bacon – is cooked in milk. This helps to counteract the saltiness, keeps the meat beautifully moist, and imparts a delicious and unusual flavour. The leftover milk stock can be used to make soup.

Serves 4–6

1.3kg/3lb piece of gammon or boiling bacon

30ml/2 tbsp oil

2 large onions, sliced

1 bay leaf

750ml/1¼ pints/3 cups milk, plus extra if necessary

15ml/1 tbsp cornflour (cornstarch), dissolved in 15ml/1 tbsp milk

45ml/3 tbsp wholegrain mustard

15–30ml/2–3 tbsp single (light) cream (optional)

1 head of cabbage, such as Savoy, trimmed, ribs removed and leaves finely sliced

ground black pepper

3 Remove the meat from the pan and keep warm. Strain the cooking liquid. Reserve 300ml/½ pint/1¼ cups for the sauce and put the remainder aside.

4 Add the cornflour mixture to the reserved liquid and bring up to the boil, stirring constantly. As it begins to thicken, stir in the wholegrain mustard and cream, if using.

5 Rinse the cabbage in cold running water and drain well. Heat the remaining oil in a wok or large frying pan and stir-fry the cabbage for 2–3 minutes until cooked but still crunchy. Slice the ham and serve on warmed serving plates with the mustard sauce and crisply cooked cabbage.

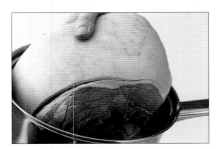

1 Soak the bacon joint in cold water overnight. To cook, heat 15ml/1 tbsp oil in a large pan, add the onions and cook gently for a few minutes.

2 Place the joint on the bed of onions. Add the bay leaf and milk, and season with pepper. Bring to the boil, cover with a tight-fitting lid and cook over a gentle heat for about 1½ hours. When the meat is cooked, the skin will peel off easily.

Energy 541Kcal/2253kJ; Protein 58.4g; Carbohydrate 7.4g, of which sugars 5g; Fat 30.8g, of which saturates 9.4g; Cholesterol 77mg; Calcium 76mg; Fibre 2.1g; Sodium 2.87g

Somerset cider-glazed ham

William the Conqueror is credited with bringing the art of cider-making to England from Normandy in 1066. This wonderful West Country ham glazed with cider is traditionally served with cranberry sauce and is ideal for Christmas or Boxing Day.

Serves 8–10

2kg/4½lb middle gammon (smoked or cured ham) joint

2 small onions

about 30 whole cloves

3 bay leaves

10 black peppercorns

1.3 litres/2¼ pints/5⅔ cups medium-dry (hard) cider

45ml/3 tbsp soft light brown sugar

For the cranberry sauce

350g/12oz/3 cups cranberries

175g/6oz/¾ cup soft light brown sugar

grated rind and juice of 2 clementines

30ml/2 tbsp port

1 Weigh the ham and calculate the cooking time at 20 minutes per 450g/1lb. Place in a large pan. Stud the onions with 10 cloves and add the bay leaves and peppercorns.

2 Add 1.2 litres/2 pints/5 cups of the cider and enough water just to cover the ham. Heat until simmering and skim off the scum that rises to the surface.

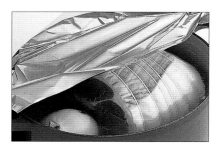

3 Start timing the cooking from the moment the stock begins to simmer. Cover with a lid or foil and simmer gently for the calculated time. Towards the end of the cooking time, preheat the oven to 220°C/425°F/Gas 7.

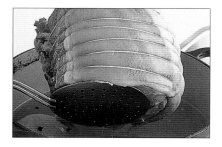

4 Lift the ham out of the pan. Leave to stand until cool enough to handle.

5 Heat the sugar and remaining cider in a pan until the sugar dissolves. Bubble gently for about 5 minutes to make a dark glaze. Remove the pan from the heat and leave to cool for 5 minutes.

6 Carefully and evenly, cut off the rind of the ham, then score the fat to make a neat diamond pattern. Place the ham in a roasting tin. Press a clove into the centre of each diamond, then carefully spoon the glaze over. Put into the hot oven and cook for 20–25 minutes, or until brown, glistening and crisp.

7 To make the cranberry sauce, simmer all the ingredients in a heavy pan for 15–20 minutes, stirring frequently, until the fruit bursts and the sauce thickens. Pour into a serving dish.

8 Serve the ham hot or cold with the cranberry sauce.

Cook's tips
• If the ham is very salty, soak it overnight in cold water before cooking. Your butcher will advise you.
• Reserve the stock used to cook the ham and use it to make a hearty split pea or lentil soup.

Energy 368kcal/1541kJ; Protein 39.6g; Carbohydrate 15.2g, of which sugars 15.2g; Fat 16.9g, of which saturates 5.6g; Cholesterol 52mg; Calcium 25mg; Fibre 0.6g; Sodium 1982mg

Haggis with clapshot cake

Haggis is probably the best known of all Scottish traditional dishes, not least because of the famous Burns poem which is recited the world over in front of a haggis at suppers celebrating the poet. This is the traditional haggis recipe served with turnip and potato clapshot – a variation on the "haggis with neeps and tatties" theme.

Serves 4

1 large haggis, approximately 800g/1¾lb

450g/1lb peeled turnip or swede (rutabaga)

225g/8oz peeled potatoes

120ml/4fl oz/½ cup milk

1 garlic clove, crushed with 5ml/1 tsp salt

175ml/6fl oz/¾ cup double (heavy) cream

freshly grated nutmeg

ground black pepper

butter, for greasing

1 Preheat the oven to 180°C/350°F/ Gas 4. Wrap the haggis in foil, covering it completely and folding over the edges of the foil.

Cook's tip If you are serving haggis on Burns Night (January 25th), you need to bring the haggis whole to the table on a platter and cut it open reciting the famous Burns poem. This is done in honour of Robert Burns, the celebrated Scottish poet.

2 Place the haggis in a roasting pan with about 2.5cm/1in water. Heat through in the preheated oven for 30–40 minutes.

3 Slice the turnip or swede and potatoes quite finely. A mandolin or food processor is quite handy for the turnip or swede as both vegetables tend to be hard and difficult to cut finely with a knife.

4 Put the sliced vegetables in a large pan and add the milk and garlic. Stir gently and continuously over a low heat until the potatoes begin to break down and exude their starch and the liquid thickens slightly.

5 Add the cream and nutmeg and grind some black pepper into the mixture. Stir gently but thoroughly. Slowly bring to the boil, reduce the heat and simmer gently for a few minutes.

6 Butter a deep round 18cm/7in dish or a small roasting pan. Transfer the vegetable mixture to the dish or pan. It shouldn't come up too high as it will rise slightly and bubble.

7 Bake in the oven for about 1 hour, or until you can push a knife easily through the cake. The top should be nicely browned by this time. If it is becoming too brown on top, cover it with foil and continue baking. If it is not browned enough after 1 hour of cooking, place it under a hot grill (broiler) for a few minutes.

8 Remove the foil from the haggis, place on a warmed serving dish and bring out to the table for your guests to witness the cutting. Use a sharp knife to cut through the skin then spoon out the haggis on to warmed plates. Serve the clapshot cake in slices with the haggis, spooning any juices over.

Energy 918kcal/3819kJ; Protein 24.9g; Carbohydrate 55.3g, of which sugars 8.5g; Fat 67.9g, of which saturates 30.2g; Cholesterol 244mg; Calcium 180mg; Fibre 3.1g; Sodium 1586mg

Rissoles

In a 16th-century English recipe for "rissheshewes", finely chopped cooked meat was mixed with breadcrumbs and bound into little cakes with beaten eggs, which were then cooked on the griddle and served with a thick gravy. These contemporary rissoles include mashed potato as well as breadcrumbs, which makes the mixture easier to shape.

Serves 4

675g/1½lb potatoes, peeled

350g/12oz cooked beef or lamb, such as the remains of a joint, trimmed of excess fat

1 small onion

5ml/1 tsp Worcestershire sauce

30ml/2 tbsp chopped fresh herbs, such as parsley, mint and chives

30ml/2 tbsp plain (all-purpose) flour

2 eggs, beaten

115g/4oz/2 cups fresh breadcrumbs

oil for frying

salt and ground black pepper

1 Cook the whole potatoes in boiling water for about 20 minutes or until completely soft. Meanwhile, mince (grind) or chop the meat very finely. Finely chop the onion.

2 Drain the potatoes and mash them thoroughly by pushing the warm potatoes through a ricer, passing them through a mouli (grater), or mashing them with a potato masher or fork.

3 In a large mixing bowl combine the meat and onion with the potatoes, Worcestershire sauce, herbs and seasoning, beating well. Shape the mixture into eight patties or sausages.

4 Dip in the flour, then in the beaten egg and finally in the breadcrumbs, gently shaking off any excess.

5 Heat enough oil to cover the base of a large frying pan and cook the rissoles over a medium heat, turning once or twice, until crisp and golden brown. Drain and serve with brown sauce.

Cook's tip
• Chilling the potato and meat mixture before shaping the rissoles will make it easier to handle.
• A peppery leaf, such as watercress or rocket makes a good accompaniment to the rissoles.

Energy 519kcal/2184kJ; Protein 27.4g; Carbohydrate 56.7g, of which sugars 4.1g; Fat 22g, of which saturates 6.5g; Cholesterol 162mg; Calcium 86mg; Fibre 2.8g; Sodium 363mg

Welsh faggots with onion gravy

In the days when most households reared a pig at the bottom of the garden, these faggots – Ffagod – were made with the fresh liver on slaughter day. The paté-like mixture was wrapped in the lacy netting of the pig's caul, which held the contents together during the cooking process. Serve the faggots with peas and mashed potato.

Serves 4

450g/1lb pig's liver, trimmed and roughly chopped

300g/11oz belly pork, roughly chopped

2 onions, roughly chopped

100g/3½oz/1 cup fresh breadcrumbs

1 egg, beaten

2 sage leaves, chopped

5ml/1 tsp salt

2.5ml/½ tsp ground mace

1.5ml/¼ tsp ground black pepper

150ml/¼ pint/⅔ cup beef or vegetable stock

butter for greasing

For the onion gravy:

50g/2oz/¼ cup butter

4 onions (white, red or a mixture), thinly sliced

generous 10ml/2 tsp sugar

15ml/1 tbsp plain (all-purpose) flour

300ml/½ pint/1¼ cups good beef stock

300ml/½ pint/1¼ cups good vegetable stock

salt and black pepper

1 Preheat the oven to 180°C/350°F/Gas 4. Put the liver, pork and onions in a food processor and process until finely chopped. Then turn the mixture out into a large mixing bowl and stir in the breadcrumbs, egg, sage, salt, mace and pepper until thoroughly combined.

2 With wet hands, shape the mixture into 10–12 round faggots and lay them in a shallow ovenproof dish. Pour in the stock.

3 Use a buttered sheet of foil to cover the dish, butter side down. Crimp the edges around the dish to seal them.

4 Cook in the oven for 45–50 minutes (the juices should run clear when the faggots are pierced with a sharp knife).

5 For the onion gravy, melt the butter in a large pan and add the onions and sugar. Cover and cook gently for at least 30 minutes, until the onions are soft and evenly caramelized to a rich golden brown.

6 Stir in the flour, remove from the heat and stir in both types of stock. Return the pan to the heat and, stirring continuously, bring just to the boil. Simmer gently for 20-30 minutes, stirring occasionally (if the liquid looks like reducing too much, add a splash of water). Season to taste with salt and pepper.

7 Once cooked, remove the foil covering the faggots and increase the oven temperature to 200°C/400°F/Gas 6. Cook for a further 10 minutes until lightly browned. Serve with the onion gravy.

Energy 664kcal/2768kJ; Protein 41.4g; Carbohydrate 31.2g, of which sugars 9.8g; Fat 42.5g, of which saturates 17.9g; Cholesterol 421mg; Calcium 84mg; Fibre 2.2g; Sodium 434mg

Oven-cooked potatoes with bacon

This Welsh dish from Carmarthenshire is often called Miser's Feast. Originally, the potatoes, onions and slices of bacon would have been layered in the cooking pot with water and then cooked over an open fire. Here, a flameproof casserole is put on the hob. Serve with a crisp salad or stir-fried vegetables, or as an accompaniment to grilled sausages.

2 The next stage is to add the thinly sliced onions to the bacon in the casserole. Cook for 5–10 minutes, stirring occasionally, until the onions have slightly softened and turned a rich golden brown.

3 Add the potatoes and stir well. Pour in the stock and level the surface, pushing the potatoes and onions into the liquid. Season with black pepper.

Serves 4

15ml/1 tbsp oil

25g/1oz/2 tbsp butter

8 thick rindless bacon rashers (strips), chopped

2 onions, thinly sliced

1kg/2¼lb potatoes, thinly sliced

600ml/1 pint/2½ cups stock

ground black pepper

chopped fresh parsley, to garnish

1 Preheat the oven to 190°C/ 375°F/ Gas 5. Heat the oil and butter in a wide flameproof casserole, add the bacon and cook over medium heat, stirring occasionally, until the bacon is just beginning to brown at its edges.

Variations
• Use chicken stock or vegetable stock, or a mixture of both.
• Try adding a little chopped fresh sage, shredded wild garlic or leeks, or some grated mature cheese in step 4.

4 Bring to the boil, cover and put into the hot oven. Cook for 30–40 minutes or until the vegetables are soft.

5 Remove the cover. Raise the oven temperature to 220°C/425°F/Gas 7 and cook for a further 15–20 minutes, until the top is crisp and golden brown. Garnish with some chopped parsley.

Energy 385kcal/1615kJ; Protein 14.8g; Carbohydrate 48.2g, of which sugars 8.9g; Fat 16.1g, of which saturates 7.1g; Cholesterol 43mg; Calcium 44mg; Fibre 3.9g; Sodium 935mg

Welsh bacon, chicken and leek pudding

Old-fashioned suet puddings are still a favourite in Wales, and this one is bursting with flavour. The pastry is quite thin, but to make it thicker, simply increase the flour to 225g/8oz/2 cups and the suet to 100g/3½oz/⅔ cup. Serve it with seasonal vegetables or a green salad tossed lightly in an oil and vinegar dressing.

Serves 4

200g/7oz unsmoked lean, rindless bacon, preferably in one piece

400g/14oz skinless boneless chicken, preferably thigh meat

2 small or medium leeks, finely chopped

30ml/2 tbsp finely chopped fresh parsley

175g/6oz/1¼ cups self-raising (self-rising) flour

75g/3oz/½ cup shredded suet

120ml/4fl oz chicken or vegetable stock, or water

ground black pepper

butter for greasing

1 Cut the bacon and chicken into bitesize pieces into a large bowl. Mix them with the leeks and half the parsley. Season with black pepper.

2 Sift the flour into another large bowl and stir in the suet and the remaining parsley. With a round-bladed knife, stir in sufficient cold water to make a soft dough. On a lightly floured surface, roll out the dough to a circle measuring about 33cm/13in across. Cut out one quarter of the circle (starting from the centre, like a wedge), roll up and reserve.

3 Lightly butter a 1.2 litre/2 pint pudding bowl. Use the rolled out dough to line the buttered bowl, pressing the cut edges together to seal them and allowing the pastry to overlap the top of the bowl slightly.

4 Spoon the bacon and chicken mixture into the lined bowl, packing it neatly and taking care not to split the pastry. Pour the chicken or vegetable stock over the bacon mixture making sure it does not overfill the bowl.

5 Roll out the reserved pastry into a circle to form a lid and lay it over the filling, pinching the edges together to seal them well. Cover with baking parchment (pleated in the centre to allow the pudding to rise) and then a large sheet of foil (again pleated at the centre). Tuck the edges under and press them tightly to the sides of the bowl until well sealed.

6 Steam the pudding over boiling water for about 3½ hours. Check the water level occasionally. Uncover the pudding, slide a knife around the sides and turn out on to a warmed serving plate.

Energy 535kcal/2236kJ; Protein 28.2g; Carbohydrate 39.4g, of which sugars 2.9g; Fat 31.3g, of which saturates 14.8g; Cholesterol 86mg; Calcium 111mg; Fibre 4g; Sodium 999mg

Liver, bacon and onions

Simple yet so full of flavour, this dish was traditionally made with pig's liver. Here, lamb's liver is the main ingredient, although you can use pig's liver if you prefer. Serve with creamy mashed potatoes to soak up the sauce, maybe with swede, parsnip or pumpkin added.

2 Heat the oil in a large frying pan and add the bacon. Cook over medium heat until the fat runs out of the bacon and it is browned and crisp. Lift out and keep warm.

3 Add the onions and sage to the frying pan. Cook over medium heat for about 10–15 minutes, stirring occasionally, until the onions are soft and golden brown. Lift out with a draining spoon and keep warm.

4 Increase the heat under the pan and, adding a little extra oil if necessary, add the liver in a single layer. Cook for 3–4 minutes, turning once, until browned on both sides.

Serves 4

450g/1lb lamb's liver

30ml/2 tbsp plain (all-purpose) flour

15ml/1 tbsp oil, plus extra if necessary

8 rindless streaky (fatty) bacon rashers (slices)

2 onions, thinly sliced

4 fresh sage leaves, finely chopped

150ml/¼ pint/⅔ cup chicken or vegetable stock

salt and ground black pepper

1 Pat the liver with kitchen paper, then trim it and, with a sharp knife, cut on the diagonal to make thick strips. Season the flour and toss the liver in it until it is well coated, shaking off any excess flour.

5 Return the onions to the pan and pour in the stock. Bring just to the boil and bubble gently for a minute or two, seasoning to taste with salt and pepper. Serve topped with the bacon.

Energy 310kcal/1293kJ; Protein 28.7g; Carbohydrate 13.7g, of which sugars 5.7g; Fat 15.9g, of which saturates 4.4g; Cholesterol 500mg; Calcium 44mg; Fibre 1.6g; Sodium 400mg

Braised sausages with onions, celeriac and apple

Britain boasts a wealth of wonderful sausages made by artisan producers across the regions. For this recipe, choose your favourite good-quality sausages, such as traditional pork, Cumberland, or something more unusual, such as duck, venison or wild boar.

Serves 4

30ml/2 tbsp oil

8 meaty sausages

2 onions, sliced

15ml/1 tbsp plain (all-purpose) flour

400ml/14fl oz/1⅔ cups dry (hard) cider

350g/12oz celeriac, cut into chunks

15ml/1 tbsp Worcestershire sauce

15ml/1 tbsp chopped fresh sage

2 small cooking apples

salt and ground black pepper

1 Preheat the oven to 180°C/350°F/ Gas 4. Heat the oil in a frying pan, add the sausages and fry for about 5 minutes until evenly browned.

2 Transfer the sausages to an ovenproof cassserole dish and drain any excess oil from the pan to leave 15ml/1 tbsp. Add the onions and cook for a few minutes, stirring occasionally, until softened and turning golden.

3 Stir in the flour, then gradually add the cider and bring to the boil, stirring. Add the celeriac and stir in the Worcestershire sauce and sage. Season with salt and black pepper.

4 Pour the cider and celeriac mixture over the sausages. Cover, put into the hot oven and cook for 30 minutes, or until the celeriac is soft.

5 Quarter the apples, remove their cores and cut into thick slices. Stir the apple slices into the casserole, cover and cook for a further 10–15 minutes, or until the apples are just tender. Taste and adjust the seasoning if necessary before serving.

Energy 508kcal/2114kJ; Protein 12.7g; Carbohydrate 29.3g, of which sugars 13.6g; Fat 35.8g, of which saturates 12.3g; Cholesterol 45mg; Calcium 131mg; Fibre 3.3g; Sodium 1019mg

Dublin coddle

This utterly Irish dish combines bacon and sausages, two foods found in the earliest Irish literature, and is said to have been Jonathan Swift's favourite meal. Leeks and oatmeal were originally used but potatoes and onion are popular nowadays.

Makes 4 large or 8 small portions

8 x 8mm/⅓in thick ham or dry-cured bacon slices

8 best-quality lean pork sausages

4 large onions, thinly sliced

900g/2lb potatoes, peeled and sliced

90ml/6 tbsp chopped fresh parsley

salt and ground black pepper

1 Cut the ham or bacon into large chunks and cook with the sausages in 1.2 litres/2 pints/5 cups boiling water for 5 minutes. Drain, but reserve the cooking liquor.

2 Put the meat into a pan or ovenproof dish with the onions, potatoes and the parsley. Season, and add just enough of the reserved cooking liquor to cover. Cover with a tight-fitting lid; lay a piece of buttered foil or baking parchment on top before putting on the lid.

3 Simmer gently over a low heat for about 1 hour, or until the liquid is reduced by half and all the ingredients are cooked but not mushy. Serve hot with the vegetables on top; and traditional accompaniments of fresh soda bread and a glass of stout.

Energy 432Kcal/1809kJ; Protein 20.6g; Carbohydrate 52g, of which sugars 10.2g; Fat 17.2g, of which saturates 6.1g; Cholesterol 45mg; Calcium 83mg; Fibre 5.7g; Sodium 1.27g

Toad in the hole

Early versions of toad in the hole, in the 18th century, were made with pieces of meat rather than sausages: one very grand recipe even called for fillet steak. Today the "toads" are sausages and the batter is that used for Yorkshire pudding. There is an English pub game of the same name, where discs are thrown at a hole in the table.

Serves 6

175g/6oz/1½ cups plain (all-purpose) flour

2.5ml/½ tsp salt

2 eggs

300ml/½ pint/1¼ cups milk

30ml/2 tbsp oil

500g/1¼lb meaty butcher's sausages

1 Preheat the oven to 220°C/425°F/ Gas 7. To make the batter, sift the flour and salt into a bowl, make a well in the centre and break the eggs into it.

2 Mix the milk with 300ml/½ pint/ 1¼ cups cold water. Using a whisk, gradually stir the milk mixture into the bowl with the eggs, incorporating the flour and beating well to make a smooth batter. Leave to stand.

3 Pour the oil into a roasting pan and add the sausages (cut in half crosswise if large). Put into the hot oven and cook for about 10 minutes until the oil is very hot and the sausages begin to brown.

4 Stir the batter, quickly pour it around the sausages and return to the oven. Cook for about 45 minutes or until the batter is puffed up, set and golden brown. Serve immediately.

Energy 497kcal/2070kJ; Protein 14.5g; Carbohydrate 32.1g, of which sugars 3.8g; Fat 35.4g, of which saturates 13.6g; Cholesterol 109mg; Calcium 141mg; Fibre 1.3g; Sodium 616mg

Casseroled venison with stout

Venison, both wild and (more usually) farmed, is widely available in Britain. It is popular on restaurant menus and, increasingly, available to home cooks from butchers and the better supermarkets. Serve with boiled or baked potatoes and red cabbage.

Serves 6

900g/2lb stewing venison, such as shoulder

45ml/3 tbsp seasoned flour

30ml/2 tbsp olive oil

2 or 3 large onions, sliced

5 or 6 juniper berries, crushed

3 allspice berries

rind of ½ lemon or orange

25g/1oz/2 tbsp butter

about 300ml/½ pint/1¼ cups chicken or beef stock

150ml/¼ pint/⅔ cup red wine vinegar or cider vinegar

300ml/½ pint/1¼ cups stout or red wine

salt and ground black pepper

1 Preheat the oven to 180°C/350°F/Gas 4. Cut the meat into 5cm/2in cubes. Toss the meat in the seasoned flour. Shake off and reserve the excess flour.

2 Heat the oil in a heavy frying pan and fry the meat in it until well browned all over. Lift out the pieces with a slotted spoon and put them into a casserole. Add the onions to the casserole with the juniper berries and allspice, a little salt and black pepper and the lemon or orange rind.

3 Melt the butter in the pan in which the meat was browned, add the reserved flour, and stir and cook for 1 minute. Mix the stock, vinegar and stout or red wine together and gradually add to the pan, stirring until it boils and thickens.

4 Pour the sauce over the meat in the casserole, cover closely and cook in the oven for 1 hour. Reduce the temperature to 150°C/300°F/Gas 2 and cook for a further 2 hours, or until the venison is tender. Check the casserole occasionally and add a little extra stock or water if required. Serve piping hot.

Cook's tip Venison is not difficult to cook but, like other game, it is lean, so marinating, basting and braising all help to offset any tendency to dryness.

Energy 294Kcal/1233kJ; Protein 34.7g; Carbohydrate 9.3g, of which sugars 4.9g; Fat 10.6g, of which saturates 3.9g; Cholesterol 84mg; Calcium 37mg; Fibre 1.3g; Sodium 114mg

Roast Scottish venison

Venison has been eaten in Scotland for generations, by kings, lairds and ordinary people, hunted and poached in equal measure. Today there are a number of deer farms, which produce high quality meat. This recipe marinates the meat for two days.

Serves 4

1 venison haunch, approximately 2.75kg/6lb

30ml/2 tbsp olive oil

25g/1oz/2 tbsp butter

225g/8oz bacon, diced

salt and ground black pepper

For the marinade

1 onion, sliced

2 carrots, peeled and sliced

60ml/4 tbsp olive oil

1 bottle red wine

2 garlic cloves, crushed

1 bay leaf

5 black peppercorns

sprig of rosemary

6 juniper berries

For the sauce

15ml/1 tbsp plain (all-purpose) flour

15ml/1 tbsp butter, softened

150ml/¼ pint/⅔ cup port

15ml/1 tbsp Scottish Rowan Jelly

1 Marinate the meat two days before cooking. Cook the onion and carrots in the olive oil, without allowing them to colour. Then put the mixture into a non-metallic container that is large enough to hold the venison.

2 Add the other ingredients, put the haunch in and leave for two days, turning regularly to coat all sides.

3 When ready to cook, preheat the oven to 160°C/325°F/Gas 3. Remove the haunch from the marinade and dry with kitchen paper.

4 Put a large casserole, into which the haunch will fit with the lid on, over a high heat and add the oil and butter. Brown the bacon and then the haunch, browning it all over.

5 In another pan, reduce the marinade by half by boiling it rapidly and then strain over the haunch. Cover and cook for 30 minutes per 450g/1lb. When cooked, remove and keep warm, covered in foil so it does not dry out.

6 Strain the juices into a pan and boil rapidly. Make a beurre manié by mixing the flour and butter together then whisk it into the boiling liquor. Simmer until reduced by half. Add the port and the rowan jelly, adjust the seasoning, if necessary, and serve.

Energy 978kcal/4132kJ; Protein 167.1g; Carbohydrate 11.1g, of which sugars 7.3g; Fat 25.2g, of which saturates 8.8g; Cholesterol 383mg; Calcium 52mg; Fibre 0.2g; Sodium 442mg

Scottish venison pie

This is a variation on cottage or shepherd's pie using rich venison, and the result is particularly tasty – a hearty treat after an energetic day hiking through the Highlands. Serve with lightly steamed green vegetables such as kale or cabbage.

Serves 6

30ml/2 tbsp olive oil

2 leeks, washed, trimmed and chopped

1kg/2¼lb minced (ground) venison

30ml/2 tbsp chopped fresh parsley

300ml/½ pint/1¼ cups game consommé

salt and ground black pepper

For the topping

1.4kg/3¼lb mixed root vegetables, such as sweet potatoes, parsnips and swede (rutabaga), coarsely chopped

15ml/1 tbsp horseradish sauce

25g/1oz/2 tbsp butter

1 Heat the oil in a pan over a medium heat. Add the leeks and cook for about 8 minutes, or until they are softened and beginning to brown.

2 Add the minced venison to the pan and cook over a medium heat, stirring frequently, for about 10 minutes or until the venison is thoroughly browned all over.

3 Add the chopped fresh parsley and stir it in thoroughly, then add the consommé and salt and ground black pepper. Stir well. Bring the mixture to the boil over a medium heat, then reduce the heat to low, cover and simmer gently for about 20 minutes, stirring occasionally.

4 Meanwhile, preheat the oven to 200°C/400°F/Gas 6 and prepare the pie topping. Cook the chopped root vegetables in boiling salted water to cover for 15–20 minutes.

Variation
• This pie can be made with other minced (ground) meats, such as beef, lamb or pork. You may need to adapt the cooking times for these, depending on the type that you use, although the basic recipe remains the same.
• You can also use other types of game meats for this pie, such as finely chopped or minced rabbit or hare.

5 Drain the vegetables and put them in a bowl. Mash them together with the horseradish sauce, butter and plenty of ground black pepper.

6 Spoon the venison mixture into a large ovenproof dish and cover the top evenly with the mashed vegetables. It is often easier to spoon it over in small quantities rather than pouring it on and then smoothing it out.

7 Bake in the preheated oven for 20 minutes, or until piping hot and beginning to brown. Serve immediately, with steamed green vegetables.

Cook's tip
• Use wild venison if possible as it has more flavour and the lowest fat level. If you can't get it, then use farmed venison, which will work well in this dish. Look for organic farmed vension.
• If leeks aren't available, then use a large onion and chop it coarsely.

Energy 307kcal/1291kJ; Protein 39.8g; Carbohydrate 13.2g, of which sugars 12.5g; Fat 12g, of which saturates 4.1g; Cholesterol 93mg; Calcium 154mg; Fibre 5.8g; Sodium 176mg

Collops of venison with rowan sauce

A slice of meat is called a collop in Scotland, where it makes a popular, easy-to-prepare and nutritious meal. Rowan berries come from the mountain ash, which grows all over Britain, in parts of Europe and as a shade tree in the USA. The berries make a light red jelly with a sharp flavour that partners venison perfectly.

Serves 4

4 venison haunch steaks, about 200g/7oz each

15ml/1 tbsp vegetable oil

50g/2oz/¼ cup butter

15ml/1 tbsp Scottish Rowan Jelly

120ml/4fl oz/½ cup red wine

salt and ground black pepper

1 Bring the steaks out of the refrigerator a few hours prior to cooking, so that they will cook more quickly. Before cooking, dry the steaks on kitchen paper and season with salt and ground black pepper.

2 Heat a heavy pan and add the oil and half the butter. Cook the haunch steaks as you would a sirloin or fillet, browning both sides and then reducing the heat to complete the cooking.

3 When cooked to your liking, remove the steaks from the pan, set them aside and keep warm.

4 Mix together the rowan jelly and wine and then add to the pan, stirring to bring up the meat juices and dissolve the jelly. Once the jelly has melted, season the sauce with salt and ground black pepper then, off the heat, swirl in the remaining butter. Serve the steaks on warmed plates with the sauce poured over.

Energy 355kcal/1488kJ; Protein 44.5g; Carbohydrate 2.7g, of which sugars 2.7g; Fat 17.4g, of which saturates 8.4g; Cholesterol 127mg; Calcium 15mg; Fibre 0g; Sodium 189mg

Smoked venison with creamy potato bake

Smoked venison is one of Scotland's lesser known treasures, and it can be used in many different ways. The best smoked venison is, of course, from wild animals taken from the moors and hills. The only smokery in Scotland to smoke wild venison is Rannoch Smokery in Perthshire. This warming dish makes an ideal supper or lunch.

Serves 4

675g/1½lb peeled potatoes

175ml/6fl oz/¾ cup milk

olive oil, for greasing and to serve

1 garlic clove

10ml/2 tsp sea salt

75ml/2½fl oz/⅓ cup double (heavy) cream

115g/4oz sliced smoked venison

salad leaves, to garnish

1 Preheat the oven to 180°C/350°F/ Gas 4. Slice the potatoes thinly using a sharp knife or mandolin. Place in a pan and pour in the milk. Grease a large gratin dish with olive oil.

2 Crush the garlic in the sea salt with the side of a knife. Add to the potatoes. Bring to the boil over a gentle heat, until the milk begins to thicken.

3 Add the cream to the potatoes and, stir. Allow to just come to the boil again then pour into the gratin dish. Place the dish in the preheated oven for about 1 hour until lightly browned and tender.

4 To serve, divide the smoked venison on to 4 warmed plates, dress with a splash of olive oil. then add a spoonful of potato to each plate.

Energy 281kcal/1180kJ; Protein 15.6g; Carbohydrate 29.5g, of which sugars 4.5g; Fat 12g, of which saturates 6.1g; Cholesterol 25mg; Calcium 80mg; Fibre 1.7g; Sodium 1050mg

Poultry and game

Every countrywoman used to keep poultry – with birds and eggs providing an extra source of income as well as food for the family table – and goose, turkey and chicken have long been associated with celebratory meals and seasonal feasts such as Michaelmas and Christmas. Game – both furred and feathered – is plentiful when in season, and there are lovely traditional recipes here for every kind.

Stuffed roast chicken with bread sauce

Chicken today is a popular choice in Britain for roasting. Free-range and organic birds taste best and are more like the birds that previous generations regarded as a luxury food. Add sausages and potatoes to the tin and roast with the chicken for a complete meal.

Serves 6

1 chicken weighing about 1.8kg/4lb, with giblets and neck if possible

1 small onion, sliced

1 small carrot, sliced

small bunch of parsley and thyme

15g/½oz/1 tbsp butter

30ml/2 tbsp oil

6 rashers (strips) fatty bacon

15ml/1 tbsp plain (all-purpose) flour

300ml/½ pint/1¼ cups chicken stock

salt and ground black pepper

For the stuffing

1 onion, finely chopped

50g/2oz/4 tbsp butter

150g/5oz/2½ cups fresh white breadcrumbs

15ml/1 tbsp chopped fresh parsley

15ml/1 tbsp chopped fresh herbs, such as thyme, marjoram and chives

grated rind and juice of ½ lemon

For the bread sauce

1 small onion, sliced

1 bay leaf

6 black peppercorns

2 whole cloves

pinch of mace or grated nutmeg

400ml/14fl oz/1⅔ cups milk

50g/2oz/1 cup fresh breadcrumbs

25g/1oz/2 tbsp butter

1 Put the giblets and neck into a pan with the sliced onion and carrot and the bunch of parsley and thyme. Season with salt and pepper. Cover generously with cold water, bring to the boil and simmer gently for about 1 hour. Strain the stock, discarding the giblets. Preheat the oven to 200°C/400°F/Gas 6.

2 To make the stuffing, cook the onion in the butter in a large pan over low heat until soft. Remove from the heat and stir in the breadcrumbs, herbs, lemon rind and juice, salt and pepper.

3 Spoon the stuffing into the neck cavity of the chicken and secure the opening with a small skewer. Weigh the stuffed chicken and calculate the cooking time at 20 minutes per 450g/1lb plus 20 minutes extra. Spread the chicken breast with the butter, then put the oil into a roasting pan and sit the bird in it. Season and lay the bacon rashers over the breast.

4 Put the chicken into the hot oven. After 20 minutes, reduce the temperature to 180°C/350°F/Gas 4 and cook for the remaining time. To check the chicken is cooked, insert a sharp knife between the body and the thigh: if the juices run clear with no hint of blood, it is done.

5 Meanwhile, make the bread sauce. Into a pan, put the onion, bay leaf, peppercorns, cloves, mace and milk. Bring slowly to the boil, remove from the heat, cover and leave to stand for 30 minutes or longer to infuse. Strain and return the milk to the cleaned pan, add the breadcrumbs and seasoning. Heat until bubbling and simmer gently for about 10 minutes until thick and creamy. Stir in the butter and it is ready to serve.

6 Transfer the cooked chicken to a serving dish and allow it to rest for 10 minutes in a warm place while you make the gravy.

7 To make the gravy, pour off the excess fat from the roasting pan, then sprinkle in the flour. Cook gently, stirring, for 1–2 minutes. Gradually add the stock, scraping the pan to lift the residue and stirring well until smooth. Bring to the boil, stirring and adding extra stock if necessary. Adjust the seasoning to taste.

8 Carve the chicken, and serve with the gravy and bread sauce.

Cook's tip If you prefer not to stuff the chicken, the stuffing can be formed into small balls and baked around the bird for the last 20–30 minutes of the cooking time.

Energy 823kcal/3420kJ; Protein 55.7g; Carbohydrate 21.1g, of which sugars 19.1g; Fat 57.8g, of which saturates 19.7g; Cholesterol 383mg; Calcium 113mg; Fibre 4.9g; Sodium 252mg

Mustard baked chicken

In this Irish recipe, a mild, aromatic wholegrain mustard makes a tasty way of cooking chicken. Speciality mustards are made by several companies in Ireland, although the mustard seeds are imported. Serve with new potatoes and peas or mangetouts.

Serves 4–6

8–12 chicken joints, or 1 medium chicken, about 1kg/2¼lb, jointed

juice of ½ lemon

15–30ml/2–3 tbsp whiskey mustard

10ml/2 tsp chopped fresh tarragon

sea salt and ground black pepper

Variation A whole chicken can also be baked this way. Allow about 1½ hours in an oven preset to 180°C/350°F/ Gas 4. When cooked, the juices will run clear without any trace of blood.

1 Preheat the oven to 190°C/375°F/ Gas 5. Put the chicken joints into a large shallow baking dish in a single layer and sprinkle the lemon juice over the chicken to flavour the skin. Season well with sea salt and black pepper.

2 Spread the mustard over the joints and sprinkle with the chopped tarragon. Bake in the preheated oven for 20–30 minutes or until thoroughly cooked, depending on the size of the chicken pieces. Serve immediately.

Energy 426Kcal/1768kJ; Protein 40.3g; Carbohydrate 0g, of which sugars 0g; Fat 29.3g, of which saturates 8.1g; Cholesterol 215mg; Calcium 13mg; Fibre 0g; Sodium 146mg

Irish hen in a pot with parsley sauce

Many Irish familes keep hens for eggs, and the older ones are destined for the table. Although harder to find nowadays, a boiling fowl will feed a family well. A large chicken could replace the boiling fowl. Serve with potatoes, boiled in their skins, and cabbage.

Serves 6

1.6–1.8kg/3½–4lb boiling fowl

½ lemon, sliced

small bunch of parsley and thyme

675g/1½lb carrots, cut into large chunks

12 shallots or small onions, left whole

For the sauce

50g/2oz/¼ cup butter

50g/2oz/½ cup plain (all-purpose) flour

15ml/1 tbsp lemon juice

60ml/4 tbsp finely chopped fresh parsley

150ml/¼ pint/⅔ cup milk

salt and ground pepper

fresh parsley sprigs, to garnish

1 Put the fowl into a large pan with enough water to cover. Add the sliced lemon and parsley and thyme, and season well with salt and pepper.

2 Cover the pan and bring to the boil, then reduce the heat and simmer over a gentle heat for 2½ hours, turning several times during cooking.

3 Add the carrots and whole onions to the pot and cook for another 30–40 minutes, or until the fowl and the vegetables are tender.

4 Using a slotted spoon, lift the fowl on to a warmed serving dish, arrange the vegetables around it and keep warm. Remove the herbs and lemon slices from the cooking liquor and discard.

5 Bring the liquor back to the boil and boil it, uncovered, to reduce the liquid by about a third. Strain and leave to settle for 1–2 minutes, then skim the fat off the surface.

6 Melt the butter in a pan, add the flour and cook, stirring, for 1 minute. Gradually stir in the stock (there should be about 600ml/1 pint/2½ cups) and bring to the boil. Add the lemon juice, parsley and the milk. Adjust the seasoning and simmer the sauce for another 1–2 minutes.

7 To serve, pour a little of the sauce over the fowl and the carrots and onions, then garnish with a few sprigs of fresh parsley and take to the table for carving. Pour the rest of the sauce into a heated sauceboat and hand round separately.

Energy 509Kcal/2114kJ; Protein 36.2g; Carbohydrate 20.1g, of which sugars 12.2g; Fat 31.9g, of which saturates 11.4g; Cholesterol 195mg; Calcium 109mg; Fibre 4g; Sodium 214mg

Scottish stoved chicken

The word "stoved" is derived from the French *étuver* – to cook in a covered pot – and originates from the time of the Franco/Scottish Alliance in the 17th century. Instead of buying chicken legs, you can also choose either chicken thighs or chicken drumsticks.

Serves 4

900g/2lb potatoes, cut into 5mm/¼in slices

2 large onions, thinly sliced

15ml/1 tbsp chopped fresh thyme

25g/1oz/¼ stick butter

15ml/1 tbsp oil

2 large bacon rashers (strips), chopped

4 large chicken legs, halved

1 bay leaf

600ml/1 pint/2½ cups chicken stock

salt and ground black pepper

1 Preheat the oven to 150°C/300°F/ Gas 2. Make a thick layer of half the potato slices in the base of a large, heavy casserole, then cover with half the onion. Sprinkle with half the thyme and salt and ground black pepper.

2 Heat the butter and oil in a large frying pan then brown the bacon and chicken. Using a slotted spoon, transfer the chicken and bacon to the casserole. Reserve the fat in the pan.

3 Tuck the bay leaf in between the chicken. Sprinkle the remaining thyme over, then cover with the rest of the onion, followed by a neat layer of overlapping potato slices. Season.

4 Pour the stock into the casserole. Brush the top layer of the sliced potatoes with the reserved fat from the frying pan, then cover tightly and cook in the preheated oven for about 2 hours, until the chicken is thoroughly cooked and tender.

5 Preheat the grill (broiler) to high. Uncover the casserole and place under the grill and cook until the slices of potato are beginning to brown and crisp. Serve hot.

Variation You can use tarragon instead of the thyme: French tarragon has a superior flavour to the Russian variety.

Energy 630kcal/2653kJ; Protein 69.2g; Carbohydrate 48.2g, of which sugars 8.9g; Fat 19.2g, of which saturates 7.2g; Cholesterol 195mg; Calcium 57mg; Fibre 3.9g; Sodium 574mg

Hunter's chicken

This tasty dish sometimes has strips of green pepper in the sauce instead of the mushrooms. It is excellent served with creamy mashed potatoes, and can be great for a lunch or late supper with a good chunk of fresh crusty bread.

Serves 4

30ml/2 tbsp olive oil

15g/½oz/1 tbsp butter

4 chicken portions, on the bone

1 large onion, thinly sliced

400g/14oz can chopped tomatoes

150ml/¼ pint/⅔ cup red wine

1 garlic clove, crushed

1 rosemary sprig, finely chopped, plus extra whole sprigs to garnish

115g/4oz fresh field (portabello) mushrooms, thinly sliced

salt and ground black pepper

1 Heat the oil and butter in a large, flameproof casserole until foaming. Add the chicken portions and fry for 5 minutes. Remove the chicken pieces and drain on kitchen paper.

2 Add the sliced onion and cook gently, stirring frequently, for about 3 minutes then stir in the tomatoes and red wine.

3 Add the crushed garlic and chopped rosemary and season. Bring to the boil, stirring continuously.

4 Return the chicken to the casserole and turn to coat with the sauce. Cover with a tightly fitting lid and simmer gently for 30 minutes.

5 Add the fresh mushrooms to the casserole and stir well to mix into the sauce. Continue simmering gently for 10 minutes, or until the chicken is tender. Taste and add more salt and ground black pepper if necessary. Garnish with the fresh rosemary sprigs. Serve hot, with creamy mashed potatoes or crusty white bread and butter, if you like.

Energy 386kcal/1622kJ; Protein 53.6g; Carbohydrate 4.5g, of which sugars 4.1g; Fat 14.5g, of which saturates 4.5g; Cholesterol 155mg; Calcium 28mg; Fibre 1.5g; Sodium 141mg

Roast chicken with leek, laver and lemon stuffing

In this Welsh dish, leek, laver and lemon complement each other beautifully to make a light stuffing that goes perfectly with chicken. You can also add finely grated cheese to the stuffing, choose a hard cheese, such as Welsh Caerphilly, which is white and crumbly.

Serves 4–6

1.4–1.8kg/3–4lb oven-ready chicken

1 small onion, quartered

½ lemon, roughly chopped

2 garlic cloves, halved

olive oil or melted butter

For the stuffing

30ml/2 tbsp olive oil

2 rindless bacon rashers (slices), finely chopped

1 small leek, thinly sliced

1 garlic clove, crushed or finely chopped

30ml/2 tbsp laverbread

150g/5½oz/1¼ cups fresh breadcrumbs

finely grated rind and juice of ½ lemon

salt and ground black pepper

1 To make the stuffing, put the oil and bacon into a pan and cook over medium heat, stirring occasionally, for about 3 minutes without browning.

2 Add the leek and garlic and cook for 3–5 minutes, stirring occasionally, until soft and just beginning to brown. Remove from the heat and stir in the laverbread, breadcrumbs, lemon rind and juice. Season and leave to cool.

Cook's tip This stuffing is also excellent for spooning under the skin of chicken breasts, or piling on to fillets of fish before oven cooking.

3 Preheat the oven to 200°C/400°F/Gas 6. Rinse the chicken inside and out, and then pat dry with kitchen paper. Spoon the cooled stuffing into the neck cavity of the chicken and fold the skin over and under. Any excess stuffing can be put under the breast skin – loosen it carefully by sliding your fingers underneath and then fill the resulting pocket evenly.

4 Put the onion, lemon and garlic into the main cavity of the chicken. Sit the bird in a roasting tin (pan) and brush it all over with olive oil or melted butter. Cover the breast area with a small piece of foil.

5 Put into the hot oven and cook for about 1½ hours, or until the chicken is cooked through (when a sharp knife is inserted in the thick part of the thigh next to the breast, the juices should run clear, not pink). Remove the foil for the final 30 minutes of cooking to allow the skin to brown and crisp.

6 Remove from the oven and leave to rest in a warm place for 15–20 minutes before carving. Reheat the pan juices and serve them spooned over the chicken.

Energy 486kcal/2027kJ; Protein 33.4g; Carbohydrate 22.3g, of which sugars 1.2g; Fat 29.7g, of which saturates 8.1g; Cholesterol 154mg; Calcium 54mg; Fibre 1g; Sodium 461mg

Chicken with red cabbage

Red cabbage is not just for pickling, though that seems to be the only way it was eaten in England until the late 20th century. Teamed with chicken and braised, it makes a delicious autumn or winter meal. Cooked chestnuts are available canned, vacuum packed or frozen.

Serves 4

50g/2oz/4 tbsp butter

4 chicken thighs

4 chicken drumsticks

1 onion, chopped

500g/1¼lb red cabbage, finely shredded

4 juniper berries, crushed

12 peeled, cooked chestnuts

125ml/4fl oz/½ cup red wine

salt and ground black pepper

1 Heat the butter in a heavy flameproof casserole and lightly brown the chicken pieces. Lift out. Add the onion to the casserole and cook gently until soft and golden. Stir in the cabbage and juniper berries, season and cook for 6–7 minutes, stirring once or twice.

2 Add the chestnuts, then tuck the chicken under the cabbage on the bottom of the casserole. Add the wine.

3 Cover and cook gently for 40 minutes until the cabbage is very tender. Adjust the seasoning to taste.

Energy 405kcal/1697kJ; Protein 44.9g; Carbohydrate 18.6g, of which sugars 9.2g; Fat 14.9g, of which saturates 7.7g; Cholesterol 189mg; Calcium 94mg; Fibre 4.1g; Sodium 229mg

Coronation chicken

Originally devised as part of the feast to celebrate the coronation of Elizabeth II in 1953, this chicken salad has been appearing on English buffet tables countrywide ever since.

Serves 8

½ lemon

2.25kg/5lb chicken

1 onion, quartered

1 carrot, quartered

1 large bouquet garni

8 black peppercorns, crushed

salt

watercress sprigs, to garnish

For the sauce

1 small onion, chopped

15g/½oz/1 tbsp butter

15ml/1 tbsp curry paste

15ml/1 tbsp tomato purée (paste)

125ml/4fl oz/½ cup red wine

1 bay leaf

juice of ½ lemon, or to taste

10–15ml/2–3 tsp apricot jam

300ml/½ pint/1¼ cups mayonnaise

125ml/4fl oz/½ cup whipping cream

salt and ground black pepper

1 Put the lemon half in the chicken cavity, then place it in a close-fitting pan. Add the vegetables, bouquet garni, peppercorns and a little salt.

2 Add water to come two-thirds of the way up the chicken, bring just to the boil, cover and cook very gently for 1½ hours, until the chicken juices run clear. Leave to cool. When the chicken is cold remove all the skin and bones and chop the flesh.

Cook's tips A few walnut pieces or slices of celery would add some crunch and texture to the dish.

3 To make the sauce, cook the onion in the butter until soft. Add the curry paste, tomato purée, wine, bay leaf and lemon juice, then cook gently for 10 minutes. Add the jam, press through a sieve (strainer) and cool.

4 Beat the sauce into the mayonnaise. Whip the cream and fold it in; add seasoning and lemon juice, then stir in the chicken. Garnish and serve.

Energy 587kcal/2429kJ; Protein 10.1g; Carbohydrate 17.1g, of which sugars 4.7g; Fat 51.6g, of which saturates 8.8g; Cholesterol 228mg; Calcium 97mg; Fibre 1.1g; Sodium 401mg

Devilled chicken

Applying hot or spicy seasonings to food before cooking, known as devilling, became very popular in the 1800s, and was used to revive cold, cooked meat for serving the next day.

Serves 4–6

6 chicken drumsticks

6 chicken thighs

15ml/1 tbsp oil

45ml/3 tbsp chutney, finely chopped

15ml/1 tbsp Worcestershire sauce

10ml/2 tsp English (hot) mustard

1.5ml/¼ tsp cayenne pepper

1.5ml/¼ tsp ground ginger

salt and ground black pepper

3 Preheat the oven to 200°C/400°F/ Gas 6. Arrange the chicken pieces in a single layer on a non-stick baking sheet, brushing them with any extra sauce.

Variation Instead of chutney, try using the same quantity of tomato ketchup or mushroom ketchup.

4 Put the chicken pieces into the hot oven and cook for about 35 minutes until crisp, deep golden brown and cooked through (test by inserting a small sharp knife or skewer – the juices should run clear). Turn them over once or twice during cooking to encourage even browning.

1 With a sharp knife, make several deep slashes in the chicken pieces, cutting down to the bone.

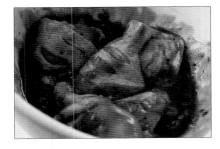

2 In a large bowl, mix the oil, chutney, Worcestershire sauce, mustard, cayenne, ginger and seasoning. Add the chicken pieces and toss them in the mixture, until well coated. Cover and leave to stand for 1 hour.

Energy 299kcal/1254kJ; Protein 47.4g; Carbohydrate 0.3g, of which sugars 0.3g; Fat 12g, of which saturates 2.6g; Cholesterol 236mg; Calcium 41mg; Fibre 0.6g; Sodium 207mg

Welsh roast duck with apples

Apple makes a delicious accompaniment to both duck and goose, helping to offset their rich flavour. Duck is eaten throughout the year, while goose (in season September to December) has always been a meal for special occasions – New Year's Day, Michaelmas Day and Christmas. The duck is particularly famous in the mid-Wales town of Presteigne, where a trial for duck-stealing in 1866 is recreated in The Judge's Lodging Victorian Museum.

Serves 6

20g/¾oz/1½ tbsp butter

1 onion, finely chopped

5ml/1 tsp finely chopped fresh sage or 2.5ml/½ tsp dried

75g/3oz/1½ cups fresh breadcrumbs

1 oven-ready duck, weighing about 1.8–2.25kg/4–5lb

3 crisp eating apples

salt and ground black pepper

1 To make the stuffing melt the butter in a pan, add the onion and cook gently for about 5 minutes, stirring occasionally, until soft but not browned. Then remove from the heat and stir in the sage, breadcrumbs, salt and pepper.

2 Preheat the oven to 200°C/400°F/ Gas 6. Remove any lumps of fat from inside the duck. With a fork, prick the skin all over then rub the skin all over with salt.

3 Spoon the stuffing into the neck end of the bird and, with a small skewer, secure the skin over the opening.

4 Sit the duck on a rack in a roasting tin (pan) and pour in 150ml/¼ pint/⅔ cup cold water. Cover the breast area of the duck with foil. Roast in the hot oven for 30 minutes.

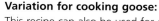

5 Quarter and core the apples and cut them into thick wedges.

6 Remove the roasting tin from the oven. Lift the duck and then the rack out of the tin and drain off excess fat from the tin, leaving a little fat, and all the sediment and meat juices.

7 Add the apple wedges to the roasting tin, stirring until they are all evenly coated with fat and juices. Replace the rack over the apples.

8 Replace the duck on the rack over the apples. Continue cooking for 30 minutes, turning the apples over once, until the apples are soft and the duck is crisp, golden brown.

9 At the end of cooking time, check the duck is done by inserting a skewer into the thickest part of the leg next to the breast – if the juices run clear, with no pink, the duck is done.

10 Before carving, leave the duck in warm place to rest for 10–15 minutes.

Variation for cooking goose:
This recipe can also be used for goose, when it is available.
• When buying a goose, allow about 675g/1½lb per person – a bird weighing about 5.5kg/12lb will feed eight.
• For eight servings, make twice as much stuffing and use about 6 apples.
• Prick the skin of the goose all over with a fork or skewer – try not to pierce the meat beneath.
• Any fat removed from the cavity can be placed on the breast of the goose before covering with foil and cooking.
• Cook at 190°C/375°F/Gas 5.
• A 5.5kg/12lb goose will take about 2½–3 hours to cook. Check it is cooked through by inserting a skewer into the thickest part of the leg next to the breast – the juices should run clear.
• Before carving, leave the goose in a warm place to rest for 20 minutes.
• Lots of fat will drain off the goose during cooking. Save it for roasting potatoes. It freezes well packed in small polythene boxes or freezer bags.

Energy 270kcal/1138kJ; Protein 23.7g; Carbohydrate 23.3g, of which sugars 6g; Fat 9.9g, of which saturates 3.9g; Cholesterol 119mg; Calcium 51mg; Fibre 1.6g; Sodium 303mg

Duck with damson and ginger sauce

Probably the most celebrated duck dish in Wales must be Lady Llanover's 19th-century recipe, which involved salting a whole bird for three days before cooking and serving with damson sauce. This simpler version gives the same sweet and sour taste combination.

Serves 4

250g/9oz fresh damsons

5ml/1 tsp ground ginger

45ml/3 tbsp sugar

10ml/2 tsp wine vinegar or sherry vinegar

4 duck breast portions

15ml/1 tbsp oil

salt and ground black pepper

1 Put the damsons in a pan with the ginger and 45ml/3 tbsp water. Bring to the boil, cover and simmer gently for about 5 minutes, or until the fruit is soft. Stir frequently and add a little extra water if the fruit looks as if it is drying out or sticking to the bottom of the pan.

2 Stir in the sugar and vinegar. Press the mixture through a sieve to remove stones (pits) and skin. Taste the sauce and add more sugar (if necessary) and seasoning to taste.

3 Meanwhile, with a sharp knife, score the fat on the duck breast portions in several places without cutting into the meat. Brush the oil over both sides of the duck. Sprinkle a little salt and pepper on the fat side only.

4 Preheat a heavy frying pan. When hot, add the duck breast portions, skin side down, and cook for 5 minutes.

5 When the fat is evenly browned and crisp, turn the duck over and cook the meat side for 4–5 minutes. Lift out and leave to rest for 5–10 minutes.

6 Slice the duck on the diagonal and serve with the sauce.

Cook's tip Both the duck and the sauce are too good served cold too. Serve with simple steamed vegetables or crisp salads.

Energy 275kcal/1157kJ; Protein 29.9g; Carbohydrate 17.5g, of which sugars 17.5g; Fat 12.5g, of which saturates 2.4g; Cholesterol 165mg; Calcium 39mg; Fibre 1.1g; Sodium 167mg

Scottish braised pigeon with elderberry wine

Elderberry wine is made commercially by several companies in Scotland and is just one of many things that can be made from the tree. The berries are bitter on their own but make a deep, rich, almost port-like wine. Pigeons are best in the autumn.

Serves 4

4 pigeons

15ml/1 tbsp plain (all-purpose) flour

30ml/2 tbsp olive oil, plus extra if needed

1 onion, chopped

225g/8oz button (white) mushrooms, sliced

250ml/8fl oz/1 cup dark stock

100ml/3½fl oz/scant ½ cup elderberry wine

salt and ground black pepper

kale, to serve (optional)

1 Preheat the oven to 170°C/325°F/ Gas 3. Season the pigeons inside and out with salt and black pepper and roll liberally in the flour. Heat a heavy pan over a medium heat, add the olive oil and wait for it to bubble slightly. Brown the pigeons lightly all over, then transfer them to a casserole dish.

2 Brown the onion and then the mushrooms in the same pan, still over a medium heat, adding more oil if necessary. Add the vegetables to the casserole with the pigeon and mix around well.

3 Pour in the stock, elderberry wine and just enough water to cover. Bring to the boil, cover tightly with a lid and cook in the preheated oven for 2 hours, until the pigeons are tender.

4 Remove the birds from the casserole and keep warm. Boil the cooking liquor rapidly to thicken slightly. Return the pigeons to the pan and heat through. Serve with kale, if you like.

Variation This recipe suits most game birds, so if you can't find pigeon, or it is the wrong season, you can use partridge, woodcock, pheasant or even duck or goose legs.

Energy 296kcal/1237kJ; Protein 31g; Carbohydrate 6.8g, of which sugars 2.5g; Fat 14.3g, of which saturates 0.1g; Cholesterol 0mg; Calcium 35mg; Fibre 1g; Sodium 117mg

Grey partridge with lentils and sausage

The grey partridge is indigenous to Scotland, although it is often called the English partridge, and is slightly smaller than the European red-legged variety. The wonderful rich flavour is complemented by the lovely earthy flavour of the Puy lentils.

Serves 4

450g/1lb/2 cups Puy lentils

75g/3oz/6 tbsp butter

15ml/1 tbsp vegetable oil

4 grey partridges

2 venison sausages

1 garlic clove, peeled but left whole

250ml/8fl oz/1 cup stock

salt and ground black pepper

1 Preheat the oven to 180°C/350°F/ Gas 4. Wash the lentils then simmer them in water for about 10 minutes to soften slightly. Drain then set aside.

2 Melt one-third of the butter with the oil in a large ovenproof frying pan and place the partridges, breast side down, in the pan. Brown both breasts lightly.

3 Set the partidges on their backs, season lightly with salt and ground black pepper and cook in the preheated oven for 15 minutes.

4 When cooked, remove the partridges from the oven, allow to cool for a few minutes then remove the legs. Keep the rest warm.

5 Put the large frying pan back on the hob and brown the two sausages. Add the Puy lentils and garlic and stir to coat in the juices from the partridges and the sausages. Then add the stock and simmer for a few minutes. Place the partridge legs on top of the lentil mixture and return to the oven for a further 15 minutes.

6 Remove the pan from the oven and set aside the partridge legs and sausages. Discard the garlic. Season the lentils with salt and ground black pepper, and if there is still a lot of liquid remaining, boil over a low heat to evaporate a little of the excess moisture. Then, off the heat, gradually swirl in the remaining butter.

7 Remove the breasts from the carcasses and set aside. Cut the sausages into pieces and stir into the lentil mixture.

8 To serve, place a leg on individual warmed plates, put the lentils on top and then the breast, sliced lengthways, on top of the lentils.

Energy 1309kcal/5495kJ; Protein 152.1g; Carbohydrate 59.4g, of which sugars 2.2g; Fat 53g, of which saturates 20.1g; Cholesterol 55mg; Calcium 255mg; Fibre 10.2g; Sodium 761mg

Quail with apples

Nowadays, quail often appear on restaurant menus, and they are increasingly used by domestic cooks too. As they are very tiny, the cooking time is short and it is necessary to allow one for each person as a first course and two for a main course.

**Serves 2 as a main course or
4 as a first course**

4 oven-ready quail

120ml/4fl oz/½ cup olive oil

2 firm eating apples

115g/4oz/½ cup butter

4 slices white bread

salt and ground black pepper

1 Preheat the oven to 220°C/425°F/ Gas 7.

2 Core the apples and slice them thickly (leave the peel on if it is attractive and not too tough).

3 Brush the quail with half the olive oil and roast them in a pan in the oven for 10 minutes, or until brown and tender.

4 Meanwhile, heat half the butter in a frying pan and sauté the apple slices for about 3 minutes until they are golden but not mushy. Season with pepper, cover and keep warm until required.

5 Remove the crusts from the bread. Heat the remaining olive oil and the butter in a frying pan and fry the bread on both sides until brown and crisp.

6 Lay the fried bread on heated plates and place the quail on top. Arrange the fried apple slices around them, and serve immediately.

Energy 814Kcal/3389kJ; Protein 53.3g; Carbohydrate 33.3g, of which sugars 10.5g; Fat 43.6g, of which saturates 23.4g; Cholesterol 69mg; Calcium 169mg; Fibre 2.4g; Sodium 644mg

Michaelmas goose with apple stuffing

The feast of St Michael falls on 29 September, when goose and apples are both in season, so this dish was traditionally served on the day. Small, crisp English apples make a refreshing foil to the richness of the goose and black pudding.

Serves 6–8

1 goose, 4.5kg/10lb, with giblets

1 onion, sliced

2 carrots, sliced

2 celery sticks, sliced

a small bunch of parsley and thyme

450g/1lb black pudding (blood sausage), crumbled or chopped

2 large cooking apples, peeled, cored and finely chopped

1 large garlic clove, crushed

250ml/8fl oz/1 cup dry (hard) cider

15ml/1 tbsp plain (all-purpose) flour

salt and ground black pepper

watercress or parsley, to garnish

1 Remove the goose liver from the giblets and put the remainder into a pan with the onion, carrots, celery and herbs. Cover with cold water, season and simmer for 30–45 minutes. Strain, discarding the meat and keeping the stock for the gravy. Preheat the oven to 200°C/400°F/Gas 6.

2 Meanwhile, chop the liver finely and mix it with the black pudding, garlic and apples. Add salt and pepper, and 75ml/2½fl oz/⅓ cup cider to bind.

3 Stuff the goose with the liver mixture being careful not to pack it too tightly. Prick the skin all over with a fork, sprinkle with salt and pepper. Now weigh the goose and calculate the cooking time at 15 minutes per 450g/1lb plus 15 minutes over. Put on a rack in a large roasting pan, cover with foil and place in the oven.

4 After 1 hour, remove the goose from the oven and carefully pour off the fat. You may need to do this more than once. Pour the remaining cider into the tin and return to the oven.

5 Half an hour before the end of the cooking time, remove the foil and baste the goose with the juices. Return to the oven, uncovered, and allow the bird to

brown, basting occasionally. When cooked, transfer the goose to a serving dish and put it in a warm place to rest.

6 Meanwhile, make the gravy. Pour off excess fat from the roasting pan, leaving 30ml/2 tbsp, sprinkle in enough plain flour to absorb it. Cook over a medium heat for a minute, scraping the pan to loosen the sediment. Add the giblet stock, bring to the boil and simmer for a few minutes, stirring. Add any juices that have accumulated under the cooked goose, season to taste and pour the gravy into a heated sauceboat.

7 Garnish the goose with the parsley or watercress. Carve into slices at the table and serve with the gravy, roast potatoes and some seasonal vegetables.

Energy 795Kcal/3297kJ; Protein 32.8g; Carbohydrate 17.1g, of which sugars 2.3g; Fat 65.4g, of which saturates 20.6g; Cholesterol 171mg; Calcium 109mg; Fibre 0.4g; Sodium 800mg

Pan-fried pheasant with oatmeal and cream sauce

Rolled oats are often used in Scotland for coating fish before pan-frying, but this treatment is equally good with tender poultry, game and other meats. Sweet, slightly tangy redcurrant jelly is used to bind the oatmeal to the pheasant breast fillets.

Serves 4

115g/4oz/generous 1 cup medium rolled oats

4 skinless, boneless pheasant breasts

45ml/3 tbsp redcurrant jelly, melted

50g/2oz/¼ cup butter

15ml/1 tbsp olive oil

45ml/3 tbsp wholegrain mustard

300ml/½ pint/1¼ cups double (heavy) cream

salt and ground black pepper

1 Place the rolled oats on a plate and season with salt and ground black pepper. Brush the skinned pheasant breasts with the melted redcurrant jelly, then turn them in the oats to coat evenly. Shake off any excess oats and set aside.

2 Heat the butter and oil in a frying pan until foaming. Add the pheasant breasts and cook over a high heat, turning frequently, until they are golden brown on all sides. Reduce the heat to medium and cook for a further 8–10 minutes, turning once or twice, until the meat is thoroughly cooked.

3 Add the mustard and cream, stirring to combine with the cooking juices. Bring slowly to the boil then simmer for 10 minutes over a low heat, or until the sauce has thickened to a good consistency. Serve immediately.

Energy 847kcal/3520kJ; Protein 37.1g; Carbohydrate 30.1g, of which sugars 9.1g; Fat 59g, of which saturates 35.1g; Cholesterol 129mg; Calcium 105mg; Fibre 2g; Sodium 205mg

Pheasant and wild mushroom ragoût

Pheasant are an established part of the autumnal landscape all over Britain, and it is hard to imagine them not there. With their proud strutting and brilliant plumage they are stunning to look at. They also make very good eating.

Serves 4

4 pheasant breasts, skinned

12 shallots, halved

2 garlic cloves, crushed

75g/3oz wild mushrooms, sliced

75ml/2½fl oz/⅓ cup port

150ml/¼ pint/⅔ cup chicken stock

sprigs of fresh parsley and thyme

1 bay leaf

grated rind of 1 lemon

200ml/7fl oz/scant 1 cup double (heavy) cream

salt and ground black pepper

1 Dice and season the pheasant breasts. Heat a little oil in a heavy pan and colour the pheasant meat quickly. Remove from the pan and set aside.

2 Add the shallots to the pan, fry quickly to colour a little then add the garlic and sliced mushrooms. Reduce the heat and cook gently for 5 minutes.

3 Pour the port and stock into the pan and add the herbs and lemon rind. Reduce a little. When the shallots are nearly cooked add the cream, reduce to thicken then return the meat. Allow to cook for a few minutes before serving.

Cook's Tip Serve with pilaff rice: fry a chopped onion, stir in 2.5cm/1in cinnamon stick, 2.5ml/½ tsp crushed cumin seeds, 2 crushed cardamom pods, a bay leaf and 5ml/1 tsp turmeric. Add 225g/8oz/generous 1 cup long grain rice. Stir until well coated. Pour in 600ml/1 pint/2½ cups boiling water, cover then simmer for 15 minutes. Transfer to a serving dish, cover with a dish towel and leave for 5 minutes.

Energy 530kcal/2200kJ; Protein 34.1g; Carbohydrate 7.4g, of which sugars 5.9g; Fat 33g, of which saturates 20.2g; Cholesterol 69mg; Calcium 91mg; Fibre 1.1g; Sodium 114mg

Roast pheasant with matchstick chips

The British pheasant season begins on 1 October, when pheasant hens are in their prime. The addition of bacon, covering the breast, helps to keep the moisture in the roasted meat. Crisp-fried matchstick chips are the traditional, and perfect, accompaniment.

Serves 2

1 hen pheasant

25g/1oz/2 tbsp butter

115g/4oz rindless streaky (fatty) bacon rashers (strips)

2 medium potatoes

oil, for deep-frying

salt and ground black pepper

For the stuffing

25g/1oz/2 tbsp butter

1 leek, chopped

115g/4oz peeled, cooked chestnuts, coarsely chopped (see Cook's tip)

30ml/2 tbsp chopped fresh flat-leaf parsley

For the gravy

15ml/1 tbsp cornflour (cornstarch)

300ml/½ pint/1¼ cups well-flavoured chicken stock

50ml/2fl oz/¼ cup port

1 Preheat the oven to 190°C/375°F/ Gas 5. Pick any stray quills or stubs of feathers from the pheasant and season the bird inside and out with salt and black pepper.

Cook's tip For convenience, use vacuum-packed or frozen chestnuts rather than fresh, which are fiddly to peel and cook. Simply rinse the chestnuts thoroughly with boiling water and drain before using. Whole, unsweetened canned chestnuts could be used, but they tend to be fairly dense and can be soft.

2 Carefully loosen and lift the skin covering the breast and rub the butter between the skin and flesh.

3 To make the stuffing, melt the butter in a pan and cook the leek for about 5 minutes until softened but not coloured. Remove from the heat and mix in the chopped chestnuts, parsley and seasoning to taste.

4 Spoon the stuffing into the cavity of the pheasant and secure the opening with skewers. Arrange the bacon over the breast and place in a roasting pan.

5 Put into the hot oven and cook for 1–1½ hours, or until the juices run clear when the bird is pierced with a skewer in the thickest part of the leg.

6 Lift out and cover closely with foil, then leave to stand in a warm place for 15 minutes before carving.

7 On the stove, heat the juices in the roasting pan and stir in the cornflour. Gradually stir in the stock and port. Bring to the boil, then reduce the heat and simmer for about 5 minutes, until the sauce is slightly thickened and glossy. Strain the sauce and keep warm.

8 Peel the potatoes and cut into matchsticks. Heat the oil in a deep-fat fryer or large pan to 190°C/375°F and fry the chips until crisp, golden and cooked through. Drain on kitchen paper.

9 Carve the pheasant and serve with the stuffing, gravy and chips.

Energy 897kcal/3742kJ; Protein 70.6g; Carbohydrate 34.3g, of which sugars 9.1g; Fat 50.8g, of which saturates 20g; Cholesterol 524mg; Calcium 127mg; Fibre 4.5g; Sodium 946mg

Braised rabbit

Rabbit now features frequently on restaurant menus. It is delicious served with potatoes boiled in their skins and a lightly-cooked green vegetable.

Serves 4–6

1 rabbit, prepared and jointed by the butcher

30ml/2 tbsp seasoned flour

30ml/2 tbsp olive oil or vegetable oil

25g/1oz/2 tbsp butter

115g/4oz streaky (fatty) bacon

1 onion, roughly chopped

2 or 3 carrots, sliced

1 or 2 celery sticks, trimmed and sliced

300ml/½ pint/1¼ cups chicken stock

300ml/½ pint/1¼ cups dry (hard) cider or stout

a small bunch of parsley leaves, chopped

salt and ground black pepper

1 Soak the joints in cold salted water for at least two hours, then pat them dry with kitchen paper and toss them in seasoned flour. Preheat the oven to 200°C/400°F/Gas 6.

2 Heat the oil and butter together in a heavy flameproof casserole. Shake off (and reserve) any excess flour from the rabbit joints and brown them on all sides. Lift out and set aside.

3 Add the bacon to the casserole and cook for a few minutes, then remove and set aside with the rabbit. Add the vegetables to the casserole and cook gently until just colouring, then sprinkle over any remaining seasoned flour to absorb the fats in the casserole. Stir over a low heat for 1 minute, to cook the flour. Add the stock and cider or stout, stirring, to make a smooth sauce.

4 Return the rabbit and bacon to the casserole, and add half of the chopped parsley and a light seasoning of salt and pepper. Mix gently together, then cover with a lid and put into the preheated oven. Cook for 15–20 minutes, then reduce the temperature to 150°C/300°F/Gas 2 for about 1½ hours, or until the rabbit is tender. Add the remaining parsley and serve.

Cook's tip Buy rabbit whole or jointed, from butchers and good supermarkets.

Energy 368Kcal/1535kJ; Protein 32.9g; Carbohydrate 10.5g, of which sugars 5.8g; Fat 19.7g, of which saturates 8g; Cholesterol 133mg; Calcium 88mg; Fibre 1.4g; Sodium 567mg

Saddle of rabbit with Scottish asparagus

Some of the best Scottish asparagus comes from near Glamis in Angus in the east of the country, where a little extra sunlight produces stems with juicy, succulent flavours.

Serves 4

2 saddles of rabbit

75g/3oz/6 tbsp butter

sprig of fresh rosemary

45ml/3 tbsp olive oil

10 asparagus spears

200ml/7fl oz/scant 1 cup chicken stock, plus extra for cooking the asparagus (see Step 5)

salt and ground black pepper

1 Preheat the oven to 200°C/400°F/ Gas 6. Trim the rabbit saddles, removing the membrane and the belly flaps.

2 Heat an ovenproof pan then add 50g/2oz/4 tbsp of the butter. Season the saddles and brown them lightly all over, by frying them gently in the butter for a few minutes on each side.

3 Tuck the rosemary underneath the saddles, with the fillets facing up, and put in the oven for 10 minutes.

4 Meanwhile, in a second pan, heat the olive oil then add the asparagus spears. Make sure they are coated in the oil and leave them to sweat gently for a few minutes.

5 Add enough stock to just cover the asparagus and bring to a gentle boil. Allow the liquid to evaporate to a light glaze and the asparagus will be cooked.

6 Remove the rabbit from the oven and leave to rest for 5 minutes. Remove any fat from the pan then add the measured stock. Bring to the boil, scraping up any bits from the base of the pan. Reduce the liquid by about a half, then remove from the heat and whisk in the remaining butter. Strain through a sieve and set aside.

7 Take the meat off the saddles in slices lengthways and place on a warmed serving dish. Serve with the asparagus on top and the sauce spooned over.

Energy 406kcal/1684kJ; Protein 33.7g; Carbohydrate 0.6g, of which sugars 0.6g; Fat 29.8g, of which saturates 13.4g; Cholesterol 146mg; Calcium 43mg; Fibre 0.4g; Sodium 215mg

Rabbit with apricots

A delicious meat, rabbit is richer and more tasty than chicken, but with a similar colouring and texture. The gamey flavours go very well in many dishes, especially those with fruits and berries. Once a staple of the countryside, enjoyed by farmers and hunting parties alike, it is now available from good butchers and some fishmongers too.

Serves 4

2 rabbits

30ml/2 tbsp plain (all-purpose) flour

15ml/1 tbsp vegetable oil

90g/3½oz streaky (fatty) bacon, cut into thin pieces

10 baby (pearl) onions, peeled but kept whole

200ml/7fl oz/scant 1 cup dry white wine

1 bay leaf

12 dried apricots

salt and ground black pepper

1 Ask your butcher to joint the rabbits, providing two legs and the saddle cut in two. Sprinkle the flour over a dish, season with salt and ground black pepper and mix well into the flour. Roll the rabbit pieces in it one by one to coat lightly all over, shaking off any excess flour. Set aside.

2 Heat a heavy pan and add the oil. Brown the rabbit pieces all over then remove from the pan. Brown the bacon followed by the onions.

3 Place the browned rabbit pieces, bacon and onions in a casserole. Pour the wine into the heavy pan and, over a low heat, scrape up all the bits from the base of the pan. Add a little water, bring to the boil and pour over the rabbit in the casserole, adding more water if needed to just cover.

4 Add the bay leaf and bring to the boil. Allow to simmer gently for 40 minutes until the rabbit is tender.

5 Remove the rabbit and onions from the pan and set aside, keeping them warm. Put the apricots into the pan and boil rapidly until the cooking liquor thickens slightly. Remove the bay leaf and check the seasoning. You can now either return the rabbit and onions to the pan as it is and heat before serving, or you can purée the apricots in the cooking liquor and pour the resulting rich sauce over the rabbit.

Cook's tip This dish is best reheated and served the next day so that the flavours can develop overnight.

Energy 481kcal/2022kJ; Protein 60.2g; Carbohydrate 22.5g, of which sugars 21.4g; Fat 13.8g, of which saturates 6.1g; Cholesterol 223mg; Calcium 153mg; Fibre 3.9g; Sodium 417mg

Roast Scottish hare with beetroot and crowdie

Hares are not the easiest of things to get hold of but in some parts of Scotland they are often available. This sauce goes well with venison too. Crowdie is a cream cheese that was made on every homestead up to the middle of the last century. For a less rich dish you could use plain yogurt in place of the crowdie at the end.

Serves 4

2 saddles of hare

10ml/2 tsp olive oil

350g/12oz cooked beetroot (beets)

30ml/2 tbsp chopped shallot

30ml/2 tbsp white wine vinegar

50g/2oz/¼ cup crowdie

5ml/1 tsp English mustard

salt and ground black pepper

For the marinade

600ml/1 pint/2½ cups red wine

1 carrot, finely diced

1 onion, finely diced

generous pinch of mixed herbs

pinch of salt

8 peppercorns

8 juniper berries

2 cloves

1 Using a flexible knife, remove the membrane covering the saddles. Mix all the ingredients for the marinade together and coat the saddles then leave for one day, turning occasionally.

2 Preheat the oven to 240°C/475°F/ Gas 9. Take out and dry the saddles with kitchen paper. Strain the marinade through a sieve and set aside.

3 Heat the olive oil in a large ovenproof pan. Brown the saddles all over then cook in the preheated oven for 10–15 minutes. They should still be pink. Leave in a warm place to rest.

4 Remove most of the fat from the pan then add the beetroot. Cook for 1–2 minutes then add the shallot and cook for about 2 minutes to soften.

5 Add the vinegar and 30ml/2 tbsp of the marinade and stir in thoroughly. Reduce the liquid until a coating texture is nearly achieved. Reduce the heat to low and add the crowdie. Whisk it in until completely melted, then add the mustard and season to taste. Set aside and keep warm.

6 To serve, remove the fillets from the top and bottom of the saddles and slice lengthways. Place on four warmed plates and arrange the beetroot mixture on top. Reheat the sauce, without boiling, and hand round separately.

Energy 352kcal/1471kJ; Protein 41g; Carbohydrate 9.6g, of which sugars 8.7g; Fat 13.1g, of which saturates 6.5g; Cholesterol 136mg; Calcium 84mg; Fibre 1.9g; Sodium 255mg

Scottish loin of wild boar with bog myrtle

Wild boar used to roam the hills of Britain centuries ago and when the kings of Scotland travelled to Falkland Palace, Fife, for the summer months they would go out hunting them. Today they are farmed as a rare breed of pig. Bog myrtle is a fragrant wild herb that thrives in Scotland and was used in medieval times for brewing beer.

Serves 4

1 loin of wild boar, approximately 2.75kg/6lb

10ml/2 tsp salt

1 onion, roughly chopped

1 carrot, peeled and roughly chopped

150ml/¼ pint/⅔ cup dry vermouth

10ml/2 tsp English (hot) mustard

handful of bog myrtle, or a few sprigs of fresh rosemary, if you prefer

salt and ground black pepper

1 Ask your butcher to take the loin off the bone and then to tie it back on and to make 2cm/¾in cuts through the skin from top to bottom at 5cm/2in intervals. This will make the crackling easier to slice when you come to carve. Allow the loin to sit at room temperature for at least an hour prior to cooking. Preheat the oven to 220°C/425°F/Gas 7.

2 Rub the salt all over the skin of the boar, easing it slightly into the cuts made by the butcher.

3 Place the chopped vegetables and herbs in a lightly oiled roasting pan.

4 Put the loin on top of the vegetables and herbs, with the skin facing up, and roast in the oven for 40 minutes.

5 Reduce the oven temperature to 180°C/350°F/Gas 4 and cook for another 40 minutes. Remove from the oven and cut the meat from the bones – this should just be a matter of cutting the string. Set the meat aside to rest for at least 20 minutes.

6 Meanwhile make the gravy. Pour or spoon off the excess fat from the roasting pan but try to retain the juices, which will be under the fat.

7 Put the roasting pan on the stove over a low heat and add the vermouth and mustard. Stir well to mix thoroughly, scraping the base of the pan to incorporate the cooked flavours.

8 Just as it comes to the boil, pour the gravy into a clean pan, along with the bones, herbs and vegetables. Swill out the roasting pan with a little water and add this to the new pan, making sure that you have all the juices. Simmer the gravy in the new pan for about 5 minutes.

9 Remove the bones and strain the juices into the gravy pan. Test the seasoning, adding salt and ground black pepper if necessary.

10 Serve the loin in slices, each slice with a strip of the crackling, and pass around the gravy in a separate dish.

Cook's tip The crisp and crunchy crackling is particularly good and can be broken off in chunks because of the scoring made prior to cooking. The meat should be carved separately.

Energy 530kcal/2221kJ; Protein 81.9g; Carbohydrate 6.7g, of which sugars 5.7g; Fat 15.5g, of which saturates 5.3g; Cholesterol 236mg; Calcium 109mg; Fibre 1.9g; Sodium 1309mg

Vegetable dishes and salads

Britain's temperate climate produces delicious seasonal vegetables, particularly the glories of summer such as tiny new potatoes, tender asparagus and freshly gathered peas and beans, as well as wonderful salad crops. But the old recipes also make the most of staples such as cabbages, leeks, onions and carrots, which saw hungry families through the cold winter months with warming stews and braises.

English asparagus with hollandaise sauce

Since the 16th century England has produced this "queen of vegetables", at its finest for a short season in early summer. Serve it simply – drizzled with melted unsalted butter, with lightly boiled eggs (dip the asparagus into the egg) or with hollandaise sauce.

Serves 4

2 bunches of asparagus

30ml/2 tbsp white wine vinegar

2 egg yolks

115g/4oz butter, melted

juice of ½ lemon

salt and ground black pepper

Cook's tips

• Asparagus should be cooked and eaten as soon as possible, preferably on the day it is picked.

• Asparagus is also good served cold with mayonnaise.

• Make stock with the woody ends of the asparagus and use it for vegetable soups or sauces.

1 Snap off the tough ends of the asparagus. Drop the spears into fast boiling water, cooking for 1–2 minutes until just tender. Test the thickest part of the stalk with a small sharp knife; take care not to overcook.

2 In a pan, bring the vinegar to the boil and bubble until it has reduced to just 15ml/1 tbsp. Remove from the heat and add 15ml/1 tbsp cold water.

3 Whisk the egg yolks into the vinegar and water mixture, then put the pan over a very low heat and continue whisking until the mixture is frothy and thickened.

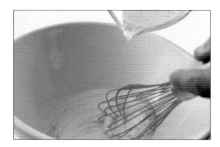

4 Remove from the heat again and slowly whisk in the melted butter. Add the lemon juice and seasoning to taste. Serve the sauce immediately with the drained asparagus.

Energy 276kcal/1135kJ; Protein 5.3g; Carbohydrate 2.7g, of which sugars 2.6g; Fat 27.1g, of which saturates 15.9g; Cholesterol 162mg; Calcium 51mg; Fibre 2.1g; Sodium 180mg

Cauliflower cheese

The use of flour to thicken sauces began in France in the 17th century – hence the French name "roux" for the mixture of flour and fat that forms the base of a white sauce. Cheese sauce made in this way has now become a staple of British cookery.

Serves 4

1 medium cauliflower

25g/1oz/2 tbsp butter

25g/1oz/4 tbsp plain (all-purpose) flour

300ml/½ pint/1¼ cups milk

115g/4oz mature Cheddar or Cheshire cheese, grated

salt and ground black pepper

1 Trim the cauliflower and cut it into florets. Bring a pan of lightly salted water to the boil, drop in the cauliflower and cook for 5–8 minutes or until just tender. Drain and tip the florets into an ovenproof dish.

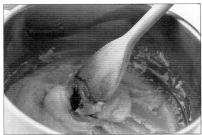

2 To make the sauce, melt the butter in a pan, stir in the flour and cook gently, stirring constantly, for about 1 minute (do not allow it to brown). Remove from the heat and gradually stir in the milk. Return the pan to the heat and cook, stirring, until the mixture thickens and comes to the boil. Simmer gently for 1–2 minutes.

3 Stir in three-quarters of the cheese and season to taste. Spoon the sauce over the cauliflower and scatter the remaining cheese on top. Put under a hot grill (broiler) until golden brown.

Cook's tip Boost the cheese flavour by adding a little English (hot) mustard to the cheese sauce.

Energy 318kcal/1318kJ; Protein 17.4g; Carbohydrate 4.4g, of which sugars 3.9g; Fat 25.8g, of which saturates 16.3g; Cholesterol 71mg; Calcium 371mg; Fibre 1.8g; Sodium 453mg

Braised leeks with carrots

Sweet carrots and leeks go well together and are good finished with a little chopped mint, chervil or parsley. This is an excellent accompaniment to roast beef, lamb or chicken. Boiling the buttery cooking liquid away leaves the vegetables with a lovely glaze.

2 Uncover the pan and boil until the juices have evaporated, leaving the carrots moist and glazed. Remove from the pan and set aside.

3 Melt 25g/1oz/2 tbsp of the remaining butter in the pan. Add the leeks and cook over a low heat for 4–5 minutes, without allowing them to brown.

4 Add seasoning, a good pinch of sugar, the wine and half the chopped herbs. Heat until simmering, then cover and cook gently for 5–8 minutes, until the leeks are tender but not collapsed. Uncover and turn the leeks in the buttery juices, then increase the heat and boil the liquid rapidly until reduced to a few tablespoonfuls.

Serves 4

70g/2½oz/5 tbsp butter

675g/1½lb carrots, thickly sliced

2 fresh bay leaves

pinch of sugar

675g/1½lb leeks, cut into 5cm/2in lengths

125ml/4fl oz/½ cup white wine

30ml/2 tbsp chopped fresh mint, chervil or parsley

salt and ground black pepper

1 Melt 25g/1oz/2 tbsp of the butter in a wide, heavy pan and cook the carrots, without allowing them to brown, for about 5 minutes. Add the bay leaves, seasoning, a pinch of sugar and 75ml/ 5 tbsp water. Bring to the boil, cover and cook for 10 minutes, or until the carrots are just tender.

5 Add the carrots to the leeks and reheat gently, stirring occasionally, then add the remaining butter. Adjust the seasoning. Transfer to a warmed serving dish and serve sprinkled with herbs.

Energy 163kcal/677kJ; Protein 3.8g; Carbohydrate 18.5g, of which sugars 16.4g; Fat 6.5g, of which saturates 3.6g; Cholesterol 13mg; Calcium 87mg; Fibre 7.8g; Sodium 85mg

Colcannon

This traditional Irish dish is especially associated with Hallowe'en, when it was made with curly kale and would have a ring hidden in it – predicting marriage during the coming year for the person who found it. It is also served through the winter, when cabbage is used.

Serves 3–4 as a main dish, 6–8 as an accompaniment

450g/1lb potatoes, peeled and boiled

450g/1lb curly kale or cabbage, cooked

milk, if necessary

50g/2oz/2 tbsp butter, plus extra for serving

1 large onion, finely chopped

salt and ground black pepper

3 Add the remainder of the butter to the hot pan. When very hot, turn the potato mixture on to the pan and spread it out. Fry until brown, then cut it roughly into pieces and continue frying until they are crisp and brown.

4 Serve in bowls or as a side dish, with plenty of butter.

Right A rustic temple in a walled garden, Glin Castle, County Limerick.

1 Mash the potatoes. Chop the kale or cabbage, add it to the potatoes and mix. Stir in a little milk if the mash is too stiff.

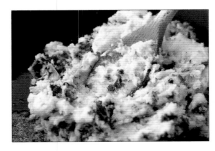

2 Melt a little butter in a frying pan over a medium heat and add the onion. Cook until softened. Remove and mix well with the potato and kale or cabbage.

Energy 306Kcal/1281kJ; Protein 5.4g; Carbohydrate 40.6g, of which sugars 13.6g; Fat 14.6g, of which saturates 8.8g; Cholesterol 36mg; Calcium 104mg; Fibre 5.9g; Sodium 127mg

Leeks in cream sauce

This versatile vegetable makes a great winter standby and leeks find their way into many dishes, including casseroles and soups. Simple buttered leeks are underrated as a side dish, and this recipe makes a tasty accompaniment for plain grilled food, such as chops or chicken, or it can be served as a light lunch or supper on its own.

Serves 4–6

4 large or 8 medium leeks, cleaned and sliced into chunks

300ml/½ pint/1¼ cups milk

8 streaky (fatty) rashers (strips) of bacon, trimmed and sliced (optional)

1 egg, lightly beaten

150ml/¼ pint/⅔ cup single (light) cream

15ml/1 tbsp mild mustard

75g/3oz/¾ cup grated cheese (optional)

salt and ground black pepper

1 Put the leeks into a pan with the milk. Season and bring to the boil. Reduce the heat and simmer for 15–20 minutes, or until tender. Drain, reserving the cooking liquor and turn the leeks into a buttered shallow baking dish.

2 Meanwhile, if using the bacon, put it into a frying pan and cook gently to allow the fat to run, then turn up the heat a little and cook for a few minutes until it crisps up. Remove from the pan with a slotted spoon and sprinkle the bacon over the leeks. Preheat the oven to 200°C/400°F/Gas 6.

3 Rinse the pan used for the leeks. Blend the beaten egg, single cream and Irish mustard together and mix it with the reserved cooking liquor.

4 Return the sauce to the pan and heat gently without boiling, allowing the sauce to thicken a little. Taste and adjust the seasoning with salt and freshly ground black pepper.

5 Pour the sauce over the leeks and bacon. Sprinkle with grated cheese, if using. Place in the hot oven and bake for 20–25 minutes until heated through and browned on top.

6 Serve with plain grilled meat or poultry, if you like.

Variation The bacon may be grilled and served separately, if you prefer.

Energy 238Kcal/993kJ; Protein 18.6g; Carbohydrate 9g, of which sugars 7.9g; Fat 14.4g, of which saturates 7.3g; Cholesterol 90mg; Calcium 172mg; Fibre 3.5g; Sodium 830mg

Broad beans with bacon and mint

In early summer, tender young broad beans are a treat, and fresh mint and a smattering of crisply cooked bacon are their perfect partners. At other times of year, this recipe works well with frozen broad beans. Serve warm or at room temperature as a salad with crusty bread, or hot as an accompaniment to roast duck or chicken.

Serves 4–6

30ml/2 tbsp olive oil

175g/6oz streaky (fatty) bacon, cut into narrow strips

1 medium onion, thinly sliced

2.5ml/½ tsp sugar

450g/1lb shelled broad (fava) beans

15ml/1 tbsp cider vinegar

small handful of fresh mint, finely chopped

salt and ground black pepper

1 Heat half the oil in a large pan and cook the bacon until crisp. Lift out with a slotted spoon and set aside.

2 Add the onion to the hot pan with the sugar and cook over a medium heat until soft and golden brown.

3 Meanwhile, bring a pan of water to the boil and add the beans. Cook for 5–8 minutes until tender. Drain well.

4 Add the cooked beans and bacon to the onions. Stir in the remaining oil, vinegar, seasonings and mint and serve.

Energy 162kcal/674kJ; Protein 7.9g; Carbohydrate 9.6g, of which sugars 1.8g; Fat 10.5g, of which saturates 2.2g; Cholesterol 9mg; Calcium 45mg; Fibre 4.5g; Sodium 190mg

Braised red cabbage

Red cabbage is a robust winter vegetable that takes on a beautiful colour and texture when cooked slowly and gently. This spiced version goes particularly well with pork, duck or game, and is also often served with cold meats at Christmas time.

Serves 4–6

1kg/2¼lb red cabbage

2 onions, chopped

2 cooking apples, peeled, cored and coarsely grated

5ml/1 tsp freshly grated nutmeg

1.5ml/¼ tsp ground cloves

1.5ml/¼ tsp ground cinnamon

15ml/1 tbsp dark brown sugar

45ml/3 tbsp cider vinegar

25g/1oz/2 tbsp butter, cut into small pieces

salt and ground black pepper

1 Preheat the oven to 160°C/325°F/ Gas 3. Remove the large white ribs from the outer cabbage leaves, then shred the cabbage finely.

Cook's tip The braised cabbage can be cooked in advance and reheated in the oven for 30 minutes when needed. Leftovers can also be frozen.

2 Layer the shredded cabbage in a large ovenproof dish with the onions, apples, spices, sugar and seasoning. Pour the vinegar over and dot with the butter.

3 Cover, put into the hot oven and cook for about 1½ hours, stirring a couple of times, until the cabbage is very tender. Serve hot.

Energy 74kcal/309kJ; Protein 2.1g; Carbohydrate 10.1g, of which sugars 9.5g; Fat 3g, of which saturates 0.4g; Cholesterol 0mg; Calcium 53mg; Fibre 3.1g; Sodium 38mg

Scottish kale with mustard dressing

Traditionally, sea kale is used for this dish, available in Scotland between January and March. Its pale green fronds have a slightly nutty taste. Use curly kale if you can't get sea kale, although you will need to boil it briefly for a few minutes before chilling and serving.

Serves 4

250g/9oz sea kale or curly kale

45ml/3 tbsp light olive oil

5ml/1 tsp wholegrain mustard

15ml/1 tbsp white wine vinegar

pinch of caster (superfine) sugar

salt and ground black pepper

1 Wash the sea kale, drain thoroughly, then trim it and cut in two.

2 Whisk the oil into the mustard in a bowl. When it is blended completely, whisk in the white wine vinegar. It should begin to thicken.

3 Season the mustard dressing to taste with sugar, salt and ground black pepper. Toss the sea kale in the dressing and serve immediately.

Energy 99kcal/409kJ; Protein 2.1g; Carbohydrate 1.9g, of which sugars 1.9g; Fat 9.3g, of which saturates 1.3g; Cholesterol 0mg; Calcium 82mg; Fibre 2g; Sodium 27mg

Cabbage with bacon

Bacon, especially if smoked, makes all the difference to the flavour of the cabbage, turning it into a delicious vegetable accompaniment to serve with roast beef, chicken or even a celebration turkey. Try it with people who don't like to eat greens.

Serves 4

30ml/2 tbsp oil

1 onion, finely chopped

115g/4oz smoked bacon, finely chopped

500g/1¼lb cabbage (red, white or Savoy)

salt and ground black pepper

1 Heat the oil in a large pan over a medium heat, add the chopped onion and bacon and cook for about 7 minutes, stirring occasionally.

2 Remove any tough outer leaves and wash the cabbages. Shred them quite finely, discarding the core. Add the cabbage to the pan and season. Stir for a few minutes until the cabbage begins to lose volume.

3 Continue to cook the cabbage, stirring frequently, for 8–10 minutes until it is tender but still crisp. (If you prefer softer cabbage, then cover the pan for part of the cooking time.) Serve immediately.

Variations
• This dish is equally delicious if you use spring greens (collards) instead of cabbage. You could also use curly kale.
• To make a more substantial dish to serve for lunch or supper, add more bacon, some chopped button (white) mushrooms and skinned, seeded and chopped tomatoes.

Energy 151kcal/623kJ; Protein 6.7g; Carbohydrate 7.4g, of which sugars 7g; Fat 10.5g, of which saturates 2.6g; Cholesterol 15mg; Calcium 67mg; Fibre 2.8g; Sodium 452mg

New potatoes with bacon dressing

This tasty summer salad becomes a favourite with all who try it. Choose dry-cured bacon and real new-season potatoes rather than all-year "baby" potatoes, if possible.
Using superior ingredients makes this a special dish, and it's ideal for a barbecue or party.

Serves 4–6

900g/2lb small new potatoes

sprig of mint

15–30ml/1–2 tbsp olive oil

1 onion, thinly sliced

175g/6oz smoked bacon, cut into small strips

2 garlic cloves, crushed

30ml/2 tbsp chopped fresh parsley

1 small bunch of chives, chopped

15ml/1 tbsp wine vinegar or cider vinegar

15ml/1 tbsp wholegrain mustard

salt and ground black pepper

1 Scrape the new potatoes and cook in salted water with the mint for about 10 minutes, until just tender. Drain and cool a little, then tip into a salad bowl.

2 Heat the oil in a frying pan, add the onion and cook gently until just softening, stirring occasionally. Add the bacon to the pan and cook for 3–5 minutes, until it begins to crisp.

3 Add the garlic and cook for another minute or so, then remove from the heat and add the chopped herbs, vinegar, mustard and seasoning to taste, remembering that the bacon may be salty.

4 Pour the dressing over the potatoes. Toss gently to mix, and serve the salad while still warm.

Energy 318kcal/1319kJ; Protein 12.4g; Carbohydrate 10.9g, of which sugars 2.2g; Fat 25.4g, of which saturates 4g; Cholesterol 198mg; Calcium 106mg; Fibre 2.3g; Sodium 268mg

Irish champ

This traditional dish is especially associated with Northern Ireland. Flavourings for champ include a wide range of greens – freshly chopped chives or parsley, onions or spring onions and even green peas. The chopped onions can be boiled with the milk.

Serves 2–3 as a main dish

675g/1½lb potatoes

1 bunch spring onions (scallions), chopped

about 300ml/½ pint/1¼ cups milk

salt and ground black pepper

butter, to serve

1 Peel and boil the potatoes in salted water until tender. Drain and return to the pan.

2 Simmer the spring onions for 5 minutes in the milk. (Alternatively, bring the milk to boiling point on its own, if you prefer the onions raw.)

3 Cover the potatoes with a clean cloth and dry them at the side of the stove for a few minutes before mashing well.

4 Beat the boiling milk into the mashed potatoes until the consistency is smooth and creamy. Add more hot milk if necessary.

5 Stir in the spring onions. Serve the champ in heated bowls with a knob (pat) of butter on top.

Energy 334Kcal/1415kJ; Protein 13.2g; Carbohydrate 66.6g, of which sugars 10.5g; Fat 3.5g, of which saturates 1.7g; Cholesterol 9mg; Calcium 217mg; Fibre 5.2g; Sodium 92mg

Potatoes and parsnips with garlic and cream

For the best results, cut the potatoes and parsnips very finely – use a mandolin if you have one. This method is also ideal for cooking sweet potatoes, which Tudor cooks in England would have been more likely to slice and crystallize, to serve as a sweetmeat.

Serves 4–6

3 large potatoes, total weight about 675g/1½ lb

350g/12oz small to medium-sized parsnips

200ml/7fl oz/scant 1 cup single (light) cream

100ml/3½fl oz/scant ½ cup milk

2 garlic cloves, crushed

butter, for greasing

about 5ml/1 tsp freshly grated nutmeg

75g/3oz/¾ cup coarsely grated Cheddar or Red Leicester cheese

salt and ground black pepper

1 Peel the potatoes and parsnips and cut them into thin slices. Cook in a large pan of salted boiling water for 5 minutes. Drain and cool slightly.

2 Meanwhile, pour the cream and milk into a heavy pan and add the crushed garlic. Bring to the boil over a medium heat, then remove from the heat and leave to stand for about 10 minutes.

3 Preheat the oven to 180°C/350°F/ Gas 4 and lightly butter the bottom and sides of a shallow ovenproof dish.

4 Arrange the potatoes and parsnips in the dish, sprinkling each layer with a little freshly grated nutmeg, salt and ground black pepper.

5 Pour the liquid into the dish and press the potatoes and parsnips down into it. Cover with lightly buttered foil and cook in the hot oven for 45 minutes.

6 Remove the foil and sprinkle the grated cheese over the vegetables in an even layer.

7 Return the dish to the oven and continue cooking, uncovered, for a further 20–30 minutes, or until the potatoes and parsnips are tender and the top is golden brown.

Energy 241kcal/1012kJ; Protein 7.8g; Carbohydrate 27.2g, of which sugars 6.4g; Fat 11.7g, of which saturates 7.2g; Cholesterol 31mg; Calcium 173mg; Fibre 3.9g; Sodium 126mg

Young vegetables with tarragon

This is almost a salad, but the vegetables here are just lightly cooked to bring out their different flavours. The tarragon adds a wonderful depth to this bright, fresh dish. It goes well as a light accompaniment to fish and seafood dishes.

Serves 4

5 spring onions (scallions)

50g/2oz/¼ cup butter

1 garlic clove, crushed

115g/4oz asparagus tips

115g/4oz mangetouts (snowpeas), trimmed

115g/4oz broad (fava) beans

2 Little Gem (Bibb) lettuces

5ml/1 tsp finely chopped fresh tarragon

salt and ground black pepper

1 Cut the spring onions into quarters lengthways and fry gently over a medium-low heat in half the butter with the garlic.

2 Add the asparagus tips, mangetouts and broad beans. Mix in, covering all the pieces with oil.

3 Just cover the base of the pan with water, season, and allow to simmer gently for a few minutes.

4 Cut the lettuce into quarters and add to the pan. Cook for 3 minutes then, off the heat, swirl in the remaining butter and the tarragon, and serve.

Energy 149kcal/619kJ; Protein 4.7g; Carbohydrate 6.1g, of which sugars 3g; Fat 12g, of which saturates 7.3g; Cholesterol 29mg; Calcium 55mg; Fibre 3.5g; Sodium 89mg

Celeriac purée

A most delicious vegetable, celeriac is ignored too often. This is sad as it is so good grated raw with mayonnaise and served with smoked salmon. Here it is made into a delicious purée that goes very well with game, poultry or roast pork or boar.

Serves 4

1 celeriac bulb, cut into chunks

1 lemon

2 potatoes, cut into chunks

300ml/½ pint/1¼ cups double (heavy) cream

salt and ground black pepper

chopped chives, to garnish

1 Place the celeriac in a pan. Cut the lemon in half and squeeze it into the pan, dropping the two halves in too.

2 Add the potatoes to the pan and just cover with cold water. Place a disc of greaseproof (waxed) paper over the vegetables. Bring to the boil, reduce the heat and simmer until tender, about 20 minutes.

3 Remove the lemon halves and drain through a colander. Return to the pan and allow to steam dry for a few minutes over a low heat.

4 Remove from the heat and purée in a food processor. This mixture can be set aside until you need it and can be kept in the refrigerator for a few days, covered with clear film (plastic wrap).

5 When ready to use, pour the cream into a pan and bring to the boil. Add the celeriac mixture and stir to heat through. Season, garnish wth snipped chives and serve.

Energy 403kcal/1661kJ; Protein 2.2g; Carbohydrate 7.9g, of which sugars 2.3g; Fat 40.5g, of which saturates 25.1g; Cholesterol 103mg; Calcium 65mg; Fibre 1.1g; Sodium 58mg

Creamed leeks

This dish is a real Scottish favourite, delicious with a full roast dinner, or on its own. Look for young, tender leeks, and use just the white and light green parts of the vegetable. Use the trimmed tops in soup or stock. The Scottish Musselburgh variety is excellent.

Serves 4

2 Musselburgh leeks, tops trimmed and roots removed

50g/2oz/½ stick butter

200ml/7fl oz/scant 1 cup double (heavy) cream

salt and ground black pepper

Cook's Tip
When buying leeks, choose smaller and less bendy ones as they are more tender.

1 Split the leeks down the middle, then cut across so you make pieces approximately 2cm/¾in square. Wash thoroughly and drain in a colander.

2 Melt the butter in a large pan and when quite hot throw in the leeks, stirring to coat them in the butter, and heat through. They will wilt but should not exude water. Keep the heat high but don't allow them to colour. You need to create a balance between keeping the temperature high so the water steams out of the vegetable, keeping it bright green, whilst not burning the leeks.

3 Keeping the heat high, pour in the cream, mix in thoroughly and allow to bubble and reduce. Season with salt and ground black pepper. When the texture is smooth, thick and creamy, the leeks are ready to serve.

Variation Although these leeks have a wonderful taste themselves, you may like to add extra flavourings, such as a little chopped garlic or some chopped fresh tarragon or thyme.

Energy 363kcal/1496kJ; Protein 2.5g; Carbohydrate 3.8g, of which sugars 3.1g; Fat 37.6g, of which saturates 23.3g; Cholesterol 95mg; Calcium 51mg; Fibre 2.2g; Sodium 89mg.

Baked tomatoes with mint

This is a dish for the height of the summer when the tomatoes are falling off the vines and are very ripe, juicy and full of flavour. Mint flourishes in British gardens and is prolific during the summer. This tomato dish goes especially well with lamb.

Serves 4

6 large ripe tomatoes

300ml/½ pint/1¼ cups double (heavy) cream

2 sprigs of fresh mint

olive oil, for brushing

a few pinches of caster (superfine) sugar

30ml/2 tbsp grated Bonnet cheese

salt and ground black pepper

1 Preheat the oven to 220°C/425°F/ Gas 7. Bring a pan of water to the boil and have a bowl of iced water ready. Cut the cores out of the tomatoes and make a cross at the base. Plunge the tomatoes into the boiling water for 10 seconds and then straight into the iced water. Leave to cool completely.

2 Put the cream and mint in a pan and bring to the boil. Reduce the heat and allow to simmer until it has reduced by about half.

3 Peel the cooled tomatoes and slice them thinly.

Cook's Tip Bonnet is a hard goat's cheese but any hard, well-flavoured cheese will do.

4 Brush a shallow gratin dish lightly with a little olive oil. Layer the sliced tomatoes in the dish, overlapping slightly, and season with salt and ground black pepper. Sprinkle a little sugar over the top.

5 Strain the reduced cream evenly over the top of the tomatoes. Sprinkle on the cheese and bake in the preheated oven for 15 minutes, or until the top is browned and bubbling. Serve immediately in the gratin dish.

Energy 443kcal/1831kJ; Protein 5g; Carbohydrate 6.7g, of which sugars 6.7g; Fat 44.1g, of which saturates 27.4g; Cholesterol 113mg; Calcium 123mg; Fibre 1.8g; Sodium 105mg.

Brussels sprouts with chestnuts

Native to southern Europe, chestnuts arrived in England with the Romans. The fresh nuts
are available in early winter and are an indispensable feature of Christmas dinner.

Serves 6

350g/12oz fresh chestnuts

300ml/½ pint/1¼ cups chicken or
vegetable stock (optional)

5ml/1 tsp sugar

675g/1½lb Brussels sprouts

50g/2oz/4 tbsp butter

115g/4oz bacon, cut into strips

1 Cut a cross in the pointed end of
each chestnut, then cook in boiling
water for 5–10 minutes.

2 Drain the chestnuts, then peel off
both the tough outer skin and the fine
inner one. Return the chestnuts to the
pan, add the stock (if using) or water
and sugar and simmer gently for
30–35 minutes, until the chestnuts
are tender, then drain thoroughly.

3 Meanwhile, cook the sprouts in lightly
salted boiling water for 8–10 minutes,
until tender, then drain well.

4 Melt the butter, add the bacon, cook
until becoming crisp, then stir in the
chestnuts for 2–3 minutes. Add the hot
sprouts, toss together and serve.

Roast potatoes

Roast potatoes can be cooked around a joint of meat, where they will absorb the juices.
For crisp potatoes with a soft, fluffy interior, roast them in a separate dish in a single layer.

Serves 4

1.3kg/3lb floury potatoes

90ml/6 tbsp oil, lard or goose fat

salt

1 Preheat the oven to 200°C/400°F/
Gas 6. Peel the potatoes and cut into
chunks. Boil in salted water for about
5 minutes, drain, return to the pan, and
shake them to roughen the surfaces.

2 Put the fat into a large roasting pan
and put into the hot oven to heat the
fat. Add the potatoes, coating them in
the fat. Return to the oven and cook
for 40–50 minutes, turning once or
twice, until crisp and cooked through.

Energy 256kcal/1070kJ; Protein 8.3g; Carbohydrate 26g, of which sugars 7.6g; Fat 13.9g, of which saturates 6.6g; Cholesterol 30mg; Calcium 59mg; Fibre 7g; Sodium 364mg

Energy 484kcal/2048kJ; Protein 9.4g; Carbohydrate 84.2g, of which sugars 2g; Fat 14.6g, of which saturates 5.9g; Cholesterol 13mg; Calcium 26mg; Fibre 5.9g; Sodium 29mg

Roast parsnips with honey and nutmeg

The Romans considered parsnips to be a luxury, at which time they were credited with a variety of medicinal and aphrodisiac qualities. Today, they are especially enjoyed when roasted around a joint of beef. Their sweetness mingles well with spices and honey.

Serves 4–6

4 medium parsnips

30ml/2 tbsp plain (all-purpose) flour seasoned with salt and pepper

60ml/4 tbsp oil

15–30ml/1–2 tbsp clear honey

freshly grated nutmeg

1 Preheat the oven to 200°C/400°F/ Gas 6. Peel the parsnips and cut each one lengthways into quarters, removing any woody cores. Drop into a pan of boiling water and cook for 5 minutes until slightly softened.

2 Drain the parsnips thoroughly, then toss in the seasoned flour, shaking off any excess.

3 Pour the oil into a roasting pan and put into the oven until hot. Add the parsnips, tossing them in the oil and arranging them in a single layer.

4 Return the pan to the oven and cook the parsnips for about 30 minutes, turning occasionally, until crisp, golden brown and cooked through.

5 Drizzle with the honey and sprinkle a little grated nutmeg. Return the parsnips to the oven for 5 minutes before serving.

Mushy peas

Dried marrowfat peas, cooked and served in their own juice, are believed to have originated in the north of England. Today, they are popular all over the country, especially with fish and chips. In the West Riding of Yorkshire mushy peas are served with pork pie.

Serves 4–6

250g/9oz dried peas

1 small onion

1 small carrot

2.5ml/½ tsp sugar

25g/1oz/2 tbsp butter

salt and ground black pepper

1 Put the peas in a bowl and pour over boiling water to cover them well. Soak for about 12 hours or overnight.

2 Drain and rinse the peas and put into a pan. Add the onion, carrot, sugar and 600ml/1pint/2½ cups cold water.

3 Bring to the boil and simmer gently for about 20 minutes or until the peas are soft and the water absorbed.

4 Remove the onion and carrot from the pan. Mash the peas, seasoning to taste with salt and black pepper, and stir in the butter.

Cook's tip Cooking the peas in a muslin (cheesecloth) bag in step 2 stops them disintegrating.

Energy 144kcal/600kJ; Protein 2g; Carbohydrate 16.2g, of which sugars 6.7g; Fat 8.3g, of which saturates 1g; Cholesterol 0mg; Calcium 41mg; Fibre 4g; Sodium 9mg

Energy 68kcal/288kJ; Protein 4.8g; Carbohydrate 11.5g, of which sugars 1.4g; Fat 0.6g, of which saturates 0.1g; Cholesterol 0mg; Calcium 12mg; Fibre 1.5g; Sodium 283mg

Clapshot

This Scottish vegetable dish is excellent with haggis or on top of shepherd's pie in place of just potato. Turnips give an earthy flavour, and swede introduces a sweet accent. It is also slightly less heavy than mashed potato, which is good for a lighter meal or supper.

Serves 4

450g/1lb potatoes

450g/1lb turnips or swede (rutabaga)

50g/2oz/¼ cup butter

50ml/2fl oz/¼ cup milk

5ml/1 tsp freshly grated nutmeg

30ml/2 tbsp chopped fresh parsley

salt and ground black pepper

1 Peel the potatoes and turnips or swede, then cut them into evenly sized small chunks. You will need a large sharp knife for the turnips.

2 Place the chopped vegetables in a pan and cover with cold water. Bring to the boil over a medium heat, then reduce the heat and simmer until both vegetables are cooked, which will take about 15–20 minutes. Test the vegetables by pushing the point of a sharp knife into one of the cubes; if it goes in easily and the cube begins to break apart, then it is cooked.

3 Drain the vegetables through a colander. Return to the pan and allow them to dry out for a few minutes over a low heat, stirring occasionally to prevent any from sticking to the base of the pan.

4 Melt the butter with the milk in a small pan over a low heat. Mash the dry potato and turnip or swede mixture, then add the milk mixture. Grate in the nutmeg, add the parsley, mix thoroughly and season to taste. Serve immediately with roast meat or game.

Energy 204kcal/852kJ; Protein 3.4g; Carbohydrate 24.1g, of which sugars 7.2g; Fat 11.2g, of which saturates 6.8g; Cholesterol 27mg; Calcium 78mg; Fibre 3.8g; Sodium 111mg

Skirlie

Oatmeal has been a staple in Scotland for centuries. Skirlie is a simple preparation and can be used for stuffings or as an accompaniment, and is especially good with roast meats. It is traditionally cooked in lard but many people prefer butter.

Serves 4

50g/2oz/¼ cup butter

1 onion, finely chopped

175g/6oz/scant 2 cups medium rolled oats

salt and ground black pepper

Variation To add a lovely rich flavour to the skirlie, grate in a little nutmeg and add a good pinch of cinnamon towards the end.

1 Melt the butter in a pan over a medium heat and add the onion. Fry gently until it is softened and very slightly browned.

2 Stir in the rolled oats and season with salt and ground black pepper. Cook gently for 10 minutes. Taste for seasoning and serve immediately.

Energy 282kcal/1182kJ; Protein 6g; Carbohydrate 34.9g, of which sugars 2.2g; Fat 14.2g, of which saturates 6.5g; Cholesterol 27mg; Calcium 36mg; Fibre 3.5g; Sodium 91mg

Welsh spiced roasted pumpkin

Until the early 1900s pumpkins were only grown in the Gower Peninsula. They were always favourites for making into pies and pickles. Here chunks of pumpkin are roasted with spices and herbs before being topped with cheese. Serve on its own with a salad of watercress and baby spinach leaves. Minus the cheese, the dish makes a good accompaniment to roast meats, sausages or lamb chops.

Serves 3-4

5ml/1 tsp fennel seeds

30ml/2 tbsp olive oil

1 garlic clove, crushed

5ml/1 tsp ground ginger

5ml/1 tsp dried thyme

pinch of chilli powder (optional)

piece of pumpkin weighing about 1.5kg/3lb 6oz

75g/3oz/¾ cup cheese, such as Caerphilly, grated

salt and ground black pepper

1 Preheat the oven to 200°C/400°F/ Gas 6. Lightly crush or bruise the fennel seeds with a pestle and mortar, a rolling pin or the back of a large spoon – this helps to release their flavour.

2 Put the oil into a large mixing bowl and stir in the fennel, garlic, ginger, thyme and chilli. Season with salt and pepper and mix well.

3 Cut the skin off the pumpkin, scrape out and discard the seeds. Cut the flesh into rough chunks of about 3.5cm/1in. Toss the chunks in the oil mixture until evenly coated, then spread them in a single layer on a large baking tray.

4 Put into the hot oven and cook for about 40 minutes or until tender and golden brown on the edges. It helps to turn them over once during cooking.

5 Sprinkle the cheese over the top and return to the oven for 5 more minutes.

6 Serve straight from the baking tray, making sure all the golden bits of cheese are scraped up with the pumpkin.

Energy 171kcal/712kJ; Protein 7.1g; Carbohydrate 8.3g, of which sugars 6.4g; Fat 12g, of which saturates 5g; Cholesterol 17mg; Calcium 238mg; Fibre 3.8g; Sodium 127mg

Onion cake

Serve this simple but delicious Welsh dish with a salad accompaniment. It's particularly good alongside sausages, lamb chops or roast chicken – in fact, any roast meat.
The cooking time will depend on the potatoes and how thinly they are sliced: use a food processor or mandolin (if you have one) to make paper-thin slices. The mound of potatoes will cook down to make a thick buttery cake.

Serves 6

900g/2lb new potatoes, peeled and thinly sliced

2 medium onions, very finely chopped

salt and ground black pepper

about 115g/4oz/½ cup butter

1 Preheat the oven to 190°C/375°F/ Gas 5. Butter a 20cm/8in round cake tin (pan) and line the base with a circle of baking parchment.

2 Arrange some of the potato slices evenly in the bottom of the tin and then sprinkle some of the onions over them. Season with salt and pepper. Reserve 25g/1oz/2 tbsp of the butter and dot the mixture with tiny pieces of the remaining butter.

3 Repeat these layers, using up all the ingredients and finishing with a layer of potatoes. Melt the reserved butter and brush it over the top.

4 Cover the potatoes with foil, put in the hot oven and cook for 1–1½ hours, until tender and golden. Remove from the oven and leave to stand, still covered, for 10–15 minutes..

5 Carefully turn out the onion cake on to a warmed plate and serve.

Cook's tip If using old potatoes, cook and serve in an earthenware or ovenproof-glass dish. Then remove the cover for the final 10–15 minutes to lightly brown the top.

Energy 272kcal/1133kJ; Protein 3.5g; Carbohydrate 29.5g, of which sugars 5.8g; Fat 16.3g, of which saturates 10.1g; Cholesterol 41mg; Calcium 29mg; Fibre 2.4g; Sodium 135mg

Baked onions

One of Britain's oldest and most widely used flavouring vegetables, the onion, also deserves to be used more as a vegetable accompaniment in its own right. Onions become sweet and mildly flavoured when boiled or baked, and can be cooked very conveniently in the oven when baking potatoes or parsnips.

Serves 4

4 large even-sized onions

Cook's tip These onions are baked in their skins, but you could peel them, if preferred, before baking. The peeled onions are best baked in a covered casserole dish instead of a roasting tin.

◀ **1** Preheat the oven to 180°C/350°F/Gas 4. Put a little cold water into a medium-size roasting pan, and arrange the unpeeled onions in it.

2 Bake in the preheated oven for about 1 hour, or until the onions feel soft when squeezed at the sides. Peel the skins and serve immediately.

Energy 90Kcal/375kJ; Protein 3g; Carbohydrate 19.8g, of which sugars 14g; Fat 0.5g, of which saturates 0g; Cholesterol 0mg; Calcium 63mg; Fibre 3.5g; Sodium 8mg

Roasted Jerusalem artichokes

Although not widely available in stores, Jerusalem artichokes grow easily in many parts of Britain and conceal a deliciously sweet white flesh inside their knobbly brown exterior. While they are best known for velvety soups, their natural sweetness enables them to glaze easily and they make a delicious side vegetable with many foods, especially game.

Serves 6

675g/1½lb Jerusalem artichokes

15ml/1 tbsp lemon juice or vinegar

salt

50g/2oz/¼ cup unsalted (sweet) butter

seasoned flour, for dusting

1 Peel the artichokes, dropping them straight into a bowl of water acidulated with lemon juice or vinegar to prevent browning. Cut up the artichokes so that the pieces are matched for size, otherwise they will cook unevenly.

2 Preheat the oven to 180°C/350°F/ Gas 4. Bring a pan of salted water to the boil, drain the artichokes from the acidulated water and boil them for 5 minutes, or until just tender. Watch them carefully, as they break up easily.

◀ **3** Melt the butter in a roasting pan, coat the artichokes in the seasoned flour and roll them around in the butter in the pan.

4 Cook the butter and flour coated artichokes in the preheated oven for 20–30 minutes, or until golden brown. Serve immediately.

Variation Puréeing is a useful fall-back if the artichokes break up during cooking: simply blend or mash the drained boiled artichokes with salt and freshly ground black pepper to taste and a little single (light) cream, if you like. Puréed artichokes are especially good served with game, which tends to be dry.

Energy 101Kcal/419kJ; Protein 0.7g; Carbohydrate 8.9g, of which sugars 8.4g; Fat 7.2g, of which saturates 4.5g; Cholesterol 18mg; Calcium 30mg; Fibre 2.7g; Sodium 242mg

New potato and chive salad

The potatoes absorb the oil and vinegar dressing as they cool, and are then tossed in mayonnaise. Small, waxy potatoes, which can be kept whole, are particularly suitable for this recipe. Serve them with cold poached salmon or roast chicken.

2 Meanwhile, finely chop the white parts of the spring onions together with a little of the green part.

3 Whisk the oil with the vinegar and mustard. Drain the potatoes. Immediately, while the potatoes are still hot and steaming, toss them lightly with the oil mixture and the spring onions. Leave to cool.

Serves 4–6

675g/1½lb small new potatoes, unpeeled

4 spring onions (scallions)

45ml/3 tbsp olive oil

15ml/1 tbsp cider vinegar or wine vinegar

2.5ml/½ tsp ready-made English (hot) mustard

175ml/6fl oz/¾ cup mayonnaise

45ml/3 tbsp chopped fresh chives

salt and ground black pepper

1 Cook the new potatoes in boiling salted water for about 15 minutes, or until tender.

Variation Add a handful of chopped parsley or mint to the salad with the mayonnaise instead of chives.

4 Stir the mayonnaise and chives into the cooled potatoes and turn into a serving bowl. Chill the salad until you are ready to serve.

Energy 182kcal/761kJ; Protein 2.5g; Carbohydrate 22.5g, of which sugars 1.9g; Fat 9.7g, of which saturates 1.5g; Cholesterol 0mg; Calcium 20mg; Fibre 1.7g; Sodium 17mg

Salmagundi

Salads, with the ingredients elaborately arranged, were fashionable in 16th-century England, containing chopped meat, anchovies and eggs, garnished with onions, lemon juice, oil and other condiments. This variation is thought to come from Northumbria.

Serves 4–6

1 large chicken, weighing about 2kg/4½lb

1 onion

1 carrot

1 celery stick

2 bay leaves

large sprig of thyme

10 black peppercorns

500g/1¼lb new or baby potatoes

225g/8oz carrots, cut into small sticks

225g/8oz sugar snap peas

4 eggs

½ cucumber, thinly sliced

8–12 cherry tomatoes

8–12 green olives stuffed with pimento

For the dressing

75ml/5 tbsp olive oil

30ml/2 tbsp lemon juice

2.5ml/½ tsp sugar

1.5ml/¼ tsp ready-made English (hot) mustard

salt and ground black pepper

1 Put the chicken in a deep pan with the onion, carrot, celery, bay leaves, thyme and peppercorns. Add water to cover by at least 2.5cm/1in. Bring to the boil and simmer gently for 45 minutes or until the chicken is cooked, then leave to cool in the stock for several hours to keep it moist.

2 Whisk together the ingredients for the dressing. Set aside.

3 Using a separate pan for each, cook the potatoes, carrots and peas in lightly salted boiling water until just tender, Drain and rinse under cold water. Halve the potatoes. Hard-boil the eggs, cool, shell and cut into quarters.

4 Lift the chicken out of the stock, remove the meat and cut or tear into bite size pieces.

5 Arrange the vegetables, chicken and eggs on a large platter, or in a large bowl, and add the tomatoes and olives. Just before serving, drizzle the salad dressing over the top.

Energy 397kcal/1664kJ; Protein 41.2g; Carbohydrate 24.9g, of which sugars 8.7g; Fat 15.5g, of which saturates 3g; Cholesterol 220mg; Calcium 63mg; Fibre 4.6g; Sodium 155mg

Beetroot and apple salad

These two typically English ingredients complement each other well to make a pretty salad, with the apple pieces turning pink on contact with the beetroot juices. The crispness of the apple contrasts well with the soft texture of the cooked beetroot.

Serves 4

6 beetroot (beets)

30ml/2 tbsp mayonnaise

30ml/2 tbsp thick natural (plain) yogurt

2 crisp eating apples

small handful of chopped fresh chives

salt and ground black pepper

salad leaves and/or watercress sprigs, to serve

Variations
• Try dill in place of the chives.
• Add some thinly sliced celery.
• Use soured cream in place of the mayonnaise and yogurt.

1 Wash the beetroot gently, without breaking their skins. Trim the stalks until very short but do not remove them completely. Put into a pan and cover well with water. Bring to the boil and simmer gently for 1–2 hours, depending on their size, or until soft throughout (check by inserting a sharp knife into the centre). Drain and leave to cool. When cold, remove the skins of the beetroot and cut into small cubes.

2 In a large bowl, stir together the mayonnaise and yogurt.

3 Peel the apples, remove their cores and cut into small cubes.

4 Add the beetroot, apples and two-thirds of the chives to the mayonnaise mixture and toss until well coated, seasoning to taste with salt and pepper. Leave to stand for 10–20 minutes.

5 Pile onto a serving dish. Add salad leaves and/or watercress sprigs and scatter with the remaining chives.

Energy 191kcal/793kJ; Protein 4.1g; Carbohydrate 9.5g, of which sugars 8.8g; Fat 15.5g, of which saturates 1.6g; Cholesterol 0mg; Calcium 54mg; Fibre 2.7g; Sodium 58mg

Coleslaw with English blue cheese

Lancashire, Lincolnshire and Kent in particular are renowned for growing cabbages. In this dish, shredded crisp white cabbage is tossed in a dressing flavoured with English blue cheese. Serve it with other salads or with hot potatoes baked in their skins.

Serves 4–8

45ml/3 tbsp mayonnaise

45ml/3 tbsp thick natural (plain) yogurt

50g/2oz blue cheese, such as Stilton or Oxford Blue

15ml/1 tbsp lemon juice or cider vinegar

about 500g/1¼lb white cabbage

1 medium carrot

1 small red onion

2 small celery sticks

1 crisp eating apple

salt and ground black pepper

watercress sprigs, to garnish

1 To make the dressing, put the mayonnaise and yogurt into a large bowl and crumble in the cheese. Stir well, adding a squeeze of lemon juice and a little seasoning to taste.

Cook's tips
• Make the dressing by whizzing the ingredients in a food processor.
• If you have a slicing attachment, the cabbage can be finely shredded using a food processor.

2 Trim and shred the cabbage finely, grate the carrot, chop the onion finely and cut the celery into very thin slices. Core and dice the apple.

Variation Try making the coleslaw with a half-and-half mixture of red cabbage with the white cabbage.

3 Add the cabbage, carrot, onion, celery and apple to the bowl and toss until all the ingredients are well mixed and coated with the dressing.

4 Cover the bowl and refrigerate for 2–3 hours or until ready to serve. Stir before serving, garnish with watercress.

Energy 86kcal/359kJ; Protein 2.7g; Carbohydrate 5.1g, of which sugars 4.8g; Fat 6.3g, of which saturates 1.9g; Cholesterol 9mg; Calcium 78mg; Fibre 1.6g; Sodium 116mg

Globe artichoke salad

The spiky artichoke plants are grown widely in British gardens and allotments in the warmer southern areas, and are valued for their architectural qualities in the garden as for the table. This salad makes a versatile first course, and is equally good served hot or cold.

Serves 4

4 artichokes

juice of 1 lemon

900ml/1 ½ pints/3¾ cups vegetable stock

2 garlic cloves, chopped

1 small bunch parsley

6 whole peppercorns

15ml/1 tbsp olive oil, plus extra for drizzling

1 Trim the stalks of the artichokes close to the base, cut the tips off the leaves and then divide them into quarters.

2 Remove the inedible hairy choke (the central part), carefully scraping the hairs away from the heart at the base of the artichoke.

3 Squeeze a little of the lemon juice over the cut surfaces of the artichokes to prevent discoloration. Put the artichokes into a pan and cover with the stock and water, garlic, parsley, peppercorns and olive oil.

4 Cover with a lid and cook gently for 1 hour, or until the artichokes are tender. They are ready when the leaves will come away easily when pulled.

5 Remove the artichokes with a slotted spoon and keep them warm if serving hot. Boil the cooking liquor hard without the lid, to reduce by half, and then strain.

6 To serve, arrange the artichokes in serving dishes, pour over the reduced juices, drizzle over a little olive oil and lemon juice. Provide finger bowls.

7 To eat, pull a leaf away from the artichoke and scrape the fleshy part at the base with your teeth. Discard the remainder of the leaves and then eat the heart at the base.

Energy 59Kcal/245kJ; Protein 0.7g; Carbohydrate 7.8g, of which sugars 7.3g; Fat 3.1g, of which saturates 0.5g; Cholesterol 0mg; Calcium 25mg; Fibre 2.4g; Sodium 61mg

Roast beetroot with horseradish cream

Beetroot was very popular in Elizabethan England, when its vibrant colour was added to elaborate salads. In this recipe, its sweet flavour is enhanced first by roasting and then by the horseradish and vinegar in the cream. Serve it with roast beef or venison.

Serves 4–6

10–12 small whole beetroot (beets)

30ml/2 tbsp oil

45ml/3 tbsp grated fresh horseradish

15ml/1 tbsp white wine vinegar

10ml/2 tsp caster (superfine) sugar

150ml/¼ pint/⅔ cup double (heavy) cream

salt

Cook's tips
• If you are unable to find any fresh horseradish root use preserved grated horseradish instead.
• For a lighter sauce, replace half the cream with thick plain yogurt.

1 Preheat the oven to 180°C/350°F/ Gas 4. Wash the beetroot without breaking their skins. Trim the stalks very short but do not remove them completely. Toss the beetroot in the oil and sprinkle with salt. Spread them in a roasting pan and cover with foil. Put into the hot oven and cook for about 1½ hours or until soft throughout. Leave to cool, covered, for 10 minutes.

2 Meanwhile, make the horseradish sauce. Put the horseradish, vinegar and sugar into a bowl and mix well. Whip the cream until thickened and fold in the horseradish mixture. Cover and chill until required.

3 When the beetroot are cool enough to handle, slip off the skins and serve with the sauce.

Energy 254kcal/1052kJ; Protein 2.1g; Carbohydrate 10g, of which sugars 9.1g; Fat 22.2g, of which saturates 3.2g; Cholesterol 1mg; Calcium 26mg; Fibre 2.3g; Sodium 143mg

Savoury pies and pastries

Pastry is a passion in Britain, whether it's used to make a portable feast such as a Cornish pasty or a Scotch mutton pie; a traditional chicken or steak and kidney pie to feed the family; or an elegant party dish such as beef Wellington or a spectacular raised game pie. Each region and period of history has produced its own favourite variations on the theme.

Fish, cockle and laverbread pie

This is a traditional fish pie with a distinct Welsh flavour, using a combination of white fish, smoked haddock and some Welsh cockles. The puff pastry topping can easily be replaced with mashed potato if you prefer. The addition of a little laverbread adds an extra twist of Welsh flavour. If you can't find any, use cooked, squeezed spinach instead.

Serves 4

225g/8oz skinless white fish, such as hake, haddock or cod

225g/8oz skinless smoked haddock or cod

425ml/¾ pint/scant 2 cups milk

25g/1oz/2 tbsp butter

25g/1oz/¼ cup plain (all-purpose) flour

good pinch of freshly grated nutmeg

1 leek, thinly sliced

200g/7oz shelled cooked cockles (small clams)

30ml/2 tbsp laverbread

30ml/2 tbsp finely chopped fresh parsley

1 sheet ready-rolled puff pastry

salt and ground black pepper

1 Preheat the oven to 200°C/400°F/ Gas 6. Put the white and smoked fish in a pan with the milk. Heat until the milk barely comes to the boil, then cover and poach gently for about 8 minutes or until the fish is just cooked.

2 Lift the fish out, reserving the liquid. Break into flakes, discarding any bones.

3 Melt the butter, stir in the flour and cook for 1–2 minutes. Remove and stir in the reserved cooking liquid. Stir over medium heat until the sauce thickens.

4 Stir in the fish flakes and their juices. Add nutmeg and season to taste.

5 Add the leek, cockles, laverbread and parsley to the sauce and spoon into a 1.2 litre/2 pint ovenproof dish.

6 Brush the edges of the dish with water. Unroll the pastry and lay it over the top of the dish, trimming it to fit.

7 Use the pastry off-cuts to make decorative fish or leaves for the top, brushing each one with a little water to help them stick.

8 Put into the hot oven and cook for about 30 minutes, or until the pastry is puffed and golden brown.

Cook's tips
• If you don't have laverbread, add some shredded sorrel or some finely grated lemon rind instead.
• The puff pastry could be replaced with shortcrust pastry. Alternatively, try using several sheets of filo pastry, each lightly brushed with melted butter, either layered on top of the pie or gently scrunched up and arranged over the surface of the filling.

Energy 573kcal/2401kJ; Protein 36.8g; Carbohydrate 41g, of which sugars 7.3g; Fat 31.2g, of which saturates 4.7g; Cholesterol 92mg; Calcium 270mg; Fibre 1.2g; Sodium 1084mg

Steak and oyster pie

In the 17th century England, oysters were so plentiful and cheap that not only could the poor afford to eat them, they were even used to feed animals. When enormous beef pies were prepared for large gatherings, oysters were added to make the beef go further. Though oysters are a luxury today, they add a wonderful flavour to the filling in this pie.

Serves 6

30ml/2 tbsp plain (all-purpose) flour

1kg/2¼lb rump (round) steak, cut into 5cm/2in pieces

45ml/3 tbsp oil

25g/1oz/2 tbsp butter

1 large onion, chopped

300ml/½ pint/1¼ cups beef stock

300ml/½ pint/1¼ cups brown ale or red wine

30ml/2 tbsp fresh thyme leaves

225g/8oz chestnut mushrooms, halved if large

12 shelled oysters

375g/13oz puff pastry, thawed if frozen

beaten egg, to glaze

salt and ground black pepper

1 Preheat the oven if using (see step 3) to 150°C/300°F/Gas 2. Season the flour with salt and pepper and toss the pieces of steak in it until well coated. Heat half the oil with half the butter in a large pan or flameproof casserole and quickly brown the meat in batches. Set it to one side.

2 Add the remaining oil and butter to the hot pan, stir in the chopped onion and cook over a medium heat, stirring occasionally, until golden brown and beginning to soften.

3 Return the meat and any juices to the pan and stir in the stock, ale or wine and thyme. Bring just to the boil then cover the pan and either simmer very gently on the stove or cook in the preheated oven for about 1½ hours, or until the beef is tender.

4 Using a slotted spoon, lift the meat and onion out of the liquid and put it into a 1.75 litre/3 pint/7½ cup pie dish. Bring the liquid to the boil and reduce to about 600ml/1 pint/2½ cups.

Cook's tip Though using rump steak for the pie is traditional, replacing it with the same amount of braising steak is acceptable.

5 Season to taste and stir in the mushrooms, then pour the mixture over the meat in the dish. Leave to cool. Preheat the oven to 200°C/400°F/Gas 6, if not already using.

6 Add the oysters to the cooled meat, pushing them down into the mixture.

7 Roll out the pastry on a lightly floured surface to a shape 2.5cm/1in larger than the dish. Trim off a 1cm/½in strip all around the edge. Brush the rim of the dish with a little beaten egg and lay the strip on it. Brush the strip with egg, lay the pastry sheet over the top, trim to fit and press the edges together well to seal them. Brush the top of the pie with beaten egg.

8 Put the pie into the hot oven and cook for about 40 minutes, until the pastry is crisp and golden brown and the filling is piping hot.

Energy 689kcal/2874kJ; Protein 49.4g; Carbohydrate 29.8g, of which sugars 1g; Fat 39g, of which saturates 9.1g; Cholesterol 144mg; Calcium 145mg; Fibre 0.4g; Sodium 674mg

Veal and ham pie

In the cold version of veal and ham pie, the filling is completely enclosed in hot water crust pastry. In this hot version, the pastry sits on top of the classic combination of meat and eggs, keeping the contents moist and the aromas sealed in until the pie is cut open.

Serves 4

450g/1lb boneless shoulder of veal, cut into cubes

225g/8oz lean gammon, cut into cubes

15ml/1 tbsp plain (all-purpose) flour

large pinch each of dry mustard and ground black pepper

25g/1oz/2 tbsp butter

15ml/1 tbsp oil

1 onion, chopped

600ml/1 pint/2½ cups chicken or veal stock

2 eggs, hard-boiled and sliced

30ml/2 tbsp chopped fresh parsley

For the pastry

175g/6oz/1½ cups plain (all-purpose) flour

pinch of salt

85g/3oz/6 tbsp butter, diced

beaten egg, to glaze

1 Preheat the oven to 180°C/350°F/ Gas 4. Mix the veal and gammon in a bowl. Season the flour with the mustard and black pepper, then add it to the meat and toss well.

2 Heat the butter and oil in a large, flameproof casserole until sizzling, then cook the meat mixture in batches until golden on all sides. Use a slotted spoon to remove the meat and set aside.

3 Cook the onion in the fat remaining in the casserole until softened but not coloured. Stir in the stock and the meat. Cover and cook in the hot oven for 1½ hours or until the veal is tender. Adjust the seasoning and leave to cool.

4 To make the pastry, sift the flour into a bowl with the salt and rub in the butter until the mixture resembles fine crumbs. Mix in just enough cold water to bind the mixture, gathering it together with your fingertips. Wrap the pastry in clear film (plastic wrap), and chill for at least 30 minutes.

Variation Use ready-made fresh or frozen puff pastry to cover the pie.

5 Spoon the veal mixture into a 1.5 litre/2½ pint/6¼ cup pie dish. Arrange the slices of hard-boiled egg on top and sprinkle with the parsley.

6 On a lightly floured surface, roll out the pastry to about 4cm/1½in larger than the top of the pie dish. Cut a strip from around the edge, dampen the rim of the dish and press the pastry strip on to it. Brush the pastry rim with beaten egg and top with the lid.

7 Trim off any excess pastry. Use the blunt edge of a knife to tap the outside edge, pressing the pastry down with your finger to seal in the filling. Pinch the pastry between your fingers to flute the edge. Roll out any trimmings and cut out shapes to decorate the pie.

8 Brush the top of the pie with beaten egg, put into the hot oven and cook for 30–40 minutes or until the pastry is well risen and golden brown. Serve hot.

Energy 621kcal/2595kJ; Protein 42.4g; Carbohydrate 39.2g, of which sugars 2.6g; Fat 33.8g, of which saturates 17.2g; Cholesterol 281mg; Calcium 128mg; Fibre 2.3g; Sodium 1007mg

Chicken and ham pie

This pie has pastry top and bottom. Though it can be served warm, it is even more delicious cold. Serve it with salad for a summer lunch or take it on a picnic.

Serves 6

For the pastry

275g/10oz/2½ cups plain (all-purpose) flour

pinch of salt

150g/5oz/⅔ cup butter, diced

For the filling

800g/1¾lb chicken breast

350g/12oz smoked or cured ham

6 spring onions (scallions), chopped

15ml/1 tbsp chopped fresh tarragon

10ml/2 tsp chopped fresh thyme

grated rind and juice of ½ lemon

60ml/4 tbsp double (heavy) cream

5ml/1 tsp ground mace or nutmeg

beaten egg, to glaze

salt and ground black pepper

1 Sift the flour into a bowl with the salt and rub in the butter until the mixture resembles fine crumbs. Mix in just enough cold water to bind the mixture, gathering it together with your fingertips. Chill for 30 minutes.

2 Preheat the oven to 190°C/375°F/ Gas 5. Roll out one-third of the pastry.

3 Line a 20cm/8in pie dish 5cm/2in deep with the pastry and place on a baking (cookie) sheet.

4 Mince (grind) or process 115g/4oz of the chicken with the gammon. Place the meat in a bowl and add the spring onions, tarragon and thyme, lemon rind, 15ml/1 tbsp lemon juice and seasoning. Stir well, adding enough cream to make a soft mixture.

5 Cut the remaining chicken into 1cm/½in pieces and mix with the remaining lemon juice, the mace or nutmeg and seasoning.

6 Put one-third of the gammon mixture in the pastry base and cover with half the chopped chicken. Repeat the layers, then top with the remaining gammon.

7 Dampen the edges of the pastry base. Roll out the remaining pastry and cover the pie, sealing the edges firmly.

8 Use the trimmings to decorate the top. Make a small hole in the centre and brush with beaten egg. Cook for 20 minutes then turn the oven down to 160°C/325°F/Gas 3 and cook for a further 1–1¼ hours. Cover with foil if the pastry becomes too brown.

Energy 431kcal/1804kJ; Protein 34.8g; Carbohydrate 23.8g, of which sugars 0.8g; Fat 22.5g, of which saturates 8.3g; Cholesterol 98mg; Calcium 57mg; Fibre 1.1g; Sodium 648mg

Chicken and mushroom pie

This traditional pie is a favourite throughout Britain, especially in the Lowlands of Scotland where farmyard chickens provide a plentiful supply of fresh, free-range birds. If you can find them, use wild mushrooms, such as ceps, to intensify the flavours.

Serves 6

50g/2oz/¼ cup butter

30ml/2 tbsp plain (all-purpose) flour

250ml/8fl oz/1 cup hot chicken stock

60ml/4 tbsp single (light) cream

1 onion, coarsely chopped

2 carrots, sliced

2 celery sticks, coarsely chopped

50g/2oz fresh (preferably wild) mushrooms, quartered

450g/1lb cooked chicken meat, cubed

50g/2oz/½ cup fresh or frozen peas

salt and ground black pepper

beaten egg, to glaze

For the pastry

225g/8oz/2 cups plain (all-purpose) flour

1.5ml/¼ tsp salt

115g/4oz/½ cup cold butter, diced

65g/2½oz/⅓ cup white vegetable fat (shortening), diced

90–120ml/6–8 tbsp chilled water

1 To make the pastry, sift the flour and salt into a bowl. Rub in the butter and white vegetable fat until the mixture resembles breadcrumbs. Sprinkle with 90ml/6 tbsp chilled water and mix until the dough holds together. If the dough is too crumbly, add a little more water, 15ml/1 tbsp at a time.

2 Gather the dough into a ball and flatten it into a round. Wrap in clear film (plastic wrap) so that it is airtight and chill in the refrigerator for at least 30 minutes.

3 Preheat the oven to 190°C/375°F/ Gas 5. To make the filling, melt half the butter in a heavy pan over a low heat. Whisk in the flour and cook until bubbling, whisking constantly. Add the hot stock and whisk over a medium heat until the mixture boils. Cook for 2–3 minutes, then whisk in the cream. Season to taste with salt and ground black pepper, and set aside.

4 Heat the remaining butter in a large non-stick frying pan and cook the onion and carrots over a low heat for about 5 minutes. Add the celery and mushrooms and cook for a further 5 minutes, until they have softened. Add the cooked chicken and peas and stir in thoroughly.

5 Add the chicken mixture to the hot cream sauce and stir to mix. Adjust the seasoning if necessary. Spoon the mixture into a 2.5 litre/4 pint/2½ quart oval baking dish.

6 Roll out the pastry on a floured surface to a thickness of about 3mm/ ⅛in. Cut out an oval 2.5cm/1in larger all around than the dish. Lay the pastry over the filling. Gently press around the edge of the dish to seal, then trim off the excess pastry. Crimp the edge of the pastry by pushing the forefinger of one hand into the edge and, using the thumb and forefinger of the other hand, pinch the pastry. Continue all round the pastry edge.

7 Press together the pastry trimmings and roll out again. Cut out mushroom shapes with a sharp knife and stick them on to the pastry lid with a little of the beaten egg. Glaze the lid with beaten egg and cut several slits in the pastry to allow the steam to escape.

8 Bake the pie in the preheated oven for about 30 minutes, until the pastry has browned. Serve hot.

Cook's tip Using a combination of butter and white vegetable fat gives shortcrust pastry a lovely crumbly texture with good flavour.

Energy 600kcal/2501kJ; Protein 23.7g; Carbohydrate 38.8g, of which sugars 3.7g; Fat 40g, of which saturates 21.8g; Cholesterol 132mg; Calcium 92mg; Fibre 2.7g; Sodium 226mg

Pigeon pie

This country dish is adaptable and could be made with whatever game birds are available. Serve the pie with seasonal vegetables: potatoes boiled in their skins, puréed Jerusalem artichokes and winter greens, such as purple sprouting broccoli or Brussels sprouts.

Serves 8–10

4 pheasant and/or pigeon skinless breast portions

225g/8oz lean stewing steak

115g/4oz streaky (fatty) bacon, trimmed

butter, for frying

2 medium onions, finely chopped

1 large garlic clove, crushed

15ml/1 tbsp plain (all-purpose) flour

about 300ml/½ pint/¼ cup pigeon or pheasant stock

15ml/1 tbsp tomato purée (paste) (optional)

15ml/1 tbsp chopped fresh parsley

a little grated lemon rind

15ml/1 tbsp rowan or redcurrant jelly

50–115g/2–4oz button (white) mushrooms, halved or quartered if large

a small pinch of freshly grated nutmeg or ground cloves (optional)

milk or beaten egg, to glaze

sea salt and ground black pepper

For the rough-puff pastry

225g/8oz/2 cups plain (all-purpose) flour

2.5ml/½ tsp salt

5ml/1 tsp lemon juice

115g/4oz/½ cup butter, in walnut-sized pieces

1 To make the rough-puff pastry, sift the flour and salt into a large mixing bowl. Add the lemon juice and the butter pieces and just enough cold water to bind the ingredients together. Turn the mixture on to a floured board and roll the pastry into a long strip. Fold it into three and press the edges together. Half-turn the pastry, rib it with the rolling pin to equalize the air in it and roll it into a strip once again. Repeat this folding and rolling process three more times.

2 Slice the pheasant or pigeon breasts from the bone and cut the meat into fairly thin strips. Trim away any fat from the stewing steak and slice it in the same manner. Cut the streaky (fatty) bacon into thin strips, and then cook it very gently in a heavy frying pan until the fat runs. Add some butter and brown the sliced pigeon or pheasant and stewing steak in it, a little at a time.

3 Remove the meats from the pan and set aside. Cook the onions and garlic in the fat for 2–3 minutes over a medium heat. Remove and set aside with the meats, then stir the flour into the remaining fat. Cook for 1–2 minutes, and then gradually stir in enough stock to make a fairly thin gravy. Add the tomato purée, if using, parsley, lemon rind and rowan or redcurrant jelly and the mushrooms. Season to taste and add the nutmeg or cloves, if you like.

4 Return the browned meats, chopped onion and garlic to the pan containing the gravy, and mix well before turning into a deep 1.75 litre/3 pint/7½ cup pie dish. Leave to cool. Meanwhile, preheat the oven to 220°C/425°F/Gas 7.

5 Roll the prepared pastry out to make a circle 2.5cm/1in larger all round than the pie dish, and cut out to make a lid for the pie. Wet the rim of the pie dish and line with the remaining pastry strip. Dampen the strip and cover with the lid, pressing down well to seal.

6 Trim away any excess pastry and knock up the edges with a knife. Make a hole in the centre for the steam to escape and use any pastry trimmings to decorate the top. Glaze the top of the pie with milk or beaten egg. Bake in the oven for about 20 minutes, until the pastry is well-risen, then reduce the oven to 150°C/300°F/Gas 2 for another 1½ hours, until cooked. Protect the pastry from over-browning if necessary by covering it with a double layer of wet baking parchment. Serve.

Cook's tip Frozen puff pastry could replace the home-made rough-puff pastry, if you prefer.

Energy 448Kcal/1871kJ; Protein 28.3g; Carbohydrate 29.5g, of which sugars 5.3g; Fat 24.9g, of which saturates 9.5g; Cholesterol 55mg; Calcium 67mg; Fibre 1.5g; Sodium 393mg

Welsh leek, bacon and egg pie

In this dish, leeks (a national emblem of Wales) are used to make a sauce that is teamed with bacon and eggs to make a delicious family meal. Here the pie is topped off with puff pastry, although shortcrust pastry would be just as good.

Serves 4-6

15ml/1 tbsp olive oil

200g/7oz back bacon rashers (strips)

250g/9oz/2 cups leeks, thinly sliced

40g/1½oz/⅓ cup plain (all-purpose) flour

1.5ml/¼ tsp freshly grated nutmeg

425ml/¾ pint/scant 2 cups milk

4 eggs

1 sheet ready-rolled puff pastry

salt and ground black pepper

1 Preheat the oven to 200°C/400°F/ Gas 6. With a sharp knife, trim the bacon rashers of rind and any excess fat. Cut the bacon into thin strips.

2 Put the oil and bacon strips in a pan and cook the bacon for 5 minutes, stirring occasionally, until the bacon is golden brown.

3 Add the leeks to the bacon. Stir, cover and cook over medium heat for 5 minutes until slightly softened, stirring once or twice.

4 Stir in the flour and nutmeg. Remove from the heat and gradually stir in the milk. Return the pan to the heat and cook, stirring, until the sauce thickens and boils. Season lightly with salt and pepper.

5 Tip the mixture into a shallow ovenproof pie dish, measuring about 25cm/10in in diameter. Using the back of a spoon, make four wells in the sauce and break an egg into each one.

6 Brush the edges of the dish with milk. Lay the pastry over the dish. Trim off the excess pastry and use it to make the trimmings. Brush the backs with milk and stick them on the top of the pie.

7 Brush the pastry with milk and make a small central slit to allow steam to escape.

8 Put into the oven and cook for about 40 minutes until the pastry is puffed up and golden, and the eggs have set.

Energy 202kcal/842kJ; Protein 13.4g; Carbohydrate 9.7g, of which sugars 4.4g; Fat 12.5g, of which saturates 4.2g; Cholesterol 149mg; Calcium 125mg; Fibre 1.1g; Sodium 592mg

Shropshire fidget pie

The name of this pie is said to have come from the fact that it was originally "fitched" or five-sided in shape. It would have been typical of the thrifty and filling food eaten at the end of a long, hard day in the fields of the English county of Shropshire.

Serves 4–5

75g/3oz plain (all-purpose) flour

75g/3oz plain wholemeal (whole-wheat) flour

pinch of salt

40g/1½oz/3 tbsp lard, diced

40g/1½oz/3 tbsp butter, diced

15ml/1 tbsp oil

225g/8oz lean bacon or gammon (smoked or cured ham), cut into small strips

2 medium onions, thinly sliced

450g/1lb potatoes, thinly sliced

10ml/2 tsp sugar

2 medium cooking apples

4 fresh sage leaves, finely chopped

salt and ground black pepper

300ml/½ pint/1¼ cups vegetable stock or medium dry (hard) cider

beaten egg or milk, to glaze

1 Sift the two flours and salt into a bowl and rub in the fats until the mixture resembles fine crumbs. Mix in enough cold water to bind the mixture, gathering it into a ball of dough. Chill for 30 minutes.

2 Preheat the oven to 180°C/350°F/ Gas 4. Heat the oil in a large non-stick pan and cook the bacon until crisp. Transfer to a large mixing bowl.

3 Add the onions, potatoes and sugar to the hot pan and brown until beginning to soften. Add to the bowl.

4 Peel, core and slice the apples and add to the bowl. Stir in the sage, season with salt and pepper and mix well. Tip the mixture into a 1.5 litre/ 2½ pint/6¼ cup pie dish, level the surface and pour the stock or cider over.

5 Roll out the pastry on a lightly floured surface to a shape large enough to cover the dish. Brush the edges of the dish with milk or beaten egg. Lay the pastry lid over the top, trim the edges and make a slit in the centre. Brush the lid with beaten egg or milk.

6 Put into the hot oven and cook for about 1 hour, until the crust is golden brown and the filling is cooked through.

Energy 436kcal/1824kJ; Protein 12.7g; Carbohydrate 42.7g, of which sugars 8.2g; Fat 25g, of which saturates 10.7g; Cholesterol 48mg; Calcium 43mg; Fibre 4g; Sodium 754mg

Dingle pies

These pies are traditional on the Dingle peninsula, in south-west Ireland, for special occasions, especially Lammas Day, 1 August, which marked the first day of the harvest. There are many recipes for the filling; this version contains more vegetables than usual.

Makes 6 small pies

450g/1lb boneless mutton or lamb

1 large onion, diced

2 carrots, diced

1 potato, diced

2 celery sticks, diced

1 egg, beaten

salt and ground black pepper

For the shortcrust pastry

500g/1¼lb/5 cups plain (all-purpose) flour

250g/9oz/generous 1 cup butter, or half butter and half white vegetable fat (shortening)

120ml/4fl oz/½ cup very cold water

1 To make the pastry, sieve the flour into a large bowl and add the butter. Rub the butter into the flour with the fingertips or a pastry blender, lifting the mixture as much as possible to aerate. Add the chilled water. Mix with a knife or fork until the mixture clings together. Turn it on to a floured worktop and knead lightly once or twice until smooth. Wrap in baking parchment or foil and leave in the refrigerator to relax for 20 minutes before using.

2 Trim any fat or gristle from the meat and cut it up into very small pieces. Place in a large bowl and add the diced onion, carrots, potato and celery. Mix well and season with salt and freshly ground black pepper.

3 Preheat the oven to 180°C/350°F/ Gas 4. Cut a third off the ball of pastry and reserve to make the lids of the pies. Roll out the rest and, using a small plate as a guide and re-rolling the pastry as necessary, cut out six circles. Divide the meat and vegetable mixture between the circles, piling it in the middle of each.

4 Roll out the remaining pastry and cut out six smaller circles, about 10cm/4in across. Lay these on top. Dampen the edges of the pastry bases, bring the pastry up around the meat, pleat it to fit the lid and pinch the edges together.

5 Make a small hole in the top of each pie to let out the steam, brush them with beaten egg and slide the pies on to baking sheets. Bake in the preheated oven for an hour. Serve warm.

Variations
• If there is any lamb gravy left over from a roast, mix a little in with the raw ingredients: it makes the pies juicier.
• Pies are commonly baked in the oven, and regular shortcrust pastry is usual, although some restaurants make the pies in individual dishes topped with puff pastry.

Left The picturesque town of Dingle and the Irish coastline, County Kerry.

Per pie Energy 784Kcal/3275kJ; Protein 25.1g; Carbohydrate 74.6g, of which sugars 5.2g; Fat 44.9g, of which saturates 26.1g; Cholesterol 178mg; Calcium 155mg; Fibre 4g; Sodium 345mg

Beef Wellington

This dish, a British dinner party favourite, is derived from the classic French boeuf en croûte. The English name was applied to it in honour of the Duke of Wellington, following his victory at the Battle of Waterloo in 1815. Begin preparing the dish well in advance to allow time for the meat to cool before it is wrapped in pastry.

Serves 6

1.5kg/3lb 6oz fillet of beef

45ml/3 tbsp oil

115g/4oz mushrooms, chopped

2 garlic cloves, crushed

175g/6oz smooth liver pâté

30ml/2 tbsp chopped fresh parsley

400g/14oz puff pastry

beaten egg, to glaze

salt and ground black pepper

1 Tie the fillet at intervals with string. Heat 30ml/2 tbsp of the oil, and brown on all sides over a high heat. Transfer to a roasting tin and cook in the oven for 20 minutes. Leave to cool.

2 Heat the remaining oil and cook the mushrooms and garlic for 5 minutes. Beat the mushrooms into the pâté. Add the parsley, season and leave to cool.

3 Roll out the pastry, reserving a small amount, into a rectangle large enough to enclose the beef. Spread the pâté mixture down the middle, untie the beef and lay it on the pâté.

4 Preheat the oven to 220°C/425°F/ Gas 7. Brush the pastry edges with beaten egg and fold it over the meat. Place, seam down, on a baking sheet. Cut leaves from the reserved pastry and decorate the top. Brush the parcel with beaten egg. Chill for 10 minutes or until the oven is hot.

5 Cook for 50–60 minutes, covering loosely with foil after about 30 minutes to prevent the pastry burning. Cut into thick slices to serve.

Energy 511kcal/2131kJ; Protein 41.7g; Carbohydrate 19.3g, of which sugars 1.2g; Fat 30.6g, of which saturates 7.2g; Cholesterol 128mg; Calcium 41mg; Fibre 0.4g; Sodium 320mg

Mutton pies

Small savoury pies were one of Britain's first fast foods, sold in the street during the 16th and 17th centuries on market days and holidays. Mutton pies were popular all over the country, and in Victorian times were served as appetizers at Buckingham Palace. Using muffin tins to shape them may be unconventional but it's very convenient.

Makes 6

For the filling

450g/1lb minced (ground) mutton or lamb, such as shoulder

3 spring onions (scallions), chopped

1.5ml/¼ tsp freshly grated nutmeg

90ml/6 tbsp meat stock

salt and ground black pepper

For the pastry

250g/9oz/2¼ cups plain (all-purpose) flour

generous pinch of salt

50g/2oz/4 tbsp lard

60ml/4 tbsp milk

beaten egg, to glaze

1 Preheat the oven to 190°C/375°F/ Gas 5. Combine the meat with the spring onions and seasoning. Mix well then stir in the stock and set aside.

2 To make the pastry, sift the flour and salt into a bowl and make a well in the centre. Heat the lard, milk and 75ml/ 5 tbsp water until just boiling. Immediately pour it into the flour and beat quickly to make a soft dough.

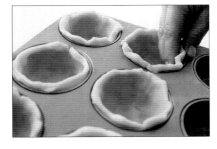

3 Knead the dough lightly on a floured surface until smooth, adding a little more boiling water if necessary. Working quickly, divide two-thirds of the pastry into six pieces. Press each into a hole in a non-stick muffin tray, with the pastry slightly above the rim.

4 Divide the meat mixture equally between the pastry cases.

5 Use the remaining pastry to make lids for the pies. Moisten the pastry edges with water and top each with a lid, pressing the edges together to seal them well. Make a small slit in the centre of each lid and brush with beaten egg.

6 Put the pies into the hot oven and cook for about 35 minutes until the pastry is crisp, golden brown and cooked through. Cool in the tin for 5 minutes then transfer to a wire rack. Serve warm or cold.

Energy 369kcal/1547kJ; Protein 18.7g; Carbohydrate 33g, of which sugars 1.2g; Fat 19g, of which saturates 8.2g; Cholesterol 66mg; Calcium 85mg; Fibre 1.4g; Sodium 58mg

Pork and bacon picnic pies

In the days when most country people carried their lunch with them to eat in the fields or journeying on foot along the lanes, small pies made tasty parcels that could be packed in the pocket, held in the hand and eaten anywhere.

Makes 12

10ml/2 tsp oil

1 onion, finely chopped

225g/8oz pork, coarsely chopped

115g/4oz cooked bacon, chopped

45ml/3 tbsp chopped mixed fresh herbs, such as sage, parsley and oregano

6 eggs, hard-boiled and halved

1 egg yolk, beaten

20g/¾oz packet powdered aspic

300ml/½ pint/1¼ cups boiling water

salt and ground black pepper

For the hot water crust pastry

450g/1lb/4 cups plain (all-purpose) flour

115g/4oz/½ cup lard

275ml/9fl oz/generous 1 cup water

1 Preheat the oven to 200°C/400°F/ Gas 6. Sift the flour into a bowl and make a well in the centre. Heat the lard and water until melted, then bring to the boil and pour into the flour, stirring. Press the mixture into a smooth ball of dough using the back of a spoon. Cover the bowl and set it aside.

2 Heat the oil and cook the onion until soft. Stir in the pork and bacon and cook until browned. Remove from the heat and add the herbs and seasoning.

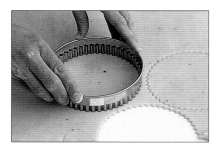

3 Roll out two-thirds of the pastry on a lightly floured work surface. Using a 12cm/4½in round cutter, stamp out rounds and line 12 muffin tins.

4 Place a little of the meat mixture in each case, then add half an egg and top with the remaining meat.

5 Roll out the remaining pastry and use a 7.5cm/3in round cutter to stamp out lids. Dampen the rims of the bases and press the lids in place. Seal the edges, brush with egg yolk and make a hole in the top of each pie. Bake for 30–35 minutes. Cool for 15 minutes, then transfer to a rack to cool completely.

6 Meanwhile, stir the aspic powder into the boiling water until dissolved. Using a small funnel, pour a little aspic into the hole in the top of each pie. Leave the pies to cool and set, then chill for up to 24 hours before serving.

Energy 311kcal/1302kJ; Protein 12.1g; Carbohydrate 30.4g, of which sugars 1.6g; Fat 16.4g, of which saturates 5.5g; Cholesterol 135mg; Calcium 77mg; Fibre 1.5g; Sodium 74mg

Cornish pasties

The original portable lunch, pasties made a satisfying midday meal for intrepid Cornish tin miners, who could use the crimped pastry join across the top as a handle if their hands were filthy. These contain the traditional filling of chopped steak and root vegetables.

Makes 6

500–675g/1¼–1½lb shortcrust pastry

450g/1lb chuck steak, cubed

1 potato, about 175g/6oz, cubed

175g/6oz swede (rutabaga), cubed

1 onion, finely chopped

2.5ml/½ tsp dried mixed herbs

beaten egg, to glaze

salt and ground black pepper

3 Brush the edges with water, then fold the pastry over the filling. Crimp the edges firmly together.

4 Use a fish slice to transfer the pasties to a non-stick baking (cookie) sheet, then brush each one with beaten egg.

5 Put into the hot oven and cook for 15 minutes, then reduce the oven temperature to 160°C/325°F/Gas 3 and cook for a further 1 hour.

Cook's tip Swede (rutabaga) is the traditional vegetable in Cornish pasties, but turnip, carrot or celery could be used in its place, if you prefer.

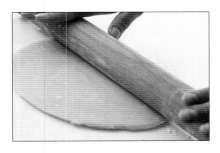

1 Preheat the oven to 220°C/425°F/Gas 7. Divide the pastry into six equal pieces, then roll out each piece to form a rough circle, measuring about 20cm/8in.

2 Mix together the steak, vegetables, herbs and seasoning, then spoon an equal amount on to one half of each pastry circle.

Energy 414kcal/1731kJ; Protein 10.4g; Carbohydrate 38.8g, of which sugars 1.4g; Fat 25.3g, of which saturates 9.2g; Cholesterol 51mg; Calcium 93mg; Fibre 1.4g; Sodium 620mg

English game pie

A raised game pie makes an impressive centrepiece, especially if made in a fluted raised pie mould. Not only does it look magnificent, it tastes wonderful. These pies used to be made in the country and sent to London for Christmas, so the crust had to be stoutly built.

Serves 10

25g/1oz/2 tbsp butter

1 onion, finely chopped

2 garlic cloves, finely chopped

900g/2lb mixed boneless game, such as pheasant and/or pigeon breast, venison and rabbit, diced

30ml/2 tbsp chopped fresh herbs such as parsley, thyme and marjoram

salt and ground black pepper

For the pâté

50g/2oz/¼ cup butter

2 garlic cloves, finely chopped

450g/1lb chicken livers, rinsed, trimmed and chopped

60ml/4 tbsp brandy

5ml/1 tsp ground mace

For the hot water crust pastry

675g/1½lb/6 cups strong plain (all-purpose) flour

5ml/1 tsp salt

115ml/3½fl oz/scant ½ cup milk

115ml/3½fl oz/scant ½ cup water

115g/4oz/½ cup lard, diced

115g/4oz/½ cup butter, diced

beaten egg, to glaze

For the jelly

300ml/½ pint/1¼ cups game or beef consommé

2.5ml/½ tsp powdered gelatine

1 Melt the butter until foaming and cook the onion and garlic until softened but not coloured. Remove from the heat and mix with the meat and herbs. Season well, cover and chill.

2 To make the pâté, melt the butter in a pan until foaming, add the garlic and chicken livers and cook until just browned. Remove from the heat and stir in the brandy and mace. Purée the mixture in a blender or food processor until smooth, then leave to cool.

3 To make the pastry, sift the flour and salt into a bowl and make a well in the centre. Gently heat the milk, water, lard and butter together until melted. Bring to the boil, removing from the heat as soon as the mixture begins to bubble. Pour the hot liquid into the well in the flour and beat until smooth. Cover and leave until cool enough to handle.

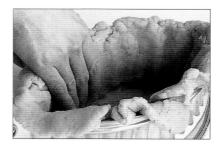

4 Preheat the oven to 200°C/400°F/ Gas 6. Roll out two-thirds of the pastry and use to line a 23cm/9in raised pie mould, pressing it in with your fingers. Spoon in half the game mixture and press it down evenly. Add the pâté, then top with the remaining game.

Cook's tip If you don't have a raised pie mould, use a 20cm/8in springform cake tin (pan).

5 Roll out the remaining pastry to form a lid. Brush the edge of the pastry lining the tin with a little water and cover the pie with the lid. Trim off excess pastry and pinch the edges together to seal. Make two holes in the centre of the lid and brush the top with egg. Use the trimmings to roll out leaves to garnish the pie and brush them with egg.

6 Put into the hot oven and cook for 20 minutes, then cover with foil and cook for 10 minutes. Reduce the oven temperature to 150°C/300°F/Gas 2. Brush the pie again with egg and cook for a further 1½ hours, keeping the top covered loosely with foil.

7 Remove from the oven and leave to stand for 15 minutes. Increase the oven temperature to 200°C/400°F/Gas 6. Stand the tin on a baking sheet and remove its sides. Quickly brush the sides of the pie with beaten egg, cover the top with foil, then cook for another 15 minutes to brown the sides. Leave to cool completely, then chill overnight.

8 To make the jelly, heat the consommé in a small pan until hot but not boiling, whisk in the gelatine until dissolved and leave to cool until just setting. Using a small funnel, carefully pour the jellied consommé into the holes in the pie. Chill until set.

Energy 448kcal/1871kJ; Protein 28.3g; Carbohydrate 29.5g, of which sugars 5.3g; Fat 24.9g, of which saturates 9.5g; Cholesterol 55mg; Calcium 67mg; Fibre 1.5g; Sodium 393mg

Haggis, potato and apple tart

Here is another way to serve your haggis, with just a little refinement and the extra sumptuousness of puff pastry. Apple combines very well with haggis as its tart and sweet taste cuts through the richness of the meat.

3 Place the smaller pastry disc on a baking tray and spread half the potatoes over it, leaving a rim of about 2cm/¾in all the way round.

4 Cut the haggis open and crumble the meat on top. Slice the apple into circles and spread all over the haggis. Then top with the rest of the potatoes.

Serves 4

450g/1lb peeled potatoes, sliced

1 garlic clove, crushed with 1 tsp salt

freshly grated nutmeg

400g/14oz ready-made puff pastry

300g/11oz haggis

2 cooking apples, cored

1 egg, beaten

salt and ground black pepper

1 Preheat the oven to 220°C/425°F/ Gas 7. Slice the potatoes and mix with the crushed garlic. Season with a little freshly grated nutmeg and salt and ground black pepper.

2 Roll out the puff pastry into two discs, one about 25cm/10in in diameter and the other a little larger.

Cook's Tip Use a fairly sharp-tasting variety of apple, such as Cox's Orange Pippin or cooking apples.

5 Brush the egg all around the exposed pastry rim then place the other pastry circle on top, pushing down on the rim to seal. Use a fork to tidy up the edges and then press down around the edge again to create a firm seal. Leave to rest for 10 minutes.

6 Brush over with more egg and bake the tart in the preheated oven for 10 minutes to set the pastry. Then reduce the oven temperature to 200°C/400°F/Gas 6 and bake for a further 40 minutes until evenly browned and cooked. Serve in slices.

Energy 698kcal/2919kJ; Protein 15.8g; Carbohydrate 72.9g, of which sugars 6.1g; Fat 41.2g, of which saturates 5.8g; Cholesterol 68mg; Calcium 88mg; Fibre 1.9g; Sodium 901mg

Angus pasties

Scottish Aberdeen Angus beef is the traditional filling for these pasties, as it is such a well-known breed, but any really good-quality beef may be used. These pasties are perfect served either cold or warmed for lunch or as a snack, and make great picnic food.

Makes 10

For the pastry

900g/2lb/8 cups plain (all-purpose) flour

225g/8oz/1 cup butter

225g/8oz/1cup lard or white cooking fat

pinch of salt

For the filling

1.2kg/2½lb rump (round) steak

225g/8oz/1¾ cups beef suet (US chilled, grated shortening)

5 onions, finely chopped

salt and ground black pepper

1 Preheat the oven to 200°C/400°F/ Gas 6. Using a mixer, place the flour in the mixing bowl and blend in the butter and lard or white cooking fat using the dough hook. Add salt and mix to a stiff dough, adding water gradually as needed. Leave the pastry ball to rest in clear film (plastic wrap) for 30 minutes.

2 Meanwhile, trim the meat of any excess fat and cut into 1cm/½in squares. Chop the suet finely then mix with the meat and onions. Season.

3 Divide the pastry into ten equal sized pieces. Roll out each piece into an oval, not too thinly, and divide the meat mixture among them at one end, leaving an edge for sealing. Dampen the edges of each oval with cold water and fold the pastry over the filling.

4 Seal carefully – use a fork to make sure the edges are stuck together securely. Make a hole in the top of each pasty. Place on a greased baking sheet and bake in the preheated oven for 45 minutes. Serve hot, or allow to cool and refrigerate.

Energy 1131kcal/4714kJ; Protein 37.7g; Carbohydrate 84.8g, of which sugars 4.5g; Fat 74.5g, of which saturates 37.9g; Cholesterol 171mg; Calcium 162mg; Fibre 3.9g; Sodium 232mg

Welsh katt pie

This oddly-named, but delicious sweet-savoury pie was traditionally made for the annual fair at Templeton in Pembrokeshire. The lamb, sugar and currants would have been layered inside pies made with suet pastry. This recipe uses a crisp shortcrust pastry made with equal quantities of lard and butter. Serve with a salad of watercress, baby spinach leaves and red onion.

Serves 6

250g/9oz/2¼ cups plain (all-purpose) flour

75g/3oz/6 tbsp chilled lard,

75g/3oz/6 tbsp chilled butter

300g/11oz lean minced (ground) lamb, such as shoulder

75g/3oz/⅓ cup currants

75g/3oz/6 tbsp dark muscovado (molasses) sugar

salt and ground black pepper

milk for brushing

1 To make the pastry, sift the flour and salt into a bowl. Cut the lard and butter into cubes. Add to the bowl. With the fingertips, rub the fat into the flour until it resembles breadcrumbs. Alternatively, you can process the mixture in a food processor.

2 Stir in about 60–75ml/4–5 tbsp cold water until the mixture can be gathered together into a smooth dough. Then wrap and refrigerate the dough for about 20–30 minutes.

3 Preheat the oven to 190°C/375°F/ Gas 5. Mix together the lamb, currants and sugar with a little salt and pepper.

4 On a lightly floured surface, roll out two-thirds of the dough into a circle.

5 Use the rolled-out dough to line a 20–23cm/ 8–9in tart tin (pan). Then spread the lamb mixture over the pastry. Roll out the remaining pastry to make a lid and lay this on top of the lamb filling.

6 Trim the excess pastry all around the top of the pie, and pinch the edges together to seal them. Make a small slit in the centre of the pastry and then brush the top with milk or beaten egg.

7 Put the pie into the hot oven and cook for about 40 minutes, until the pastry is crisp and golden brown and the filling is cooked through. Serve warm or at room temperature.

Energy 527kcal/2206kJ; Protein 13.9g; Carbohydrate 54g, of which sugars 22.2g; Fat 29.9g, of which saturates 14.7g; Cholesterol 77mg; Calcium 88mg; Fibre 1.5g; Sodium 114mg

Welsh goat's cheese, leek and hazelnut tart

The skills of making wonderful goat's cheeses have been revived in Wales today, from soft cheese and soft-rind logs to hard varieties that are ideal for cooking. If your cheese is particularly strong you may want to use the smaller quantity listed in the ingredients. This tart is best served hot or at room temperature.

Serves 6

85g/3oz/¾ cup hazelnuts, skinned

175g/6oz/1½ cups plain (all-purpose) flour

115g/4oz/½ cup butter, chilled and cut into small cubes

15ml/1 tbsp olive oil

350g/12oz/3 cups leeks, thinly sliced

5 eggs, lightly beaten

425ml/¾ pint single (light) cream

2.5ml/1½ tbsp wholegrain mustard

175–225g/6–8oz/1½–2 cups hard goat's cheese, such as Merlin, grated

salt and ground black pepper

1 Toast the hazelnuts in a dry frying pan, in a hot oven or under the grill (broiler), until golden. Leave to cool, roughly chop half and finely chop the rest.

2 Sift the flour and seasoning into a large bowl and stir in the finely chopped nuts. Add the butter. Using your fingertips, rub the butter into the flour until the mixture resembles fine breadcrumbs. Sprinkle over about 45ml/3 tbsp cold water, mix until the crumbs begin to stick together and then gather the mixture into a ball.

3 Roll out the pastry and line a 25cm/10in flan tin (pan). Put in the refrigerator for 10–25 minutes to rest (or leave it there until required).

4 Put a baking sheet in the oven and preheat to 200°C/400°F/Gas 6.

5 Put the oil and leeks into a pan and cook until soft, stirring occasionally. (Alternatively, place in a microwave-proof dish, cover and microwave on full power for about 5 minutes, stirring once).

Variation This dish is equally good made with crumbled Caerphilly cheese: use the larger quantity listed in the ingredients as it has a mild flavour.

6 Prick the base of the pastry case and line with baking parchment and dried beans. Put on to the hot baking sheet and cook for 10 minutes. Remove the paper and beans and brush the pastry with beaten egg. Return to the oven for 3–4 minutes.

7 Meanwhile, mix together the remaining eggs with the cream, mustard, half the cheese and a little seasoning. Stir the mixture into the leeks and pour into the hot pastry case. Sprinkle the rest of the cheese on top and scatter the remaining (roughly chopped) hazelnuts over the top or around the edges.

8 Put into the hot oven and cook for about 30 minutes until set and golden.

Energy 683kcal/2835kJ; Protein 20.7g; Carbohydrate 26.9g, of which sugars 4g; Fat 55g, of which saturates 27.3g; Cholesterol 267mg; Calcium 381mg; Fibre 3.1g; Sodium 409mg

Cheese and asparagus flan

The British asparagus season is short, so you need to make the most of it. The distinctive taste of fresh asparagus comes through in this flan and makes a small amount go further. It has an affinity with cheese, with each ingredient enhancing the flavour of the other.

Serves 5–6

175g/6oz/1½ cups plain (all-purpose) flour

pinch of salt

40g/1½oz/3 tbsp lard, diced

40g/1½oz/3 tbsp butter, diced

300g/11oz small asparagus spears weighed after trimming

75g/3oz mature Cheddar cheese, grated

3 spring onions (scallions), thinly sliced

2 eggs

300ml/½ pint/1¼ cups double (heavy) cream

freshly grated nutmeg

salt and ground black pepper

1 To make the pastry, sift the flour and salt into a bowl and add the lard and butter. With your fingertips, rub the fats into the flour until the mixture resembles fine breadcrumbs.

2 Stir in about 45ml/3 tbsp cold water until the mixture can be gathered together into a ball of dough. (Or use a food processor.) Wrap the pastry and chill for 30 minutes.

3 Put a flat baking sheet in the oven and preheat to 200°C/400°F/Gas 6. Roll out the pastry on a lightly floured work surface and use it to line a 20cm/8in flan tin (pan).

4 Line the pastry case (pie shell) with baking parchment or foil and add a layer of baking beans. Put the flan tin on to the heated baking sheet in the oven and cook for 10–15 minutes until set. Carefully remove the beans and parchment or foil, return the pastry to the oven and cook for a further 5 minutes, until light golden brown on the edges. Remove the flan and reduce the temperature to 180°C/350°F/Gas 4.

5 Meanwhile, cook the asparagus spears in lightly salted boiling water for 2–3 minutes or until only just tender. Drain, rinse under cold water and dry on kitchen paper. Cut the asparagus spears into 2.5cm/1in lengths, leaving the tips whole.

6 Scatter half the cheese in the base of the cooked pastry case and add the asparagus and the spring onions.

7 Beat the eggs with the cream and season with salt, pepper and nutmeg.

8 Pour over the asparagus and top with the remaining cheese.

9 Return the flan to the hot baking sheet in the oven and cook for about 30 minutes or until just set. Leave the flan to settle for 5 minutes before cutting and serving.

Energy 547kcal/2266kJ; Protein 10.4g; Carbohydrate 24.7g, of which sugars 2.4g; Fat 45.6g, of which saturates 26.2g; Cholesterol 165mg; Calcium 184mg; Fibre 1.8g; Sodium 167mg

Scottish smoked haddock flan

The classic combination of potatoes and smoked fish is reworked in pastry. Always ask your fishmonger for "pale" smoked rather than "yellow" haddock as the latter tends to have been dyed to look bright and often has not been smoked properly at all.

Serves 4

For the pastry

225g/8oz/2 cups plain (all-purpose) flour

pinch of salt

115g/4oz/1½ cup cold butter, cut into chunks

cold water, to mix

For the filling

2 pale smoked haddock fillets (approximately 200g/7oz)

600ml/1 pint/2½ cups full-fat (whole) milk

3–4 black peppercorns

sprig of fresh thyme

150ml/¼ pint/⅔ cup double (heavy) cream

2 eggs

200g/7oz potatoes, peeled and diced

ground black pepper

1 Preheat the oven to 200°C/400°F/ Gas 6. Use a food processor to make the pastry. Put the flour, salt and butter into the food processor bowl and process until the mixture resembles fine breadcrumbs. Pour in a little cold water (you will need about 40ml/8 tsp but see Cook's tip) and continue to process until the mixture forms a ball. If this takes longer than 30 seconds add a dash or two more water. Take the pastry ball out of the food processor, wrap in clear film (plastic wrap) and leave to rest in a cool place for about 30 minutes.

2 Roll out the dough and use to line a 20cm/8in flan tin (quiche pan). Prick the base of the pastry all over with a fork then bake blind in the preheated oven for 20 minutes.

3 Put the haddock in a pan with the milk, peppercorns and thyme. Poach for 10 minutes. Remove the fish from the pan and flake into small chunks. Allow the poaching liquor to cool.

4 Whisk the cream and eggs together thoroughly, then whisk in the cooled poaching liquid.

5 Layer the flan case with the flaked fish and diced potato, seasoning with black pepper.

6 Pour the cream mixture over the top. Put the flan in the oven and bake for 40 minutes, until lightly browned on top and set.

Cook's tip Different flours absorb water at different rates. A traditional rule of thumb is to use the same number of teaspoons of water as the number of ounces of flour, but some flours will require less water and others more, so add the water gradually. If you add too much water, the pastry will become unworkable and you will need to add more flour.

Variation This recipe is also delicious if you add hard boiled eggs, chopped into quarters or eighths before adding the potatoes.

Energy 734kcal/3064kJ; Protein 23.8g; Carbohydrate 58.4g, of which sugars 8.2g; Fat 46.8g, of which saturates 27.9g; Cholesterol 225mg; Calcium 280mg; Fibre 2.3g; Sodium 636mg

Puddings and warm desserts

Everyone loves a pudding, and there is a wealth of traditional British recipes to choose from when you want to end a meal with a treat. Many use orchard fruits, stewed or baked, in tarts, crumbles, pies and dumplings. There are also nursery classics such as milk puddings, roly-poly and syrup sponge, and rich mixtures containing spices and dried fruits including, of course, Christmas pudding.

Welsh whinberry and apple tart

The traditional wild harvest of whinberries or, as many Welsh people insist, "whimberries", has always been gathered with great excitement from the hillsides in summer. The tiny dark purple berries (elsewhere called bilberries, blueberries or whortleberries) were most often made into tarts. It was customary to first bake the tart before carefully lifting the lid, adding the sugar and putting it all back together again. Incidentally, in Wales a tart is called a tart (never a pie) even when it has pastry top and bottom.

Serves 6

2 cooking apples, total weight about 400g/14oz

10ml/2 tsp cornflour (cornstarch)

350g/12oz/3 cups whinberries

40–50g/3–4 tbsp caster (superfine) sugar, plus extra for sprinkling

milk for brushing

For the pastry

250g/9oz/2¼ cups plain (all-purpose) flour

25g/1oz/2 tbsp caster (superfine) sugar

150g/5oz/10 tbsp butter, chilled and cut into small cubes

1 egg

2 Preheat the oven to 190°C/375°F/ Gas 5. On a lightly floured surface, roll out half the dough to make a circle and use it to line a deep 23cm/9in tart tin (pan) or ovenproof dish, gently pressing it into the corners and allowing the pastry to hang over the sides slightly. Roll out the remaining pastry to a circle large enough to make a lid and check it for size.

3 Peel the apples, remove their cores and chop them into small pieces. Toss the apple pieces with the cornflour until evenly coated and arrange them in the bottom of the pastry case. Scatter the whinberries (or blueberries) on top and sprinkle the sugar over. Lightly brush the edges of the pastry with water.

4 Lay the pastry lid over the fruit filling. Trim off the excess pastry and pinch the edges together to seal them well. Make a small slit in the centre, then brush the top with milk and sprinkle with a little sugar.

5 Put into the hot oven and cook for 30–40 minutes until the pastry is crisp and golden brown and the filling is cooked through. While the pastry is still hot, sprinkle with more caster sugar.

1 Sift the flour into a bowl and stir in the sugar. Add the butter and rub into the flour until the mixture resembles fine crumbs. Stir in the egg and enough cold water until the mixture forms clumps, then gather it together to make a smooth dough. Wrap the pastry and refrigerate for 20–30 minutes.

Cook's tip Whinberries give out a lot of juice, so don't be tempted to use a loose-bottomed tin (pan) in case it leaks out and over the floor of the oven.

Energy 403kcal/1688kJ; Protein 5.76g; Carbohydrate 51.4g, of which sugars 18.15g; Fat 20.8g, of which saturates 12.5g; Cholesterol 81.5mg; Calcium 98.6mg; Fibre 3,5g; Sodium 157.5mg

Apple pie

Britain's most popular dessert is on every informal menu in the country and, when well made, there is nothing to beat it. Bake in a traditional metal pie plate so that the pastry base will be perfectly cooked. Serve with chilled whipped cream, or vanilla ice cream.

Serves 6

225g/8oz/2 cups plain (all-purpose) flour

130g/4½oz/generous ½ cup butter, or mixed butter and white vegetable fat (shortening)

25g/1oz/2 tbsp caster (superfine) sugar

45ml/3 tbsp very cold milk or water

For the filling

675g/1½lb cooking apples

75g/3oz/½ cup sultanas (golden raisins) (optional)

a little grated lemon rind (optional)

75g/3oz/6 tbsp caster (superfine) sugar

a knob (pat) of butter or 15ml/ 1 tbsp of water

a little milk, to glaze

icing (confectioners') sugar and whipped cream, to serve

1 Sieve the flour into a large mixing bowl, add the butter and cut it into small pieces. Rub the butter into the flour with the fingertips, or using a pastry (cookie) cutter, lifting the mixture as much as possible to keep the pastry aerated.

2 Mix the caster sugar with the chilled milk or water, add to the bowl and mix with a knife or fork until the mixture clings together. Turn on to a floured worktop and knead lightly once or twice until smooth.

3 Wrap in baking parchment or foil and leave in the refrigerator to relax for 20 minutes before using. Meanwhile, preheat the oven to 200°C/400°F/Gas 6.

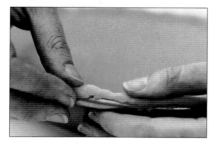

4 Roll out one-third of the pastry and use to line a 23cm/9in pie plate. Use any trimmings to make a second layer of pastry around the top edge of the pie plate.

5 To make the filling, peel, core and slice the apples and arrange half of them on the pastry base, then sprinkle over the sultanas and lemon rind, if using. Top with the caster sugar, the remaining apples and butter or water.

6 Roll out the remainder of the pastry to make a circle about 2.5cm/1in larger than the pie plate. Dampen the pastry edging on the rim and lay the top over the apples, draping it gently over any lumps to avoid straining the pastry. Press the rim well to seal. Knock up the edge with a knife, and pinch the edges neatly with the fingers to make a fluted edge.

7 Brush the pastry lightly with milk and bake the pie in the preheated oven for about 30 minutes, or until the pastry is nicely browned and crisp, and the fruit is cooked.

8 To serve, dust the pastry with icing sugar and serve hot, warm or cold, but not straight from the refrigerator.

Variation The same filling may be used to make a deep pie in a 25cm/10in deep oval pie dish, although only about three-quarters of the quantity of pastry will be needed for the topping.

Energy 393Kcal/1650kJ; Protein 4.1g; Carbohydrate 56.3g, of which sugars 27.7g; Fat 18.4g, of which saturates 11.4g; Cholesterol 46mg; Calcium 68mg; Fibre 2.5g; Sodium 136mg

Plum pie

Fruit pies can be made either in a pie dish with a deep filling or on a plate with a crust both top and bottom. A range of fruits can be used, such as apples, gooseberries, blackberries, rhubarb or, as here, plums. Serve the pie with whipped cream or custard.

Serves 6

200g/7oz/1¾ cups plain (all-purpose) flour

25g/1oz/4 tbsp icing (confectioner's) sugar

115g/4oz/½ cup butter, diced

1 egg, lightly beaten

800g/1¾lb plums, stoned (pitted)

about 75g/3oz caster (superfine) sugar, plus extra for sprinkling

beaten egg white, to frost

1 Sift the flour and icing sugar into a bowl and rub in the butter until the mixture resembles fine crumbs. Stir in the egg and gather together into a smooth dough. Chill for 30 minutes.

2 Preheat the oven to 190°C/375°F/ Gas 5. Place half the plums in a 1 litre/ 1¾ pint/4 cup pie dish. Sprinkle the caster sugar over them, adjusting the amount according to the sweetness of the fruit, then add the remaining plums.

3 Roll out the pastry on a lightly floured surface to a shape slightly larger than the dish. Dampen the edges of the dish with a little egg white and cover with the pastry.

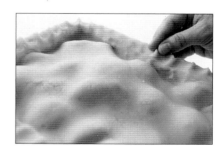

4 Trim the edges and pinch to make a decorative edging. Brush the top with egg white and sprinkle with a little caster sugar. Make a small slit in the centre to allow steam to escape.

5 Cook in the oven for 35–40 minutes until the pastry is golden brown and the plums are soft (check by inserting a knife through the slit). Serve sprinkled with extra caster sugar.

Energy 360kcal/1516kJ; Protein 4.1g; Carbohydrate 57g, of which sugars 25.5g; Fat 14.5g, of which saturates 7.5g; Cholesterol 26mg; Calcium 73mg; Fibre 2.9g; Sodium 61mg

Border tart

The Border region of Scotland is particularly associated with sweet tarts that are often eaten for mid-morning snacks, as well as satisfying desserts. This currant and walnut version is delicious served hot or cold with cream.

Serves 4

250g/9oz sweet pastry (*see* Auld Alliance Apple Tart)

1 egg

75g/3oz/scant ½ cup soft light brown sugar

50g/2oz/¼ cup butter, melted

10ml/2 tsp white wine vinegar

115g/4oz/½ cup currants

25g/1oz/¼ cup chopped walnuts

double (heavy) cream, to serve (optional)

1 Line a 20cm/8in flan tin (tart pan) with sweet pastry. Preheat the oven to 190°C/375°F/Gas 5. Mix the egg, sugar and melted butter together.

2 Stir the vinegar, currants and walnuts into the egg mixture.

3 Pour the mixture into the pastry case and bake in the preheated oven for 30 minutes. Remove from the oven when thoroughly cooked, take out of the flan tin and leave to cool on a wire rack for at least 30 minutes. Serve on its own or with a dollop of fresh cream.

Energy 312kcal/1307kJ; Protein 3.4g; Carbohydrate 41.1g, of which sugars 41g; Fat 16.1g, of which saturates 7.3g; Cholesterol 74mg; Calcium 54mg; Fibre 0.8g; Sodium 99mg

Scottish raspberry and almond tart

Raspberries grow best in a cool, damp climate, making them a natural choice for Scottish gardeners. Juicy ripe raspberries and almonds go very well together. This is a rich tart, ideal for serving at the end of a special lunch or at a dinner party.

Serves 4

200g/7oz sweet pastry (*see* Auld Alliance Apple Tart)

2 large (US extra large) eggs

75ml/2½fl oz/⅓ cup double (heavy) cream

50g/2oz/¼ cup caster (superfine) sugar

50g/2oz/½ cup ground almonds

20g/¾oz/4 tsp butter

350g/12oz/2 cups raspberries

1 Line a 20cm/8in flan tin (tart pan) with the pastry. Prick the base all over and leave to rest for at least 30 minutes. Preheat the oven to 200°C/400°F/Gas 6.

2 Put the eggs, cream, sugar and ground almonds in a bowl and whisk together briskly. Melt the butter and pour into the mixture, stirring to combine thoroughly.

3 Sprinkle the raspberries evenly over the pastry case. The ones at the top will appear through the surface, so keep them evenly spaced. You can also create a pattern with them.

4 Pour the egg and almond mixture over the top. Once again ensure that it is spread evenly throughout the tart.

5 Bake in the preheated oven for 25 minutes. Serve warm or cold.

Variation Peaches also make a very attractive tart. Use 6 large, ripe peaches and remove the skin and stone (pit). Cut into slices and use in the same way as the raspberries above.

Energy 548kcal/2284kJ; Protein 10.9g; Carbohydrate 41.7g, of which sugars 18.4g; Fat 38.8g, of which saturates 14.8g; Cholesterol 158mg; Calcium 128mg; Fibre 4.1g; Sodium 282mg

Auld Alliance apple tart

The Auld Alliance is a friendship that has existed between France and Scotland for some 600 years and as well as sharing friendship the two countries have also shared ideas on food. This is a classic French pudding that has been adopted by the Scots.

Serves 4

200g/7oz/1¾ sticks butter

200g/7oz/1 cup caster (superfine) sugar

6 large eating apples

For the sweet pastry

150g/5oz/10 tbsp butter

50g/2oz/¼ cup caster (superfine) sugar

225g/8oz/2 cups plain (all-purpose) flour

1 egg

1 Make the sweet pastry. Cream the butter with the caster sugar together in a food processor. Add the plain flour and egg. Mix until just combined, being careful not to overprocess. Leave in a cool place for an hour before use.

2 Preheat the oven to 200°C/400°F/ Gas 6. Make the filling. Cut the butter into small pieces. Using a shallow, 30cm/12in ovenproof frying pan, heat the sugar and butter and allow to caramelize over a low heat, stirring gently continuously. This will take about 10 minutes.

3 Meanwhile peel and core the apples then cut them into eighths. When the butter and sugar are caramelized, place the apples in the pan in a circular fan, one layer around the outside then one in the centre. The pan should be full. Reduce the heat and cook the apples for 5 minutes then remove from heat.

4 Roll out the pastry to a circle big enough to fit the pan completely with generous edgings.

5 Spread the pastry over the fruit and tuck in the edges. Bake in the oven for about 30 minutes, or until the pastry is browned and set.

6 When cooked remove the tart from the oven and leave to rest. When ready to serve, gently reheat on the stove for a few minutes then invert on to a warmed serving plate, so that the pastry becomes the base and the caramelized apples are on top.

Energy 904kcal/3774kJ; Protein 4.6g; Carbohydrate 95.2g, of which sugars 66.5g; Fat 58.8g, of which saturates 31.5g; Cholesterol 116mg; Calcium 95mg; Fibre 3.6g; Sodium 559mg

Bakewell tart

This is a modern version of the Bakewell pudding, which is made with puff pastry and has a custard-like almond filling. It is said to be the result of a 19th-century kitchen accident and is still baked in the original shop in Bakewell, Derbyshire. This very popular, tart-like version is simpler to make and is a favourite dessert and teatime treat all over England.

Serves 4

For the pastry

115g/4oz/1 cup plain (all-purpose) flour

pinch of salt

50g/2oz/4 tbsp butter, diced

For the filling

30ml/2 tbsp raspberry or apricot jam

2 whole eggs and 2 extra yolks

115g/4oz/generous ½ cup caster (superfine) sugar

115g/4oz/½ cup butter, melted

55g/2oz/⅔ cup ground almonds

few drops of almond extract

icing (confectioners') sugar, to dust

1 Sift the flour and salt and rub in the butter until the mixture resembles fine crumbs. Stir in about 20ml/2 tbsp cold water and gather into a smooth ball of dough. Wrap and chill for 30 minutes. Preheat the oven to 200°C/400°F/Gas 6.

2 Roll out the pastry and use to line an 18cm/7in loose-based flan tin (pan). Spread the jam over the pastry.

3 Whisk the eggs, egg yolks and sugar together in a large bowl until the mixture is thick and pale.

4 Gently stir in the melted butter, ground almonds and almond extract.

5 Pour the mixture over the jam in the pastry case (pie shell). Put the tart into the hot oven and cook for 30 minutes until just set and browned. Sift a little icing sugar over the top before serving warm or at room temperature.

Energy 700kcal/2919kJ; Protein 10.8g; Carbohydrate 57.1g, of which sugars 36.7g; Fat 49.9g, of which saturates 17.1g; Cholesterol 257mg; Calcium 110mg; Fibre 0.9g; Sodium 394mg

Blackcurrant tart

Blackcurrants grow in the wild, are cultivated throughout Europe, and are widely available. This tart makes the most of these exquisite summer fruits, and is quick and easy to prepare using ready-made puff pastry. Serve with whipped cream.

Serves 4

500g/1¼lb/5 cups blackcurrants

115g/4oz/generous ½ cup caster (superfine) sugar

250g/9oz ready-made puff pastry

50g/2oz/½ cup icing (confectioners') sugar

whipped cream, to serve

1 Preheat the oven to 220°C/425°F/ Gas 7. Trim the blackcurrants, making sure you remove all the stalks and any hard parts in the middle. Add the caster sugar and mix well.

2 Roll out the pastry to about 3mm/ ⅛in thick and cut out four discs roughly the size of a side plate or a large cereal bowl. Then using a smaller plate (or bowl) lightly mark with the point of a knife a circle about 2cm/¾in inside each disc.

3 Spread the blackcurrants over the discs, keeping them within the marked inner circle. Bake in the oven for 15 minutes. Dust generously with the icing sugar before serving. Serve hot with a large dollop of whipped cream, or serve cold as a tea-time snack.

Energy 426kcal/1798kJ; Protein 4.9g; Carbohydrate 73.2g, of which sugars 50.9g; Fat 15.3g, of which saturates 0g; Cholesterol 0mg; Calcium 133mg; Fibre 4.5g; Sodium 200mg

Lemon meringue pie

This popular dessert is a 20th-century development of older English cheesecakes – open tarts with a filling of curds. It was particularly relished in the 1950s after the years of wartime rationing, when sugar, lemons and eggs became plentiful once more. The pie is best served at room temperature, with or without cream.

Serves 6

For the pastry

115g/4oz/1 cup plain (all-purpose) flour

pinch of salt

25g/1oz/2 tbsp lard, diced

25g/1oz/2 tbsp butter, diced

For the filling

50g/2oz/¼ cup cornflour (cornstarch)

175g/6oz/¾ cup caster (superfine) sugar

finely grated rind and juice of 2 lemons

2 egg yolks

15g/½oz/1 tbsp butter, diced

For the meringue topping

2 egg whites

75g/3oz/½ cup caster (superfine) sugar

1 To make the pastry, sift the flour and salt into a bowl and add the lard and butter. With the fingertips, lightly rub the fats into the flour until the mixture resembles fine crumbs.

2 Stir in about 20ml/2 tbsp cold water until the mixture can be gathered together into a smooth ball of dough. (Alternatively make the pastry using a food processor.) Wrap the pastry and refrigerate for at least 30 minutes. Meanwhile, preheat the oven to 200°C/400°F/Gas 6.

3 Roll out the pastry on a lightly floured surface and use to line a 20cm/8in flan tin (pan). Prick the base with a fork, line with baking parchment or foil and add a layer of baking beans to prevent the pastry rising.

4 Put the pastry case (pie shell) into the hot oven and cook for 15 minutes. Remove the beans and parchment or foil, return the pastry to the oven and cook for a further 5 minutes until crisp and golden brown. Reduce the oven temperature to 150°C/300°F/Gas 2.

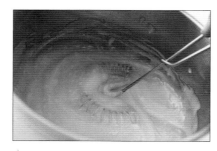

5 To make the lemon filling, put the cornflour into a pan and add the sugar, lemon rind and 300ml/½ pint/ 1¼ cups water. Heat the mixture, stirring continuously, until it comes to the boil and thickens. Reduce the heat and simmer very gently for 1 minute. Remove the pan from the heat and stir in the lemon juice.

6 Add the the egg yolks to the lemon mixture, one at a time and beating after each addition, and then stir in the butter. Tip the mixture into the baked pastry case and level the surface.

7 To make the meringue topping, whisk the egg whites until stiff peaks form then whisk in half the sugar. Fold in the rest of the sugar using a metal spoon.

8 Spread the meringue over the lemon filling, covering it completely. Cook for about 20 minutes until lightly browned.

Energy 357kcal/1497kJ; Protein 6.8g; Carbohydrate 42.8g, of which sugars 25.1g; Fat 18.9g, of which saturates 9g; Cholesterol 129mg; Calcium 108mg; Fibre 0.7g; Sodium 137mg

Treacle tart

The name of this English favourite is somewhat misleading, since golden syrup, not treacle, is used for the filling. Golden syrup became available only in the late 19th century, making this plate tart a relatively recent invention. Serve it warm or cold, with custard or cream.

3 Mix the breadcrumbs with the ginger, if using, and spread the mixture over the bottom of the pastry. Gently warm the syrup with the lemon rind and juice (on the stove or in the microwave) until quite runny and pour evenly over the breadcrumbs.

4 Gather the reserved pastry trimmings into a ball, roll out on a lightly floured surface and cut into long, narrow strips. Twist these into spirals and arrange them in a lattice pattern on top of the tart, pressing them on to the edge to secure. Trim the ends.

5 Put into the hot oven and cook for about 25 minutes until the pastry is golden brown and cooked through and the filling has set.

Serves 6

175g/6oz/1½ cups plain (all-purpose) flour

pinch of salt

40g/1½oz/3 tbsp lard

40g/1½oz/3 tbsp butter, diced

75g/3oz/1½ cups fresh breadcrumbs

2.5ml/½ tsp ground ginger (optional)

225g/8oz/1 cup golden (corn) syrup

grated rind and juice of 1 lemon

1 Sift the flour and salt into a bowl and add the lard and butter. With the fingertips, rub the fats into the flour until the mixture resembles fine breadcrumbs. Stir in about 45ml/3 tbsp cold water until the mixture can be gathered together into a smooth ball of dough. Wrap the pastry and refrigerate for 30 minutes. Meanwhile, preheat the oven to 190°C/375°F/Gas 5.

2 Roll out the pastry on a lightly floured surface and use to line a 20cm/8in flan tin (pan) or pie plate, reserving the trimmings.

Variation Omit the lemon rind and juice if you prefer. Sometimes finely crushed cornflakes are used in place of the breadcrumbs.

Energy 420kcal/1764kJ; Protein 4.1g; Carbohydrate 63.5g, of which sugars 35.1g; Fat 18.4g, of which saturates 11.3g; Cholesterol 46mg; Calcium 62mg; Fibre 1.1g; Sodium 344mg

Yorkshire curd tart

Also known as Yorkshire cheesecake, this tart was originally made with curds made at home from creamy raw milk by adding buttermilk and heating gently. The traditional flavour comes from allspice or "clove pepper". Serve it plain or with cream.

Serves 8

For the pastry

115g/4oz/½ cup butter, diced

225g/8oz/2 cups plain (all-purpose) flour

1 egg yolk

For the filling

large pinch of ground allspice

90g/3½oz/½ cup soft brown sugar

3 eggs, beaten

grated rind and juice of 1 lemon

40g/1½oz/3 tbsp butter, melted

450g/1lb curd (farmer's) cheese

85g/3oz/scant ½ cup raisins or sultanas (golden raisins)

3 To make the filling, mix the allspice with the sugar in a bowl, then stir in the eggs, lemon rind and juice, butter, curd cheese and raisins or sultanas.

4 Pour the filling into the pastry case (pie shell). Bake for about 40 minutes until the filling is lightly set and golden. Serve slightly warm, cut into wedges.

1 Rub the butter into the flour until the mixture resembles fine crumbs. Stir in the egg yolk, with a little water if necessary, and gather the mixture into a smooth ball of dough.

2 On a floured surface, roll out the pastry and use to line a 20cm/8in fluted loose-bottomed flan tin (quiche pan). Chill for 15 minutes. Preheat the oven to 190°C/375°F/Gas 5.

Energy 480kcal/2005kJ; Protein 16.2g; Carbohydrate 48.2g, of which sugars 23.7g; Fat 27g, of which saturates 15.8g; Cholesterol 173mg; Calcium 153mg; Fibre 1.2g; Sodium 451mg

Apple and blackberry crumble

The origins of crumble are unclear. It did not appear in recipe books until the 20th century, but has become a firm favourite all over the country. Autumn heralds the harvest of apples and their perfect partners, blackberries. The oatmeal adds even more delicious crunch.

Serves 6–8

115g/4oz/½ cup butter

115g/4oz/1 cup wholemeal (whole-wheat) flour

50g/2oz/½ cup fine oatmeal

50g/2oz/¼ cup soft light brown sugar

a little grated lemon rind (optional)

900g/2lb cooking apples

450g/1lb/4 cups blackberries

squeeze of lemon juice

175g/6oz/scant 1 cup caster (superfine) sugar

1 Preheat the oven to 190°C/375°F/ Gas 5. To make the crumble, rub the butter into the flour, until it resembles fine breadcrumbs. Add the oatmeal and brown sugar and continue to rub in until the mixture begins to stick together, forming large crumbs. Mix in the lemon rind if using. Peel, core and slice the cooking apples.

2 Put the apples, blackberries, lemon juice, 30ml/2 tbsp water and caster sugar in a shallow ovenproof dish, about 2 litres/3½ pints/9 cups capacity.

3 Cover the fruit with the crumble topping. Put into the hot oven and cook for 30–40 minutes until the fruit is soft and the top is golden brown.

Energy 336kcal/1413kJ; Protein 4g; Carbohydrate 53.1g, of which sugars 30.8g; Fat 13.4g, of which saturates 6.8g; Cholesterol 27mg; Calcium 72mg; Fibre 3g; Sodium 81mg

Winter fruit crumble

This crumble uses pears and dried fruit in its base, making it ideal for the winter months. Serve it with custard or whipped cream. At other times of the year, try gooseberries or rhubarb flavoured with orange zest. The almond topping adds a delicious rich texture.

Serves 6

175g/6oz/1½ cups plain (all-purpose) flour

50g/2oz/½ cup ground almonds

175g/6oz/¾ cup butter, diced

115g/4oz/½ cup soft light brown sugar

40g/1½oz flaked (sliced) almonds

1 orange

about 16 ready-to-eat dried apricots

4 firm ripe pears

1 Preheat the oven to 190°C/375°F/ Gas 5. To make the topping, sift the flour into a bowl and stir in the ground almonds. Add the butter and rub it into the flour until the mixture resembles rough breadcrumbs. Stir in 75g/3oz/ ⅓ cup sugar and the flaked almonds.

2 Finely grate 5ml/1 tsp rind from the orange and squeeze out its juice. Halve the apricots and put them into a shallow ovenproof dish. Peel the pears, remove their cores and cut the fruit into small pieces. Scatter the pears over the apricots. Stir the orange rind into the orange juice and sprinkle over the fruit. Scatter the remaining brown sugar over the top.

3 Cover the fruit completely with the crumble mixture and smooth over. Put into the hot oven and cook for about 40 minutes until the topping is golden brown and the fruit is soft (test with the point of a sharp knife).

Energy 615kcal/2569kJ; Protein 9.4g; Carbohydrate 65.7g, of which sugars 42.9g; Fat 36.7g, of which saturates 16.2g; Cholesterol 62mg; Calcium 150mg; Fibre 6.6g; Sodium 190mg

Bread and butter pudding

Plates of white bread and butter were for many years a standard feature of an English tea or nursery supper, and frugal cooks needed to come up with ways to use up the leftovers. Bread and butter pudding was a family favourite until, surprisingly, in the late 20th century it was given a makeover using cream and brioche, and began to appear on the menus of upmarket restaurants. This is the original version, which traditionalists prefer.

Serves 4–6

50g/2oz/4 tbsp soft butter

about 6 large slices of day-old white bread

50g/2oz dried fruit, such as raisins, sultanas (golden raisins) or chopped dried apricots

40g/1½oz/3 tbsp caster (superfine) sugar

2 large eggs

600ml/1 pint/2½ cups full cream (whole) milk

3 Arrange half the bread pieces, buttered side up, in the prepared dish and sprinkle the dried fruit and half of the sugar over the top.

4 Lay the remaining bread slices, again buttered side up, evenly on top of the fruit. Sprinkle the remaining sugar evenly over the top.

1 Preheat the oven to 160°C/325°F/ Gas 5. Lightly butter a 1.2 litre/2 pint/ 5 cup ovenproof dish.

2 Butter the slices of bread and cut them into small triangles or squares.

5 Beat the eggs lightly together, just to break up the yolks and whites, and stir in the milk.

6 Strain the egg mixture and pour it over the bread in the dish. Push the top slices down into the liquid if necessary so that it is evenly absorbed.

7 Leave the pudding to stand for 30 minutes to allow the bread to soak up all the liquid (this is an important step so don't be tempted to skip it).

8 Put the dish into the hot oven and cook for about 45 minutes or until the custard is set and the top is crisp and golden brown. Serve the pudding immediately with pouring cream.

Variation
• To make a special occasion chocolate bread and butter pudding, complete steps 1–4, omitting the dried fruit. Break 150g/5oz 70% dark (bittersweet) chocolate into 500ml/17fl oz/generous 2 cups milk and heat gently (on the stove, or on low in the microwave) until the milk is warm and the chocolate has melted. Stir frequently during heating and do not allow the milk to boil. Stir the warm chocolate milk into the beaten eggs in step 5, and then continue with the remaining steps.
• You could replace the dried fruit in either version of the pudding with slices of fresh banana.

Energy 622kcal/2597kJ; Protein 10.5g; Carbohydrate 55.6g, of which sugars 37.8g; Fat 39g, of which saturates 23g; Cholesterol 186mg; Calcium 203mg; Fibre 1.6g; Sodium 350mg

Scottish scone and fresh fruit pudding

This luscious dessert incorporates good Scottish ingredients – sweet, juicy strawberries and raspberries in season, cream crowdie (a curd cheese) and a scone topping. Served with fresh cream or custard, it is perfect to finish a dinner party or hearty Sunday lunch.

3 Dot spoonfuls of the crowdie over the fruit. If you can't get crowdie, use a good thick Greek (US strained plain) yogurt instead.

Serves 4

450g/1lb/4 cups strawberries

250g/9oz/1½ cups raspberries

50g/2oz/¼ cup soft light brown sugar

For the scone topping

175g/6oz/1½ cups self-raising (self-rising) flour

5ml/1 tsp baking powder

50g/2oz/¼ cup soft light brown sugar

grated rind of 1 lemon

50g/2oz/¼ cup butter, melted

1 egg, beaten

250g/9oz cream crowdie

1 Preheat the oven to 220°C/425°F/ Gas 7. Gently mix the fruit with the sugar then place in a bowl in an ovenproof dish.

2 For the scone topping, combine the flour, baking powder and sugar in a bowl with the grated lemon rind then add the melted butter and beaten egg and mix thoroughly.

4 Place a scoop of the scone dough on top of each spoon of crowdie. Bake for about 20 minutes. The crowdie or yogurt should be oozing out of the scone topping. Serve immediately, and pass around a dish of crowdie (or yogurt) for those who want more.

Variations
• Many other fruits can be used for this wonderful and easy dessert. If you prefer, try orchard fruits such as apples, pears, apricots and peaches. Plums work particularly well, and the flavour can be enhanced with the juice of an orange or lemon.
• If you prefer, you can prepare the recipe without the crowdie (or yogurt) baked into the pie. Serve it on the side, or use custard or thick cream instead.

Energy 474kcal/1996kJ; Protein 11.6g; Carbohydrate 70.2g, of which sugars 37.7g; Fat 19g, of which saturates 10.4g; Cholesterol 79mg; Calcium 304mg; Fibre 4.2g; Sodium 307mg

Scone and butter pudding

The word scone originated in 16th-century Scotland. Scones are extremely easy to make but when you're short of time you can usually buy them from a bakery. Another good Scottish ingredient in this dessert is, of course, the whisky.

Serves 4

50g/2oz/scant ½ cup sultanas (golden raisins)

50g/2oz/¼ cup dried apricots, cut into small pieces

50ml/2fl oz/¼ cup whisky

300ml/½ pint/1¼ cups milk

300ml/½ pint/1¼ cups double (heavy) cream

5 egg yolks

50g/2oz/¼ cup caster (superfine) sugar

2 drops vanilla extract

6 scones

75g/3oz/6 tbsp butter

60ml/4 tbsp apricot jam, warmed

2 Whisk the milk, cream, egg yolks, sugar and vanilla extract. Slice the tops off the scones and then slice each into three rounds. Butter each round and then layer with the fruit and custard in buttered ramekins. Set aside for 1 hour.

3 Bake in a bain-marie (see Cook's tip) in the preheated oven for 40 minutes until risen slightly and golden-brown in colour.

4 Remove from the oven and brush with the warmed apricot jam. Serve immediately in the ramekins, or carefully pass a small sharp knife around the inside of each and gently ease the puddings out into bowls or on to individual plates.

Variation If you prefer, you can use the same quantity of Drambuie or brandy in place of the whisky.

1 Place the dried fruit and whisky in a small bowl, cover and leave to soak overnight or for at least 2 hours. Preheat the oven to 200°C/400°F/Gas 6.

Cook's tip A bain-marie is a water bath used for cooking delicate dishes, such as custards. Place the ramekin dishes in a large, shallow pan of hot water before putting in the oven.

Energy 796kcal/3305kJ; Protein 8.1g; Carbohydrate 43.2g, of which sugars 43.2g; Fat 63.9g, of which saturates 37.6g; Cholesterol 399mg; Calcium 178mg; Fibre 0.5g; Sodium 187mg

Syrup sponge pudding

England is famous for its steamed puddings and this one is a classic. The light sponge with its golden coat of syrup brings back memories of childhood when, for many, syrup sponge pudding (probably in a more stodgy version) was one of the highlights of school dinners. Serve this one with freshly made custard or cold pouring cream.

Serves 4–6

45ml/3 tbsp golden (light corn) syrup

115g/4oz/8 tbsp soft butter

115g/4oz/½ cup caster (superfine) sugar

2 eggs

5ml/1 tsp finely grated lemon rind

175g/6oz/1½ cups self-raising (self-rising) flour

30ml/2 tbsp milk

1 Butter a 1.2 litre/2 pint/5 cup heatproof bowl and spoon the golden syrup into the bottom of it.

2 In a large bowl, beat the butter and sugar until pale, light and fluffy.

3 In a separate bowl, beat the eggs and then gradually beat them into the butter-and-sugar mixture together with the lemon rind.

Variations
• Replace the golden syrup with orange or lemon marmalade, or jam such as raspberry or plum.
• Add a few drops of vanilla extract to the sponge mixture in place of the lemon rind.

4 Sift the flour over the mixture and fold it in lightly using a metal spoon. Gently stir in the milk to give a soft dropping consistency.

5 Spoon the sponge mixture over the golden syrup in the bowl.

6 Cover the pudding with a sheet of greaseproof (waxed) paper or baking parchment, making a pleat in the centre to give the pudding room to rise. Cover this with a large sheet of foil (again pleated in the centre).

7 Tie a length of string securely around the bowl, under the lip, to hold the foil and paper in place.

8 Half-fill a large pan with water and bring it to the boil. Place an inverted saucer or trivet in the bottom and stand the bowl on it. Cover the pan and steam the pudding for about 1½ hours, topping up the pan with more boiling water if necessary.

9 Remove the pudding from the steamer and leave it standing for about 5 minutes before turning out on to a warm plate to serve.

Cook's tips
• To cook the pudding in the microwave, cover the bowl with baking parchment (but do not tie it on) and cook on medium (500–600W) for 6–8 minutes until the sponge is just cooked through. Leave to stand for 5 minutes before serving.
• The pudding can also be baked for a dryer, cakier texture. Preheat the oven to 190°C/375°F/Gas 5. Cover the bowl with buttered foil and cook for 35–40 minutes. Meanwhile, heat 45ml/3tbsp golden syrup gently with 30ml/2tbsp water. Pour this hot sauce into a jug (pitcher) and serve alongside the pudding for pouring over.

Energy 480kcal/2005kJ; Protein 16.2g; Carbohydrate 48.2g, of which sugars 23.7g; Fat 27g, of which saturates 15.8g; Cholesterol 173mg; Calcium 153mg; Fibre 1.2g; Sodium 451mg

Christmas pudding

Plum pudding and figgy pudding were the forerunners of today's concoction of mixed dried fruits. This pudding is eaten on Christmas Day, brought to the table doused in warm brandy or whisky and set alight. Serve with pouring cream and brandy butter.

Makes 2 puddings, each serving 6–8

280g/10oz/5 cups fresh breadcrumbs

225g/8oz/1 cup light muscovado (brown) sugar

225g/8oz/1 cup currants

280g/10oz/2 cups raisins

225g/8oz/1⅓ cups sultanas (golden raisins)

50g/2oz/⅓ cup chopped (candied) mixed peel

115g/4oz/½ cup glacé (candied) cherries

225g/8oz suet, shredded (or vegetarian equivalent)

2.5ml/½ tsp salt

10–20ml/2–4 tsp mixed (apple pie) spice

1 carrot, peeled and coarsely grated

1 apple, peeled, cored and finely chopped

grated rind and juice of 1 orange

2 large eggs, lightly whisked

450ml/¾ pint/scant 2 cups stout

butter, for greasing

1 Put the breadcrumbs, sugar, dried fruit and peel in a large mixing bowl. Add the suet, salt, mixed spice, carrot, apple and orange rind. Mix well.

Cook's tip When a pudding is required, steam it for another 2–3 hours and serve hot. Christmas puddings are made at least a month in advance (traditionally on "stir-up Sunday" at the end of November).

2 Stir the orange juice, eggs and stout into the breadcrumbs. Leave overnight, stirring occasionally, if possible.

3 Butter two 1.2 litre/2 pint/5 cup heatproof bowls and put a circle of baking parchment in the bottoms. Stir the mixture and turn into the bowls.

4 Top with buttered circles of baking parchment, cover tightly with more layers of parchment and foil, tied securely under the rim. Steam for about 6–7 hours, top with boiling water as necessary. When the puddings are cooked and cooled, re-cover them with foil and store in a cool, dry place.

Energy 448kcal/1902kJ; Protein 2.4g; Carbohydrate 99.8g, of which sugars 92.5g; Fat 7.1g, of which saturates 3.6g; Cholesterol 20mg; Calcium 67mg; Fibre 0.9g; Sodium 123mg

Queen of puddings

This delicate English dessert has a base made with custard and breadcrumbs flavoured with lemon. Once it is set, a layer of jam is added and covered with a light meringue topping. Mrs Beeton called this Queen of Bread Pudding. It's good served just as it is or with cream.

Serves 4

80g/3oz/1½ cups fresh breadcrumbs

60ml/4 tbsp caster (superfine) sugar, plus 5ml/1 tsp

grated rind of 1 lemon

600ml/1 pint/2½ cups milk

4 eggs

45ml/3 tbsp raspberry jam, warmed

1 Stir the breadcrumbs, 30ml/2 tbsp of the sugar and the lemon rind together in a bowl. Bring the milk to the boil in a pan, then stir it into the breadcrumb and sugar mixture.

2 Separate three of the eggs and beat the yolks with the remaining whole egg. Stir the eggs into the breadcrumb mixture, then pour into a buttered ovenproof dish and leave to stand for 30 minutes.

3 Meanwhile, preheat the oven to 160°C/325°F/Gas 3. Cook the pudding for 50–60 minutes, until set.

4 Whisk the egg whites in a large, clean bowl until stiff but not dry, then gradually whisk in the remaining 30ml/ 2 tbsp caster sugar until the mixture is thick and glossy, be careful not to overwhip the mixture.

Cook's tip The traditional recipe stipulates that raspberry jam should be used, but you could ring the changes by replacing it with a different jam, such as strawberry or plum, or with lemon curd, marmalade or fruit purée.

5 Spread the jam over the set custard, then spoon over the meringue to cover the top. Sprinkle the remaining 5ml/ 1 tsp sugar over the meringue, then return to the oven for a further 15 minutes, until the meringue is light golden. Serve warm.

Energy 297kcal/1259kJ; Protein 13.7g; Carbohydrate 45g, of which sugars 31g; Fat 8.5g, of which saturates 3.2g; Cholesterol 199mg; Calcium 242mg; Fibre 0.4g; Sodium 281mg

Jam roly poly

This warming winter pudding, with its nursery-sounding name, first appeared on English tables in the 1800s. A savoury version, known as Plough Pudding, had a filling of bacon, onion and sage, and was eaten by Victorian stable lads for their supper on chilly days. While boiling is the traditional cooking method for jam roly poly, baking produces a lovely crisp golden crust and a sticky jam filling. Serve it thickly sliced with custard.

Serves 4–6

175g/6oz/1½ cups self-raising (self-rising) flour

pinch of salt

75g/3oz shredded suet (or vegetarian equivalent)

finely grated rind of 1 small lemon

90ml/6 tbsp jam

1 Preheat the oven to 180°C/350°F/Gas 4 and line a baking sheet with baking parchment.

2 Sift the flour and salt into a bowl and stir in the suet and lemon rind. With a round-ended knife, stir in just enough cold water to enable you to gather the mixture into a ball of soft dough, finishing off with your fingers.

3 Remove the ball of dough from the bowl, and on a lightly floured work surface or board, knead it very lightly until smooth.

Cook's tip For the lightest suet pastry, use as little cold water as possible to mix the dough, and handle it as gently and lightly as you can.

4 Gently roll out the pastry into a rectangle that measures approximately 30 x 20cm/12 x 8in.

5 Using a palette knife or metal spatula, spread the jam evenly over the pastry, leaving the side edges and ends clear.

6 Brush the edges of the pastry with a little water and, starting at one of the short ends, carefully roll up the pastry. Try to keep the roll fairly loose so that the jam is not squeezed out.

7 Place the roll, seam side down, on the prepared baking sheet. Put into the hot oven and cook for 30–40 minutes until risen, golden brown and cooked through. Leave the pudding to cool for a few minutes before cutting into thick slices to serve.

To boil the roly poly
1 Shape the mixture into a roll and wrap loosely (to allow room for the pudding to rise) first in baking parchment and then in a large sheet of foil. Twist the ends of the paper and foil to seal them securely and tie a string handle from one end to the other.

2 Lower the package into a wide pan of boiling water on the stove, cover and boil for about 1½ hours. Check the water level occasionally and top up with boiling water if necessary.

Variation To make a similar traditional nursery favourite, Spotted Dick, replace half the flour with 115g/4oz/2 cups fresh white breadcrumbs; add 50g/2oz/½ cup caster (superfine) sugar and 175g/6oz/¾ cup currants to the flour in step 2. Instead of water to mix, use about 75ml/5 tbsp milk. Leave out the jam and just form into a sausage shape without rolling.

Energy 240kcal/1008kJ; Protein 2.8g; Carbohydrate 33.7g, of which sugars 10.7g; Fat 11.3g, of which saturates 5.7g; Cholesterol 0mg; Calcium 104mg; Fibre 0.9g; Sodium 111mg

Eve's pudding

The name "Mother Eve's pudding", from the biblical Eve, was first used in the 19th century for a boiled suet pudding filled with apples, from which this lighter sponge version developed.

Serves 4–6

115g/4oz/½ cup butter

115g/4oz/½ cup caster (superfine) sugar

2 eggs, beaten

grated rind and juice of 1 lemon

90g/3¼oz/scant 1 cup self-raising (self-rising) flour

40g/1½oz/⅓ cup ground almonds

115g/4oz/scant ½ cup brown sugar

550–675g/1¼–1½lb cooking apples, cored and thinly sliced

25g/1oz/¼ cup flaked (sliced) almonds

1 Preheat the oven to 180°C/350°F/ Gas 4. Beat together the butter and caster sugar in a large mixing bowl until the mixture is very light and fluffy.

2 Gradually beat the eggs into the butter mixture, beating well after each addition, then fold in the lemon rind, flour and ground almonds.

3 Mix the brown sugar, apples and lemon juice and tip the mixture into an ovenproof dish, spreading it out evenly.

4 Spoon the sponge mixture over the top in an even layer and right to the edges. Sprinkle the almonds over. Put into the hot oven and cook for 40–45 minutes until risen and golden brown.

Energy 507kcal/2128kJ; Protein 6.9g; Carbohydrate 65.5g, of which sugars 52.7g; Fat 26.1g, of which saturates 12g; Cholesterol 114mg; Calcium 91mg; Fibre 2.8g; Sodium 159mg

Yorkshire lemon surprise

During cooking a tangy lemon sauce collects beneath a light sponge topping. It's important to bake this dish while it is standing in the bath of hot water, otherwise it will not work.

Serves 4

50g/2oz/¼ cup butter, plus extra for greasing

grated rind and juice of 2 lemons

115g/4oz/½ cup caster (superfine) sugar

2 eggs, separated

50g/2oz/½ cup self-raising (self-rising) flour

300ml/½ pint/1¼ cups milk

1 Preheat the oven to 190°C/375°F/ Gas 5. Use a little butter to grease a 1.2 litre/2 pint/5 cup ovenproof dish.

2 Beat the remaining butter, lemon rind and caster sugar in a bowl until pale and fluffy. Add the egg yolks and flour and beat together well. Gradually whisk in the lemon juice and milk (the mixture may curdle horribly, but don't be alarmed). In a clean bowl, whisk the egg whites until they form stiff peaks.

3 Fold the egg whites lightly into the lemon mixture using a metal spoon, then pour into the prepared dish.

4 Place the dish in a roasting pan pour in hot water to fill halfway up the sides, put into the hot oven and cook for 45 minutes until golden.

Energy 319kcal/1341kJ; Protein 7g; Carbohydrate 43.1g, of which sugars 33.8g; Fat 14.5g, of which saturates 8.1g; Cholesterol 126mg; Calcium 166mg; Fibre 0.4g; Sodium 190mg

Baked rice pudding

Rice pudding can be traced back to medieval England, when rice and sugar were expensive imports. Much later it was recommended for nursing mothers, gained a reputation as an aphrodisiac and, most enduringly, became a nursery favourite, served with a dollop of jam.

Serves 4

50g/2oz/4 tbsp butter, diced, plus extra for greasing

50g/2oz/¼ cup pudding rice

30ml/2 tbsp soft light brown sugar

900ml/1½ pints/3¾ cups milk

small strip of lemon rind

freshly grated nutmeg

Variations
• Add sultanas (golden raisins), raisins or dried apricots and cinnamon.
• Serve with fresh fruit such as sliced peaches, raspberries or strawberries.

1 Preheat the oven to 150°C/300°F/ Gas 2. Butter a 1.2 litre/2 pint/5 cup shallow ovenproof dish.

2 Put the rice, sugar and butter into the dish and stir in the milk. Add the strip of lemon rind and sprinkle a little nutmeg over the surface. Put the pudding into the hot oven.

3 Cook the pudding for about 2 hours, stirring after 30 minutes and another couple of times during the next 1½ hours, until the rice is tender and the pudding is thick and creamy.

4 If you prefer skin on top, leave the pudding undisturbed for the final 30 minutes, or stir again. Serve with jam.

Energy 298kcal/1252kJ; Protein 8.8g; Carbohydrate 54.3g, of which sugars 21.5g; Fat 5.2g, of which saturates 1.4g; Cholesterol 143mg; Calcium 71mg; Fibre 0g; Sodium 185mg

Kentish cherry batter pudding

The south of England was already famous for its cherry orchards in the 16th century. Pink and white cherry blossom heralded the arrival of spring, and Kent was dubbed the "garden of England". The cherry season is short, and puddings like this help to make the most of it.

Serves 4

45ml/3 tbsp cherry brandy or kirsch (optional)

450g/1lb dark cherries, pitted

50g/2oz/½ cup plain (all-purpose) flour

50g/2oz/4 tbsp caster (superfine) sugar, plus extra to serve

2 eggs, separated

300ml/½ pint/¼ cups milk

75g/3oz/5 tbsp butter, melted

1 Sprinkle the cherry brandy or kirsch, if using, over the cherries and leave to soak for about 30 minutes.

2 Stir the flour and sugar together in a mixing bowl, then slowly stir in the egg yolks and milk to make a smooth batter. Stir half the melted butter into the mixture and leave it to rest for 30 minutes.

3 Preheat the oven to 220°C/425°F/Gas 7. Pour the remaining melted butter over the bottom of a 600ml/1 pint/2½ cup ovenproof dish and put it in the oven to heat up.

4 Stiffly whisk the egg whites and fold into the batter with the cherries. Pour into the dish, and bake for 15 minutes. Reduce the heat to 180°C/350°F/Gas 4 and cook for 20 minutes until golden and set. Serve sprinkled with sugar.

Energy 357kcal/1493kJ; Protein 8.1g; Carbohydrate 39.4g, of which sugars 29.8g; Fat 19.7g, of which saturates 11.4g; Cholesterol 140mg; Calcium 147mg; Fibre 1.4g; Sodium 183mg

Clootie dumpling

This rich, dense Scottish pudding was traditionally cooked in a "cloot", a cloth, boiled in water over the fire. Clootie dumplings are traditionally made for the festive season.

Serves 8

225g/8oz/2 cups plain (all-purpose) flour, plus 15ml/1 tbsp for the cloot

115g/4oz/scant 1 cup suet (US chilled, grated shortening)

115g/4oz/generous 1 cup rolled oats

75g/3oz/scant ½ cup caster (superfine) sugar

5ml/1 tsp baking powder

225g/8oz/generous 1½ cups mixed sultanas (golden raisins) and currants

5ml/1 tsp each ground cinnamon and ground ginger

15ml/1 tbsp golden (light corn) syrup

2 eggs, lightly beaten

45–60ml/3–4 tbsp milk

1 Sift the flour into a dry bowl then add the suet to the flour. Using your fingertips, rub the fat into the flour until it is the texture of breadcrumbs. Add the rolled oats, sugar, baking powder, fruit and spices. Mix in well then add the syrup and eggs. Stir thoroughly, using enough milk to form a firm batter.

If using an ovenproof bowl

2 Lightly grease the inside of the bowl and put the mixture in, allowing at least 2.5cm/1in space at the top. Cover with baking parchment and tie down well.

3 Put an inverted plate or saucer in the base of a deep pan, place the dumpling on top and cover with boiling water. Cook for 2½–3 hours over a low heat.

If using a cloot

2 The cloot – or cloth – should be either cotton or linen, about 52cm/21in square. Plunge it into boiling water, remove it carefully from the pan, wring it out and lay it out on a flat surface.

3 Sprinkle 15ml/1 tbsp flour evenly over the cloot. Place the pudding mixture in the middle of the floured cloth then bring each of the four corners into the middle above the mixture and tie them up with a piece of strong, clean string, leaving plenty of space for the pudding to expand.

4 Place in a bain-marie (a roasting pan filled with water and placed in the oven) or steam over a double boiler. Cook over a low heat for 2½–3 hours.

5 When the dumpling is cooked, turn out on to a large warmed plate. Serve in slices with hot jam and cream. It can also be eaten cold and will keep in an airtight container for a month.

Energy 902kcal/3798kJ; Protein 15.1g; Carbohydrate 143.3g, of which sugars 69.2g; Fat 35g, of which saturates 16.6g; Cholesterol 121mg; Calcium 183mg; Fibre 5.5g; Sodium 81mg

Dunfillan bramble pudding

This warming pudding comes from Dunfillan in Perthshire. It is easy to make, if you have a little time, and is perfect with fresh cream as a tasty dessert or teatime indulgence.

Serves 4

For the Dunfillan pastry

50g/2oz/¼ cup butter

50g/2oz/¼ cup caster (superfine) sugar

1 large egg, well beaten

115g/4oz/1 cup plain (all-purpose) flour, sifted

pinch of baking powder

30ml/2 tbsp milk

grated rind of 2 lemons

For the filling

450g/1lb/4 cups blackberries

75g/3oz/scant ½ cup caster (superfine) sugar

squeeze of lemon juice

sprinkling of cornflour (cornstarch)

1 Preheat the oven to 180°C/350°F/ Gas 4. Put the blackberries in a pan and barely cover with water, then add the sugar and lemon juice. Cook until soft, about 5 minutes.

2 Transfer the blackberries to an ovenproof dish in layers, sprinkling each layer with a little cornflour.

3 To make the pastry, cream the butter and sugar then add the beaten egg. Mix the flour and baking powder then add it alternately with the milk to the butter mixture, mixing well after each addition. Finally stir in the lemon rind.

4 Spread the pastry evenly over the fruit, taking small batches from the bowl and spreading carefully. Cook in the preheated oven for 20–30 minutes, or until the top is golden brown. Serve hot or cold.

Energy 366kcal/1539kJ; Protein 6.2g; Carbohydrate 60.2g, of which sugars 39.2g; Fat 12.8g, of which saturates 7.2g; Cholesterol 90mg; Calcium 122mg; Fibre 4.4g; Sodium 107mg

Snowdon pudding

Reminiscent of the Welsh snow-capped mountain, this light pudding was allegedly created for a hotel situated at the base of Wales' highest peak. Use the softest, juiciest raisins you can find – they are more likely to stick to the basin than small dry ones. The pudding is often served with a wine sauce – to make it, simply replace the milk with white wine.

Serves 6

15–25g/½–1oz/1–2 tbsp butter, softened

100g/3½oz/⅔ cup raisins

175g/6oz/3 cups fresh white breadcrumbs

75g/3oz/½ cup shredded suet (US chilled, grated shortening)

75g/3oz/6 tbsp soft brown sugar

25g/1oz/¼ cup cornflour (cornstarch)

finely grated rind of 1 lemon

2 eggs

60ml/4 tbsp orange marmalade

30ml/2 tbsp fresh lemon juice

For the sauce:

1 lemon

25g/1oz/¼ cup cornflour (cornstarch)

300ml/½ pint/1¼ cups milk

50g/2oz/¼ cup caster (superfine) sugar

25g/1oz/2 tbsp butter

2 Mix together the breadcrumbs, suet, brown sugar, cornflour, lemon rind and the remaining raisins. Beat the eggs with the marmalade and lemon and stir into the dry ingredients.

3 Spoon the mixture into the bowl, without disturbing the raisins.

4 Cover with baking parchment (pleated) and then a large sheet of foil (also pleated). Tuck the edges under and press tightly to the sides. Steam over a pan of boiling water for 1¾ hours.

5 Pare two or three large strips of lemon rind and put into a pan with 150ml/¼ pint/⅔ cup water. Bring to the boil and simmer for 10 minutes. Discard the rind. Blend the cornflour with the milk and stir into the pan. Squeeze the juice from half the lemon and add to the pan with the sugar and butter. Heat until the sauce thickens and comes to the boil.

6 Turn the pudding out on to a warmed plate, spooning a little sauce over the top.

1 Smear the butter on the inside of a 1.2-litre/2-pint pudding bowl and press half the raisins on the buttered surface.

Energy 456kcal/1922kJ; Protein 7.7g; Carbohydrate 74.4g, of which sugars 43.4g; Fat 16.8g, of which saturates 8.6g; Cholesterol 82mg; Calcium 131mg; Fibre 1.1g; Sodium 304mg

Baked apples with mincemeat

This quintessential British fruit was once thought to have magical powers and, to this day, apples are linked with many English traditions and festivals. Here, they are baked in the oven with a filling of sweetened dried fruit. They are best served straight from the oven, while still puffed up and before they begin to crumple. Serve with custard or cream.

Serves 4

25g/1oz/2 tbsp butter, plus extra for greasing

4 cooking apples

about 60ml/4 tbsp mincemeat

30ml/2 tbsp honey

1 Preheat the oven to 180°C/350°F/ Gas 4. Butter a shallow ovenproof dish.

Variation Replace the mincemeat with chopped dried apricots or dates.

2 With an apple corer or a small sharp knife, remove the cores from the apples. Run a sharp knife around the middle of each apple, cutting through the skin but not deep into the flesh. Stand the apples in the dish.

3 Fill the hollow centres of the apples with mincemeat. Drizzle the honey over the top and dot with butter. Add 60ml/ 4 tbsp water to the dish. Bake for about 45 minutes until soft throughout, and serve at once.

Energy 70kcal/301kJ; Protein 0.7g; Carbohydrate 17.4g, of which sugars 17.4g; Fat 0.3g, of which saturates 0g; Cholesterol 0mg; Calcium 30mg; Fibre 2.4g; Sodium 9mg

Welsh apple pudding

In rural areas of south-east Wales, most homes would have had an apple tree in the back garden, often alongside damsons, plums or medlars. The fruits would be made into puddings, cakes and preserves. Today old-fashioned, single-variety apple crops are being made into preserves and the fruit is being made into award-winning apple juices.

2 Put the milk, butter and flour in a pan. Stirring continuously with a whisk, cook over medium heat until the sauce thickens and comes to the boil. Let it bubble gently for 1–2 minutes, stirring well to make sure it does not stick and burn on the bottom of the pan. Pour into a bowl, add the sugar and vanilla extract, and then stir in the egg yolks.

3 In a separate bowl, whisk the egg whites until stiff peaks form. With a large metal spoon fold the egg whites into the custard. Pour the custard mixture over the apples in the dish.

4 Put into the hot oven and cook for about 40 minutes until puffed up, deep golden brown and firm to the touch.

5 Serve straight out of the oven, before the soufflé-like topping begins to fall.

Serves 4

4 crisp eating apples

a little lemon juice

300ml/½ pint/1¼ cups milk

40g/1½oz/3 tbsp butter

40g/1½oz/⅓ cup plain (all-purpose) flour

25g/1oz/2 tbsp caster (superfine) sugar

2.5ml/½ tsp vanilla extract

2 eggs, separated

1 Preheat the oven to 200°C/400°F/ Gas 6. Butter a dish measuring 20–23cm/8–9in diameter and 5cm/2in deep. Peel, core and slice the apples and put in the dish.

Variation Stewed fruit, such as cooking apples, plums, rhubarb or gooseberries sweetened with honey or sugar, would also make a good base for this pudding, as would fresh summer berries (blackberries, raspberries, redcurrants and blackcurrants).

Energy 240kcal/1006kJ; Protein 7g; Carbohydrate 26.8g, of which sugars 19.2g; Fat 12.5g, of which saturates 6.8g; Cholesterol 121mg; Calcium 127mg; Fibre 1.9g; Sodium 131mg

Bread pudding

Thrifty cooks all over Britain were extremely inventive with finding ways to use the stale ends of loaves, and bread pudding is one example. This dish is spicy, rich and very filling – and is therefore an ideal winter food. Serve the pudding warm with custard or cream, or if you prefer it's just as nice left until cold.

Makes 9 squares

225g/8oz/4 cups stale bread, weighed after removing crusts

300ml/½ pint/1¼ cups milk

butter, for greasing

50g/1¾oz/4 tbsp dark muscovado (molasses) sugar

85g/3oz/½ cup shredded suet (US chilled, grated shortening) or grated chilled butter

225g/8oz/1⅓ cups mixed dried fruit, including currants, sultanas (golden raisins), finely chopped citrus peel

15ml/1 tbsp mixed (apple pie) spice

2.5ml/½ tsp freshly grated nutmeg

finely grated rind of 1 small orange and 1 small lemon, plus a little orange or lemon juice

1 egg, lightly beaten

caster (superfine) sugar for sprinkling

3 Using a fork, break up the bread before stirring in the sugar, suet, dried fruit, spices and citrus rinds. Beat in the egg, adding some orange or lemon juice to make a soft mixture.

Cook's tip Although suet is traditionally used for this pudding, you may prefer to use grated chilled butter.

4 Spread the mixture into the prepared dish and level the surface.

5 Put into the hot oven and cook for about 1¼ hours or until the top is brown and firm to the touch.

6 Sprinkle caster sugar over the surface and cool before cutting into squares.

1 Break the bread into small pieces. Place in a large mixing bowl, pour the milk over and leave for about 30 minutes.

2 Preheat the oven to 180°C/350°F/ Gas 4. Butter an 18cm/7in square and 5cm/2in deep ovenproof dish.

Energy 254kcal/1072kJ; Protein 4.3g; Carbohydrate 39.7g, of which sugars 27g; Fat 10.2g, of which saturates 5.3g; Cholesterol 31mg; Calcium 103mg; Fibre 1.4g; Sodium 147mg

Irish apple cake

This moist cake – also known as Kerry Apple Cake in the south of the country – is perhaps best in autumn, when home-grown apples are in season. It has a lovely crunchy top and can be served cold, as a cake, or warm with chilled cream or custard as a dessert.

Makes 1 cake

225g/8oz/2 cups self-raising (self-rising) flour

good pinch of salt

pinch of ground cloves

115g/4oz/½ cup butter, at room temperature

3 or 4 cooking apples, such as Bramley's Seedling

115g/4oz/generous ½ cup caster (superfine) sugar

2 eggs, beaten

a little milk to mix

granulated sugar to sprinkle over

1 Preheat the oven to 190°C/375°F/Gas 5 and butter a 20cm/8in cake tin (pan).

2 Sieve the flour, salt and ground cloves into a bowl. Cut in the butter and rub in until the mixture is like fine breadcrumbs. Peel and core the apples. Slice them thinly and add to the rubbed in mixture with the sugar.

3 Mix in the eggs and enough milk to make a fairly stiff dough, then turn the mixture into the prepared tin and sprinkle with granulated sugar.

4 Bake in the preheated oven for 30–40 minutes, or until springy to the touch. Cool on a wire rack. When cold store in an airtight tin until ready to serve.

Per cake Energy 2315Kcal/9717kJ; Protein 37g; Carbohydrate 312.5g, of which sugars 145.3g; Fat 110.9g, of which saturates 64.1g; Cholesterol 702mg; Calcium 948mg; Fibre 10.7g; Sodium 1.68g

Pratie apple cake

Both sweet and savoury versions of this potato apple cake exist; the sweet one, here, was the high point of many a farmhouse high tea. Adding the sugar and butter after most of the cooking is done means the cake has a lovely rich sauce when it is served.

Makes 2 farls; serves 4–6

450g/1lb freshly cooked potatoes in their skins, preferably still warm

pinch of salt

25g/1oz/2 tbsp butter, melted

about 115g/4oz/1 cup plain (all-purpose) flour

For the filling

3 large or 4 small cooking apples, such as Bramley's Seedlings

a little lemon juice (optional)

about 50g/2oz/¼ cup butter in thin slices

50–115g/2–4oz/¼ –generous ½ cup caster (superfine) sugar, or to taste

1 Preheat the oven to 200°C/400°F/ Gas 6. Peel the potatoes and mash them in a large heavy pan until very smooth. Season to taste with the salt, and drizzle the melted butter over.

2 Knead in as much plain flour to the potato as necessary to make a pliable dough (waxy potatoes will need more flour than floury ones). The dough should be elastic enough to roll out, but do not knead more than necessary.

3 Roll the potato mixture out into a large circle and cut into four farls (triangular pieces).

4 Peel, core and thinly slice the apples and pile slices of the raw apple on to two of the farls. Sprinkle a little lemon juice, if you like. Dampen the edges of the farls, place the other two on top.

5 With your fingers, "nip" around all sides of the two farl cakes to seal. Cook in the preheated oven for about 15–20 minutes. Remove from the oven, slit each cake around the side and lift the top back. Lay slices of butter over the apples, until almost covered, then sprinkle with sugar. Replace the top. Return to the oven for a further 5 minutes to melt the butter and sugar. Cut each farl into pieces and serve.

Per farl Energy 786Kcal/3307kJ; Protein 9.5g; Carbohydrate 121.9g, of which sugars 40.5g; Fat 32.4g, of which saturates 19.9g; Cholesterol 80mg; Calcium 117mg; Fibre 6.1g; Sodium 253mg

Chilled and cold desserts

On large country estates, the dairy maid was responsible not just for making cream, butter and fresh cheese, but also for delectable cold confections such as fools, flummeries, junkets and syllabubs, and there is a rich heritage of such creamy desserts. In summer, soft fruits would be turned into pretty jellies and trifles, topped with luscious whipped cream, and ice cream was a special treat.

Summer pudding

This pudding has only been a British favourite since the 20th century, but was no doubt devised as a thrifty way to use up stale bread, and make the most of the wonderful summer berries that are available in Britain for such a short time.

Serves 4–6

8 x 1cm/½ in thick slices of day-old white bread, crusts removed

800g/1¾lb/6–7 cups mixed berries, such as strawberries, raspberries, blackcurrants, redcurrants and blueberries

50g/2oz/¼ cup golden caster (superfine) sugar

lightly whipped double (heavy) cream or crème fraîche, to serve

1 Trim a slice of bread to fit in the base of a 1.2 litre/2 pint/5 cup bowl, then trim another 5–6 slices to line the sides of the bowl, making sure the bread comes up above the rim.

2 Place the fruit and sugar in a pan. Do not add water. Cook gently for 4–5 minutes until the juices begin to run.

3 Allow the mixture to cool then spoon the berries, and enough of their juices to moisten, into the bread-lined bowl. Reserve any remaining juice to serve with the pudding.

4 Fold over the excess bread from the side of the bowl, then cover the fruit with the remaining bread, trimming to fit. Place a small plate or saucer that fits inside the bowl directly on top of the pudding. Weight it down with a 900g/2lb weight, if you have one, or use a couple of full cans.

5 Chill the pudding in the refrigerator for at least 8 hours or overnight. To serve, run a knife between the pudding and the bowl and turn out on to a serving plate. Spoon any reserved juices over the top.

Energy 230kcal/977kJ; Protein 6.2g; Carbohydrate 51.7g, of which sugars 26.5g; Fat 1.2g, of which saturates 0g; Cholesterol 0mg; Calcium 98mg; Fibre 3g; Sodium 294mg

Irish apple and barley flummery

Although the name of this pudding comes from the Welsh, the Celtic countries all share this soft, sweet pudding. In Scotland it is based on oatmeal, but this Irish variation uses barley, and also includes apples; sago or tapioca could replace the barley.

Serves 4–6

90ml/6 tbsp pearl barley

675g/1½lb cooking apples, such as Bramley's Seedling

50g/2oz/¼ cup caster (superfine) sugar

juice of 1 lemon

45–60ml/3–4 tbsp double (heavy) cream

1 Put 1 litre/1¾ pints/4 cups of water into a pan. Add the barley and bring gently to the boil.

2 Peel, core and slice the apples. Add them to the pan and continue cooking gently until the barley is soft and apples are cooked.

3 Liquidize (blend) the mixture, or press through a sieve, and return to the rinsed pan.

4 Add the sugar and lemon juice and bring back to the boil.

5 Remove from the heat and allow to cool. Turn into individual glasses or a serving dish, and chill until required. Stir in the cream and serve cold.

Variations
• Other garden produce, such as blackcurrants, blackberries or rhubarb, could be used instead of apple.
• For an extra special flavour add 30ml/2 tbsp Irish whiskey to the flummery with the double cream.

Energy 245Kcal/1040kJ; Protein 2.5g; Carbohydrate 47.1g, of which sugars 28.3g; Fat 6.6g, of which saturates 3.8g; Cholesterol 15mg; Calcium 24mg; Fibre 2.7g; Sodium 7mg

Burnt cream

Now more elegantly known as crème brulée, this classic sweet appears on many an British restaurant menu – and the contrast between the crunchy topping and the smooth luxuriously creamy custard underneath it is irresistible.

Serves 6

4 egg yolks

15ml/1 tbsp caster (superfine) sugar plus 115–150g/4–6oz for the topping

600ml/1 pint/2½ cups double (heavy) cream

1 vanilla pod (bean), or a few drops of vanilla essence (extract)

Cook's tip A long iron rod with a cast-iron disk at one end that was heated on the range – was once used to brown the top of the burnt cream. You can now buy a special propane kitchen blow torch for a really crunchy topping.

1 Preheat the oven to 140°C/275°F/ Gas 1. Mix the yolks well with 15ml/ 1 tbsp sugar. Put the cream and vanilla pod, if using, in a pan, bring up to scalding point, remove the pod and pour the hot cream on to the yolks, blending well. Add the vanilla essence, if using.

2 Return the mixture to a double boiler, or a bowl over a pan of hot water, and cook carefully, stirring or whisking constantly, until the mixture thickens; do not allow it to boil.

3 Strain the custard into a gratin dish, or divide it among six ramekins. Cook the custard in the oven for 15 minutes or just long enough to let a skin form on the top, but do not allow it to colour. This stage may be omitted if you wish, as the custard is already cooked. Cooking in the oven will set it further.

4 Allow to cool, then leave to chill for several hours, preferably overnight.

5 To finish: preheat the grill (broiler). Sprinkle the custard evenly with the remaining sugar so that it is completely covered, but not too thick. Grill (broil) as close as possible to the heat for 2–3 minutes, or until the sugar melts and caramelizes, then remove from the heat and leave in a cold place for up to 2–3 hours before serving.

Variation This rich dessert is traditionally served with fresh or poached fruit. Alternatively, add a few teaspoons of a soft fruit, such as bilberries (fraughan), strawberries or raspberries to each ramekin before adding the vanilla custard.

Energy 547Kcal/2251kJ; Protein 3.6g; Carbohydrate 4.3g, of which sugars 4.3g; Fat 57.4g, of which saturates 34.4g; Cholesterol 272mg; Calcium 66mg; Fibre 0g; Sodium 28mg

Baked caramel custard

The British have long enjoyed baked custards either served on their own with a sprinkling of grated nutmeg or to accompany simple poached fruits. Baked caramel custard is a dressed-up version with a soft caramel top. Serve it as it is, or with cream.

Serves 6

75g/3oz/scant ½ cup granulated sugar

600ml/1 pint/2½ cups milk

vanilla pod (bean) or a few drops of vanilla essence (extract)

6 eggs

75g/3oz/scant ½ cup caster (superfine) sugar

1 Preheat the oven to 160°C/325°F/ Gas 3. Put the sugar into a heavy pan and stir over medium heat to make a golden caramel syrup. Remove from the heat and very carefully stir in 15ml/ 1 tbsp water. Return to the heat.

2 Pour the caramel into an ungreased, heated 900ml/1½ pints/3¾ cup baking dish, or divide among six ramekins. Using oven gloves or a cloth, tilt the dish to coat the base evenly with the hot caramel, then place in a shallow roasting pan.

3 To make the custard, scald the milk in a small pan with the vanilla pod, if using. Lightly beat the eggs and caster sugar in a bowl and, when it is nearly boiling, remove the vanilla pod and whisk in the hot milk. Add the vanilla essence, if using. Pour the custard into the prepared dish.

4 Fill the roasting pan to a depth of about 2.5cm/1in with cold water, cover the dishes with buttered baking parchment and bake in the centre of the oven until the custard has set, about 1–1½ hours, if baking one large dish, or about 30 minutes for individual ones. Leave to cool, and then chill.

5 To serve, loosen around the edge with a knife and tip the dish to ease the custard away from the sides.

6 Select a serving dish that is flat in the middle but with a deep enough rim to contain the caramel syrup. Invert the serving dish over the baking dish and turn upside down. If using ramekins, turn out on to small plates. Serve.

Cook's tip Baked caramel custard is popular throughout Europe and is very similar to the French pudding *crème caramel*. In Italy it is known as *crema caramella*, and in Spain as *flan*.

Energy 233Kcal/983kJ; Protein 11g; Carbohydrate 30.8g, of which sugars 30.8g; Fat 8.4g, of which saturates 2.9g; Cholesterol 234mg; Calcium 168mg; Fibre 0g; Sodium 129mg

Fruit and wine jelly

In 17th-century England, when making jelly was a lengthy process that involved the boiling of calf's hoof, hartshorn or isinglass, it was a centrepiece at high-class banquets. Though jelly now tends to be associated with children's parties it can still make a light and elegant dessert. You need to allow plenty of time for sieving the fruit and cooling the jelly.

Serves 6

600g/1lb 6oz fresh raspberries

140g/5oz/¾ cup white sugar

300ml/½ pint/1¼ cups medium-dry white wine

5 sheets of gelatine (6 if the jelly is to be set in a mould and turned out)

Cook's tip Instead of making your own fruit juice, use a carton of juice, such as mango, cranberry or orange, sweetened to taste.

1 Put the raspberries and sugar in a pan with 100ml/3½fl oz/scant ½ cup water and heat gently until the fruit releases its juices and becomes very soft, and the sugar has dissolved.

2 Remove the pan from the heat, tip the mixture into a fine nylon sieve (strainer) or jelly bag over a large bowl, and leave to strain – this will take some time but do not squeeze the fruit or the resulting juice may be cloudy.

3 When the juice from the fruit has drained into the bowl, make it up to 600ml/1 pint/2½ cups with water if necessary. Soak the gelatine in cold water for about 5 minutes to soften it.

4 Heat half the juice until very hot but not quite boiling. Remove from the heat. Squeeze the softened gelatine to remove excess water, then stir it into the hot juice until dissolved. Stir in the remaining raspberry juice and the wine.

5 Pour into stemmed glasses and chill until set. Alternatively, set the jelly in a wetted mould and turn out on to a pretty plate for serving.

Energy 178kcal/758kJ; Protein 8.6g; Carbohydrate 29.3g, of which sugars 29.3g; Fat 0.3g, of which saturates 0.1g; Cholesterol 0mg; Calcium 42mg; Fibre 2.5g; Sodium 6mg

Almond and rosewater blancmange

In the Middle Ages blancmange (literally 'white food') was a banqueting dish that contained chicken and rice as well as almonds and sugar. Later, arrowroot and cornflour were used as thickeners (and indeed are often still used). During Victoria's reign the dessert began to be set with gelatine in fancy moulds and became very fashionable.

Serves 6

5 sheets of gelatine

1 lemon

450ml/¾ pint/1⅔ cups milk

115g/4oz/½ cup caster (superfine) sugar

450ml/¾ pint/scant 2 cups single (light) cream

85g/3oz/¾ cup ground almonds

about 2.5ml/1 tsp triple-strength rosewater

fresh or sugared rose petals, to decorate (optional)

1 Soak the gelatine leaves in cold water for about 5 minutes to soften them.

2 Thinly pare strips of rind from the lemon, taking care not to include the white pith. Heat the milk gently with the lemon rind until it just comes to the boil. Discard the rind.

Variations
• Omit the lemon rind and add 2.5ml/1 tsp vanilla extract at step 3.
• Instead of rosewater, use your favourite liqueur.

3 Lift the softened sheets of gelatine out of the soaking water, squeezing out the excess. Stir the gelatine into the hot milk until dissolved. Stir in the sugar until it has dissolved. Add the cream, almonds and rosewater to taste and mix well.

4 Pour into one large or six individual wetted moulds, put into the refrigerator and chill until completely set.

5 Turn the blancmange out of its mould(s) just before serving. Decorate with rose petals if you wish.

Energy 350kcal/1462kJ; Protein 10.2g; Carbohydrate 26.2g, of which sugars 25.8g; Fat 23.5g, of which saturates 10.6g; Cholesterol 46mg; Calcium 201mg; Fibre 1.1g; Sodium 57mg

Scottish whisky mac cream

The warming Scottish drink, whisky mac, is a combination of equal quantities of Scotch whisky and ginger wine. This recipe takes the drink and transforms it into a rich, smooth, creamy dessert – very delicious and very decadent.

Serves 4

4 egg yolks

15ml/1 tbsp caster (superfine) sugar, plus 50g/2oz/¼ cup

600ml/1 pint/2½ cups double (heavy) cream

15ml/1 tbsp whisky

green ginger wine, to serve

1 Whisk the egg yolks thoroughly with the first, smaller amount of caster sugar. Whisk briskly until they are light and pale.

2 Pour the cream into a pan with the whisky and the rest of the caster sugar. Bring to scalding point but do not boil, then pour on to the egg yolks, whisking continually. Return to the pan and, over a low heat, stir until the custard thickens slightly.

3 Pour into individual ramekin dishes, cover each with clear film (plastic wrap) and leave overnight to set.

4 To serve, pour just enough green ginger wine over the top of each ramekin to cover the cream.

Energy 892kcal/3682kJ; Protein 5.4g; Carbohydrate 19.7g, of which sugars 19.7g; Fat 86.1g, of which saturates 51.7g; Cholesterol 407mg; Calcium 107mg; Fibre 0g; Sodium 44mg

Gooseberry and elderflower fool

Little can be simpler than swirling cooked fruit into whipped cream. Rhubarb is another favourite seasonal flavour to use in this recipe. Be sure to serve fool in pretty glasses or dishes, accompanied by crisp biscuits to add a contrast of texture.

Serves 4

500g/1¼lb gooseberries

300ml/½ pint/1¼ cups double (heavy) cream

about 115g/4oz/1 cup icing (confectioners') sugar, to taste

30ml/2 tbsp elderflower cordial

mint sprigs, to decorate

crisp biscuits (cookies), to serve

1 Place the gooseberries in a heavy saucepan, cover and cook over a low heat, shaking the pan occasionally, until tender. Tip the gooseberries into a bowl, crush them with a fork or potato masher, then leave to cool completely.

2 Whip the cream until soft peaks form, then fold in half the crushed fruit. Add sugar and elderflower cordial to taste, and sweeten the remaining fruit.

3 Layer the cream mixture and the crushed gooseberries in four dessert dishes or tall glasses, then cover and chill until ready to serve. Decorate the fool with mint sprigs and serve with crisp sweet biscuits.

Variations
• When elderflowers are in season, cook 2–3 flower heads with the gooseberries and omit the cordial.
• For rhubarb fool use squeezed orange juice in place of elderflower cordial.

Energy 366kcal/1521kJ; Protein 3.5g; Carbohydrate 24.2g, of which sugars 21.8g; Fat 28.4g, of which saturates 16.7g; Cholesterol 70mg; Calcium 111mg; Fibre 1.9g; Sodium 41mg

Eton mess

The "mess" consists of whipped cream, crushed meringue and sliced or mashed
strawberries, all mixed together before serving. The pudding gets its name from the
English public school, Eton College, where it is served at the summer picnic on 4 June.

Serves 4

450g/1lb ripe strawberries

45ml/3 tbsp elderflower cordial or
orange liqueur

300ml/½ pint/1¼ cups double
(heavy) cream

4 meringues or meringue baskets

Cook's tips
• Serve Eton mess just as it is or
accompanied by crisp biscuits (cookies).
• Make the dish with other soft fruit,
such as lightly crushed raspberries
or blackcurrants.
• This is a useful recipe to know if you
are trying to make a large meringue
and it cracks, as you can just break it up
completely and serve it this way.

1 Remove the green hulls from the
strawberries and slice the fruit into a
bowl, reserving a few for decoration.

2 Sprinkle with the elderflower cordial
or fruit liqueur. Cover the bowl and chill
for about 2 hours.

3 Whip the cream until soft peaks form.
Crush the meringue into small pieces.
Add the fruit and most of the meringue
to the cream and fold in lightly. Spoon
into serving dishes and chill until
required. Before serving, decorate with
the reserved strawberries and meringue.

Energy 526kcal/2182kJ; Protein 3.5g; Carbohydrate 32.8g, of which sugars 32.8g; Fat 40.4g, of which saturates 25.1g; Cholesterol 103mg; Calcium 60mg; Fibre 1.4g; Sodium 53mg

Syllabub

This dish can be traced back to the 17th century, when it is said to have been made by pouring fresh milk, straight from the cow, on to spiced cider or ale, creating a frothy foam. Later, cream and wine were used to make an impressive and luxurious dessert.

Serves 6

1 orange

65g/2½oz/⅓ cup caster (superfine) sugar

60ml/4 tbsp medium dry sherry

300ml/½ pint/1¼ cups double (heavy) cream

strips of crystallized orange, to decorate

sponge fingers or crisp biscuits (cookies) to serve

1 Finely grate 2.5ml/½ tsp rind from the orange, then squeeze out its juice.

2 Put the orange rind and juice, sugar and sherry into a large bowl and stir until the sugar is completely dissolved. Stir in the cream. Whip the mixture until thick and soft peaks form.

3 Spoon the syllabub into wine glasses.

4 Chill the glasses of syllabub until ready to serve, then decorate with strips of crystallized orange. Serve with sponge fingers or crisp biscuits.

Cook's tips
• Syllabub is lovely spooned over a bowl of fresh soft fruit such as strawberries, apricots, raspberries or blackberries.
• Add a pinch of ground cinnamon to the mixture in step 2.

Energy 310kcal/1282kJ; Protein 1.1g; Carbohydrate 14.5g, of which sugars 14.5g; Fat 26.9g, of which saturates 16.7g; Cholesterol 69mg; Calcium 41mg; Fibre 0.3g; Sodium 15mg

Fruit trifle

Everyone's favourite, trifle is a classic British dessert. The earliest trifles were creamy confections rather like fools, but in the 18th century the dish took the form familiar today, with layers of sponge soaked in whisky or sherry, topped with syllabub or whipped cream.

Serves 6–8

1 x 15–18cm/6–7in plain sponge cake

225g/8oz/¾ cup raspberry jam

150ml/¼ pint/⅔ cup medium or sweet sherry

450g/1lb ripe fruit, such as pears and bananas, peeled and sliced

300ml/½ pint/1¼ cups whipping cream

toasted flaked (sliced) almonds, to decorate or glacé (candied) cherries and angelica, (optional)

For the custard

450ml/¾ pint/scant 2 cups full cream (whole) milk

1 vanilla pod (bean)

3 eggs

25g/1oz/2 tbsp caster (superfine) sugar

1 To make the custard, put the milk into a pan with the vanilla pod, split along its length, and bring almost to the boil. Remove from the heat. Leave to cool a little while you whisk the eggs and sugar together lightly. Remove the vanilla pod from the milk and gradually whisk the milk into the egg mixture.

2 Rinse out the pan with cold water and return the mixture to it.

3 Stir over a low heat until it thickens enough to coat the back of a wooden spoon; do not allow the custard to boil. Turn the custard into a bowl, cover and set aside while you assemble the trifle.

4 Halve the sponge cake horizontally, spread with the raspberry jam and sandwich together. Cut into slices and use to line the bottom and lower sides of a large glass serving bowl. Sprinkle the sponge cake with the sherry.

Variation The sherry could be replaced with whisky or a fruit liqueur.

5 Spread the fruit over the sponge in an even layer. Pour the custard on top, cover with clear film (plastic wrap) to prevent a skin forming, and leave to cool and set. Chill until required.

6 To serve, whip the cream and spread it over the custard. Decorate with the almonds, cherries and angelica, if using.

Energy 631kcal/2615kJ; Protein 8.4g; Carbohydrate 24.9g, of which sugars 18.4g; Fat 53.1g, of which saturates 28.4g; Cholesterol 258mg; Calcium 155mg; Fibre 1.4g; Sodium 116mg

Welsh spiced plums with flummery topping

The English word flummery stems from *llymru*, which is Welsh for the method of cooking oats in water. The recipe has since developed, first with the addition of milk and then whipped cream and toasted oats. This version is laced with whisky.

Serves 4

8–12 plums

2.5ml/½ tsp mixed (apple pie) spice

25g/1oz/2 tbsp sugar, or to taste

30g/1oz/4 tbsp medium oatmeal

300ml/½ pint/1¼ cups double (heavy) cream

30ml/2 tbsp clear honey

30ml/2 tbsp Welsh whisky

1 Quarter the plums and remove their stones (pits). Put the fruit in a pan with 60ml/4 tbsp water and the mixed spice.

2 Bring just to the boil, cover and cook gently until the plums are soft, stirring occasionally and adding a little extra water if necessary to keep them moist (cooking time will depend on the ripeness of the fruit). Remove from the heat and stir in the sugar to taste. Leave to cool.

3 Heat a frying pan, add the oatmeal and toss or stir it until golden brown. Tip on to a plate and leave to cool.

Variation In place of plums, try fresh ripe berries or apricot slices sprinkled with brown sugar, or soft-cooked apples or pears.

4 Whip the cream until thick but not stiff. Blend the honey with the whisky and add to the cream. Continue whipping until the cream thickens again and soft peaks form. Stir in three-quarters of the toasted oatmeal (take care not to over mix).

5 Spoon the plums and their juices into the bottom of the serving glasses and then top each one with a layer of the cream and oatmeal mixture. Sprinkle the remaining toasted oatmeal over the top and chill the glasses in the refrigerator.

Energy 540kcal/2243kJ; Protein 3.8g; Carbohydrate 35.5g, of which sugars 24.5g; Fat 41.7g, of which saturates 25.1g; Cholesterol 103mg; Calcium 64mg; Fibre 2.8g; Sodium 25mg

Devonshire junket

Junkets, or Curds, were enjoyed by the medieval nobility and became universally popular in Tudor England. The name comes from a Norman word, *jonquette*, meaning cream cheese. Junket is also known as Damask Cream, perhaps because of its smooth, silky consistency.

Serves 4

600ml/1 pint/2½ cups milk

45ml/3 tbsp caster (superfine) sugar

several drops of triple-strength rosewater

10ml/2 tsp rennet

60ml/4 tbsp double (heavy) cream

sugared rose petals, to decorate (optional)

1 Gently heat the milk with 30ml/2 tbsp of the sugar, stirring, until the sugar has dissolved and the temperature reaches body heat (37°C/98.4°F).

2 Remove from the heat and stir in rosewater to taste, then the rennet.

3 Pour the junket into serving dishes and leave undisturbed at room temperature for 2–3 hours, until set. Do not move it during this time, otherwise it will separate into curds and whey.

4 Stir the remaining sugar into the cream, then carefully spoon the mixture over the surface of the set junket. Decorate with sugared rose petals, if you wish.

Energy 196kcal/824kJ; Protein 7.5g; Carbohydrate 19.1g, of which sugars 19.1g; Fat 10.6g, of which saturates 6.6g; Cholesterol 29mg; Calcium 193mg; Fibre 0g; Sodium 69mg

Bailey's carrageen pudding

Carrageen, also known as Irish moss, is a purplish variety of seaweed which is found all along the west coast of Ireland. When cooked it produces a jelly, which is used as the setting agent in this pudding that is still widely made in Ireland. Gelatine can be substituted.

Serves 8–10

15g/½oz carrageen

1.5 litres/2½ pints/6¼ cups milk

300ml/½ pint/1¼ cups Bailey's Irish Cream

2 eggs, separated

about 60ml/4 tbsp caster (superfine) sugar

1 Soak the carrageen in tepid water for 10 minutes. Put the milk into a pan with the drained carrageen. Bring to the boil and simmer very gently for 20 minutes, stirring occasionally.

2 Strain the mixture and rub all the jelly through the strainer; discard anything remaining in the sieve. Rinse out the pan and return the mixture to it, over a very low heat. Blend in the Bailey's.

3 Heat the mixture very gently to just below boiling point, and then remove from the heat.

4 Mix the egg yolks and the sugar together and blend in a little of the hot mixture, then stir, or whisk, the egg yolks and sugar into the hot mixture. When the sugar has dissolved, leave the mixture to cool a little, and then whisk the egg whites stiffly and fold in gently.

5 Turn into a serving bowl and leave in the refrigerator to set. Serve alone, or with a dessert selection.

Cook's tip When dried, carrageen is a good thickening agent for puddings, ice cream and soups.

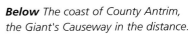

Below The coast of County Antrim, the Giant's Causeway in the distance.

Energy 2078Kcal/8724kJ; Protein 66.3g; Carbohydrate 201.6g, of which sugars 201.6g; Fat 85.3g, of which saturates 19.8g; Cholesterol 545mg; Calcium 1.95g; Fibre 0g; Sodium 1.08g

Welsh bara brith ice cream

Bara brith is Welsh for "speckled bread". This delicious ice-cream recipe combines a teabread version of bara brith with cream, custard and brandy. It is simple to make and thoroughly decadent. You need to make the custard in advance so it has time to cool before you make the ice cream mixture.

About 6–8 servings

300ml/½ pint/1¼ cups double (heavy) cream, chilled

30ml/2 tbsp brandy or whisky

225g/8oz/2 cups Bara Brith

For the custard

300ml/½ pint/ 1¼ cups full cream milk

vanilla pod

3 large eggs

85g/3oz/½ cup caster sugar

300ml/½ pint/1¼ cups double (heavy) cream

1 Make the custard: pour the milk into a heavy pan and add the vanilla pod (first split with the point of a sharp knife along its length and the seeds scraped straight into the milk). Bring the milk almost to the boil, remove from the heat and leave to stand for 10–20 minutes.

2 In a bowl, beat the eggs with the sugar, stir in the warm milk and remove the vanilla pod. Clean the pan, pour the milk mixture into it and cook over a gentle heat, stirring with a wooden spoon until the custard thickens enough to coat the back of the spoon.

3 Once the custard has thickened, transfer to a bowl, and leave to cool. When cool, add the double cream and chill until ready to use.

4 When you are ready to make the ice cream, switch your freezer to its very coldest setting.

5 Tip the cream, custard and whisky into a large plastic bowl or freezer box and, with a whisk, stir well.

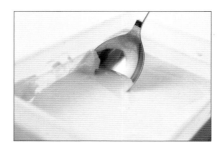

6 Cover and freeze for 1½–2 hours. Every 30 minutes or so take the box out of the freezer and stir well to move the ice crystals from around the edges to the centre of the bowl (you can set a timer to remind you to stir).

7 Meanwhile, crumble or chop the bara brith into very small pieces.

Variations
• If you prefer, you can use 550g/1lb 2oz carton ready made custard instead of making it yourself.
• Replace the bara brith with other teabread or cake.
• In place of brandy or whisky try using a Welsh liqueur such as Black Mountain, made with blackcurrants and apples.

8 When the mixture is slushy, break up the ice crystals with a fork, electric hand-mixer or food processor, and quickly return it to the freezer for about 1 hour.

9 Each time the mixture thickens and becomes slushy, repeat the mashing procedure once or twice more until the ice cream is thick and creamy.

10 Stir in the crumbled or chopped bara brith, cover and freeze the ice cream until required.

Cook's tip For easy freezing, the individual ingredients should be well chilled before they are mixed together at step 2. So if time allows, set the freezer to its coldest setting several hours earlier (or overnight) and then leave the mixed ingredients in the refrigerator to chill.

Energy 340kcal/1415kJ; Protein 4.5g; Carbohydrate 25.6g, of which sugars 13.1g; Fat 22.8g, of which saturates 13.1g; Cholesterol 53mg; Calcium 106mg; Fibre 0.7g; Sodium 123mg

Cakes and teatime treats

Afternoon tea became an elegant ritual in the 19th century, to fill the long gap between the midday meal and dinner in the evening. It is still a charming way to entertain friends, with a pretty tablecloth and the best china. A pot of tea can be accompanied by freshly made scones with clotted cream and jam, or an array of dainty sandwiches, tarts, biscuits and cakes.

Anchovy toasts

The Victorians loved anchovies in all kinds of dishes. In the late 19th century it became fashionable to serve anchovy butter spread on fried bread and topped with Cornish clotted cream – but simple toast fingers are more suited to modern tastes.

Serves 4–6

50g/2oz can of anchovy fillets in olive oil, well drained

75g/3oz/6 tbsp soft unsalted butter

15ml/1 tbsp finely chopped fresh parsley

generous squeeze of lemon juice

ground black pepper

4–6 slices of bread

1 Using a mortar and pestle, crush the anchovies to make a thick paste. Add the butter, parsley and lemon juice and mix well, seasoning to taste with black pepper. (Alternatively, put all the ingredients into a food processor and blend to a smooth paste.) Cover and chill until required.

2 Just before serving, toast the bread on both sides. Spread the anchovy butter on the hot toast, cut into fingers and serve immediately.

Sausage rolls

Small sausage rolls rank high in the league of popular teatime and party foods. They are delicious when homemade, particularly if quality butcher's sausagemeat is used to fill them. Serve them hot or cold. They also make an ideal addition to a picnic or packed lunch.

Makes about 16

175g/6oz/1½ cups plain (all-purpose) flour

pinch of salt

40g/1½oz/3 tbsp lard, diced

40g/1½oz/3 tbsp butter, diced

250g/9oz pork sausagemeat (bulk sausage)

beaten egg, to glaze

1 To make the pastry, sift the flour and salt and add the lard and butter. Rub the fats into the flour until the mixture resembles fine crumbs. Stir in about 45ml/3 tbsp cold water until the mixture can be gathered into a smooth ball of dough. Wrap and chill for 30 minutes.

2 Preheat the oven to 190°C/375°F/ Gas 5. Roll out the pastry on a lightly floured surface to make a rectangle about 30cm/12in long. Cut lengthways into two long strips.

3 Divide the sausagemeat into two pieces and, on a lightly floured surface, shape each into a long roll the same length as the pastry. Lay a roll on each strip of pastry. Brush the pastry edges with water and fold them over the meat, pressing the edges together to seal them well.

4 Turn the rolls over and, with the seam side down, brush with beaten egg. Cut each roll into eight and place on a baking sheet. Bake in the hot oven for 30 minutes until crisp and golden brown. Cool on a wire rack.

Energy 159kcal/661kJ; Protein 4g; Carbohydrate 10.4g, of which sugars 0.7g; Fat 11.5g, of which saturates 6.7g; Cholesterol 32mg; Calcium 55mg; Fibre 0.4g; Sodium 512mg

Energy 125kcal/521kJ; Protein 2.5g; Carbohydrate 10.3g, of which sugars 0.5g; Fat 8.4g, of which saturates 3.9g; Cholesterol 14mg; Calcium 23mg; Fibre 0.4g; Sodium 142mg

Cheese straws

Cheese-flavoured pastries became popular when it was customary (for gentlemen, particularly) to eat a small savoury at the end of a long, sophisticated meal. Now we are more likely to enjoy cheese straws as an appetizer or with sandwiches at tea time.

Makes about 10

75g/3oz/⅔ cup plain (all-purpose) flour

40g/1½oz/3 tbsp butter, diced

40g/1½oz mature hard cheese, such as Cheddar, finely grated

1 egg

5ml/1 tsp ready-made mustard

salt and ground black pepper

1 Preheat the oven to 180°C/350°F/ Gas 4. Line a baking sheet with baking parchment.

2 Sift the flour and seasoning and add the butter. Rub the butter into the flour until the mixture resembles fine crumbs. Stir in the cheese.

3 Lightly beat the egg with the mustard. Add half the egg to the flour, stirring in until the mixture can be gathered into a smooth ball of dough.

4 Roll the dough out to make a square measuring about 15cm/6in. Cut into ten lengths. Place on the baking sheet and brush with the remaining egg. Put into the hot oven and cook for about 12 minutes until golden brown. Transfer to a wire rack and serve warm.

Cucumber sandwiches

Think of Edwardian England and invariably afternoon tea with dainty cucumber sandwiches come to mind. Cucumbers were first grown in English hothouses in the 16th century, just waiting for the sandwich to be invented two hundred years later.

Serves 4

½ cucumber

soft unsalted butter

8 slices of white bread

salt and ground white pepper

1 Peel the cucumber and cut it into thin slices. Sprinkle with salt, place in a colander and leave for about 20 minutes to drain. Butter the slices of bread on one side. Lay the cucumber over four slices of bread and sprinkle with pepper.

2 Top with the remaining bread, press down lightly and trim off the crusts

3 Cut the sandwiches into squares, fingers or triangles. Serve immediately.

Energy 49kcal/206kJ; Protein 1.5g; Carbohydrate 3.9g, of which sugars 0.1g; Fat 3.1g, of which saturates 1.9g; Cholesterol 13mg; Calcium 32mg; Fibre 0.2g; Sodium 39mg

Energy 174kcal/735kJ; Protein 6.8g; Carbohydrate 29.2g, of which sugars 3.3g; Fat 4.2g, of which saturates 1.1g; Cholesterol 5mg; Calcium 92mg; Fibre 1g; Sodium 307mg

Scones with jam and cream

For most people, afternoon tea without a plate of scones would be unthinkable. Scones have been eaten in all parts of Britain for centuries, but the name comes from Scotland. It's important that scones are freshly baked, but they are quick and easy to make.

Makes about 12

450g/1lb/4 cups self-raising (self-rising) flour

5ml/1 tsp salt

55g/2oz/¼ cup butter, chilled and cut into small cubes

15ml/1 tbsp lemon juice

about 400ml/14fl oz/1⅔ cups milk, plus extra to glaze

jam and cream, to serve

1 Preheat the oven to 230°C/450°F/ Gas 8. Sift the flour, baking powder (if using) and salt into a mixing bowl, and stir to mix through.

2 Add the butter and rub it lightly into the flour with your fingertips until the mixture resembles fine, even-textured breadcrumbs.

3 Whisk the lemon juice into the milk and leave for about 1 minute to thicken slightly, then pour into the flour mixture and mix quickly to make a soft but pliable dough. The softer the mixture, the lighter the resulting scones will be, but if it is too sticky they will spread during baking and lose their shape.

4 Knead the dough briefly, then roll it out on a lightly floured surface to a thickness of at least 2.5cm/1in.

5 Using a 5cm/2in biscuit (cookie) cutter, and dipping it into flour each time, stamp out 12 rounds. Place the dough rounds on a well-floured baking sheet. Re-roll the trimmings and cut out more scones.

6 Brush the tops of the scones with a little milk then put into the hot oven and cook for about 20 minutes, or until risen and golden brown.

7 Remove from the oven and wrap the scones in a clean dish towel to keep them warm and soft until ready to eat. Eat the scones with plenty of jam and a generous dollop of clotted or whipped double cream.

Variation To make savoury cheese scones, add 115g/4oz/1 cup of grated cheese (preferably mature (sharp) Cheddar or another strong hard cheese) to the dough and knead it in thoroughly before rolling out and cutting into shapes. Cheese scones make a good accompaniment to soup.

Energy 177kcal/749kJ; Protein 4.7g; Carbohydrate 30.7g, of which sugars 2.2g; Fat 4.8g, of which saturates 2.8g; Cholesterol 12mg; Calcium 93mg; Fibre 1.2g; Sodium 43mg

Crumpets

Toasting crumpets in front of an open fire became particularly popular during the reign of Queen Victoria. They are made with a yeast batter, cooked in metal rings on a griddle. Serve them freshly toasted and spread with butter and maybe a drizzle of golden syrup.

Makes about 10

225g/8oz/2 cups plain (all-purpose) flour

2.5ml/½ tsp salt

2.5ml/½ tsp bicarbonate of soda (baking soda)

5ml/1 tsp fast-action yeast granules

150ml/¼ pint/⅔ cup milk

oil, for greasing

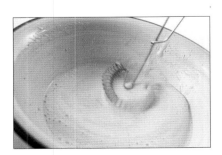

1 Sift the flour, salt and bicarbonate of soda into a bowl and stir in the yeast. Make a well in the centre. Heat the milk with 200ml/7fl oz/scant 1 cup water until lukewarm and tip into the well.

2 Mix well with a whisk or wooden spoon, beating vigorously to make a thick smooth batter. Cover and leave in a warm place for about 1 hour until the mixture has a spongy texture.

3 Heat a griddle or heavy frying pan. Lightly oil the hot surface and the inside of three or four metal rings, each measuring about 8cm/3½in in diameter. Place the oiled rings on the hot surface and leave for 1–2 minutes until hot.

4 Spoon the batter into the rings to a depth of about 1cm/½in. Cook over a medium-high heat for about 6 minutes until the top surface is set and bubbles have burst open to make holes.

5 When set, carefully lift off the metal rings and flip the crumpets over, cooking the second side for just 1 minute until lightly browned.

6 Lift off and leave to cool completely on a wire rack. Repeat with the remaining crumpet mixture. Just before serving, toast the crumpets on both sides and butter generously.

Energy 93kcal/393kJ; Protein 3g; Carbohydrate 16.5g, of which sugars 1g; Fat 2.1g, of which saturates 1g; Cholesterol 21mg; Calcium 48mg; Fibre 0.6g; Sodium 21mg

Welsh crumpets

These yeast pancakes can be served hot and buttered, with sweet or savoury accompaniments. Cook them in buttered metal rings or make them free-form. The best results come from using strong bread flour, but ordinary plain flour can be used. Try the crumpets buttered and sprinkled with cinnamon sugar to accompany a cup of tea.

Makes 8–10

225g/8oz/2 cups strong (bread) or plain (all-purpose) flour

2.5ml/½ tsp fine sea salt

6.25ml/1¼ tsp quick or easy-bake yeast

150ml/¼ pint/⅔ cup milk

15g/½oz/1 tbsp butter

1 egg

Melted butter, for brushing

1 Sift the flour and salt into a large jug (pitcher) or bowl and stir in the yeast. Combine the milk with 150ml/¼ pint/⅔ cup water and add the butter. Warm gently (on the hob or in the microwave) until the liquid is lukewarm when tested with your little finger. With a whisk, beat in the egg. Still with the whisk, stir the liquid into the flour to make a thick smooth batter. Cover and leave to stand at room temperature for about 1 hour to allow the yeast to start working.

2 Preheat a bakestone or heavy frying pan over medium to medium-low heat.

3 Brush melted butter on the inside of three or four metal rings (each measuring about 9cm/3½in) and lightly butter the hot bakestone or pan.

4 Place the metal rings on the hot surface. Pour a generous spoonful of batter into each one. Alternatively, drop generous spoonfuls of batter on to the hot buttered surface to make pancakes about 9cm/3½in in diameter, allowing some space between each one for the spreading of the batter.

5 Cook for a minute or two until the underside is golden brown, bubbles have burst on the surface and the top is just set. Carefully remove the metal rings and with a spatula, gently turn the crumpets over.

6 Cook the second side until light golden brown. Lift off and keep warm. Repeat with the remaining batter. Serve warm with butter and honey or jam, or another sweet or savoury topping.

Cook's tip These crumpets are also delicious for breakfast, warmed and served with crispy bacon, butter and maple syrup.

Energy 102kcal/432kJ; Protein 3.3g; Carbohydrate 18.2g, of which sugars 1.1g; Fat 2.3g, of which saturates 1.1g; Cholesterol 23mg; Calcium 53mg; Fibre 0.7g; Sodium 23mg

Newcastle singin' hinnies

In Tyneside, "hinny" is a term of endearment for friends or children, but these hinnies are thin, scone-like little cakes and "singin'" refers to the sound they make as they cook on the hot buttered griddle. Use a flat griddle if you have one, but a frying pan can also be used. Serve the hinnies while still warm, split and spread with butter.

Makes about 20

400g/14 oz/3½ cups self-raising (self-rising) flour

7.5ml/1½ tsp baking powder

5ml/1 tsp salt

50g/2oz butter, diced, plus extra for greasing

50g/2oz lard, diced

50g/2oz/¼ cup caster (superfine) sugar

75g/3oz/⅓ cup currants, raisins or sultanas (golden raisins)

about 150ml/¼ pint/⅔ cup milk

1 Sift the flour, baking powder and salt into a large bowl. Add the butter and lard and, with your fingertips, rub them into the flour until the mixture resembles fine breadcrumbs.

2 Stir in the sugar and dried fruit. Add the milk and, with a flat-ended knife, stir the mixture until it can be gathered into a ball of soft dough.

Variation Instead of making small cakes, try cooking the dough in a large, pan-sized circle, cutting it into wedges first to facilitate easy turning.

3 Transfer to a lightly floured surface and roll out to about 5mm/¼in thick. With a 7.5cm/3in cutter, cut into rounds, gathering up the offcuts and re-rolling to make more.

4 Heat a heavy frying pan or griddle. Rub with butter and cook the scones in batches for 3–4 minutes on each side until well browned. Lift off and keep warm until all are cooked.

Energy 132kcal/557kJ; Protein 2.3g; Carbohydrate 21.1g, of which sugars 5.8g; Fat 4.9g, of which saturates 2.4g; Cholesterol 8mg; Calcium 42mg; Fibre 0.7g; Sodium 118mg

English drop scones

Another form of traditional griddle cake, so popular in Britain, these thin, light and spongy drop scones (because the batter is 'dropped' onto the griddle), are also known as girdlecakes, griddlecakes and Scotch pancakes. They can be served hot or cold with butter and honey, syrup or jam. They are good with whipped cream and fresh soft fruit too.

3 Make a well in the centre of the flour mixture, then stir in the egg. Stir in the milk a little at a time, adding enough to give a thick creamy consistency.

4 Cook in batches. Drop three or four even spoonfuls of the mixture, spaced slightly apart, on the griddle or frying pan. Cook over a medium heat for 2–3 minutes, until bubbles rise to the surface and burst.

5 Turn the scones over and cook for a further 2–3 minutes on the other side, until golden. Place the cooked scones between the folds of a clean dish towel while cooking the remaining batter. Serve warm with butter and honey.

Cook's tip Placing the freshly cooked drop scones in a clean folded dish towel keeps them soft, warm and moist, and also makes an attractive way to serve them at the table.

Makes 8–10

115g/4oz/1 cup plain (all-purpose) flour

5ml/1 tsp bicarbonate of soda (baking soda)

5ml/1 tsp cream of tartar

25g/1oz/2 tbsp butter, cut into small cubes

1 egg, beaten

about 150ml/¼ pint/⅔ cup milk

butter and clear honey, to serve

1 Sift the flour, bicarbonate of soda and cream of tartar into a mixing bowl. Rub the butter into the flour until the mixture resembles fine breadcrumbs.

2 Lightly grease a griddle pan or heavy frying pan, and heat it.

Energy 60kcal/252kJ; Protein 2g; Carbohydrate 11.1g, of which sugars 1.8g; Fat 1.1g, of which saturates 0.2g; Cholesterol 11mg; Calcium 66mg; Fibre 0.4g; Sodium 56mg

Welsh tinker's cakes

These delicate little cakes, *teisenni tincar*, could be rustled up in next to no time for eating hot off the bakestone when visitors or the travelling pot mender or tinker, called. The quantities have been kept small because they really must be eaten while still really fresh. To make more, simply double up on the measures.

Makes 8–10

125g/4½oz/1 cup self-raising (self-rising) flour

small pinch of salt

70g/2½oz/5 tbsp butter, cut into small cubes

50g/2oz/4 tbsp demerara (raw) or light muscovado (brown) sugar

1 small cooking apple, weighing about 150g/5oz

about 30ml/2 tbsp milk

caster (superfine) sugar, for dusting

1 Preheat the bakestone or heavy frying pan over low to medium heat.

2 Sift the flour and salt into a mixing bowl. Add the butter and, with your fingertips, rub it into the flour until the mixture resembles fine breadcrumbs. Alternatively, whizz the ingredients in a food processor. Stir in the sugar.

3 Peel and grate the apple, discarding the core, and stir the grated apple into the flour mixture with enough milk to make a mixture than can be gathered into a ball of soft, moist dough. Work it slightly to make sure the flour is mixed in well.

4 Transfer to a lightly floured surface and roll out the dough to about 5mm/¼in thick. With a 6–7.5cm/2½–3in cutter, cut out rounds, gathering up the offcuts and re-rolling them to make more.

5 Smear a little butter on the hot bakestone or pan and cook the cakes, in batches, for about 4–5 minutes on each side or until golden brown and cooked through.

6 Lift on to a wire rack and dust with caster sugar. Serve warm.

Cook's tip Add a good pinch of ground cinnamon or mixed spice to the flour. The rolled-out dough could just as easily be cut into squares or triangles for a change.

Energy 121kcal/508kJ; Protein 1.4g; Carbohydrate 16.5g, of which sugars 6.9g; Fat 6g, of which saturates 3.7g; Cholesterol 15mg; Calcium 26mg; Fibre 0.6g; Sodium 45mg

Shropshire soul cakes

These little cakes were served on All Souls' Day (2 November), when it was customary to go "souling" or singing prayers for the dead. In return, the singers received a soul cake. The original recipe would have included plain flour but self-raising produces a lighter result.

Makes about 20

450g/1lb/4 cups self-raising (self-rising) flour

5ml/1 tsp ground mixed (apple pie) spice

2.5ml/½ tsp ground ginger

175g/6oz/¾ cup soft butter

175g/6oz/¾ cup caster (superfine) sugar, plus extra for sprinkling

2 eggs, lightly beaten

50g/2oz/¼ cup currants, raisins or sultanas (golden raisins)

about 30ml/2 tbsp milk

1 Preheat the oven to 180°C/350°F/ Gas 4. Lightly grease two baking sheets or line with baking parchment. Sift the flour and spices into a bowl, and set aside. In a large bowl, beat the butter with the sugar until the mixture is light, pale and fluffy.

2 Gradually beat the eggs into the mixture. Fold in the flour mixture and the dried fruit, then add sufficient warm milk to bind the mixture and gather it up into a ball of soft dough.

3 Transfer to a lightly floured surface and roll out to about 5mm/¼in thick. With a floured 7.5cm/3in cutter, cut into rounds, gathering up the offcuts and re-rolling to make more.

4 Arrange the cakes on the prepared baking sheets. Prick the surface of the cakes lightly with a fork then, with the back of a knife, mark a deep cross on top of each.

5 Put the cakes into the hot oven and cook for about 15 minutes until risen and golden brown.

6 Sprinkle the cooked cakes with a little caster sugar and then transfer to a wire rack to cool.

Energy 191kcal/803kJ; Protein 2.9g; Carbohydrate 28.4g, of which sugars 11.3g; Fat 8.1g, of which saturates 4.8g; Cholesterol 38mg; Calcium 45mg; Fibre 0.7g; Sodium 62mg

Shortbread

The quintessential Scottish biscuit, shortbread is a great speciality and favourite all round the British Isles. It is wonderfully satisfying and moreish at any time of the day or night.

Makes about 48 fingers

oil, for greasing

275g/10oz/2½ cups plain (all-purpose) flour

25g/1oz/¼ cup ground almonds

225g/8oz/1 cup butter, softened

75g/3oz/scant ½ cup caster (superfine) sugar

grated rind of ½ lemon

1 Preheat the oven to 180°C/350°F/ Gas 4 and oil a large Swiss roll tin (jelly roll pan) or baking tray.

2 Put the remaining ingredients into a blender or food processor and pulse until the mixture comes together.

3 Place the mixture on the oiled tray and flatten it out with a palette knife or metal spatula until evenly spread. Bake in the preheated oven for 20 minutes, or until pale golden brown.

Variation You can replace the lemon rind with the grated rind of two oranges for a tangy orange flavour, if you prefer.

4 Remove from the oven and immediately mark the shortbread into fingers or squares while the mixture is soft. Allow to cool a little, and then transfer to a wire rack and leave until cold. If stored in an airtight container, the shortbread should keep for up to two weeks.

Cook's tip To make by hand, sift the flour and almonds on to a pastry board or work surface. Cream together the butter and sugar in a mixing bowl and then turn the creamed mixture on to the pastry board with the flour and almonds. Work the mixture together using your fingertips. It should come together to make a smooth dough. Continue as above from step 3.

Per finger Energy 64kcal/266kJ; Protein 0.7g; Carbohydrate 6.1g, of which sugars 1.8g; Fat 4.2g, of which saturates 2.5g; Cholesterol 10mg; Calcium 11mg; Fibre 0.2g; Sodium 29mg

Maids of honour

These little delicacies were allegedly being enjoyed by Anne Boleyn's maids of honour when Henry VIII first met her in Richmond Palace in Surrey, and he is said to have named them. Originally they would have been made with strained curds, made by adding rennet to milk.

3 Put the curd cheese into a bowl and add the almonds, sugar and lemon rind. Lightly beat the eggs with the butter and add to the cheese mixture. Mix well.

4 Spoon the mixture into the pastry cases. Bake for about 20 minutes, until the pastry is well risen and the filling is puffed up, golden brown and just firm to the touch.

5 Transfer to a wire rack (the filling will sink down as it cools). Serve warm or at room temperature, dusted with a little sifted icing sugar.

Makes 12

250g/9oz ready-made puff pastry

250g/9oz/1¼ cups curd (farmer's) cheese

60ml/4 tbsp ground almonds

45ml/3 tbsp caster (superfine) sugar

finely grated rind of 1 small lemon

2 eggs

15g/½ oz/1 tbsp butter, melted

icing (confectioner's) sugar, to dust

Variation Sprinkle the filling with a little freshly grated nutmeg at the end of step 4.

1 Preheat the oven to 200°C/400°F/ Gas 6. Grease a 12-hole bun tray.

2 Roll out the puff pastry very thinly on a lightly floured surface and, using a 7.5cm/3in cutter, cut out 12 circles. Press the pastry circles into the prepared tray and prick well with a fork. Chill while you make the filling.

Energy 182kcal/758kJ; Protein 5.2g; Carbohydrate 12.6g, of which sugars 5.1g; Fat 12.9g, of which saturates 3g; Cholesterol 43mg; Calcium 31mg; Fibre 0.4g; Sodium 85mg

Jam tarts

"The Queen of Hearts, she made some tarts, all on a summer's day; the Knave of Hearts, he stole those tarts, and took them quite away!" goes the English nursery rhyme. Jam tarts are a must at birthday parties, and are often a British child's first attempt at baking.

Makes 12

175g/6oz/1½ cups plain (all-purpose) flour

pinch of salt

30ml/2 tbsp caster (superfine) sugar

85g/3oz/6 tbsp butter, diced

1 egg, lightly beaten

jam

1 Sift the flour and salt and stir in the sugar. Rub in the butter until the mixture resembles fine crumbs. Stir in the egg and gather into a smooth dough ball.

2 Chill the pastry ball for 30 minutes. Meanwhile, preheat the oven to 220°C/425°F/Gas 7 and lightly grease a 12-hole bun tray.

3 Roll out the pastry on a lightly floured surface to about 3mm/⅛in thick and, using a 7.5cm/3in fluted biscuit (cookie) cutter, cut out 12 circles. Press the pastry circles into the prepared tray. Put a teaspoonful of jam into each.

4 Put into the hot oven and cook for 15–20 minutes until the pastry is cooked and light golden brown. Carefully lift the tarts on to a wire rack and leave to cool before serving.

Mince pies

Mincemeat has its orgins in medieval time, and did once contain meat. To eat one mince pie a day for the 12 days of Christmas was thought to bring happiness for the coming year.

Makes 12

225g/8oz/2 cups plain (all-purpose) flour

pinch of salt

45ml/3 tbsp caster (superfine) sugar, plus extra for dusting

115g/4oz/½ cup butter, diced

1 egg, lightly beaten

about 350g/12oz mincemeat

1 Sift the flour and salt and stir in the sugar. Rub in the butter until the mixture resembles fine crumbs. Stir in the egg and gather into a smooth dough.

2 Chill the pastry for 30 minutes. Meanwhile, preheat the oven to 220°C/425°F/Gas 7 and lightly grease a 12-hole bun tray.

3 Roll out the pastry on a lightly floured surface to about 3mm/⅛in thick and, using a 7.5cm/3in cutter, cut out 12 circles. Press into the prepared tray. Gather up the offcuts and roll out again, cutting slightly smaller circles to make 12 lids. Spoon mincemeat into each case, dampen the edges and top with a pastry lid. Make a small slit in each pie.

4 Bake for 15–20 minutes until light golden brown. Transfer to a wire rack to cool and serve dusted with sugar.

Energy 114kcal/479kJ; Protein 1.1g; Carbohydrate 18.8g, of which sugars 12.5g; Fat 4.3g, of which saturates 2.6g; Cholesterol 18mg; Calcium 16mg; Fibre 0.3g; Sodium 39mg

Energy 236kcal/993kJ; Protein 2.5g; Carbohydrate 36.7g, of which sugars 22.4g; Fat 9.8g, of which saturates 5.2g; Cholesterol 37mg; Calcium 43mg; Fibre 1g; Sodium 70mg

Yorkshire fat rascals

These delicious teacakes from the north of England are a cross between a scone and a rock cake and are really simple to make. They would originally have been baked in a small pot oven standing over an open fire. Serve them warm or cold, just as they are or with butter.

Makes 10

350g/12oz/3 cups self-raising (self-rising) flour

175g/6oz/¾ cup butter, diced

115g/4oz/½ cup caster (superfine) sugar

75g/3oz/⅓ cup mixed currants, raisins and sultanas (golden raisins)

25g/1oz/1½ tbsp chopped mixed peel

50g/2oz/⅓ cup glacé (candied) cherries

50g/2oz/⅓ cup blanched almonds, roughly chopped

1 egg

about 75ml/5 tbsp milk

1 Preheat the oven to 200°C/400°F/ Gas 6. Line a baking sheet with baking parchment.

2 Sift the flour into a large bowl. Add the butter and, with your fingertips, rub it into the flour until the mixture resembles fine breadcrumbs (alternatively whizz the ingredients briefly in a food processor).

3 Stir in the sugar, dried fruit, peel, cherries and almonds.

4 Lightly beat the egg and stir into the flour mixture with sufficient milk to gather the mixture into a ball of dough.

5 With lightly floured hands, divide the dough into ten balls, press them into rough circles about 2cm/¾in thick and arrange on the prepared baking sheet.

6 Cook for 15–20 minutes until risen and golden brown. Transfer to a wire rack to cool.

Energy 375kcal/1574kJ; Protein 5.6g; Carbohydrate 50g, of which sugars 23.2g; Fat 18.4g, of which saturates 9.6g; Cholesterol 57mg; Calcium 93mg; Fibre 1.8g; Sodium 129mg

Ginger snaps

It was once customary to serve ginger snaps and spiced ale on Twelfth Night, the evening of 5 January and a night of parties and practical jokes. Since then, many an English tale has been told over a plate of ginger snaps and a pot of strong tea.

Makes about 24

115g/4oz/½ cup butter, diced

115g/4oz/½ cup caster (superfine) sugar

115g/4oz/½ cup golden (corn) syrup

225g/8oz/2 cups plain (all-purpose) flour

10ml/2 tsp ground ginger

5ml/1 tsp bicarbonate of soda (baking soda)

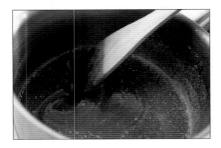

1 Preheat the oven to 180°C/350°F/ Gas 4. Line two or three baking sheets with baking parchment. Gently heat the butter, sugar and syrup until the butter has melted and the sugar has dissolved. Leave to cool slightly.

2 Sift the flour, ginger and bicarbonate of soda and stir into the mixture in the pan to make a soft dough.

3 Arrange balls of the dough on the prepared baking sheets, well spaced out. Flatten each ball slightly with a palette knife or metal spatula.

Cook's tip Measuring syrup is easier if you dip a metal spoon in very hot water first, then quickly dry it.

4 Put one tray into the hot oven and cook for about 12 minutes until golden brown (take care not to overcook them – they burn easily). Leave to cool on the baking sheet for 1–2 minutes then carefully transfer to a wire rack to crisp up and cool completely while you cook the remaining biscuits.

Energy 101kcal/424kJ; Protein 1g; Carbohydrate 16.1g, of which sugars 9g; Fat 4.1g, of which saturates 2.5g; Cholesterol 10mg; Calcium 17mg; Fibre 0.3g; Sodium 43mg

Oat biscuits

In England oats have been one of the principal crops since the days of the Anglo-Saxons and King Alfred the Great. By the 14th century, the grain had become a major export. Nutritious and delicious, oats are a major ingredient in these biscuits.

3 Sift the flour and stir into the mixture in the pan, together with the oats, to make a soft dough.

4 Roll the dough into small balls and arrange them on the prepared baking sheets, leaving plenty of room for them to spread. Flatten each ball slightly with a palette knife or a metal spatula.

5 Put one tray into the hot oven and cook for 12–15 minutes until golden brown and cooked through.

6 Leave to cool on the baking sheet for 1–2 minutes then carefully transfer to a wire rack to crisp up and cool completely, while you cook the remaining batches.

Makes about 18

115g/4oz/½ cup butter

115g/4oz/½ cup soft brown sugar

115g/4oz/½ cup golden (corn) syrup

150g/5oz/1¼ cups self-raising (self-rising) flour

150g/5oz rolled porridge oats

1 Preheat the oven to 180°C/350°F/ Gas 4. Line two or three baking (cookie) sheets with baking parchment, or grease them with butter.

2 Gently heat the butter, sugar and golden syrup until the butter has melted and the sugar has dissolved. Remove from the heat and leave to cool slightly.

Variation Add 25g/1oz/¼ cup finely chopped toasted almonds or walnuts, or a small handful of dried fruit (raisins or sultanas) in step 3.

Energy 151kcal/637kJ; Protein 1.8g; Carbohydrate 23.9g, of which sugars 11.9g; Fat 6g, of which saturates 3.3g; Cholesterol 14mg; Calcium 22mg; Fibre 0.8g; Sodium 59mg

Melting moments

As the name suggests, these crisp biscuits really do melt in the mouth. They have a texture like shortbread but are covered in rolled oats to give a crunchy surface and extra flavour, and traditionally topped with a nugget of glacé cherry.

Makes 16–20

40g/1½oz/3 tbsp soft butter

65g/2½oz/5 tbsp lard

85g/3oz/6 tbsp caster (superfine) sugar

1 egg yolk, beaten

few drops of vanilla or almond extract

150g/5oz/1¼ cups self-raising (self-rising) flour

rolled oats, for coating

4–5 glacé (candied) cherries

3 Spread rolled oats on a sheet of baking parchment and toss the balls in them until evenly coated.

4 Place the balls, spaced slightly apart, on two baking (cookie) sheets. Flatten each ball a little with your thumb. Cut the cherries into quarters and place a piece of cherry on top of each biscuit (cookie). Put into the hot oven and cook for 15–20 minutes, until they are lightly browned.

5 Allow the biscuits to cool for a few minutes on the baking sheets before transferring them to a wire rack to cool completely.

1 Preheat the oven to 180°C/350°F/ Gas 4. Beat together the butter, lard and sugar, then gradually beat in the egg yolk and vanilla or almond extract.

2 Sift the flour over and stir to make a soft dough. Roll into 16–20 small balls.

Energy 88kcal/370kJ; Protein 0.7g; Carbohydrate 10.9g, of which sugars 5.4g; Fat 5g, of which saturates 2.4g; Cholesterol 7mg; Calcium 30mg; Fibre 0.3g; Sodium 40mg

Easter biscuits

These sweet, lightly spiced cookies have fluted edges and are flecked with currants. In England's West Country they are also known as Easter cakes rather than biscuits.

Makes 16–18

115g/4oz/½ cup soft butter

85g/3oz/6 tbsp caster (superfine) sugar, plus extra for sprinkling

1 egg

200g/7oz/1¾ cups plain (all-purpose) flour

2.5ml/½ tsp mixed (apple pie) spice

2.5ml/½ tsp ground cinnamon

55g/2oz/scant ½ cup currants

15ml/1 tbsp chopped mixed (candied) peel

15–30ml/1–2 tbsp milk

1 Preheat the oven to 200°C/400°F/ Gas 6. Lightly grease two baking sheets or line with baking parchment.

2 Beat together the butter and sugar until light and fluffy. Separate the egg, reserving the white, and beat the yolk into the mixture.

3 Sift the flour and spices over the mixture, then fold in the currants and peel, adding sufficient milk to make a fairly soft dough.

4 Knead the dough lightly on a floured surface then roll out to 5mm/¼in thick. Cut out circles using a 5cm/2in fluted biscuit (cookie) cutter. Arrange on the sheets and cook for 10 minutes.

5 Beat the egg white and brush gently over the biscuits (cookies). Sprinkle with caster sugar and return to the oven for 10 minutes until golden. Transfer to a wire rack to cool.

Energy 116kcal/485kJ; Protein 1.5g; Carbohydrate 15.4g, of which sugars 7g; Fat 5.7g, of which saturates 3.4g; Cholesterol 24mg; Calcium 25mg; Fibre 0.4g; Sodium 46mg

Shrewsbury cakes

Despite their traditional name, these are crisp, lemony shortbread biscuits with fluted edges, which have been made and sold in the town of Shrewsbury since the 17th century.

Makes about 20

115g/4oz/½ cup soft butter

140g/5oz/¾ cup caster (superfine) sugar

2 egg yolks

225g/8oz/2 cups plain (all-purpose) flour

finely grated rind of 1 lemon

1 Preheat the oven to 180°C/350°F/ Gas 4. Line two baking sheets with baking parchment.

2 In a mixing bowl, beat the softened butter with the sugar until pale, light and fluffy. Beat in each of the egg yolks one at a time, beating thoroughly after each addition.

3 Sift the flour over the top and add the lemon rind. Stir in and then gather up the mixture to make a stiff dough.

4 Knead the dough lightly on a floured surface then roll it out to about 5mm/ ¼in thick. Using a 7.5cm/3in pastry (cookie) cutter, cut out circles and arrange on the baking sheets.

5 Gather up the offcuts and roll out again to make more biscuits.

6 Put into the hot oven and cook for about 15 minutes, until firm to the touch and lightly browned. Transfer to a wire rack and leave to crisp up and cool completely.

Variations
• Omit the lemon rind and sift 5ml/ 1 tsp ground mixed (apple pie) spice with the flour in step 3.
• Add 25g/1oz/2 tbsp currants or raisins to the mixture in step 3.

Energy 115kcal/482kJ; Protein 1.4g; Carbohydrate 16.1g, of which sugars 7.5g; Fat 5.4g, of which saturates 3.2g; Cholesterol 32mg; Calcium 23mg; Fibre 0.4g; Sodium 37mg

Welsh honey and spice cakes

The Welsh have always enjoyed cooking with spices. These golden little cakes are fragrant with honey and cinnamon. Though their appearance is more traditional when cooked directly in a bun tin, they tend to rise higher when baked in paper cases.

3 Beat the butter with the sugar until light and fluffy. Beat in the egg yolk, then gradually add the honey.

4 With a large metal spoon and a cutting action, fold in the flour mixture plus sufficient milk to make a soft mixture that will just drop off the spoon.

5 In a separate bowl whisk the egg white until stiff peaks form. Using a large metal spoon, fold the egg white into the cake mixture.

Makes 18

250g/9oz/2 cups plain all-purpose) flour

5ml/1 tsp ground cinnamon

5ml/1 tsp bicarbonate of soda (baking soda)

125g/4½oz/½ cup butter, softened

125g/4½oz/10 tbsp soft brown sugar

1 large (US extra large) egg, separated

125g/4½oz clear honey

about 60ml/4 tbsp milk

caster (superfine) sugar for sprinkling

1 Preheat the oven to 200°C/400°F/ Gas 6. Butter the holes of a bun tin (pan) or, alternatively, line them with paper cases.

2 Sift the flour into a large mixing bowl with the cinnamon and the bicarbonate of soda.

6 Divide the mixture among the paper cases or the holes in the prepared tin. Put into the hot oven and cook for 15–20 minutes or until risen, firm to the touch and golden brown.

7 Sprinkle the tops lightly with caster sugar and leave to cool completely on a wire rack.

Energy 152kcal/639kJ; Protein 1.9g; Carbohydrate 23.6g, of which sugars 13g; Fat 6.3g, of which saturates 3.8g; Cholesterol 26mg; Calcium 30mg; Fibre 0.4g; Sodium 49mg

Irish gur cake

This spicy fruit "cake" used to be sold very cheaply by Dublin bakers, who made it with day-old bread and cakes. It is still made, now usually called "Fruit Slice", using margarine or lard rather than butter. It can be made with puff pastry, but shortcrust is more usual.

Makes 24 slices

8 slices of stale bread, or plain cake

75g/3oz/²⁄₃ cup plain (all-purpose) flour

pinch of salt

2.5ml/½ tsp baking powder

10ml/2 tsp mixed (apple pie) spice

115g/4oz/generous ½ cup granulated sugar, plus extra for sprinkling

175g/6oz/¾ cup currants or mixed dried fruit

50g/2oz/¼ cup butter, melted

1 egg, lightly beaten

milk to mix

For the shortcrust pastry

225g/8oz/2 cups plain (all-purpose) flour

2.5ml/½ tsp salt

115g/4oz/½ cup butter

1 To make the shortcrust pastry, mix together the plain flour, salt and the butter in a large mixing bowl. Using the fingertips or a pastry (cookie) cutter, rub the butter into the flour until the mixture resembles fine breadcrumbs.

2 Mix in 30–45ml/2–3 tbsp cold water and knead the mixture lightly to form a firm dough. Wrap the dough in clear film (plastic wrap) and chill in the refrigerator for 30 minutes.

3 Preheat the oven to 190°C/375°F/ Gas 5 and grease and flour a square baking tin (pan).

4 Remove the crusts from the bread and make the remainder into crumbs, or make the cake into crumbs. Put the crumbs into a mixing bowl with the flour, salt, baking powder, mixed (apple pie) spice, sugar and dried fruit. Mix well to combine.

5 Add the butter and egg to the dry ingredients with enough milk to make a fairly stiff, spreadable mixture.

6 Roll out the pastry and, using the baking tin as a guide, cut out one piece to make the lid. Use the rest, re-rolled as necessary, to line the base of the tin. Spread the pastry with the mixture then cover with the pastry lid.

7 Make diagonal slashes across the top. Bake in the oven for 50–60 minutes, or until golden. Sprinkle with sugar and leave to cool in the tin. Cut into slices.

Per slice Energy 156Kcal/656kJ; Protein 2.4g; Carbohydrate 24.2g, of which sugars 10.5g; Fat 6.2g, of which saturates 3.7g; Cholesterol 23mg; Calcium 43mg; Fibre 0.8g; Sodium 128mg

English honey cake

The earliest form of sweetener, honey has been an important ingredient in cooking throughout history, and there have been lots of different recipes baked through the centuries. Its flavour changes subtly according to the type of honey used.

Makes 16 squares

175g/6oz/¾ cup butter

175g/6oz/¾ cup clear honey

115g/4oz/½ cup soft brown sugar

2 eggs, lightly beaten

15–30ml/1–2 tbsp milk

225g/8oz/2 cups self-raising (self-rising) flour

1 Grease and line a 23cm/9in square cake tin (pan) with baking parchment. Preheat the oven to 180°C/350°F/Gas 4.

2 Gently heat the butter, honey and sugar, stirring frequently until well amalgamated. Set aside and leave to cool slightly.

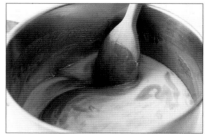

3 Beat the eggs and milk into the cooled mixture. Sift the flour over the top, stir in and beat well until smooth.

4 Tip the mixture into the prepared tin, levelling the surface. Put into the hot oven and cook for about 30 minutes until well risen, golden brown and firm to the touch.

5 Leave the cake to cool in the tin for 20 minutes then turn out, leaving the lining paper in place, onto a wire rack and leave to cool completely. Peel off the paper and cut the cake into 16 squares.

Variation Add 5ml/1tsp ground cinnamon or grated nutmeg to the flour in step 3.

Energy 152kcal/639kJ; Protein 1.9g; Carbohydrate 23.5g, of which sugars 13g; Fat 6.3g, of which saturates 3.8g; Cholesterol 26mg; Calcium 30mg; Fibre 0.4g; Sodium 49mg

Yorkshire parkin

This moist ginger cake, often eaten on Hallowe'en, probably developed in Yorkshire during the Industrial Revolution, and is particularly associated with Leeds, although there are versions in Lancashire. A fresh batch was sometimes eaten hot with apple sauce.

Makes 16–20 squares

300ml/½ pint/1¼ cups milk

225g/8oz/1 cup golden (corn) syrup

225g/8oz/¾ cup black treacle (molasses)

115g/4oz/½ cup butter

50g/2oz/scant ¼ cup dark brown sugar

450g/1lb/4 cups plain (all-purpose) flour

2.5ml/½ tsp bicarbonate of soda (baking soda)

7.5ml/1½ tsp ground ginger

350g/12oz/4 cups medium oatmeal

1 egg, beaten

icing (confectioner's) sugar, to dust

1 Preheat the oven to 180°C/350°F/ Gas 4. Gently heat together the milk, syrup, treacle, butter and sugar, stirring until smooth; do not boil.

2 Grease a 20cm/8in square cake tin (pan) and line the base and sides with baking parchment.

3 Sift the flour and bicarbonate of soda into a large mixing bowl.

4 Add the ginger and oatmeal to the flour, make a well in the centre and add the egg, then the warmed mixture, stirring to make a smooth batter.

5 Pour the batter into the tin and bake for about 45 minutes, until firm to the touch. Cool slightly in the tin, then turn out onto a wire rack to cool completely. Cut into squares and dust with icing sugar.

Cook's tip The flavour and texture of the cake improves if it is wrapped in foil and stored in an airtight container for several days.

Energy 273kcal/1152kJ; Protein 5.3g; Carbohydrate 50g, of which sugars 20.1g; Fat 7.1g, of which saturates 3.3g; Cholesterol 23mg; Calcium 127mg; Fibre 1.9g; Sodium 102mg

Almond and raspberry Swiss roll

This light and airy whisked sponge cake is rolled up with a rich and mouthwatering filling of fresh raspberries and cream, making a perfect treat for tea in the garden in summer. It is also be delicious filled with other soft fruits, such as strawberries or blackcurrants.

Serves 8

butter, for greasing

150g/5oz/1¼ cups plain (all-purpose) flour

4 eggs

115g/4oz/½ cup caster (superfine) sugar, plus extra for sprinkling

25g/1oz/2 tbsp ground almonds

225ml/8fl oz/1 cup double (heavy) cream

275g/10oz/1½ cups fresh raspberries

flaked (sliced) almonds, to decorate

1 Preheat the oven to 200°C/400°F/ Gas 6. Grease a 33 x 23cm/13 x 9in Swiss roll tin (jelly roll pan) and line with baking parchment, cut to fit. Sift the flour and set aside.

2 Beat the eggs and sugar with an electric mixer for about 10 minutes until the mixture is thick and pale. Sift the pre-sifted flour over the mixture and gently fold in with a metal spoon, together with the ground almonds.

3 Spoon the mixture into the prepared tin and bake for 10–12 minutes, until the sponge is well risen and springy to the touch.

4 Sprinkle a sheet of baking parchment liberally with caster sugar. Turn out the cake onto the paper, and leave to cool with the tin still in place.

5 Lift the tin off the cooled cake and carefully peel away the lining paper from the base of the cake.

6 Whip the cream until it holds its shape. Fold in 250g/8oz/1¼ cups of the raspberries, and spread over the cooled cake, leaving a narrow border.

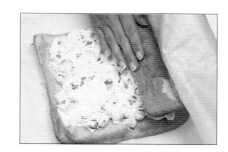

7 Carefully roll up the cake from a narrow end, using the paper to lift the sponge. Sprinkle with caster sugar. Serve decorated with the remaining raspberries and toasted flaked almonds.

Cook's tip This is a cake that needs to be eaten straight away, as cream and fresh fruit do not keep. Fill with raspberry jam or lemon curd instead of cream if you want it to last longer.

Energy 271kcal/1127kJ; Protein 4.7g; Carbohydrate 16.7g, of which sugars 11.9g; Fat 21.1g, of which saturates 11.2g; Cholesterol 114mg; Calcium 56mg; Fibre 1.2g; Sodium 35mg

West Country apple cake

The combination of sweet and tart flavours of this fruity cake is refreshing, and the cooking apples help to produce a deliciously moist cake, though you can use eating apples if you prefer for a sweeter result, or a mixture of the two.

Makes an 18cm/7in round cake

225g/8oz cooking apples, peeled, cored and chopped

juice of ½ lemon

225g/8oz/2 cups plain (all-purpose) flour

7.5ml/1½ tsp baking powder

115g/4oz/½ cup butter, cut into small pieces

165g/5½oz/scant 1 cup soft light brown sugar

1 egg, beaten

about 30–45ml/2–3 tbsp milk

2.5ml/½ tsp ground cinnamon

1 Grease and line an 18cm/7in round cake tin (pan) with baking parchment. Preheat the oven to 180°C/350°F/Gas 4.

2 Toss the apples with the lemon juice. Sift the flour and baking powder. Rub in the butter until the mixture resembles fine crumbs. Stir in 115g/4oz/¾ cup of the sugar, the apples and the egg.

3 Add enough milk to give a soft dropping consistency. Transfer to the prepared tin. Mix together the remaining sugar and the cinnamon and sprinkle over the cake mixture. Put into the hot oven and cook for 45–50 minutes, until firm to the touch. Leave to cool in the tin for 10 minutes, then transfer to a wire rack to cool.

Energy 3810kcal/16031kJ; Protein 35.7g; Carbohydrate 596.6g, of which sugars 451.9g; Fat 159g, of which saturates 68.4g; Cholesterol 260mg; Calcium 617mg; Fibre 16.4g; Sodium 839mg

Victoria sponge

This light cake was named in honour of Queen Victoria. Often referred to as a Victoria sandwich, it is based on equal quantities of fat, sugar, eggs and flour. It has come to be regarded as the classic English cake and remains a favourite for village show competitions.

Serves 6–8

3 large eggs

few drops of vanilla extract

175g/6oz/¾ cup soft butter

175g/6oz/¾ cup caster (superfine) sugar

175g/6oz/1½ cups self-raising (self-rising) flour

about 60ml/4 tbsp jam

icing (confectioner's) sugar, to dust

1 Preheat the oven to 180°C/350°F/ Gas 4. Butter two 20cm/8in sandwich tins (layer pans) and line the bases of each with baking parchment.

2 Lightly beat the eggs with the vanilla extract. In a large mixing bowl, whisk the butter with the sugar until the mixture is pale, light and fluffy.

3 Gradually add the eggs, beating well after each addition. Sift the flour over the top and, using a metal spoon, fold in lightly until the mixture is smooth.

4 Divide the mixture between the prepared tins. Cook for 20 minutes until golden and firm to the touch.

5 Leave the cakes to cool in the tins for a few minutes then carefully turn out on to a wire rack. Remove the paper and leave to cool completely.

6 When the cakes are cold, sandwich the two halves together with plenty of jam. Finally, sift a little icing sugar over the top.

Variations
• Instead of vanilla extract, beat a little finely grated lemon zest into the butter and sugar mixture in step 2. Sandwich the cake together with lemon curd.
• For a cream cake, sandwich with a thin layer of strawberry jam and a thick layer of whipped cream, topped with sliced fresh strawberries. Decorate the top of the cake with whipped cream and extra strawberries.

Energy 368kcal/1543kJ; Protein 4.6g; Carbohydrate 44.7g, of which sugars 28.5g; Fat 20.3g, of which saturates 12g; Cholesterol 118mg; Calcium 104mg; Fibre 0.7g; Sodium 241mg

Chocolate cake

The first chocolate arrived in England in the 1500s, and the 17th century saw the opening of expensive chocolate houses, which were frequented by the rich and famous. Today, chocolate cake is a staple of many a British tea table.

Serves 10–12

225g/8oz/2 cups plain (all-purpose) flour

5ml/1 tsp bicarbonate of soda (baking soda)

50g/2oz/½ cup (unsweetened) cocoa powder

125g/4½oz/9 tbsp soft butter

250g/9oz/1¼ cups caster (superfine) sugar

3 eggs, beaten

250ml/8fl oz/1 cup buttermilk

For the chocolate buttercream

175g/6oz/1½ cups icing (confectioner's) sugar

115g/4oz/½ cup soft unsalted butter

few drops of vanilla extract

50g/2oz dark chocolate

1 Butter two 20cm/8in sandwich tins (pans) and line the bases with baking parchment. Preheat the oven to 180°C/350°F/Gas 4. Sift the flour with the bicarbonate of soda and cocoa.

2 Beat the butter and sugar until light and fluffy. Gradually beat in the eggs. Add the flour and buttermilk, mix well.

3 Spoon into the prepared tins. Place into the hot oven and cook for 30–35 minutes until firm to the touch. Turn out of the tins, peel off the paper and leave on a wire rack to cool completely.

4 To make the chocolate buttercream, sift the icing sugar into a bowl. In a separate bowl, beat the butter until very soft and creamy.

5 Beat in half the sifted icing sugar until smooth and light. Gradually beat in the remaining sugar and the vanilla extract. Break the chocolate into squares. Melt in a bowl over a pan of hot water or in a microwave oven on low.

6 Mix the melted chocolate into the buttercream. Use half to sandwich the cakes together, and the rest on the top.

Energy 430kcal/1790kJ; Protein 7.8g; Carbohydrate 29.5g, of which sugars 28.8g; Fat 32.1g, of which saturates 13.6g; Cholesterol 96mg; Calcium 92mg; Fibre 1.9g; Sodium 125mg

Sponge cake with strawberries and cream

This fatless sponge is delicious in the summer, filled with soft fruit, or with the new season's jam. Have all ingredients at warm room temperature for this recipe. Unless using an electric mixer, whisk the eggs and sugar over hot water to get the required volume.

Serves 8–10

white vegetable fat (shortening), for greasing

4 eggs

115g/4oz/generous ½ cup caster (superfine) sugar, plus extra for dusting

90g/3½oz/¾ cup plain (all-purpose) flour, sifted, plus extra for dusting

icing (confectioners') sugar for dusting

For the filling

300ml/½ pint/1¼ cups double (heavy) cream

about 5ml/1 tsp icing (confectioners') sugar, sieved

450g/1lb/4 cups strawberries, washed and hulled

a little Cointreau, or other fruit liqueur (optional)

1 Preheat the oven to 190°C/375°F/ Gas 5; grease a loose-based 20cm/ 8in deep cake tin (pan) with white vegetable fat, and dust it with 5ml/ 1 tsp caster sugar mixed with 5ml/1 tsp flour. Shake off any excess sugar and flour mixture and discard.

2 Put the eggs and sugar into the bowl of an electric mixer and whisk at high speed until it is light and thick, and the mixture leaves a trail as it drops from the whisk. Alternatively, whisk by hand, or with a hand-held electric whisk; set the bowl over a pan a quarter filled with hot water and whisk until thick and creamy, then remove from the heat.

3 Sift the flour evenly over the whisked eggs and carefully fold it in with a metal spoon, mixing thoroughly but losing as little volume as possible.

4 Pour the mixture into the prepared cake tin. Level off the top and bake in the preheated oven for 25–30 minutes, or until the sponge feels springy to the touch.

5 Leave in the tin for 1–2 minutes to allow the cake to cool a little and shrink slightly from the sides, then loosen the sides gently with a knife and turn out on to a rack to cool.

6 When the sponge is completely cold, make the filling. Whip the double cream with a little icing sugar until it is stiff enough to hold its shape. Slice the sponge across the middle with a sharp knife and divide half of the cream between the two inner sides of the sandwich.

7 Select some well-shaped even-sized strawberries for the top of the cake, and then slice the rest. Lay the bottom half of the sponge on a serving plate and arrange the sliced strawberries on the cream. Sprinkle with liqueur, if using. Cover with the second half of the cake and press down gently so that it holds together.

8 Spread the remaining cream on top of the cake, and arrange the reserved strawberries, whole or halved according to size, on top. Set aside for an hour or so for the flavours to develop, then dust lightly with icing sugar and serve as a dessert.

Cook's tips
• Like all fatless sponges, this cake is best eaten on the day of baking.
• The fruits used can be varied according to availability, but strawberries and raspberries are always popular.

Energy 333Kcal/1387kJ; Protein 5.3g; Carbohydrate 27.8g, of which sugars 19.2g; Fat 23.1g, of which saturates 13.3g; Cholesterol 147mg; Calcium 65mg; Fibre 1g; Sodium 48mg

Chocolate cake with coffee icing

This easy all-in-one recipe is a favourite and can be quickly dressed up to make a cake that looks special. The coffee icing complements the rich chocolate flavour of the cake.

Makes an 18cm/7in round cake

3 large (US extra large) eggs,

175g/6oz/1½ cups self-raising (self-rising) flour

25ml/1½ tbsp cocoa powder (unsweetened)

pinch of salt

175g/6oz/¾ cup butter, softened, or easy-spread margarine

175g/6oz/¾ cup soft dark brown sugar

50g/2oz/½ cup ground almonds

For the coffee butter icing

175g/6oz/¾ cup unsalted (sweet) butter, at warm room temperature

350g/12oz/3 cups sifted icing (confectioners') sugar

30ml/2 tbsp coffee essence (extract)

whole hazelnuts or pecan nuts

1 Preheat the oven to 180°C/350°F/ Gas 4 and butter two 18cm/7in diameter sandwich tins (pans).

2 Lightly beat the eggs. Sift the flour, cocoa and salt into a mixing bowl. Cut in the butter or margarine and add the sugar, ground almonds and eggs.

Variation For a deliciously rich touch, 15–30ml/1–2 tbsp of Bailey's Irish Cream can be included in the icing – beat in with the coffee essence at the end of stage 4.

3 Beat with a wooden spoon for 2–3 minutes, until thoroughly mixed; the mixture should be smooth, with no traces of butter remaining.

4 Divide the mixture between the prepared tins and bake in the centre of the preheated oven for 25–30 minutes, or until springy to the touch. Turn out and cool on a wire rack. Meanwhile make the icing: cream the butter well, then gradually beat in the sifted icing sugar and the coffee essence.

5 When the cakes are cold, sandwich them together with some of the icing and cover the top and sides with most of the remainder.

6 Pipe the remaining icing around the top in rosettes, if you like, and decorate with whole hazelnuts or pecan nuts.

Per cake Energy 5899Kcal/24,684kJ; Protein 56.2g; Carbohydrate 691.1g, of which sugars 556.9g; Fat 343.1g, of which saturates 193.7g; Cholesterol 1.43g; Calcium 1.06g; Fibre 12.2g; Sodium 3.28g

Irish whiskey cake

This light, moist cake has the subtle flavours of lemon and cloves, rather like a hot Irish toddy – making it seem especially tempting in winter.

Makes an 18cm/7in round cake

225g/8oz/1⅓ cups sultanas (golden raisins)

grated rind of 1 lemon

150ml/¼ pint/⅔ cup Irish whiskey

175g/6oz/¾ cup butter, softened

175g/6oz/¾ cup soft brown sugar

175g/6oz/1½ cups plain (all-purpose) flour

pinch of salt

1.5ml/¼ tsp ground cloves

5ml/1 tsp baking powder

3 large (US extra large) eggs

For the icing

juice of 1 lemon

225g/8oz/2 cups icing (confectioners') sugar

crystallized lemon slices, to decorate

1 Put the sultanas and grated lemon rind into a bowl with the whiskey and leave overnight to soak.

2 Preheat the oven to 180°C/350°F/ Gas 4 and grease and base line a loose-based 18cm/7in deep cake tin (pan).

3 Cream the butter and sugar until light and fluffy. Sift the flour, salt, cloves and baking powder together into a bowl.

4 Separate the eggs, and beat the yolks into the butter and sugar one at a time, adding a little of the flour with each egg and beating well after each addition. Gradually blend in the sultana and whiskey mixture, alternating with the remaining flour. Do not overbeat at this stage.

5 Whisk the egg whites until stiff and fold them into the mixture with a metal spoon. Turn the mixture into the prepared tin and bake in the preheated oven for 1½ hours, or until well risen and springy to the touch. Turn out and cool on a rack.

6 Meanwhile, make the icing: mix the lemon juice with the sieved icing sugar and enough warm water to make a pouring consistency. Pour the icing over the cake a spoonful at a time, letting it dribble down the sides. When it has set, decorate with crystalized lemon slices.

Per cake Energy 4691Kcal/19,730kJ; Protein 48.1g; Carbohydrate 711.2g, of which sugars 577.8g; Fat 167g, of which saturates 97.1g; Cholesterol 1.06g; Calcium 735mg; Fibre 9.9g; Sodium 1.38g

Welsh boiled fruit cake

The texture of this cake is quite distinctive – moist and plump as a result of boiling the dried fruit with the butter, sugar and milk prior to baking. For special occasions replace some of the milk with sherry or brandy and arrange cherries and nuts on the surface of the uncooked cake before putting it in the oven. It makes an ideal Christmas cake, too.

Makes a 20cm/8in cake

350g/12oz/2 cups mixed dried fruit

225g/8oz/1 cup butter

225g/8oz/1 cup soft dark brown sugar

400ml/14fl oz/1⅔ cup milk

450g/1lb/4 cups self-raising (self-rising) flour

5ml/1 tsp bicarbonate of soda (baking soda)

5ml/1 tsp mixed (apple pie) spice

2 eggs, beaten

1 Preheat the oven to 160°C/325°F/ Gas 3. Lightly grease a 20cm/8in round cake tin (pan) with butter, and line it with baking parchment.

2 Put the dried fruit in a large pan and add the butter and sugar. Bring slowly to boil, stirring occasionally. When the butter has melted and the sugar has dissolved, bubble the mixture gently for about 2 minutes. Remove from the heat and cool slightly.

3 Sift the flour with the bicarbonate of soda and mixed spice. Add this and the eggs to the fruit mixture and mix together well.

4 Pour the mixture into the prepared tin and smooth the surface.

5 Bake for about 1½ hours or until firm to the touch and the cake is cooked through – a skewer inserted in the centre should come out free of sticky mixture.

6 Leave in the tin to cool for 20–30 minutes, then turn out and cool completely on a wire rack.

Per cake Energy 5150kcal/21689kJ; Protein 72.2g; Carbohydrate 796g, of which sugars 498.8g; Fat 209.1g, of which saturates 125.4g; Cholesterol 884mg; Calcium 2352mg; Fibre 20.1g; Sodium 3297mg

Welsh overnight cake

Many old recipes for cakes contained lists of ingredients with weights and proportions that were easy to remember – ideal for passing down the line from generation to generation. This one, *teisen dros nos*, has no added sugar and is at its most delicious eaten cooled on the day it is made, its crust being crisp and flaky while the inside is soft and moist.

Makes a thin 23cm/9in cake

225g/8oz/2 cups plain (all-purpose) flour

5ml/1 tsp ground cinnamon

5ml/1 tsp ground ginger

115g/4oz/½ cup butter, cut into cubes

115g/4oz/⅔ cup mixed dried fruit

2.5ml/½ tsp bicarbonate of soda (baking soda)

15ml/1 tbsp vinegar

300ml/½ pint/1¼ cups milk

1 Sift the flour and spices. Add the butter and rub in until the mixture resembles fine breadcrumbs. Stir in the dried fruit and enough milk to make a soft mix.

2 Mix the bicarbonate of soda with the vinegar and, as it froths, quickly stir it into the mixture. Cover the bowl and leave at room temperature for about 8 hours.

3 Preheat the oven to 180°C/360°F/Gas 4. Grease a shallow 23cm/9 in round cake tin (pan) and line its base with baking parchment. Spoon the cake mixture into the prepared tin and level the top.

4 Put into the hot oven and cook for about 1 hour or until firm to the touch and cooked through – a skewer inserted in the centre should come out free of sticky mixture. If the top starts to get too brown during cooking, cover it with baking parchment.

5 Leave in the tin to cool for 15–20 minutes, then turn out and cool completely on a wire rack.

Cook's tip The low-sugar content of this cake makes it ideal for serving with thin slices of crumbly cheese such as Caerphilly or Wensleydale.

Per cake Energy 2069kcal/8681kJ; Protein 34.7g; Carbohydrate 267.9g, of which sugars 96.5g; Fat 103g, of which saturates 63.6g; Cholesterol 263mg; Calcium 780mg; Fibre 9.5g; Sodium 888mg

Dundee cake

A classic Scottish fruit cake, this is made with mixed peel, dried fruit, almonds and spices. It is decorated in the traditional way, covered with whole blanched almonds. Although originally the recipe was from Scotland, this cake is popular all over the British Isles.

Serves 16–20

175g/6oz/¾ cup butter

175g/6oz/¾ cup soft light brown sugar

3 eggs

225g/8oz/2 cups plain (all-purpose) flour

10ml/2 tsp baking powder

5ml/1 tsp ground cinnamon

2.5ml/½ tsp ground cloves

1.5ml/¼ tsp freshly grated nutmeg

225g/8oz/generous 1½ cups sultanas (golden raisins)

175g/6oz/¾ cup glacé (candied) cherries

115g/4oz/⅔ cup mixed chopped (candied) peel

50g/2oz/½ cup blanched almonds, roughly chopped

grated rind of 1 lemon

30ml/2 tbsp brandy

75g/3oz/¾ cup whole blanched almonds, to decorate

Cook's tip All rich fruit cakes improve in flavour if left in a cool place for up to 3 months. Wrap the cake in baking parchment and a double layer of foil.

1 Preheat the oven to 160°C/325°F/ Gas 3. Grease and line a 20cm/8in round, deep cake tin (pan).

2 Cream the butter and sugar together in a large mixing bowl. Add the eggs, one at a time, beating thoroughly after each addition.

3 Sift the flour, baking powder and spices together. Fold into the creamed mixture alternately with the remaining ingredients. Mix until evenly blended. Transfer the mixture to the prepared tin and smooth the surface, making a dip in the centre.

4 Decorate the top by pressing the almonds in decreasing circles over the entire surface. Bake in the preheated oven for 2–2¼ hours, until a skewer inserted in the centre comes out clean.

5 Cool in the tin for 30 minutes then transfer to a wire rack to cool fully.

Energy 321kcal/1347kJ; Protein 4.7g; Carbohydrate 44.2g, of which sugars 33.3g; Fat 14.7g, of which saturates 6.4g; Cholesterol 59mg; Calcium 76mg; Fibre 1.7g; Sodium 107mg

Simnel cake

This cake dates back to medieval times, and is traditionally served at Easter, the marzipan balls on top represent the 11 faithful apostles. It is also sometimes made for Mothering Sunday, when the almond paste top is decorated with fresh or crystallized spring flowers.

Makes an 18cm/7in round cake

175g/6oz/¾ cup butter

175g/6oz/scant 1 cup soft brown sugar

3 large eggs, beaten

225g/8oz/2 cups plain (all-purpose) flour

2.5ml/½ tsp ground cinnamon

2.5ml/½ tsp freshly grated nutmeg

150g/5oz/1 cup each of currants, sultanas (golden raisins) and raisins

85g/3oz/generous ½ cup glacé (candied) cherries, quartered

85g/3oz/generous ½ cup mixed (candied) peel, chopped

grated rind of 1 large lemon

450g/1lb almond paste

1 egg white, lightly beaten

1 Grease and line an 18cm/7in round cake tin (pan) and tie a double layer of brown paper round the outside.

2 Beat the butter and sugar until pale and fluffy, then gradually beat in the eggs. Lightly fold in the flour, spices, dried fruits, cherries, mixed peel and lemon rind.

3 Preheat the oven to 160°C/325°F/ Gas 3. Roll half the almond paste to a 16cm/6½in circle on a surface dusted with caster sugar.

4 Spoon half the cake mixture into the prepared tin and place the circle of almond paste on top of the mixture. Spoon the remaining cake mixture on top and level the surface.

5 Put the cake into the hot oven and cook for 1 hour. Reduce the oven temperature to 150°C/300°F/Gas 2 and cook for another 2 hours. Leave to cool for 1 hour in the tin, then turn out and cool on a wire rack.

6 Brush the cake with egg white. Roll out half the remaining almond paste to a 28cm/11in circle and cover the cake. Roll the remaining paste into 11 balls and attach with egg white. Brush the top of the cake with more egg white and grill (broil) until lightly browned.

Energy 8108kcal/34162kJ; Protein 104g; Carbohydrate 1323.3g, of which sugars 1113.8g; Fat 303.9g, of which saturates 132.5g; Cholesterol 1442mg; Calcium 1557mg; Fibre 33.4g; Sodium 2080mg

Scottish black bun

This is a quintessential Scottish sweetmeat, eaten with a nip or two of whisky at the Hogmanay New Year festivities, and often given to guests on New Year's Day. It is different from most fruit cakes because it is baked in a pastry case. It should be made several weeks in advance to give it time to mature properly.

Makes 1 cake

For the pastry

225g/8oz/2 cups plain
(all-purpose) flour

115g/4oz/½ cup butter

5ml/1 tsp baking powder

cold water

For the filling

500g/1¼lb/4 cups raisins

675g/1½lb/3 cups currants

115g/4oz/1 cup
chopped almonds

175g/6oz/1½ cups plain
(all-purpose) flour

115g/4oz/generous ½ cup soft
light brown sugar

5ml/1 tsp ground allspice

2.5ml/½ tsp each ground ginger,
ground cinnamon and ground
black pepper

2.5ml/½ tsp baking powder

5ml/1 tsp cream of tartar

15ml/1 tbsp brandy

1 egg, beaten, plus extra
for glazing

about 75ml/5 tbsp milk

1 First make the pastry. Sift the plain flour into a mixing bowl. Remove the butter from the refrigerator ahead of time and dice it into small cubes. Leave it out of the refrigerator to soften well.

2 Add the cubes of butter to the flour. Rub the butter into the flour with your fingertips until it is the consistency of breadcrumbs. Add the baking powder and mix well. Then add small amounts of cold water, blending it in with a fork, until you can handle the mixture and knead it into a stiff dough.

3 On a floured surface, roll out the dough to a thin sheet. Grease a 20cm/8in loaf tin (pan) and line with the thin sheet of dough. Leave enough to cover the top of the cake.

4 Preheat the oven to 110°C/225°F/ Gas ¼. For the filling, put all the dry ingredients together in a dry warm bowl, including the ground spices and cream of tartar. Mix them together with a spoon until they are thoroughly blended.

5 Stir the brandy and egg into the dry filling mixture and add enough milk to moisten the mixture.

6 Put the filling into the prepared tin and cover with the remaining pastry.

7 Prick all over with a fork and brush with egg. Bake in the preheated oven for about 3 hours. Remove from the oven and leave to cool on a wire rack. Store in an airtight container.

Per cake Energy 1752kcal/7403kJ; Protein 25.8g; Carbohydrate 323.7g, of which sugars 241.9g; Fat 47.4g, of which saturates 18.5g; Cholesterol 115mg; Calcium 496mg; Fibre 11.4g; Sodium 324mg

Welsh shearing cake

To this day sheep shearing provides a good excuse for a rural get-together. The Welsh tradition was always to serve the buttery seed cake, *cacen gneifio,* as part of the shearers' well-earned refreshment. A similar cake would also be made during harvesting. It, too, contained caraway seeds and was aptly named threshing cake.

Makes a 20cm/8in cake

225g/8oz/2 cups plain (all-purpose) flour

5ml/1 tsp baking powder

175g/6oz/¾ cup butter, softened

175g/6oz/¾ cup caster (superfine) sugar

3 eggs, beaten

50g/2oz/⅓ cup chopped candied peel

10ml/2 tsp caraway seeds

30ml/2 tbsp milk or buttermilk

1 Preheat the oven to 180°C/350°F/ Gas 4. Lightly butter a 20cm/8 in round cake tin and line it with baking parchment. Sift the flour with the baking powder.

2 Beat the butter and sugar in a bowl until light and fluffy. Beat in the eggs, a little at a time. When everything is combined, using a metal spoon, fold in the flour mixture, mixed peel, caraway seeds and milk to make a soft mix.

3 Spoon the mixture into the prepared tin and level the surface. Put into the hot oven and cook for 1–1¼ hours or until firm to the touch and cooked through – a skewer inserted in the centre should come out clean.

4 Cool for 15 minutes, then turn out on to a wire rack and leave to cool completely.

Per cake Energy 3109kcal/13026kJ; Protein 43g; Carbohydrate 389.7g, of which sugars 218.3g; Fat 164.4g, of which saturates 96.6g; Cholesterol 946mg; Calcium 626mg; Fibre 9.4g; Sodium 1441mg

Old-fashioned Welsh treacle cake

This cake would have traditionally been baked on an enamel plate. rather than in a cake tin. The treacle gives it a rich colour and a deep flavour and the sight of it must have been most welcome to miners and agricultural workers when they opened their lunchbox during their well-earned meal break.

Makes a 20cm/8in cake

250g/9oz/2 cups self-raising (self-rising) flour

2.5ml/½ tsp mixed (apple pie) spice

75g/3oz/6 tbsp butter, cut into small cubes

35g/1oz/2 tbsp caster (superfine) sugar

150g/5oz/1 cup mixed dried fruit

1 egg

15ml/1 tbsp black treacle (molasses)

100ml/3½fl oz/scant ½ cup milk

1 Preheat the oven to 180°C/350°F/ Gas 5. Butter a shallow 20–23cm/ 8–9in ovenproof flan dish or baking tin (pan).

2 Sift the flour and spice into a large mixing bowl. Add the butter and, with your fingertips, rub it into the flour until the mixture resembles fine crumbs. Alternatively you could do this in a food processor. Stir in the sugar and mixed dried fruit.

Variation Use different fruit if you like: try using chopped ready-to-eat dried apricots and stem ginger, or a packet of luxury mixed dried fruit.

3 Beat the egg and, with a small whisk or a fork, stir in the treacle and then the milk. Stir the liquid into the flour to make a fairly stiff but moist consistency, adding a little extra milk if necessary.

4 Transfer the cake mixture to the prepared dish or tin with a spoon and level out the surface.

5 Bake the cake in the hot oven and cook for about 1 hour until it has risen, is firm to the touch and fully cooked through. To check if the cake is cooked, insert a small skewer in the centre – it should come out free of sticky mixture.

6 Leave the cooked treacle cake to cool completely. Serve it, cut into wedges, straight from the dish.

Per cake Energy 2089kcal/8805kJ; Protein 37.4g; Carbohydrate 343g, of which sugars 152.4g; Fat 72.8g, of which saturates 42.2g; Cholesterol 356mg; Calcium 720mg; Fibre 11.1g; Sodium 676mg

Fruit breads and breads

British cooks have devised an unrivalled repertoire of
yeast-based teabreads, filled with fruit to keep them moist,
and baked along with the bread and rolls, to be sliced and
buttered at tea times throughout the week. There is
nothing to beat home-baked bread, but when not every
kitchen had an oven, delicious bannocks and loaves
could be cooked on a bakestone over the fire.

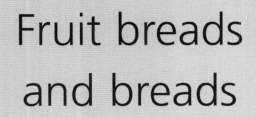

Lincolnshire plum bread

This bread, always shaped into small loaves, is particularly associated with Christmas. It is sweet and rich and is eaten with cheese, sliced and buttered or toasted like rich teacake.

Makes 2 small loaves

450g/1lb/4 cups strong white bread flour

pinch of salt

5ml/1 tsp ground cinnamon

5ml/1 tsp freshly grated nutmeg

12.5ml/2½ tsp fast-action yeast granules

60ml/4 tbsp soft light brown sugar

115g/4oz/8 tbsp butter, diced

about 100ml/3½fl oz/scant ½ cup milk

2 eggs, lightly beaten

225g/8oz/1 cup mixed dried fruit, such as currants, raisins and chopped mixed (candied) peel

1 Sift together the flour, salt and spices and stir in the yeast and sugar. Gently heat the butter and milk until just melted. Add the eggs to the flour and mix well until the mixture can be gathered into a smooth ball of dough. Cover with oiled cling film (plastic wrap) and leave in a warm place for about 1 hour until doubled in size. Grease and line two 450g/1lb loaf tins (pans) with baking parchment and preheat the oven to 190°C/375°F/Gas 5.

2 Knead the dough briefly on a lightly floured surface, working in the dried fruit evenly. Divide between the prepared tins, cover with oiled cling film and leave in a warm place for 30 minutes, or until nearly doubled in size.

3 Cook the loaves for 40 minutes, then turn them out of their tins and return to the hot oven for about 5 minutes or until they sound hollow when tapped on the base. Cool on a wire rack.

Per loaf Energy 1710kcal/7211kJ; Protein 32.2g; Carbohydrate 285.2g, of which sugars 113.7g; Fat 57.1g, of which saturates 32.5g; Cholesterol 316mg; Calcium 535mg; Fibre 9.1g; Sodium 465mg

Marmalade teabread

A cake that's perfect for serving with a cup of tea, this is especially popular in the north-west of England. The marmalade gives it a lovely flavour, at the same time keeping it moist.

Makes 1 loaf

200g/7oz/1¾ cups plain (all-purpose) flour

5ml/1 tsp baking powder

6.25ml/1¼ tsp ground cinnamon

100g/3½oz/7 tbsp butter, cut into small pieces

55g/2oz/3 tbsp soft light brown sugar

1 egg

60ml/4 tbsp chunky orange marmalade

about 45ml/3 tbsp milk

60ml/4 tbsp glacé icing, to decorate

shreds of orange and lemon rind, to decorate

1 Preheat the oven to 160°C/325°F/ Gas 3. Grease a 450g/1lb loaf tin (pan), and line with baking parchment.

2 Sift the flour, baking powder and cinnamon together, then add the butter and rub in with the fingertips until the mixture resembles fine crumbs. Stir in the sugar.

3 Beat the egg lightly in a small bowl and mix it with the marmalade and most of the milk.

4 Mix the milk mixture into the flour mixture, adding more milk if necessary to give a soft dropping consistency.

5 Transfer the mixture to the prepared tin, put into the hot oven and cook for about 1¼ hours, until the cake is firm to the touch and cooked through.

6 Leave the cake to cool for 5 minutes, then turn on to a wire rack. Carefully peel off the lining paper and leave the cake to cool completely.

7 Drizzle the glacé icing over the top of the cake and decorate with shreds of orange and lemon rind.

Energy 250kcal/1049kJ; Protein 3.5g; Carbohydrate 38g, of which sugars 19g; Fat 10.4g, of which saturates 6.2g; Cholesterol 48mg; Calcium 56mg; Fibre 0.8g; Sodium 86mg

Scottish tea loaf

It is always good to have a cake in the home, and fruit cakes are something of a tradition in Scotland. This is a simple fruit cake made by soaking dried fruits in cold tea.

Makes 1 loaf

450g/1lb/2⅔ cups mixed dried fruit

250g/9oz/generous 1 cup soft light brown sugar

200ml/7fl oz/scant 1 cup cold tea

400g/1lb/4 cups self-raising (self-rising) flour

5ml/1 tsp mixed (apple pie) spice

1 egg, beaten

1 Mix the dried fruit and sugar together, pour the cold tea over and leave to soak overnight.

2 The next day, preheat the oven to 190°C/375°F/Gas 5. Line a loaf tin (pan) with baking parchment. Add the flour and spice to the soaked fruit, stirring to combine well, then add the beaten egg and mix thoroughly.

3 Put the cake mixture in the prepared loaf tin and bake in the preheated oven for 45–50 minutes. Test with a skewer, which should come out clean. If there is any cake mixture sticking to the skewer, return the cake to the oven for a few more minutes.

Variation For something a little more special, add 10ml/2 tsp whiskey to the tea to give the loaf an aromatic and sumptuous flavour. Add more if you want a really strong flavour – some people replace the tea entirely with whiskey blended with a little water.

Per loaf Energy 1012kcal/4316kJ; Protein 15.9g; Carbohydrate 245g, of which sugars 152.1g; Fat 3.4g, of which saturates 0.6g; Cholesterol 48mg; Calcium 569mg; Fibre 6.6g; Sodium 531mg

Bara brith teabread

This Welsh loaf has become widely known as bara brith, though the method of making it is nothing like the original yeasted bread. Once the fruit has been plumped up by soaking it in tea, this version is quick to make with self-raising flour. It is eaten sliced and buttered.

Makes 1 large loaf

225g/8oz/1⅓ cups mixed dried fruit and chopped mixed (candied) peel

225ml/8fl oz/1 cup hot strong tea

225g/8oz/2 cups self-raising (self-rising) flour

5ml/1 tsp mixed (apple pie) spice

25g/1oz/2 tbsp butter

100g/3½oz/8 tbsp soft brown sugar

1 egg, lightly beaten

1 Put the fruit into a heatproof bowl and pour the hot tea over it. Cover and leave to stand at room temperature for several hours or overnight.

2 Preheat the oven to 180°C/350°F/Gas 4. Grease a 900g/2lb loaf tin (pan) and line it with baking parchment.

3 Sift the flour and the mixed spice into a large mixing bowl. Add the butter and, with your fingertips, rub it into the flour until the mixture starts to resemble fine breadcrumbs.

4 Stir in the sugar, then add the fruit and its liquid along with the beaten egg. Stir well to make a mixture with a soft consistency.

5 Transfer the mixture to the prepared loaf tin and level the surface.

6 Put into the hot oven and cook for about 1 hour or until a skewer inserted in the centre comes out clean.

7 Turn out on a wire rack and leave to cool completely.

Cook's tip The flavour of the loaf can be varied subtly by using a variety of teas – try distinctive perfumed teas such as Earl Grey.

Per loaf Energy 2024kcal/8588kJ; Protein 33.2g; Carbohydrate 432.7g, of which sugars 261.3g; Fat 29.9g, of which saturates 15g; Cholesterol 244mg; Calcium 565mg; Fibre 11.9g; Sodium 342mg

Teisen lap

A moist cake (lap means moist) with a crisp crust, teisen lap was popular with South Welsh coal miners, as it made ideal fare for their lunch boxes. Originally it would have been cooked in a Dutch oven in front of the open fire, on an enamel plate. Here, it is baked in a shallow tin.

Makes a 20–23cm/8–9in cake

250g/9oz/2 cups plain (all-purpose) flour

7.5ml/1½ tsp baking powder

pinch of salt

2.5ml/½ tsp grated nutmeg

125g/4½oz/9 tbsp butter, cut into small cubes

125g/4½oz/½ cup caster (superfine) sugar

125g/4½oz/½ cup currants or sultanas (golden raisins)

2 eggs, lightly beaten

150ml/¼ pint/⅔ cup milk or buttermilk

1 Preheat the oven to 190°C/375°F/ Gas 5. Butter a shallow 20–23cm/ 8–9in round baking tin (pan).

2 Sift the flour, baking powder, salt and nutmeg into a large mixing bowl and stir in the sugar. Add the butter and, with your fingertips, rub it into the flour until the mixture resembles fine crumbs.

3 Alternatively, do this in a food processor. Stir in the currants. Stir in the eggs with enough milk to give a mixture with a soft consistency that easily drops off the spoon.

4 Transfer the mixture to the prepared cake tin and level the surface.

5 Bake in the hot oven for 30–40 minutes, or until the cake has risen, is golden brown and cooked through. To check, a small skewer inserted in the centre should come out clean.

6 Leave in the tin for 5 minutes then turn out and cool on a wire rack.

Cook's tip Replace the currants or sultanas with chopped ready-to-eat dried apricots.

Per cake Energy 2831kcal/11903kJ; Protein 45.1g; Carbohydrate 419.3g, of which sugars 228.8g; Fat 120.1g, of which saturates 70.3g; Cholesterol 656mg; Calcium 733mg; Fibre 10.3g; Sodium 1052mg

Cornish saffron bread

This was originally made at Easter. Its beautiful yellow colour and distinctive flavour come from saffron, a precious spice from western Asia that was possibly introduced to Cornwall by Phoenicians trading in Cornish tin. Serve sliced, spread with Cornish butter.

Makes 1 loaf

good pinch of saffron threads

450g/1lb/4 cups plain (all-purpose) flour

2.5ml/½ tsp salt

50g/2oz/4 tbsp butter, diced

50g/2oz/4 tbsp lard, diced

10ml/2 tsp fast-action yeast granules

50g/2oz caster (superfine) sugar

115g/4oz/½ cup currants, raisins or sultanas (golden raisins), or a mixture

50g/2oz chopped mixed candied peel

150ml/¼ pint/⅔ cup milk

beaten egg, to glaze

1 Put the saffron in a bowl and add 150ml/¼ pint/⅔ cup boiling water. Cover and leave for several hours to allow the colour and flavour to develop.

2 Sift the flour and salt into a large bowl. Add the butter and lard and rub them into the flour until the mixture resembles fine breadcrumbs. Stir in the yeast granules, sugar, dried fruit and chopped mixed peel. Make a well in the centre.

3 Add the milk to the saffron water and warm to body heat. Pour the liquid into the flour and stir until it can be gathered into a ball. Cover with oiled plastic wrap and leave in a warm place for about 1 hour, until doubled in size.

4 Grease and line a 900g/2lb loaf tin (pan) with baking parchment. Turn the dough on to a lightly floured surface and knead gently and briefly.

5 Put the dough in the prepared tin, cover and leave in a warm place for 30 minutes until nearly doubled in size. Preheat the oven to 200°C/400°F/Gas 6.

6 Brush the top of the loaf with beaten egg and cook for 40 minutes or until risen and cooked through; cover with foil if it starts to brown too much. Leave in the tin for about 15 minutes before turning out onto a wire rack to cool.

Per loaf Energy 3041kcal/12821kJ; Protein 50.7g; Carbohydrate 516.8g, of which sugars 173.9g; Fat 99.9g, of which saturates 48.7g; Cholesterol 162mg; Calcium 1018mg; Fibre 18.5g; Sodium 541mg

Quick barm brack

This is a simplified version of the yeasted brack. The traditional Irish Hallowe'en barm brack contains all kinds of symbolic tokens, of which the best known is a ring.

Makes 2 loaves

450g/1lb/4 cups plain (all-purpose) flour

5ml/1 tsp mixed (apple pie) spice

2.5ml/½ tsp salt

2 sachets easy blend (rapid-rise) dried yeast

75g/3oz/6 tbsp soft dark brown sugar

115g/4oz/½ cup butter, melted

300ml/½ pint/1¼ cups tepid milk

1 egg, lightly beaten

375g/13oz/generous 2 cups dried mixed fruit

25g/1oz/⅓ cup chopped mixed (candied) peel

15ml/1 tbsp caster (superfine) sugar

1 Butter two 450g/1lb loaf tins (pans). Mix the flour, spice, salt, yeast and sugar in a large bowl. Mix the butter with the milk and beaten egg and add to the bowl.

2 Add the mixed fruit and peel and mix well. Turn the mixture into the loaf tins. Leave in a warm place for about 30 minutes to rise. Meanwhile, preheat the oven to 200°C/400°F/Gas 6.

3 When the dough has doubled in size, bake in the hot oven for about 45 minutes, or until the loaves begin to shrink slightly from the sides of the tins; when turned out and rapped underneath they should sound hollow.

4 Make a glaze by mixing the caster sugar with 30ml/2 tbsp boiling water. Remove the loaves from the oven and brush over with the glaze. Return them to the oven for 3 minutes, or until the tops are a rich shiny brown. Turn on to a wire rack to cool.

Per loaf Energy 2019Kcal/8524kJ; Protein 34.9g; Carbohydrate 364.6g, of which sugars 193.2g; Fat 57g, of which saturates 32.8g; Cholesterol 246mg; Calcium 704mg; Fibre 11.7g; Sodium 590mg

White soda bread

Like all Irish soda breads, this loaf is best eaten on the day of baking, but it contains a little butter helping it to keep better than fat-free versions. It is delicious with butter and jam.

Makes 1 loaf or 4 farls

450g/1lb/4 cups plain (all-purpose) flour

5ml/1 tsp bicarbonate of soda (baking soda)

7.5ml/1½ tsp cream of tartar

pinch of salt

25g/1oz/2 tbsp butter, at room temperature

1 egg whisked with 300ml/ ½ pint/1¼ cups buttermilk

1 Preheat the oven to 220°C/425°F/ Gas 7 and grease a baking sheet. Sift the dry ingredients into a big bowl. Cut in the butter and rub into the flour until the mixture resembles fine breadcrumbs.

2 Make a well in the centre and pour in the egg and buttermilk mixture. Mix thoroughly to make a soft dough.

3 Turn out on to a floured board and knead lightly for a minute or two. Shape into a round and flatten slightly. Place the loaf on the baking sheet and mark with a deep cross to help it to cook evenly. Bake in the preheated oven for about 30 minutes, until well risen and lightly browned. When cooked, it will sound hollow when tapped on the base.

4 Cool on a wire rack. If a soft crust is preferred, wrap the loaf or farls in a clean dish towel while it is cooling. Serve as soon as possible.

Cook's tip The deep cross cut into traditional round loaves ensures even cooking, and the loaf can then be easily divided into four "farls" (quarters).

Variation For fruit soda bread, a tea-bread popular in the north of Ireland, after rubbing in the butter add 15–30ml/ 1–2 tbsp sugar, 75g/3oz/½ cup each of currants and sultanas (golden raisins) and 50g/2oz/⅓ cup mixed (candied) peel. Some extra buttermilk may be needed to keep the dough soft. Allow a longer cooking time, about 45 minutes.

Per loaf Energy 1947Kcal/8242kJ; Protein 60.1g; Carbohydrate 363.9g, of which sugars 21g; Fat 38.2g, of which saturates 19g; Cholesterol 299mg; Calcium 1.03g; Fibre 13.9g; Sodium 378mg

Brown soda bread

Soda bread is best eaten on the day of baking, but it slices better if left to cool and "set" for several hours. It is delicious with good butter, farmhouse cheese and some crisp sticks of celery or a bowl of home-made soup.

Makes 1 loaf

450g/1lb/4 cups wholemeal (whole-wheat) flour

175g/6oz/1½ cups plain (all-purpose) flour

7.5ml/1½ tsp bicarbonate of soda (baking soda)

5ml/1 tsp salt

about 450ml/¾ pint/scant 2 cups buttermilk

Variation Cream of tartar can be added to the dry ingredients to provide the acid instead of buttermilk.

1 Preheat the oven to 200°C/400°F/ Gas 6, and grease a baking sheet. Combine the dry ingredients in a mixing bowl and stir in enough buttermilk to make a fairly soft dough. Turn on to a work surface dusted with wholemeal flour and knead lightly until smooth.

2 Form the dough into a circle, about 4cm/1½in thick. Lay on the baking sheet and mark a deep cross in the top with a floured knife.

3 Bake for about 45 minutes, or until the bread is browned and sounds hollow when tapped on the base. Cool on a wire rack. If a soft crust is preferred, wrap the loaf in a clean dish towel while cooling.

Above *The beautiful landscape of the river and valleys of Killorglin and Glenbeigh, County Kerry.*

Per loaf Energy 2262Kcal/9643kJ; Protein 88.5g; Carbohydrate 465.4g, of which sugars 31.4g; Fat 18.9g, of which saturates 6.5g; Cholesterol 27mg; Calcium 1.37g; Fibre 34.2g; Sodium 2.18g

Basic yeast bread

Make this dough into any shape you like, such as braids, cottage loaves or rolls. Use strong bread flour as it has a high gluten content making a more elastic dough that rises better.

Makes 4 loaves

25g/1oz fresh yeast

10ml/2 tsp caster (superfine) sugar

900ml/1½ pints/3¾ cups tepid water, or milk and water mixed

15ml/1 tbsp salt

1.3kg/3lb/12 cups strong white bread flour, preferably unbleached

50g/2oz/scant ¼ cup white vegetable fat (shortening) or 50ml/2fl oz/¼ cup vegetable oil

1 Cream the yeast and caster sugar together in a measuring jug (cup), add about 150ml/¼ pint/⅔ cup of the measured liquid and leave in a warm place for about 10 minutes to froth up.

2 Meanwhile, mix the salt into the flour and rub in the fat (if using oil, add it to the remaining liquid).

3 Using an electric mixer with a dough hook attachment or working by hand in a mixing bowl, add the yeast mixture and remaining liquid to the flour, and work it in to make a firm dough which leaves the bowl clean.

4 Knead well on a floured surface, or in the mixer, until the dough has become firm and elastic. Return to the bowl, cover lightly with a dishtowel and leave

in a warm place to rise for an hour, or until it has doubled in size. The dough will be springy and full of air. Meanwhile oil four 450g/1lb loaf tins (pans).

5 Turn the dough out on to a floured work surface and knock back (punch down), flattening it out with your knuckles to knock the air out.

6 Knead lightly back into shape, divide into four and form into loaf shapes. Place the dough in the loaf tins, pushing it down to fill into the corners, then leave to rise for another 20–30 minutes. Preheat the oven to 230°C/450°F/Gas 8.

7 When the dough has risen just above the rims of the tins, bake the loaves in the centre of the oven for 30 minutes, or until browned and shrinking a little from the sides of the tins; when turned out and rapped underneath they should sound hollow. Cool on wire racks.

Variation You can form the dough into 36 rolls and bake on greased baking trays for 15–20 minutes.

Per loaf Energy 1223Kcal/5185kJ; Protein 30.7g; Carbohydrate 256.4g, of which sugars 7.5g; Fat 15.2g, of which saturates 6.3g; Cholesterol 0mg; Calcium 457mg; Fibre 10.1g; Sodium 1.48g

Traditional bannock

This is a great Scottish loaf that makes an excellent breakfast with fresh butter and jams and jellies, a light lunch eaten with cheese and ham, a teatime staple toasted with butter and heather honey, or an accompaniment for dunking into thick soups and stews. The raisins add a slight sweetness with every other bite.

Makes 2 loaves

175g/6oz/generous ¾ cup soft light brown sugar

450ml/¾ pint/scant 2 cups milk

25g/1oz fresh yeast or 10ml/ 2 tsp dried

1kg/2¼lb/9 cups strong white bread flour

pinch of salt

115g/4oz/½ cup butter

115g/4oz/½ cup lard or white cooking fat

450g/1lb/generous 3 cups raisins

1 Preheat the oven to 220°C/425°F/ Gas 7. Dissolve 10ml/2 tsp of the sugar in a little of the milk for the glaze.

2 Warm a little milk, add the yeast with 5ml/1 tsp of sugar, mix to dissolve the sugar and yeast then leave to activate.

3 Put the flour with the salt in a warm place. Melt the butter and lard or white cooking fat with the remaining milk and keep warm. Mix the yeast mixture with the flour then add the milk and fat mixture. Mix together until a stiff dough forms. Knead for a few minutes, cover with a clean dish towel and leave in a warm place until it doubles in size.

4 Knock back (punch down) the dough then knead in the raisins and the remaining sugar. Shape into two rounds. Place on an oiled baking sheet, cover with a clean dish towel and leave to rise again in a warm place, until about twice the size.

5 Bake in the preheated oven for 10 minutes, then reduce the heat to 190°C/375°F/Gas 5 for about 30 minutes. Fifteen minutes before they are cooked, glaze the bannocks with the reserved milk and sugar mixture.

Per loaf: Energy 1924kcal/8114kJ; Protein 30.6g; Carbohydrate 330.5g, of which sugars 140g; Fat 62.5g, of which saturates 30.7g; Cholesterol 103mg; Calcium 584mg; Fibre 10g; Sodium 322mg

Bere bannocks

Beremeal is a northern barley that grows well on Orkney, and you can still buy bannocks there made from it. If you can't get beremeal, ordinary barley flour will do instead. Scottish bannocks were traditionally made on a girdle – a griddle – but baking them in the oven works very well. They make an excellent accompaniment to cheese.

Serves 6

225g/8oz/2 cups beremeal flour

50g/2oz/½ cup plain (all-purpose) flour

5ml/1 tsp cream of tartar

2.5ml/½ tsp salt

5ml/1 tsp bicarbonate of soda (baking soda)

250ml/8fl oz/1 cup buttermilk or natural (plain) yogurt

1 Preheat the oven to 180°C/350°F/Gas 4. Mix the beremeal flour, plain flour, cream of tartar and salt together in a bowl.

2 Mix the bicarbonate of soda with the buttermilk or yogurt then pour this mixture into the dry ingredients. Mix to a soft dough like a scone mix.

Variation Bere bannocks are delicious if baked with a little cheese on top. Use a harder type of cheese, such as a good mature cheddar or Bishop Kennedy, and grate about 50g/2oz/½ cup over the surface before you put it into the oven to bake. The result is very tasty hot or cold for breakfast or lunch.

3 Turn the dough out on to a floured surface and press down with your hands to make the whole dough about 1cm/½in thick.

4 Cut the dough into six segments and place on an oiled baking sheet. Bake in the oven for about 15 minutes, or until lightly browned.

Per bannock Energy 280kcal/1192kJ; Protein 8.8g; Carbohydrate 61.4g, of which sugars 4.9g; Fat 1.8g, of which saturates 0.4g; Cholesterol 1mg; Calcium 148mg; Fibre 0.4g; Sodium 54mg

Scottish morning rolls

These rolls are best served warm, as soon as they are baked. In Scotland they are a firm favourite for breakfast with a fried egg and bacon. They also go very well with a pat of fresh butter and homemade jams and jellies.

Makes 10

450g/1lb/4 cups unbleached plain (all-purpose) white flour, plus extra for dusting

10ml/2 tsp salt

20g/¾oz fresh yeast

150ml/¼ pint/⅔ cup lukewarm milk, plus extra for glazing

150ml/¼ pint/⅔ cup lukewarm water

1 Grease two baking sheets. Sift the flour and salt together into a large bowl and make a well in the centre. Mix the yeast with the milk, then mix in the water. Stir to dissolve. Add the yeast mixture to the centre of the flour and mix together to form a soft dough.

2 Knead the dough lightly then cover with lightly oiled clear film (plastic wrap) and leave to rise in a warm place for 1 hour, or until doubled in size. Turn the dough out on to a floured surface and knock back (punch down).

3 Divide the dough into 10 equal pieces. Knead each roll lightly and, using a rolling pin, shape each piece to a flat 10 x 7.5cm/4 x 3in oval or a flat 9cm/3½in round.

4 Transfer the rolls to the prepared baking sheets and cover with oiled clear film. Leave to rise in a warm place for about 30 minutes. Meanwhile, preheat the oven to 200°C/400°F/Gas 6.

5 Remove the clear film – the rolls should have risen slightly. Press each roll in the centre with your three middle fingers to equalize the air bubbles and to help prevent blistering.

6 Brush with milk and dust with flour. Bake for 15–20 minutes, or until lightly browned. As soon as you have taken the rolls out of the oven, dust with more flour and cool slightly on a wire rack. Serve warm.

Per roll Energy 160kcal/682kJ; Protein 4.7g; Carbohydrate 35.7g, of which sugars 1.4g; Fat 0.8g, of which saturates 0.3g; Cholesterol 1mg; Calcium 81mg; Fibre 1.4g; Sodium 401mg

Welsh bakestone bread

A loaf of bread that is cooked on the hob! The finished loaf has a distinctive appearance with a soft texture and scorched crust. If you have a bread machine, use it on a short programme to make the dough and then continue with steps 3–7.

Makes 1 loaf

500g/1lb 2oz/4¼ cups plain (all-purpose) flour

5ml/1 tsp fine sea salt

5ml/1 tsp sugar

7.5ml/1½ tsp easy-blend (rapid-rise) yeast

150ml/¼ pint/⅔ cup milk

15g/½oz/1 tbsp butter, cut into small pieces

5ml/1 tsp oil

1 Put the flour into a large bowl and add the salt, sugar and yeast. Combine the milk with 150ml/¼ pint/⅔ cup water and add the butter. Heat gently until the liquid is lukewarm when tested with your little finger. Stir the liquid into the flour to make a ragged mixture, then gather it together to make a dough ball.

2 Tip the dough on to a lightly floured surface and knead it until smooth, firm and elastic. Then put the oil in a large bowl and turn the dough in it until it is lightly coated. Cover the dough with cling film (plastic wrap) or a damp tea towel and leave to rise for about 1½ hours, or until just about doubled in size.

3 Tip the dough out on to a lightly floured surface and knead (gently this time) just until the dough becomes smooth – it will be soft and stretchy. On the same floured surface and using your hands or a rolling pin, press the dough into a rough circle measuring about 20cm/8in in diameter and 2cm/¾in thick. Leave to stand for 15 minutes to allow the dough to relax.

4 Meanwhile, heat a bakestone or heavy frying pan over a medium heat.

5 Using a wide spatula and your hands, lift the dough on to the warm surface and leave it to cook gently for 20 minutes.

6 Turn the bread over – it may sink, but will soon start rising again. Gently cook the second side for about 20 minutes. The top and bottom crusts should be firm and browned while the sides remain pale. When the sides are pressed with the fingers, they should feel softly firm.

7 Leave to cool on a wire rack.

Per loaf Energy 1928kcal/8179kJ; Protein 52.2g; Carbohydrate 399.8g, of which sugars 18.8g; Fat 24.4g, of which saturates 10.8g; Cholesterol 41mg; Calcium 885mg; Fibre 15.5g; Sodium 2136mg

Relishes, pickles and jams

Jams and other preserves have been part of the British culinary heritage for centuries, allowing the flavours and goodness of abundant summer fruits to be captured to add zest to winter meals. As well as orchard fruits and summer crops, wild berries gathered from hedgerows and woodlands make some of the finest pickles, and tangy chutneys are perfect accompaniments for English cheeses.

Scottish cranberry and red onion relish

This wine-enriched relish is perfect for serving with hot roast game at a celebratory meal.
It is also good served with cold meats or stirred into a beef or game casserole for a touch
of sweetness. It can be made several months in advance of any festive season.

Makes about 900g/2lb

450g/1lb small red onions

30ml/2 tbsp olive oil

225g/8oz/generous 1 cup soft light
brown sugar

450g/1lb/4 cups cranberries

120ml/4fl oz/½ cup red wine vinegar

120ml/4fl oz/½ cup red wine

15ml/1 tbsp yellow mustard seeds

2.5ml/½ tsp ground ginger

30ml/2 tbsp orange liqueur or port

salt and ground black pepper

1 Halve the red onions and slice them
very thinly. Heat the oil in a large pan,
add the onions and cook over a very
low heat for about 15 minutes, stirring
occasionally, until softened. Add 30ml/
2 tbsp of the sugar and cook for a
further 5 minutes, or until the onions
are brown and caramelized.

2 Meanwhile, put the cranberries in a
pan with the remaining sugar, and add
the vinegar, red wine, mustard seeds
and ginger. Stir in thoroughly and heat
gently, stirring continuously, until the
sugar has dissolved, then cover and
bring to the boil.

3 Simmer the relish for 12–15 minutes
then add the caramelized onions.
Stir them into the mixture. Increase the
heat slightly and cook uncovered for a
further 10 minutes, stirring the mixture
frequently, until well reduced and
nicely thickened.

4 Remove the pan from the heat then
season to taste with salt and ground
black pepper. Allow to cool completely
in the pan before pouring.

5 Transfer the relish to warmed
sterilized jars. Spoon a little of the
orange liqueur or port over the top of
each, then cover and seal. This relish
can be stored for up to 6 months.
Store in the refrigerator once opened
and use within 1 month.

Variation Redcurrants make a very
good substitute for cranberries in this
recipe. They produce a relish with a
lovely flavour and pretty colour.

Per batch Energy 1532kcal/6486kJ; Protein 8g; Carbohydrate 314.6g, of which sugars 304.2g; Fat 23.3g, of which saturates 3.1g; Cholesterol 0mg; Calcium 259mg; Fibre 13.5g; Sodium 46mg

Scottish pear and walnut chutney

This chutney recipe is ideal for using up hard windfall pears. Its mellow flavour is well suited to being brought out after dinner with a lovely selection of strong Scottish cheeses served with freshly made oatcakes or a warm traditional bannock.

Makes about 1.8kg/4lb

1.2kg/2½lb firm pears

225g/8oz cooking apples

225g/8oz onions

450ml/¾ pint/scant 2 cups cider vinegar

175g/6oz/generous 1 cup sultanas (golden raisins)

finely grated rind and juice of 1 orange

400g/14oz/2 cups granulated white sugar

115g/4oz/1 cup walnuts, roughly chopped

2.5ml/½ tsp ground cinnamon

1 Peel and core the fruit, then chop into 2.5cm/1in chunks. Peel and quarter the onions, then chop into pieces the same size as the fruit chunks. Place in a large preserving pan with the vinegar.

2 Slowly bring to the boil, then reduce the heat and simmer for 40 minutes, until the apples, pears and onions are tender, stirring the mixture occasionally.

3 Meanwhile, put the sultanas in a small bowl, pour over the orange juice and leave to soak.

4 Add the orange rind, sultanas and orange juice, and the sugar to the pan. Heat gently, stirring continuously, until the sugar has completely dissolved, then leave to simmer for 30–40 minutes, or until the chutney is thick and no excess liquid remains. Stir frequently towards the end of cooking to prevent the chutney from sticking to the base of the pan.

5 Gently toast the walnuts in a non-stick pan over a low heat for 5 minutes, stirring frequently, until lightly coloured. Stir the nuts into the chutney with the ground cinnamon.

6 Spoon the chutney into warmed sterilized jars, cover and seal. Store in a cool, dark place and leave to mature for at least 1 month. Use within 1 year.

Per batch Energy 3506kcal/14818kJ; Protein 30.9g; Carbohydrate 705.4g, of which sugars 699.5g; Fat 81.4g, of which saturates 6.4g; Cholesterol 0mg; Calcium 634mg; Fibre 40.7g; Sodium 118mg

Tomato chutney

This spicy and dark, sweet-sour chutney is delicious served with a selection of well-flavoured cheeses and crackers, oatcakes or bread. It is also popular in sandwiches and chunky lunchtime rolls packed with cold roast meats such as ham, turkey, tongue or lamb. Use it also as a condiment or table sauce for meats.

Makes about 1.8kg/4lb

900g/2lb tomatoes, skinned

225g/8oz/1½ cups raisins

225g/8oz onions, chopped

225g/8oz/generous 1 cup caster (superfine) sugar

600ml/1 pint/2½ cups malt vinegar

Variations
• Dried dates may be used in place of the raisins. Stone (pit) and chop them into small pieces. You can also buy stoned cooking dates that have been compressed in a block and these will need chopping finely.
• Red wine vinegar or sherry vinegar may be used in place of the malt vinegar, making a more delicate flavour.

1 Chop the tomatoes roughly and place in a preserving pan. Add the raisins, onions and caster sugar.

2 Pour the vinegar into the pan and bring the mixture to the boil over a medium heat. Reduce the heat and simmer for 2 hours, uncovered, until soft and thickened.

3 Transfer the chutney to warmed sterilized jars. Top with waxed discs to prevent moulds from growing. Use good airtight lids, especially if you mean to store for a long period. Store in a cool, dark place and leave to mature for at least 1 month before use.

Cook's tip The chutney will keep unopened for up to 1 year if properly airtight and stored in a cool place. Once the jars have been opened, store in the refrigerator and use within 1 month.

Per batch Energy 1733kcal/7385kJ; Protein 14.9g; Carbohydrate 436.7g, of which sugars 431.6g; Fat 4.1g, of which saturates 0.9g; Cholesterol 0mg; Calcium 342mg; Fibre 16.6g; Sodium 236mg

Mushroom sauce

This sauce is ideal as an addition to soups and stews and can be added to meat and game sauces for an extra boost of woodland flavour. You can use either wild or cultivated mushrooms for this recipe. Traditionally it would have been made in large quantities when the wild mushrooms were available, and then stored.

Makes 150ml/¼ pint/¾ cup

450g/1lb mushrooms

15ml/1 tbsp sea salt

For the spice mix

3 garlic cloves, chopped

2 red chillies, seeded and chopped

5ml/1 tsp ground allspice

2.5ml/½ tsp freshly grated nutmeg

2.5ml/½ tsp ground ginger

300ml/½ pint/1¼ cups red wine

1 Roughly chop the mushrooms and place in a large ovenproof pan, sprinkling the salt on as you go.

2 Leave, covered in clear film (plastic wrap), for 3 days to exude the juices, giving them a press occasionally.

3 Preheat the oven to 110°C/225°F/ Gas 2. Heat the pan of mushrooms in the oven for 3 hours to get the last of the moisture out.

Cook's tip The sauce will keep for a few months unopened. Once opened keep in the refrigerator and use within 1 month.

4 Strain the mushrooms. Measure the quantity of strained mushroom liquid: for every 1 litre/1¾ pints/4 cups of liquid, allow one batch of the spice mix listed in the ingredients including the wine.

5 Add the spices and wine to the mushroom liquid and bring to the boil. Return to the oven for 2–3 hours. Strain the sauce and pour into warmed sterilized jars or bottles. Use as required to flavour sauces and stews.

Per batch Energy 321kcal/1344kJ; Protein 16.5g; Carbohydrate 4.2g, of which sugars 2.4g; Fat 4.5g, of which saturates 0.9g; Cholesterol 0mg; Calcium 75mg; Fibre 9.9g; Sodium 66mg

Apple and sultana chutney

Use wine or cider vinegar for this chutney to give a subtle and mellow flavour. The chutney is perfect served with farmhouse cheese.

Makes about 900g/2lb

350g/12oz cooking apples, peeled, cored and chopped

115g/4oz/⅔ cup sultanas (golden raisins)

50g/2oz onion, finely chopped

25g/1oz/¼ cup almonds, blanched and chopped

5ml/1 tsp white peppercorns

2.5ml/½ tsp coriander seeds

175g/6oz/scant 1 cup sugar

10ml/2 tsp salt

5ml/1 tsp ground ginger

450ml/¾ pint/scant 2 cups cider vinegar

1.5ml/¼ tsp cayenne pepper

red chillies (optional)

1 Tie the peppercorns and coriander seeds in muslin (cheesecloth), using a long piece of string, and then tie to the handle of a preserving pan or stainless steel pan.

2 Put the sugar, salt, ground ginger and vinegar into the pan, with the cayenne pepper to taste. Heat gently, stirring, until the sugar has completely dissolved.

3 Add the fruit, onions and almonds to the pan. Bring to the boil and simmer for 1½–2 hours, or until most of the liquid has evaporated.

4 Spoon into warmed, sterilized jars and place one chilli in each jar, if using. Leave until cold, then cover, seal and label. Store in a cool dark place. The chutney is best left for a month, and will keep for at least 6 months.

Per batch Energy 1299Kcal/5525kJ; Protein 10.9g; Carbohydrate 299.5g, of which sugars 297.7g; Fat 14.9g, of which saturates 1.1g; Cholesterol 0mg; Calcium 254mg; Fibre 10.4g; Sodium 3.97g

Garden jam

Soft fruit is widely grown in Irish gardens and, after the first flush of early fruit is over, much of it is used for preserves, including this useful mixed fruit jam.

Makes about 3.6kg/8lb

450g/1lb/4 cups blackcurrants (stalks removed)

450g/1lb/4 cups blackberries, or whitecurrants or redcurrants

450g/1lb/2⅔ cups raspberries or loganberries

450g/1lb/4 cups strawberries

1.8kg/4lb/9 cups granulated sugar, warmed

Cook's tip To reduce the risk of mould forming during storage, cover and seal home-made preserves while they are either very hot or when absolutely cold – if covered while they are lukewarm, condensation will form and a layer of mould will grow on the surface.

1 Put the blackcurrants into a large preserving pan and add 150ml/¼ pint/⅔ cup water. Bring to the boil and simmer until almost cooked. Add the rest of the fruit and simmer gently, stirring occasionally, for about 10 minutes, or until the fruit is just soft.

2 Add the warm sugar to the pan and stir over a gentle heat until it is completely dissolved.

3 Bring to the boil and boil hard until setting point is reached. To test, put a spoonful of jam on to a cold saucer. Cool slightly, then push the surface. It is ready if a skin has formed. If not, boil for longer and keep testing until it sets.

4 Remove any scum from the jam and pour into sterilized, warm jars. Cover and seal. Store in a cool, dark place for up to 6 months.

Per batch Energy 7583Kcal/32,328kJ; Protein 23.9g; Carbohydrate 1991.7g, of which sugars 1991.7g; Fat 1.4g, of which saturates 0g; Cholesterol 0mg; Calcium 1.44g; Fibre 31.1g; Sodium 203mg

Bramble jam

Blackberrying is a much-loved British recreation and leads to a range of culinary delights too, including this jam. Serve with hot buttered toast, or scones hot from the oven and a dollop of thick clotted cream for a delicious teatime treat.

Makes 3.6kg/8lb

2.75kg/6lb/13¾ cups granulated white sugar

2.75kg/6lb/16 cups blackberries

juice of 2 lemons

150ml/¼ pint/⅔ cup water

1 Put the sugar to warm either in a low oven or in a pan over a low heat.

2 Wash the blackberries and place in a large pan with the lemon juice and water. Bring to the boil and simmer for about 5 minutes.

3 Stir in the sugar and bring back to the boil then boil rapidly. You will know when setting point is achieved as a spoonful of jam put on a plate and allowed to cool slightly will wrinkle when pressed. Ladle into warmed sterilized jam jars and seal immediately.

Cook's tip The heating of the sugar in advance helps speed up the actual jam-making process and gives a brighter, more intense flavour.

Per batch Energy 12570kcal/53550kJ; Protein 42g; Carbohydrate 3288g, of which sugars 3288g; Fat 6g, of which saturates 0g; Cholesterol 0mg; Calcium 2820mg; Fibre 93g; Sodium 240mg

Scottish damson jam

Dark, plump damsons used only to be found growing in the wild, but today they are available commercially. They produce a deeply coloured and richly flavoured jam that makes a delicious treat spread on toasted Scotch pancakes or warm crumpets at teatime.

Makes about 2kg/4½lb

1kg/2¼lb damsons or wild plums

400ml/14fl oz/1⅔ cups water

1kg/2¼lb/5 cups preserving or granulated white sugar, warmed

Cook's tip It is important to seal the jars as soon as you have filled them to ensure the jam remains sterile. However, you should then leave the jars to cool completely before labelling and storing them, to avoid the risk of burns.

1 Put the damsons in a preserving pan and pour in the water. Bring to the boil then reduce the heat and simmer gently until the damsons are soft. Add the sugar and stir it in thoroughly. Bring the mixture to the boil.

2 Skim off the stones (pits) as they rise to the surface. Boil to setting point (105°C/220°F). Remove from the heat, leave to cool for 10 minutes, then transfer to warmed sterilized jam jars. Seal immediately.

Per batch Energy 4300kcal/18360kJ; Protein 11g; Carbohydrate 1133g, of which sugars 1133g; Fat 1g, of which saturates 0g; Cholesterol 0mg; Calcium 660mg; Fibre 16g; Sodium 80mg

Raspberry jam

For many this is the best of all jams: it is delicious with scones and cream. Raspberries are low in pectin and acid, so they will not set firmly – but a soft set is perfect for this jam. Enjoy it lavishly smothered on scones or toasted tealoaf.

Makes about 3.1kg/7lb

1.8kg/4lb/10⅔ cups
firm raspberries

juice of 1 large lemon

1.8kg/4lb/9 cups sugar, warmed

Cook's tip To test if jam or jelly will set, put a spoonful of jam or jelly on to a cold saucer. Allow it to cool slightly and then push the surface of the jam with your finger. Setting point has been reached if a skin has formed and it wrinkles. If not, boil for a little longer and keep testing regularly until it sets; the flavour will be better if the boiling time is short.

1 Put 175g/6oz/1 cup of the raspberries into a preserving pan and crush them. Add the rest of the fruit and the lemon juice, and simmer until soft and pulpy. Add the sugar and stir until dissolved, then bring back to the boil and boil hard until setting point is reached, testing after 3–4 minutes.

2 Pour into warmed, sterilized jars. When cold, cover, seal and store in a cool, dark place for up to 6 months.

Variation For a slightly stronger flavour, 150ml/¼ pint/⅔ cup redcurrant juice can be used instead of the lemon juice.

Per batch Energy 7542kcal/32,220kJ; Protein 34.2g; Carbohydrate 1963.8g, of which sugars 1963.8g; Fat 5.4g, of which saturates 1.8g; Cholesterol 0mg; Calcium 1.40g; Fibre 45g; Sodium 162mg

Whisky marmalade

The word 'marmalade' appeared in English in the 15th century, and probably derives from the Latin word for 'quince', marmelo, which was cooked and preserved in honey by the Romans. By the 17th century the British used the term to apply to jam made with citrus fruits, and since then marmalade has been a breakfast favourite. This is a Scottish version.

Makes 3.6–4.5kg/8–10lb

1.3kg/3lb Seville (Temple) oranges

juice of 2 large lemons

2.75kg/6lb/13½ cups sugar, warmed

about 300ml/½ pint/1¼ cups whisky

1 Scrub the oranges thoroughly using a nylon brush and pick off the disc at the stalk end. Cut the oranges in half widthways and squeeze the juice, retaining the pips (seeds). Quarter the peel, cut away and reserve any thick white pith, and shred the peel – thickly or thinly depending on how you prefer the finished marmalade.

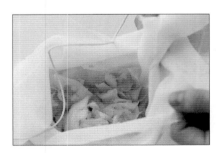

2 Cut up the reserved pith roughly and tie it up with the pips in a square of muslin (cheesecloth) using a long piece of string. Tie the bag loosely, so that water can circulate during cooking and extract the pectin. Hang the bag from the handle of the preserving pan.

3 Add the cut peel, strained juices and 3.5 litres/6 pints/15 cups water to the pan. Bring to the boil and simmer for 1½–2 hours, or until the peel is very tender (it will not soften further once the sugar has been added).

4 Lift up the bag of pith and pips and squeeze it out well between two plates over the pan to extract as much of the juices as possible as these contain valuable pectin. Add the sugar to the pan and stir over a low heat until it has completely dissolved.

5 Bring to the boil and boil hard for 15–20 minutes or until setting point is reached. To test, allow a spoon of the mixture to cool slightly, and then push the surface to see if a skin has formed. If not, boil a little longer.

6 Skim, if necessary, and leave to cool for about 15 minutes, then stir to redistribute the peel. Divide the whisky among 8–10 warmed, sterilized jars and swill it around. Using a small heatproof jug (pitcher), pour in the marmalade.

7 Cover and seal while still hot. Label when cold, and store in a cool, dark place for up to 6 months.

Per batch Energy 10,736kcal/45,734kJ; Protein 22.8g; Carbohydrate 2657.8g, of which sugars 2657.8g; Fat 1.3g, of which saturates 0g; Cholesterol 0mg; Calcium 1.74g; Fibre 15.6g; Sodium 187mg

Elderberry jelly

This country jelly uses hedgerow produce that would otherwise go to waste. It is easy to make and tastes wonderful served as an accompaniment to roast chicken or with scones.

Makes about 1.8–2.25kg/4–5lb

1.6kg/3½lb cooking apples

900g/2lb elderberries

1.2 litres/2 pints/5 cups water

450g/1lb/2¼ cups sugar to 600ml/1 pint/2½ cups juice, warmed

Cook's tip To test the jelly, put a spoonful of jam on to a cold saucer. Allow to cool slightly, and push the surface of the jam with your finger. Setting point has been reached if a skin has formed. If not, boil a little longer and keep testing until it sets.

Variation For bramble jelly follow the recipe but substitute blackberries.

1 Cut up the cooking apples roughly, without peeling the skin. Sort through the elderberries, removing any damaged berries and stalks, and wash and drain them. Put the apples into a large pan with the elderberries and add 1.2 litres/2 pints/5 cups water. Bring to the boil and cook to a pulp. Allow to cool a little, then strain the fruit mixture through a jelly bag.

2 Measure the juice and allow 450g/1lb/2¼ cups sugar for each 600ml/1 pint/2½ cups. Return the juice and sugar to the rinsed pan and heat gently until the sugar has completely dissolved. Bring to the boil. Boil hard until setting point is reached. Pour into warmed, sterilized jars. Cover, seal and store in a cool, dark place until required. The jelly will store well for 6 months.

Per batch Energy 2585Kcal/11,070kJ; Protein 15.1g; Carbohydrate 672g, of which sugars 672g; Fat 1.6g, of which saturates 0g; Cholesterol 0mg; Calcium 843mg; Fibre 58g; Sodium 86mg

Scottish rowan jelly

This astringent jelly is made from the fruit of mountain ash trees, which flourish in Scotland wherever deer run wild. It is a traditional accompaniment to game, especially venison.

Makes about 2.25kg/5lb

1.3kg/3lb/12 cups rowan berries

450g/1lb crab apples, or windfall cooking apples

450g/1lb/2¼ cups sugar per 600ml/ 1 pint/2½ cups juice, warmed

Cook's tip For a less astringent jelly, an equal quantity of apples and berries may be used, such as 900g/2lb of each.

1 Cut the rowan berries off their stalks, rinse them in a colander and put them into a preserving pan.

2 Remove any badly damaged parts from the apples before weighing them, then cut them up roughly without peeling or coring. Add the apples to the pan, with 1.2 litres/2 pints/5 cups water, which should just cover the fruit.

3 Bring to the boil and simmer for about 45 minutes, until the fruit is soft, stirring occasionally and crushing the fruit with a wooden spoon to help extract the pectin. Strain the fruit through a jelly bag or a fine sieve (strainer) into a bowl overnight.

4 Measure the juice and allow 450g/ 1lb/2¼ cups sugar per 600ml/1 pint/ 2½ cups juice. Return the juice to the rinsed preserving pan and add the measured amount of sugar.

5 Stir over a low heat until the sugar has dissolved, and then bring to the boil and boil hard for about 10 minutes until setting point is reached. To test, put a spoonful of jam on to a cold saucer. Allow to cool slightly, and then push the surface of the jam with your finger.

Setting point has been reached if a skin has formed. If not, boil a little longer and keep testing until it sets.

6 Skim, if necessary, and pour into warmed, sterilized jars. Cover, seal and store in a cool, dark place until needed. The jelly will store well for 6 months.

Variations
• The thinly peeled rind and juice of a lemon can be included for a firmer set; reduce the amount of water slightly to allow for the lemon juice.
• For sloe jelly, substitute 1.3kg/3lb sloes (black plums) for the rowan berries and use 675g/1½lb apples.

Per batch Energy 2340Kcal/9993kJ; Protein 15.8g; Carbohydrate 606.4g, of which sugars 606.4g; Fat 0.5g, of which saturates 0g; Cholesterol 0mg; Calcium 1.03g; Fibre 54g; Sodium 80mg

Sweetmeats
and drinks

The British have always had a sweet tooth, and have a long and distinguished history of home made sweets and distilated spirits. The two come together here in a collection of irresistible after-dinner treats and warming festive tipples, from heady punch and coffee laced with whiskey to an old country favourite, sloe gin. For children and drivers, there are some delicious old-fashioned soft drinks too.

Malt whisky truffles

Malt whisky has long been used to flavour Scottish dishes. Here is a new speciality, blending rich chocolate with cool cream and potent whisky for a mouthwatering end to any meal.

Makes 25–30

200g/7oz dark (bittersweet) chocolate, chopped into small pieces

150ml/¼ pint/⅔ cup double (heavy) cream

45ml/3 tbsp malt whisky

115g/4oz/1 cup icing (confectioners') sugar

cocoa powder, for coating

1 Melt the chocolate in a heatproof bowl over a pan of simmering water, stirring continuously until smooth. Allow to cool slightly.

2 Using a wire whisk, whip the cream with the whisky in a bowl until thick enough to hold its shape.

Variation
You can also make Drambuie truffles by using Drambuie instead of whisky.

3 Stir in the melted chocolate and icing sugar and leave until firm enough to handle. Dust your hands with cocoa powder and shape the mixture into bitesize balls. Coat in cocoa powder and pack into pretty cases or boxes. Store in the refrigerator for 3–4 days.

Energy 93kcal/387kJ; Protein 0.5g; Carbohydrate 10g, of which sugars 9.9g; Fat 5.5g, of which saturates 3.3g; Cholesterol 9mg; Calcium 8mg; Fibre 0.2g; Sodium 2mg

Chocolate citrus candies

Home-candied peel makes a superb sweetmeat, especially when dipped in chocolate. You can also use bought candied peel for this recipe, but make sure it is the very best quality. If you can buy it in one piece it can then be simply sliced and dipped.

Makes about 100g/4oz petits fours

1 orange or 2 lemons

25g/1oz/2 tbsp sugar

about 50g/2oz good quality plain (semisweet) chocolate

1 Using a vegetable knife, peel the rind from the fruit, without taking too much of the pith. Slice into matchsticks.

2 Blanch in boiling water for 4–5 minutes, until beginning to soften, then refresh under cold water and drain thoroughly.

3 In a small pan, heat the sugar and 30ml/2 tbsp water gently together until the sugar has dissolved. Add the strips of rind and simmer for about 8–10 minutes, or until the water has evaporated and the peel is transparent.

4 Lift out the peel with a slotted spoon and spread out on baking parchment to cool. When cold the peel can be stored in an airtight container for up to 2 days before using, if required.

5 To coat, melt the chocolate carefully in a double boiler or in a bowl over a pan of hot water. Spear each piece of peel on to a cocktail stick (toothpick) and dip one end into the chocolate.

6 To dry the candies, stick the cocktail sticks into a large potato. When the chocolate is completely dry, remove the sticks and then arrange the citrus candies attractively on a dish to serve as petits fours.

Variations
• The candied peel can be coated with caster (superfine) sugar instead of chocolate. Roll the peel in the sugar before spreading out on baking parchment to dry.
• Crystallized ginger is also good coated with melted plain chocolate: scrape off some of the rough sugar coating and dip in chocolate and dry as above.
• A mixture of the three types – chocolate- and sugar-coated peel, and ginger – makes an attractive petits fours selection for a special festive occasion such as Christmas or a large party celebration.

Per batch Energy 438Kcal/1845kJ; Protein 4.4g; Carbohydrate 74g, of which sugars 72.6g; Fat 15.8g, of which saturates 8.9g; Cholesterol 15mg; Calcium 208mg; Fibre 3.6g; Sodium 270mg

Irish yellowman

This honeycomb toffee is a bit of a curiosity and has always been associated with the Auld Lammas Fair at Ballycastle, County Antrim. The English version is known as cinder toffee.

Makes about 900g/2lb

115g/4oz/½ cup butter

30ml/2 tbsp vinegar

225g/8oz/scant ⅔ cup treacle (molasses)

225g/8oz/scant ⅔ cup golden (light corn) syrup

450g/1lb/2 cups demerara (raw) sugar

2.5ml/½ tsp bicarbonate of soda (baking soda), sieved

Cook's tip Test by dropping a small amount of the mixture into a saucer of cold water, if it is ready it should become crisp.

1 Grease a marble slab or a baking tin (pan). Melt the butter in a pan and add the vinegar, treacle, syrup and sugar. Stir over a gentle heat until the sugar has completely dissolved, and then raise the heat and bring to the boil.

2 Boil steadily until the mixture reaches soft crack stage (151°C/304°F on a sugar thermometer).

3 Remove from the heat and stir in the bicarbonate of soda. When it foams up, stir again, then pour on to a greased marble slab or baking tin and, using a spatula, keep working the edges into the centre until the mixture is pale.

4 If poured on the marble slab break into pieces, if poured into the tin, mark up into squares.

Per batch Energy 3877Kcal/16,404kJ; Protein 6.3g; Carbohydrate 799.9g, of which sugars 799g; Fat 94.5g, of which saturates 59.9g; Cholesterol 245mg; Calcium 1.53g; Fibre 0g; Sodium 1.74g

Vanilla fudge

Perennially popular, home-made fudge ends a meal beautifully when served as a petit four, – this meltingly good vanilla version is sure to become a favourite.

Makes about 60 pieces

175g/6oz/¾ cup butter

900g/2lb/4 cups soft light brown sugar

400g/14oz can sweetened condensed milk

2.5ml/½ tsp vanilla essence (extract), or to taste

1 Butter a shallow tin (pan), about 18 x 28cm/7 x 11in. Put the butter and 150ml/¼ pint/⅔ cup water into a large, heavy pan and warm very gently over a low heat until the butter melts.

2 Add the sugar and stir over a low heat until it has completely dissolved. Raise the heat and bring the mixture to the boil. Without stirring, let the mixture cook at a slow rolling boil until it reaches the soft ball stage (114°C/238°F on a sugar thermometer). This will take about 10 minutes.

3 Remove from the heat and beat in the condensed milk with a wooden spoon. Return to a medium heat, stirring, for a few minutes. Remove from the heat again, add the vanilla essence, and beat again with a spoon until glossy. Pour the mixture into the tin. Leave to cool.

4 Cut the fudge into cubes and store in an airtight tin until required. Place in petits fours cases to serve.

Variation For Coffee Fudge, add 30ml/2 tbsp coffee essence (extract).

Energy 103Kcal/435kJ; Protein 0.7g; Carbohydrate 19.4g, of which sugars 19.4g; Fat 3.1g, of which saturates 1.9g; Cholesterol 9mg; Calcium 28mg; Fibre 0g; Sodium 28mg

Lemonade

Fresh lemonade is a traditional country drink for many generations, drunk on farms to refresh the workers during harvest. Now, although still popular in rural areas, it is just as likely to be on the menu in a smart contemporary café.

Serves 4–6

3 lemons

115g/4oz/generous ½ cup sugar

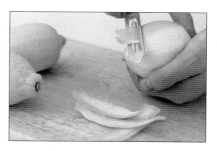

1 Pare the skin from the lemons with a vegetable peeler and squeeze the juice from the lemons.

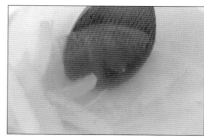

2 Put the lemon rind and sugar into a bowl, add 900ml/1½ pints/3¾ cups boiling water and stir well until the sugar has dissolved. Cover and leave until cold.

3 Add the lemon juice, mix well and strain into a jug (pitcher). Chill.

4 Serve with plenty of ice.

Variation Old-fashioned lemonade made with freshly squeezed lemons is a far cry from the carbonated commercial varieties. It can be topped up with soda water if you want some fizz.

Per glass Energy 115Kcal/489kJ; Protein 0.2g; Carbohydrate 30.4g, of which sugars 30.4g; Fat 0g, of which saturates 0g; Cholesterol 0mg; Calcium 17mg; Fibre 0g; Sodium 2mg

Barley water

Like lemonade, barley water has long been widely enjoyed as a refreshing summer drink and, until a generation ago, it would have been home-made. Barley water is usually served cold, but is also delicious hot. The concentrate will keep in the fridge for a month.

Makes about 10 glasses

50g/2oz/⅓ cup pearl barley

1 lemon

sugar, to taste

ice cubes and mint sprigs, to serve

1 Wash the pearl barley, then put it into a large stainless steel pan and cover with cold water. Bring to the boil and simmer gently for two minutes, then strain the liquid. Return the barley to the rinsed pan.

2 Wash the lemon and pare the rind from it with a vegetable peeler or a sharp knife. Squeeze the juice.

3 Add the lemon rind and 600ml/ 1 pint/2½ cups cold water to the pan containing the barley. Bring to the boil over a medium heat, then simmer the mixture very gently for 1½–2 hours, stirring occasionally.

◀ **4** Strain the liquid into a jug (pitcher), add the lemon juice, and sweeten to taste. Leave to cool. Pour the liquid into a bottle and keep in the refrigerator to use as required.

5 To serve, dilute to taste with cold water, and add ice cubes or crushed ice and a sprig of mint, if you like.

Variations
• The barley water can also be made with milk or buttermilk, in which case you should omit the lemon juice as it would curdle the milk.
• Make up the barley water with hot water to be drunk as a cold remedy, and for some extra potency add a tot of whiskey or brandy.

Per glass Energy 37.9Kcal/161.6kJ; Protein 0.43g; Carbohydrate 9.44g, of which sugars 5.26g; Fat 0.08g, of which saturates 0g; Cholesterol 0mg; Calcium 3.8mg; Fibre 0g; Sodium 0.5mg

Sparkling elderflower drink

The elder tree not only produces berries for wine but the fragrant flowers have a very pungent aroma and flavour. Unfortunately the elderflower season is short, just before the berries appear, so take advantage of them while they last.

Makes 9.5 litres/2 gallons/2.4 US gallons

24 elderflower heads

2 lemons

1.3kg/3lb/scant 7 cups granulated white sugar

30ml/2 tbsp white wine vinegar

9 litres/2 gallons/2.4 US gallons water

Cook's tips
• Collect the elderflowers in full sunshine as this means the flavour will be at its most intense.
• This drink will keep in airtight bottles for a month or so.
• If you can't find elderflowers, or it isn't the right season for them, you can use elderflower cordial, which is available in some health food stores and other specialist outlets.

1 Find a completely clean bucket that you can cover with a clean cloth. Put all the ingredients into it.

2 Cover the bucket with a plastic sheet and leave overnight.

3 Strain the elderflower drink then pour into bottles, leaving a space of about 2.5cm/1in at the top.

4 Leave sealed for about 2 weeks in a cool place. A fermentation takes place and the result is a delightful, sparkling, refreshing, non-alcoholic drink.

Per batch Energy 1282kcal/5467kJ; Protein 1.7g; Carbohydrate 339.8g, of which sugars 339.8g; Fat 0g, of which saturates 0g; Cholesterol 0mg; Calcium 173mg; Fibre 0g; Sodium 20mg

Drivers' special

This non-alcoholic drink is made with the delicious flavour combination of apple and ginger. Several small British producers make delicious natural pressed apple juice – use one of these if possible when making this bubbly apple cocktail.

Makes about 10 glasses

1.2 litres/2 pints/5 cups unsweetened apple juice

juice of 1 lemon

4 small red-skinned eating apples

1.2 litres/2 pints/5 cups ginger beer

ice cubes, to serve

lemon slices or mint sprigs, to decorate

1 Mix the apple juice and lemon juice in a large glass jug (pitcher).

2 Wash and core the apples, but do not peel them. Slice thinly and add the slices to the jug. Cover and chill.

3 Shortly before serving, add some ice cubes and the ginger beer to the jug, and decorate with lemon slices, or sprigs of mint. Serve in tall glasses.

Per glass Energy 82Kcal/352kJ; Protein 0.2g; Carbohydrate 21.4g, of which sugars 21.4g; Fat 0.2g, of which saturates 0g; Cholesterol 0mg; Calcium 15mg; Fibre 0.4g; Sodium 11mg

Irish black velvet

This modern classic always provokes a debate on whether or not this is a suitable way to drink good champagne – but those who feel it is a waste of an expensive drink usually get to like it if sparkling wine is substituted for the bubbly.

Serves 8

1 bottle of champagne, chilled

about 750ml/1¼ pints Guinness, or to taste

1 Mix the champagne with an equal quantity of Guinness, or to taste, in eight tall glasses.

2 Drink immediately, while very bubbly.

Above *Musicians playing in a pub, Derry City, County Londonderry.*

Per glass Energy 98Kcal/406kJ; Protein 0.7g; Carbohydrate 6.2g, of which sugars 6.2g; Fat 0g, of which saturates 0g; Cholesterol 0mg; Calcium 12mg; Fibre 0g; Sodium 10mg

Cranachan smoothie

Although a steaming bowl of porridge can't be beaten as a winter warmer, this sumptuous Scottish smoothie makes a great, light alternative in warmer months. Just a spoonful or so of oatmeal gives substance to this tangy, invigorating drink.

Makes 1 large glass

25ml/1½ tbsp medium rolled oats

150g/5oz/scant 1 cup raspberries

5–10ml/1–2 tsp clear honey

45ml/3 tbsp natural (plain) yogurt

1 Put the oatmeal in a heatproof bowl. Pour in 120ml/4fl oz/½ cup boiling water and leave to stand in a warm place for about 10 minutes.

2 Put the soaked oats in a food processor or blender and add all but two or three of the raspberries. Reserve the raspberries for decoration.

3 Add the honey and about 30ml/2 tbsp of the yogurt to the food processor or blender. Purée the ingredients until smooth, scraping down the side of the bowl halfway through if necessary.

4 Pour the raspberry and oatmeal smoothie into a large glass, swirl in the remaining yogurt and top with the reserved raspberries.

Cook's tips
• If you don't like raspberry pips (seeds) in your smoothies, press the fruit through a sieve to make a smooth purée, then process with the oatmeal and yogurt as above.
• If you can, prepare it ahead of time because soaking the raw oats helps to break down the starch into natural sugars that are easy to digest.
• The smoothie will thicken up in the refrigerator so you might need to stir in a little extra juice or mineral water just before serving.

Per glass Energy 186kcal/793kJ; Protein 7.5g; Carbohydrate 34.6g, of which sugars 16.4g; Fat 3.1g, of which saturates 0.4g; Cholesterol 1mg; Calcium 137mg; Fibre 5.5g; Sodium 51mg

Gaelic coffee

A good Highland or Irish coffee should be served in a tall wine glass with a 300ml/½ pint/
1¼ cup capacity. The coffee should be freshly made and very hot. The whiskey needs to be
a malt, such as Dalwhinnie or Laphroaig.

1 Pour the whiskey into the glass and add the sugar. Stir thoroughly.

2 Make a pot of fresh coffee and whilst it is still piping hot pour it into the glass with the whiskey and sugar. Stand a spoon in the glass to stop it from cracking. Leave about 2cm/¾in at the top, and stir to dissolve the sugar.

3 Using a teaspoon with its tip just touching the coffee gently pour the lightly whipped cream over the coffee until it reaches the top of the glass. Serve immediately.

Serves 1

30ml/2 tbsp malt whiskey

5ml/1 tsp soft light brown sugar

hot black coffee

50ml/2fl oz/¼ cup double (heavy) cream, lightly whipped

Cook's tips
• If the cream doesn't float well on top of the coffee, then the balance of coffee and sugar is not correct. Add a little bit more sugar, which will make the coffee more dense and the cream more likely to float.
• Use filter coffee or coffee made in a cafetière (press-pot) for the best results.

Per glass Energy 83kcal/341kJ; Protein 0.2g; Carbohydrate 1.3g, of which sugars 1.3g; Fat 6.7g, of which saturates 4.2g; Cholesterol 17mg; Calcium 7mg; Fibre 0g; Sodium 3mg

Scottish het pint

Meaning "hot pint" this is traditionally drunk at Hogmanay, with vendors in the street calling out to punters to try some. It is ideal for the night-long festivities, being both warming and sustaining with the addition of egg which also provide a rich texture.

Makes about 3 litres/5 pints

1.2 litres/2 pints/5 cups lemonade

1.2 litres/2 pints/5 cups dark beer

5ml/1 tsp ground nutmeg

75g/3oz/⅓ cup caster (superfine) sugar

3 eggs

300ml/½ pint/1¼ cups whisky

3 Whisk the eggs in a bowl and very slowly, while still beating, pour in a couple of ladlefuls of the hot mixture.

4 Gently return the egg mixture to the main pan, whisking to make sure it does not form lumps or curdle by getting too hot around the edges.

5 Add the whisky slowly, stirring continuously, and heat though to just below boiling point. Serve immediately by ladling the liquid into pint glasses (or tall glasses if you prefer) until it reaches the top. Hand it round to all the company and drink a hearty toast to Hogmanay.

1 Put the lemonade and beer into a large heavy pan over a low heat.

2 Add the nutmeg and heat gently to just below boiling point. Add the sugar and stir to dissolve.

Cook's tip This drink will only keep for a day or so, and it is better to drink it piping hot as soon as it's made. If you do want to store it, keep it in an airtight bottle.

Per glass Energy 425kcal/1888kJ; Protein 5.7g; Carbohydrate 43.6g, of which sugars 43.6g; Fat 4.2g, of which saturates 1.2g; Cholesterol 143mg; Calcium 70mg; Fibre 0g; Sodium 93mg

Prince Charlie's coffee

Bonnie Prince Charlie gave the recipe for Drambuie – a honey-flavoured whisky liquour – to the MacKinnon family, and it is now used to make this luxurious after-dinner coffee.

Serves 1

30ml/2 tbsp Drambuie

5ml/1 tsp soft light brown sugar

hot black coffee

50ml/2fl oz/¼ cup double (heavy) cream, lightly whipped

1 Pour the Drambuie into a tall wine glass with a 300ml/½ pint/1¼ cup capacity (as for the Highland Coffee). Add the sugar and stir thoroughly until completely dissolved.

2 Make a fresh pot of piping hot coffee – it is preferable to use either filter coffee or coffee made in a cafetière (press pot). It is also best to use a good, smooth coffee. Make it quite strong, although you don't want to smother the taste of the Drambuie completely.

3 Pour the hot coffee into the glass, leaving 2cm/¾in at the top, and stir.

4 Using a teaspoon with its tip just touching the coffee pour the lightly whipped cream over the coffee until it reaches the top of the glass.

Glasgow punch

Over the last few centuries, the Glaswegians enjoyed the rum that came over from the Caribbean with the sugar shipments. A number of drinks and cocktails were invented using rum as the base, the Glasgow punch being a favourite.

Makes 1.5 litres/3 pints

900ml/1½ pints/3¾ cups water

200g/6oz/scant 1 cup dark brown muscovado (molasses) sugar

1 orange

1 lemon

300ml/½ pint/1¼ cups rum

1 Put the water into a pan over a medium heat. Add the sugar and stir in thoroughly, then allow the water to come to a boil. Boil rapidly to reduce the quantity by about half. Set aside to cool competely.

2 Remove the rinds from the orange and lemon with a zester or a fine grater, avoiding the pith.

3 Pour the rum into a mixing bowl and add the rinds of the lemon and orange, reserving the fruit. Cover and leave to infuse overnight.

4 Squeeze the juice from the orange and lemon, then strain. Add to the bowl with the rum. Stir to mix, then strain the mixture to remove the rind.

5 Add the boiled water and sugar to taste and then bottle the punch. Drink the punch hot.

Per glass Energy 90kcal/371kJ; Protein 0.2g; Carbohydrate 3.1g, of which sugars 3.1g; Fat 6.7g, of which saturates 4.2g; Cholesterol 17mg; Calcium 7mg; Fibre 0g; Sodium 3mg
Per batch Energy 1474kcal/6206kJ; Protein 1.4g; Carbohydrate 214g, of which sugars 214g; Fat 0.1g, of which saturates 0g; Cholesterol 0mg; Calcium 113mg; Fibre 0.1g; Sodium 17mg

Atholl brose

The Dukes of Atholl were a powerful family in Jacobite Scotland, and legend has it that in the rebellion of 1745, the Duke overcame his enemies by filling their well with this potent brew.

Serves 4

200g/7oz/2 cups medium rolled oats

150ml/¼ pint/⅔ cup water

115g/4oz/½ cup heather honey

900ml/1½ pints/3¾ cups Highland or Island whisky

1 Place the rolled oats in a small bowl with the water and leave for 1 hour, then stir to make a paste.

2 Press the rolled oats complete with the soaking water through a sieve into a large mixing bowl. Add the heather honey and mix thoroughly until completely combined.

3 Pour in the whisky a little at a time, stirring it in completely before adding more. Finally, stir well then pour into small whisky glasses. Keep the drink in bottles and shake well before use.

Per batch Energy 3006kcal/12559kJ; Protein 25.2g; Carbohydrate 229.6g, of which sugars 84g; Fat 17.4g, of which saturates 0g; Cholesterol 0mg; Calcium 116mg; Fibre 13.6g; Sodium 78mg

Brammle kir

The French Kir and Kir Royale are made with Burgundian Chardonnay and sparkling wine respectively, mixed with cassis. This delicious Scottish version uses either white or sparkling wine mixed with Brammle, a whisky liqueur made with blackberries. Serve as an aperitif.

Serves 1

30ml/2 tbsp Brammle liqueur

dry white wine, such as Chardonnay or Sauvignon Blanc, chilled

Variation For a special occasion, make a Brammle Royale by replacing the white wine with chilled champagne or fizzy wine.

1 Pour the liqueur into the bottom of a large wine glass.

2 Top up to within 2cm/¾in of the top with the chilled white wine. Enjoy!

Per glass Energy 244kcal/1017kJ; Protein 0.3g; Carbohydrate 11.3g, of which sugars 11.3g; Fat 0g, of which saturates 0g; Cholesterol 0mg; Calcium 24mg; Fibre 0g; Sodium 14mg

Sloe gin

The small, purple sloes grow widely in the Irish hedgerows and are not much used except, perhaps, for Sloe Gin, which is drunk as a liqueur. Remember to allow at least three months for it to mature – sloes picked in September will make a special Christmas drink.

Makes 2–3 bottles

450g/1lb/4 cups ripe sloes (black plums)

225g/8oz/generous 1 cup caster (superfine) sugar

1 litre/1¾ pint/4 cups Cork Dry Gin

1 Check through the sloes and discard any damaged or unsound fruit. Rinse the sloes and remove the stalks.

2 Prick each sloe with a silver or stainless steel fork or use a cocktail stick (toothpick).

3 Select several wide-necked screw-top or easy to seal sterilized jars and arrange alternate layers of fruit and sugar in them. Top up the jars with gin, and close them tightly. Store for at least 3 months in a cool, dark place.

4 Shake the jars gently every now and then to help extract and distribute the flavour evenly. When ready, strain into a jug (pitcher) and then pour into sterilized bottles and store for another 3 months if possible.

Per bottle Energy 1554Kcal/6486kJ; Protein 0.6g; Carbohydrate 117.6g, of which sugars 117.6g; Fat 0g, of which saturates 0g; Cholesterol 0mg; Calcium 60mg; Fibre 0g; Sodium 7mg

Irish cream liqueur cocktails

Bailey's is the best known of the Irish cream liqueurs that have taken the world by storm. There are several other excellent brands available too, and they make good cocktail ingredients. These liqueurs slip down easily, however, and should be taken in moderation.

Irish flag
Serves 1

25ml/1½ tbsp green crème de menthe

25ml/1½ tbsp Bailey's Irish Cream

25ml/1½ tbsp brandy

Pour the crème de menthe and Bailey's Irish Cream into a shot glass. Slowly pour the brandy on the top so that it floats on top of the cream to mimic the green, white and orange of the Irish national flag.

Bailey's dream shake cocktail
Serves 1

50ml/2fl oz/¼ cup Bailey's Irish Cream

2 scoops vanilla ice cream

25ml/1½ tbsp single cream

Put some ice into a cocktail shaker. Add the Bailey's Irish Cream, the ice cream and the cream to the shaker. Shake until the shaker is too cold to hold. Serve the cocktail in a long, chilled glass.

Per glass Irish Flag Energy 215Kcal/896kJ; Protein 0g; Carbohydrate 11.8g, of which sugars 11.8g; Fat 3.9g, of which saturates 0g; Cholesterol 0mg; Calcium 5mg; Fibre 0g; Sodium 24mg

Bailey's Dream Shake Energy 476Kcal/1987kJ; Protein 6.2g; Carbohydrate 41.6g, of which sugars 40g; Fat 25.4g, of which saturates 12.2g; Cholesterol 50mg; Calcium 181mg; Fibre 0g; Sodium 142mg

Whiskey cocktails

Cocktails are a big hit in many of Ireland's contemporary bars, and they're a fun way to give any party a kick-start. Whiskey makes a good foundation for cocktails and these three are especially suitable for making with Jameson, which is widely available. Instructions are for one serving, but you can scale up the shaken cocktails to serve in jugs.

Jameson hourglass
Serves 1

25ml/1½ tbsp Irish whiskey

cranberry juice

orange juice

1 lime

Pour the whiskey into a tall glass and add ice. Pour in two measures of cranberry juice and two measures of orange juice. Stir to mix and finish with a squeeze and a slice of fresh lime. ▶

Jameson WTR (What's the rush?)
Serves 1

25ml/1½ tbsp whiskey

75ml/5 tbsp lemonade

dash of apple juice

orange slice

Pour the whiskey into a tall glass and add ice. Add the lemonade and a dash of apple juice. Stir to mix. and decorate with a slice of orange.

Whiskey sour
Serves 1

25ml/1½ tbsp whiskey

5ml/1 tsp caster sugar

juice of 1 lemon

Mix the whiskey, sugar and lemon juice together. Shake over ice and strain, then pour into a chilled glass. Twist a strip of lemon peel over the drink and drop into the glass. Serve with a maraschino (cocktail) cherry on a cocktail stick (toothpick).

Per glass Hourglass Energy 104Kcal/436kJ; Protein 0.3g; Carbohydrate 11.6g, of which sugars 4.4g; Fat 0.1g, of which saturates 0g; Cholesterol 0mg; Calcium 5mg; Fibre 0.1g; Sodium 5mg
Jameson WTR Energy 72Kcal/300kJ; Protein 0g; Carbohydrate 4.3g, of which sugars 4.3g; Fat 0g, of which saturates 0g; Cholesterol 0mg; Calcium 4mg; Fibre 0g; Sodium 5mg
Whiskey sour Energy 74Kcal/308kJ; Protein 0.1g; Carbohydrate 4.7g, of which sugars 4.7g; Fat 0g, of which saturates 0g; Cholesterol 0mg; Calcium 5mg; Fibre 0g; Sodium 1mg

Hot Irish whiskey, or whiskey punch

Also known as a "hot toddy" this traditional "cure" for colds is more often drunk for pleasure as a nightcap, particularly to round off a day's winter sporting activities and it is a great drink to hold and sip on cold, damp winter evenings.

Serves 1

4–6 whole cloves

60ml/4 tbsp Irish whiskey

1 thick slice of lemon, halved

5–10ml/1–2 tsp demerara (raw) sugar, to taste

Cook's tip There are three types of Irish whiskey: single malt, pure pot stilled and a column-and-pot still blend of grain and malt. All are distilled three times and matured in oak barrels.

1 Stick the cloves into the lemon slice, and put it into a large stemmed glass (or one with a handle) with the whiskey and the sugar.

2 Put a teaspoon in the glass, to prevent the hot water from cracking it, then top it up with boiling water. Stir well to dissolve the sugar and serve.

Per glass Energy 149Kcal/619kJ; Protein 0g; Carbohydrate 4.2g, of which sugars 4.2g; Fat 0g, of which saturates 0g; Cholesterol 0mg; Calcium 2mg; Fibre 0g; Sodium 0mg

Hot claret

A hot wine cup dates back hundreds of years, when it would be served to guests arriving in winter, chilled by a journey of hours – or even days – on horseback or in a carriage.

Makes about 10 glasses

1 bottle red wine

175g/6oz/scant 1 cup sugar, or to taste

1 lemon

5cm/2in piece of cinnamon stick

lemon slices, to decorate (optional)

1 Put the red wine, 300ml/½ pint/1¼ cups water and the sugar into a large stainless steel pan. Peel the lemon thinly with a vegetable peeler

2 Add the lemon peel to the pan together with the cinnamon stick. Slowly heat this mixture over a low heat, stirring to dissolve the sugar, until almost boiling.

3 Remove from the heat, cover and leave for 10 minutes to infuse (steep). Strain into a heated jug (pitcher) and pour the hot mulled wine into warmed glasses with a half-slice of lemon.

Per glass Energy 120Kcal/506kJ; Protein 0.2g; Carbohydrate 18.4g, of which sugars 18.4g; Fat 0g, of which saturates 0g; Cholesterol 0mg; Calcium 15mg; Fibre 0g; Sodium 6mg

Mulled cider

This hot cider cup is easy to make and traditional at Hallowe'en, but it makes a good and inexpensive warming brew for any winter gathering.

Makes about 20 glasses

2 lemons

1 litre/1¾ pints/4 cups apple juice

2 litres/3½ pints/9 cups medium sweet cider

3 small cinnamon sticks

4–6 whole cloves

slices of lemon, to serve (optional)

1 Wash the lemons and pare the rinds with a vegetable peeler. Blend all the ingredients together in a large stainless steel pan.

2 Set over a low heat and heat the mixture through to infuse (steep) for 15 minutes; do not allow it to boil as this reduces the alcohol content.

3 Strain the liquid and serve with extra slices of lemon, if you like.

Per glass Energy 61Kcal/258kJ; Protein 0.1g; Carbohydrate 9.3g, of which sugars 9.3g; Fat 0.1g, of which saturates 0g; Cholesterol 0mg; Calcium 12mg; Fibre 0g; Sodium 8mg

Index